The Triumph of Venus

PHILOSOPHY, SOCIAL THEORY, AND THE RULE OF LAW

General Editors
Andrew Arato, Seyla Benhabib, Ferenc Fehér, William Forbath, Agnes Heller, Arthur Jacobson, and Michel Rosenfeld

1. William Rehg, *Insight and Solidarity: A Study in the Discourse Ethics of Jürgen Habermas*
2. Alan Brudner, *The Unity of the Common Law: Studies in Hegelian Jurisprudence*
3. Peter Goodrich, *Oedipus Lex: Psychoanalysis, History, Law*
4. Michel Rosenfeld, *Just Interpretations: Law between Ethics and Politics*
5. Jeanne Lorraine Schroeder, *The Vestal and the Fasces: Hegel, Lacan, Property, and the Feminine*
6. Michel Rosenfeld and Andrew Arato, editors, *Habermas on Law and Democracy: Critical Exchanges*
7. Desmond Manderson, *Songs without Music: Aesthetic Dimensions of Law and Justice*
8. Arthur J. Jacobson and Bernhard Schlink, editors, *Weimar: A Jurisprudence of Crisis*
9. Rainer Forst, *Contexts of Justice: Political Philosophy Beyond Liberalism and Communitarianism.* Translated by John M. M. Farrell.
10. Jeanne Lorraine Schroeder, *The Triumph of Venus: The Erotics of the Market*

The Triumph of Venus

The Erotics of the Market

Jeanne Lorraine Schroeder

UNIVERSITY OF CALIFORNIA PRESS
Berkeley   Los Angeles   London

University of California Press
Berkeley and Los Angeles, California

University of California Press, Ltd.
London, England

Library of Congress Cataloging-in-Publication Data

Schroeder, Jeanne Lorraine.
The triumph of Venus : the erotics of the market / Jeanne Lorraine Schroeder.
p. cm.—(Philosophy, social theory, and the rule of law ; 10)
Includes bibliographical references and index.
ISBN 0-520-23431-6 (cloth : alk. paper)
1. Law and economics—Psychological aspects—Philosophy. 2. Sociological jusrisprudence. 3. Feminist jurisprudence. 4. Economic man. 5. Utilitarianism. 6. Romanticism. 7. Erotica. 8. Venus (Roman deity) I. Title. II. Series.

K487.E3 S38 2004
340'.115—dc21

2003012770

Manufactured in the United States of America
13 12 11 10 09 08 07 06 05 04
10 9 8 7 6 5 4 3 2 1

The paper used in this publication meets the minimum requirements of ANSI/NISO Z39.48–1992 (R 1997) (*Permanence of Paper*).

For my mother

CONTENTS

Introduction: Juno Moneta

The object of the law and the object of desire are one and the same, and remain equally concealed.

GILLES DELEUZE[1]

There is nothing which so generally strikes the imagination, and engages the affection of mankind, as the right of property. And yet there are very few, that will give themselves the trouble to consider the origin and foundation of [property]. Pleased as we are with the possession, we seem afraid to look back . . . as if fearful . . .

WILLIAM BLACKSTONE[2]

William Blackstone insisted that property, and therefore market relations, are driven by desire. This eroticism should not surprise us. Etymology tells us that money is a woman. The word "money" derives from Juno Moneta. Juno, queen of heaven, was the Roman goddess of womanhood, the personification of the feminine. Her title, "Moneta," means "she who reminds and warns." The word "money" reminds us that the feminine is a reminder—a warning.

Nevertheless, the erotic nature of law and markets is deeply repressed in American culture. We turn away from the primal scene of the passionate origins of markets with the same embarrassment and shame we experience when we contemplate our own origins in the parental bed. The ideal of the perfect market, like the idea of our own conception, is "real" in the Lacanian sense. To look back, to confront the real, is not merely frightening—it is deadly. And yet there is nothing we desire more. To be a subject is to be driven by desire. Subjectivity is the triumph of Venus.

In recent years, the study of markets in American jurisprudence has been expropriated by the self-styled "law-and-economics" movement, the dominant discourse of private law in America's most elite law schools. One of its appeals is that it gives an aura of scientific certainty and objectivity to legal analysis and normative policymaking. Despite its claim to scientific status, however, this scholarship is almost entirely devoid of methodological discussion and inter-

1. Gilles Deleuze, *Coldness and Cruelty,* MASOCHISM 9, 85 (Jean McNeil trans., 1971).

2. William Blackstone, *Two Commentaries on the Laws of England* 2 (A. W. Brian Simpson intro., 1979).

nal criticism, as though these matters were uncontroversial. Moreover, the practitioners of the "science" of law-and-economics rarely engage in empirical research. Instead, law-and-economics consists of deductions from dogmatic principles. Consequently, most law-and-economic proposals are classic cases of GIGO (garbage in—garbage out): nonfalsified theories are applied to untested assumptions in order to produce nonverifiable conclusions. Law-and-economics has all of the characteristics of a cult. Nevertheless, although it is frequently attacked in law reviews, particularly from scholars self-identified with the critical left, law-and-economics has not only prevailed; it has thrived. One reason for this is that much of this opposition to law-and-economics has taken the equally unsatisfactory form of romanticism, a viewpoint that unwittingly repeats the errors of utilitarianism. In this book, I argue that there are powerful psychoanalytic reasons why law-and-economics, as well as the romantic critique, continue to be so seductive despite their failures.

The legal economist sees market participants, and therefore the market, as essentially rational. Market participants know their preferences and take appropriate action reasonably calculated to maximize their atomistic, individualistic well-being conceived in terms of either "utility" or "wealth." Markets are deemed efficient insofar as they enable rational economic actors collectively to achieve their goals. Although individual preferences may be irrational, in the sense of pregiven and subjective, *homo oeconomicus* is rational, single-minded, predictable, and objective in the pursuit of these irrational preferences.

The romantic sees the economic vision of human nature as fundamentally flawed because it ignores, or de-emphasizes, "higher" aspects of human nature, such as spirituality, empathy, altruism, and so on. Surprisingly, these "New Age" neoromantics who emphasize the supposedly irrational aspect of human nature tend to confirm the utilitarian analysis of the market as cold and rational. Eroticism and other forms of "irrationality" are therefore seen as essentially different from and usually superior to economic relations. Their critique, however, remains impotent, precisely because it accepts a fundamental tenet of the approach they claim to condemn.

Utilitarianism and romanticism are mirror images of each other. They valorize opposites but fundamentally agree. They draw diametrically opposed conclusions from a shared erroneous assumption about law and market relations. They both assume that market relations are inherently cold, atomistic, and "rational." The utilitarian believes that "rationality" is the true essence of human nature, and therefore analyzes all human relations by analogy with the market. The romantic, in contrast, believes that human nature is essentially "irrational" in one way or another. Therefore, the market is an aberration. At best, it is a necessary evil tolerated only insofar as it is limited in scope, as a means to provide basic physical needs. At worst it is a perversion that threatens to undermine all human relations and frustrate the achievement of personhood.

This book on utilitarianism and romanticism is an encounter with Hegelian philosophy and Lacanian psychoanalysis, and an exploration of the erotics of law and the market using metaphors drawn from classical mythology. I argue that the utilitarian-romantic analysis of the law and the market is incorrect for two interrelated reasons. First, Hegelian philosophy shows us that, far from being anti-erotic, market relations are the most basic and primitive from of eroticism. Meanwhile, Lacanian theory reveals that the feminine is the primal commodity; money is Juno Moneta. Consequently, the utilitarian is correct in seeing a fundamental similarity between erotic and economic behavior, but wrong in thinking that the former can be reduced to the latter. Rather, it is the latter that can be explained in terms of the former. Venus triumphs over the market. To put this another way, both the utilitarian and the romantic see desire as external to law. In contradistinction, the Hegelian and Lacanian, following a Western philosophic tradition reaching back to Aristotelian virtue ethics, posit that law operates at the level of desire.

Second, the rational-irrational dichotomy adopted equally by utilitarians and romantics is incompetent. Dialectical reasoning reveals that reason and passion are not inalterably opposed, but rather two aspects of the same concept. It is true that human beings are rational, as argued by utilitarians. But rationality represents only the potential of human nature. This potential must be actualized through desire. Consequently, desire drives human behavior, as romantics intuit. Through reason, the abstract person comes to understand that she can only actualize herself through recognition by other subjects—through love. Therefore, she rationally desires others: logic tells her to give way to passion. This does not imply, however, that the romantic is correct in assuming that passion is superior to logic. Rather, even at the ecstatic moment of *jouissance,* the subject must preserve a moment of the rationality that makes desire possible, or submerge her personhood in the abyss.

My goal in this book is to reveal the internal, but repressed, logic of certain legal and economic concepts. I believe that the law-and-economics paradigm[3] drawn from classical price theory is decadent; in the terminology of Imre Lakatos, it is a degenerating research program.[4] I show that several attempts

3. THOMAS S. KUHN, THE STRUCTURE OF SCIENTIFIC REVOLUTIONS (2d. ed. 1970).

4. Imre Lakatos, *Falsification and the Methodology of Scientific Research Programmes,* in CRITICISM AND THE GROWTH OF KNOWLEDGE 91, 118 (Imre Lakatos & Alan Musgrave eds., 1970). Building on Karl Popper's theory of sophisticated falsification, Lakatos argues that scientists do not reject a scientific theory merely because of the empirical observation of inconsistent data. Rather they modify the theory by adopting a "protective belt" of auxiliary hypotheses designed to explain away the apparent anomaly. Eventually, the paradigm (research program) degenerates as the protective belt becomes thicker and thicker, and the core paradigm begins to shrink until it actually starts explaining less. Jeanne L. Schroeder, *Abduction From the Seraglio: Feminist Methodologies and the Logic of Imagination,* 70 TEX. L. REV. 109, 168–71 (1991).

to replace the economic paradigm are mere romanticism—utilitarianism's polarized twin. Romanticism in fact adopts utilitarianism's paradigmatic assumptions and merely rejects the utilitarian conclusions drawn from them. I attempt not only to identify the flaws of the research program that are the source of its degeneration, but also to explain why so many legal academics nevertheless continue to cling to the research program despite its flaws.

This book has two different aspects, designed for two different audiences. Part of each chapter explores a concept of legal or economic theory on its own terms in the language of lawyers and economists. The purpose of this is to reveal the internal logic and implicit paradoxes of these concepts, so that lawyers can better understand and use them. I then suggest that an understanding of these concepts can be further enriched by adding an external critique drawn from Lacanian-Hegelian analysis. I argue that Lacanian psychoanalysis can help explain why the current paradigm is so alluring despite its degeneracy.

The former discussion should be of immediate interest to legal scholars working within a traditional framework. I hope that the latter introduction to speculative theory may convince at least some readers that such theory is not merely interesting in and of itself, but potentially useful for legal and economic analysis. Indeed, I have found it invaluable as an analytic tool, not merely in my teaching and doctrinal scholarship, but in the practice of finance law. In contrast, my discussion of the relationship between Lacan and Hegel is likely initially to interest feminists and others engaged in critical theory. I hope that my discussion of law and economics may convince at least some of these readers that these disciplines are not merely useful tools of analysis, but are themselves worthy subjects for serious philosophical and psychological examination.

The one thing this book does not do is make specific policy recommendations for interpreting or changing the law. This book is a sustained critique of the consequentialist, policy-oriented turn in American legal scholarship. As a practicing lawyer and a legal scholar, I obviously do not oppose pragmatic advice or policy making in principle. Indeed, I on occasion engage in doctrinal scholarship on commercial law, and I discussed certain legal doctrines in my earlier book, *The Vestal and the Fasces: Hegel, Lacan, Property and the Fasces.*[5] One of the primary points I wish to make here, however, is that legal economists on the one hand and romantic legal scholars on the other purport to derive policy advice from theories that are analytically insupportable. If one wants to use theory to give advice, as these scholars do, one should first be sure of the validity and internal coherence of one's theory.

Moreover, following Hegel, I believe that theory can explain the underlying logic of social systems only at a very high level of abstraction. Specific

5. University of California Press (1998).

policy recommendations require practical reasoning.[6] Consequently, pragmatism is the necessary corollary to Hegelian idealism. Although it has become fashionable for both legal economists and romantics to characterize themselves as pragmatists, in fact they rarely engage in the type of detailed empirical research that would be necessary in order to support their recommendations. Rather, they base their recommendations on unsupported assumptions. Consequently, insofar as I have a policy recommendation, it is that legal scholars should be more modest in making policy recommendations.

Finally, and most importantly, my approach towards critical scholarship springs from discourse theory.[7] In Lacanian terminology, policy-oriented scholarship, including law-and-economics, speaks within the "university's discourse."[8] In this discourse, the speaker claims the position of the expert with superior knowledge and addresses the goals and desires of the law. According to Lacan, however, the purpose of this type of scholarship is not a sincere search for truth. Rather, the hidden truth of the university's discourse is that it is a veiled attempt to justify the status quo and exercise power over others. That is, policy scholarship views law from the position of the governor. The product of the university's discourse is the subjects who are subjected to and manipulated by the law in order to serve the expert's purposes.

In contrast, the critical scholar, like the practicing lawyer, speaks within the "hysteric's discourse"—the "other side" or reverse of the university's dis-

6. *See* G. W. F. HEGEL, ELEMENTS OF THE PHILOSOPHY OF RIGHT 21, 81 (Allen W. Wood ed. & H. B. Nisbet trans., 1991). As such, Hegelianism, properly understood, sails a middle ground between the pro- and anti-theory movements of contemporary legal academia.

7. For an extended application of Lacanian discourse theory to law, *see* Jeanne L. Schroeder, *The Four Discourses of Law: A Lacanian Analysis of Legal Practice and Scholarship*, 79 TEX. L. REV. 15 (2000).

In his seventeenth seminar, entitled *The Other Side of Psychoanalysis*, Lacan proposes that there are at least four discourses, which may be graphically represented as:

$$\frac{\text{agent}}{\text{truth}} \longrightarrow \frac{\text{other}}{\text{product / loss}}$$

BRUCE FINK, THE LACANIAN SUBJECT: BETWEEN LANGUAGE AND JOUISSANCE 131 (1995). The upper left corner represents the agent who speaks in the discourse. The upper right corner is the other, that which is addressed or interrogated in the discourse. The arrow between them indicates the relationship between the two. Beneath and barred from the agent is his hidden truth. Beneath the other is that which is intentionally or unintentionally produced in the discourse. Four terms rotate through these four positions, represented by the mathemes S_1 (the master signifier), S_2 (knowledge, or the signifying chain), *a* (the *objet petit a*, or object cause of desire), and $\$$ (split subject). *Id.* at 123. The meaning of these terms should become apparent in the following discussions.

8. The university's discourse is graphically represented as:

$$\frac{S_2}{S_1} \longrightarrow \frac{a}{\$}$$

course.[9] The speaker does not position herself as an expert, but rather identifies with the alienated, split subject produced by the university's discourse. The speaker views law from the position of the governed, not the governor. The hidden truth of this position is not power, as in the university's discourse, but the subjective desires and pain of the speaker herself and of those with whom the speaker identifies. The hysteric's discourse is addressed not to the law's goals, but to its power—the hidden truth of the university's discourse. If successful, the result of a hysteric's discourse is knowledge. This is not, however, the knowledge claimed by the expert who wishes to tell other people what to do in order to achieve society's "objective" purposes. Rather, it is an internal self-knowledge of the speaking subject concerning her relationship to the law and how to use or change the law for her own subjective purposes.

9. The hysteric's discourse is graphically represented as:

$$\frac{\$}{a} \longrightarrow \frac{S_1}{S_2}$$

Note that the hysteric's discourse is produced by rotating the university's discourse 180 degrees clockwise. I present this analysis in detail in Jeanne L. Schroeder; *The Stumbling Block, Freedom, Rationality and Legal Scholarship,* 44 WM. & MARY LAW REVIEW 263 (2002).

Chapter 1

Pandora's Amphora

The Eroticism of Contract and Gift[1]

PROLOGUE: THE MYTH OF ALLGIFTS

Almost three thousand years ago, Hesiod warned against gifts.[2]

In ancient times, the titan Forethought (Prometheus) taught mankind how to cheat the gods out of the profits of sacrifice.[3] Later, when Zeus punished man by taking away fire,[4] Forethought once again cheated the gods, by restoring fire to man. Zeus, seeking a more effective punishment, decided to give men a gift "in which they will all delight as they embrace their own misfortune."[5]

Zeus ordered Hephaestus, the divine smith, to forge the first woman. The goddesses bestowed her with their finest attributes—skill in crafts and weav-

1. An earlier version of this chapter was published as Jeanne L. Schroeder, *Pandora's Amphora: The Ambiguity of Gift,* 46 UCLA L. Rev. 815 (1999).

2. My account is based primarily on Hesiod's. *See* Hesiod, Theogony and Works and Days ll. 47–105, at 38–40, ll. 570–600, at 20–21 (M. L. West trans., Oxford Univ. Press 1988).

3. At the first sacrifice, Forethought divided the carcass of the sacrificial animal into two parts. Zeus agreed that his choice would be the gods' portion for all time. Forethought cleverly placed all of the meat and edible organs in one pile and covered it with the unappealing skin and stomach. The other pile consisted of the bones, lungs, and other worthless bits, covered with glistening fat. Although Hesiod incongruously insists that Zeus saw through the ruse, the story clearly indicates the opposite: Zeus chose the inedible pile. From that day on, the sacrifice was a ritual feast in which the worshippers ate mankind's portion. Bound by Zeus's foolish bargain, the gods had to be satisfied with the scent of burning fat.

4. Zeus was so furious that he deprived mankind of fire so that we could not cook our portion of the sacrificial victim and thereby benefit from Forethought's deceit.

5. *Id.* ll. 58–59, at 38. Forethought was punished by being chained to a mountain, where an eagle plucked out his liver. Being immortal, Forethought grew a new liver each day. He was eventually freed by Heracles.

ing, charm, grace, beauty, fragrance, as well as clothes and jewelry. But there also were other, less welcome gifts. Aphrodite's gift of charm came laden with "painful yearning and consuming obsession."[6] Hermes gave her the mind and knavish nature of a dog[7] and "fashioned lies and wily pretenses"[8] in her breast.

The gods named the woman Allgifts (Pandora) because she was the gift of all the gods, "a calamity for men,"[9] a "precipitous, unmanageable trap."[10] They offered her to Forethought as a wife. Understanding the danger of gifts, Forethought refused her and warned his brother, Afterthought (Epimetheus), "never to accept a gift from Olympian Zeus but to send it back lest some affliction befall mortals."[11] Afterthought paid no heed to this advice and accepted Allgifts. From this union "descended the female sex, a great affliction to mortals as they dwell with their husbands—no fit partners for accursed Poverty, but only for Plenty."[12]

Additional divine gifts compounded these woes. Allgifts was given an amphora, or storage jar, as her trousseau.[13] When Allgifts opened the amphora, out flew "grievous sicknesses that are deadly to men," "grim cares," and "countless troubles."[14]

Hesiod ostensibly presents the gift of Pandora and her amphora as an unmitigated calamity. A careful reading, however, reveals that the nature of the gift is ambiguous. First, although this tragic sequence of events was exacerbated by Prometheus's gift of fire, fire itself has been a great boon to mankind. Second, although Pandora is described as lying and knavish, she was not merely charming, graceful, and beautiful, but also highly skilled. Indeed, the gods themselves "were seized with wonder" when they saw her.[15]

6. *Id.* ll. 65–66, at 39.

7. *See id.* ll. 66–69, at 39. This strange detail reflects the fact that Hermes' sobriquet was "Killer of Dogs." This odd title is explained by the fact that Hermes was not only the messenger of the gods but also the god of thieves. As both divine thief and mailman, he was the bane of watchdogs. Presumably, Hermes used the soul of one of his canine victims to animate Allgifts.

8. *Id.* ll. 77–78, at 39.

9. *Id.* ll. 81–83, at 39.

10. *Id.* ll. 84–85, at 39.

11. *Id.* ll. 89–91, at 39.

12. *Id.* ll. 591–93, at 20.

13. We can thank Erasmus for the familiar mistranslation "Pandora's box." *See* M. L. West, *Introduction* to THEOGONY AND WORKS AND DAYS, *supra* note 2, at vii, xiv.

14. HESIOD, *supra* note 2, ll. 92–94, at 39–40. Although Pandora was the mother of all mankind and brought mortality to the world, one should not Christianize this myth by making Pandora into a form of Eve. Eve was forbidden to eat of the Tree of the Knowledge of Good and Evil and was driven out of the Garden for her sins of disobedience and pride. Pandora was never forbidden from opening the amphora. Rather, the jar was given as a wedding gift with the expectation that it would be opened.

15. *Id.* l. 589, at 20.

Third, while Hesiod describes women as afflictions,[16] he reluctantly admits that "a good wife who is sound and sensible" will save a man from the misery of a lonely old age and assure that upon his death his wealth will descend to his children, and that his distant relatives will not be laughing heirs.[17] Moreover, Hesiod's inference that Pandora was an unproductive burden contradicts his earlier statement that she had been instructed in crafts and weaving by Athena.

Fourth, by making Pandora literally a bitch, Hesiod intentionally invoked the cunning and voracious nature of dogs. But he also unwittingly implied that woman is the most loving and faithful of all creatures—man's best friend.

Finally and most importantly, although Hesiod blames Pandora for releasing all of mankind's ills, she must be thanked for preserving our greatest treasure. "Hope remained there inside in her secure dwelling, under the lip of the jar, and did not fly out, because the woman put the lid back in time."[18] In order for mankind to obtain the inestimable gift of hope, it was necessary for us first to experience the pain that makes hope necessary. The feminine is both the cause of desire and its object.

The lesson of this myth is that gifts are ambiguous. The gifts of the gods were given neither out of altruism nor out of affection. They were an aggressive, punitive attempt to reestablish godly superiority over mankind. Nevertheless, despite divine malice, the gifts brought great joy in addition to great suffering. In any event, the relationship established by such divine gifts can only be that of hierarchy. Men can curse or bless the Greek gods, submit to them or rebel, but not love them as equals or aspire to become like them.

In this chapter, I explore the nature of gift. The scope of this chapter is very specific. Much scholarship on gift promiscuously lumps together a variety of gratuitous transfers—including personal gifts, testamentary bequests, and public charity—along with a variety of altruistic behavior, such as "donations" of blood, organs, and time. This approach assumes, but does not demonstrate, a shared essence among these different practices, customs, and institutions. This can lead to flawed conclusions.

I believe, in contradistinction, that each of these different forms of human relations must be analyzed on its own terms. Only then can we

16. He compares women to drones idly consuming the fruits of productive bee-men's labors. *See id.* ll. 593–610, at 20–21. Science, of course, reverses Hesiod's sexual stereotype. Worker bees are all female; the drones are the only males in the hive.

17. *See id.* ll. 611–16, at 21.

18. *Id.* ll. 96–98, at 39–40. Hesiod tries to rob Pandora of her well-deserved credit by stating that she closed the jar "by the providence of Zeus." *Id.* ll. 96–99, at 39–40. But by this standard, she should also be acquitted of responsibility for releasing the ills when she innocently opened the wedding gift given to her by the deceitful gods.

identify essential similarities and differences, and make appropriate moral, ethical, political, and legal judgments. Hegel argues that the particular altruism that characterizes family relationships must be distinguished from the universal altruism that characterizes the relationship of citizens in the modern constitutional state.[19] Moreover, the judgment that particular and universal altruism are appropriately allocated to the family and the state, respectively, in no way suggests that the particular egoism of the state of nature or the universal egoism of the market (i.e., civil society) should be disparaged, so long as they are relegated to appropriate spheres of society. Rather, egoism complements altruism as an equally true and necessary moment of human nature.

Consequently, I limit the scope of this chapter in two ways. First, I only analyze one category of gratuitous transfers: "gift," as understood in the everyday, literal sense of one identified individual personally giving an object of desire directly to another identified individual. I do not use the term expansively or metaphorically to include all forms of altruism, such as the care given by the nurse to the afflicted or the sacrifice made by the soldier for his country. Nor do I refer to anonymous or public charity. Indeed, I challenge the unexamined assumptions that gifts are always, or even usually, altruistic in nature.

Second, I only analyze the nature of gift and do not set forth an exegesis, analysis, or critique of the existing substantive law of gift or a comprehensive survey of the considerable literature on the subject.[20] I only mention in passing one of the most important substantive legal issues governing gifts that is discussed in the literature—namely, the different treatment of completed gifts (donative transfers) and executory gifts (gratuitous promises). Although I offer a principled argument concerning another closely related and frequently debated issue (whether there is a meaningful distinction between contractual and gratuitous promises), I suggest neither a simple test for characterizing specific promises as an empirical matter nor any other specific legislative proposal.

As a Hegelian, I do not believe that philosophy alone can legitimately be used to justify positive legislation. Positive law is the bailiwick of practical, not logical, reasoning.[21] This is necessitated by the Hegelian doctrine that the

19. *See* SHLOMO AVINERI, HEGEL'S THEORY OF THE MODERN STATE 134 (1972).

20. For a useful survey of the copious literature on the law of gift, *see* Melvin Aron Eisenberg, *The World of Contract and the World of Gift*, 85 CAL. L. REV. 821 (1997).

21. *See* G. W. F. HEGEL, ELEMENTS OF THE PHILOSOPHY OF RIGHT 41, 81 (Allen W. Wood ed. & H. B. Nisbet trans., Cambridge Univ. Press 1991) [hereinafter, HEGEL, THE PHILOSOPHY OF RIGHT]. A good example of confusing the logical process of jurisprudential analysis with the pragmatic problem of rule making can be seen in Jane Baron's analysis of gifts. In her comment on Carol M. Rose's paper, *Giving, Trading, Thieving, and Trusting: How and Why Gifts Become Exchanges, and (More Importantly) Vice Versa*, 44 FLA. L. REV. 295 (1992), Baron concludes from

essence of human nature is radical freedom. If determinative logic dictated all aspects of human behavior, then we would be bound, not free.[22] The organization of human relations must therefore always reflect a fundamental moment of subjectivity—i.e., judgment. This means that idealism always requires pragmatism as its corollary.

Philosophy, however, is by no means irrelevant to law. Indeed, it serves a crucial function. Philosophy is a means of identifying and analyzing those abstract moral and ethical ideals—such as the nature of human personhood, freedom, and relationship—that the lawyer, legislator, and judge need to consider in making pragmatic decisions as to the concrete legal rules that are needed to produce a just society.

Consequently, my goal is to set forth a coherent account of the roles played by gift and contract in the creation of legal and psychoanalytic subjectivity and the creation of the regime of abstract right (i.e., private law, the market). I argue that subjectivity, contract, and law are mutually constituting. Gift is a failed attempt at the creation of legal subjectivity. Gift is therefore of questionable legal status in the private-law regime of abstract right, although it might have other, nonlegal justifications in the regimes of morality and ethics and the institutions of the family and the state. This analysis reveals that there is, therefore, some implicit philosophic logic underlying American law's traditional solicitude towards contract and suspicion of gift.

THE NATURE OF GIFT

The average person probably thinks of gifts as untrammeled good. Many legal theorists adopt this prejudice and assume that gift relationships are

---

the observation that empirical relations often cannot be neatly fit into the two categories of gift and contracts, but fall somewhere in between, that the categories themselves are incoherent. Jane B. Baron, *Do We Believe in Generosity?: Reflections on the Relationship Between Gifts and Exchanges*, 44 U. FLA. L. REV. 355, 357 (1992) [hereinafter, Baron, *Generosity*]. The implication she seems to draw from this is that gratuitous promises should be enforced like contract. See generally Jane Baron, *Gifts, Bargains, and Form*, 64 IND. L. J. 155 (1988–1989) [hereinafter, Baron, *Gifts*].

To be more accurate, Baron does not clearly state her conclusions. I infer that Baron believes that gratuitous promises should be enforceable based on her argument that gift and contract share the same essential aspect of exchange, her assertion that attempts to justify law's differential treatment of contract and gift are unsuccessful, and her conclusion that for society not to enforce gratuitous promises would be a denigration of generosity.

Baron incorrectly suggests that the fact that the distinction between gift and contract is quantitative as an empirical matter (i.e., concrete real-life events fall over a continuum between abstract legal categories) means that the two categories are not qualitatively different as a logical matter. Lawyers and judges often deal with the practical problems of line drawing and the legal characterization of the messy facts of life.

22. *See* Richard Hyland, *Hegel: A User's Manual*, 10 CARDOZO L. REV. 1735, 1741 (1989).

morally superior to contracts and market relationships. In this view, gift is seen as erotic and creative[23] in contrast to the cold sterility of contract.[24] Nevertheless, the law is notoriously suspicious of gifts, giving them less protection than contracts. In the words of one legal scholar:

> The law discriminates between gifts and exchanges in odd and interesting ways. A promisee can sue to enforce an ordinary commercial promise, but not a promise to give a gift. Creditors can force a donee to disgorge gifts received from insolvent debtors, but they cannot usually force a purchaser to disgorge goods purchased from insolvent debtors. In England and the United States, disinherited spouses can sometimes reverse inter vivos gifts that diminish their statutory share of the estate; in civil jurisdictions, disinherited spouses and children can do this routinely. But in none of these places can disinherited relatives reverse commercial exchanges that have diminished the value of the estate.[25]

Most notably, the formalities for an enforceable contract—offer, acceptance, consideration, and, in some circumstances, the statute of frauds—are minimal and flexible. In contrast, to be enforceable, gratuitous promises must frequently comply with complex formalities.[26]

23. *See, e.g.*, LEWIS HYDE, THE GIFT: IMAGINATION AND THE EROTIC LIFE OF PROPERTY (1983).

24. See Blake D. Morant, *The Teachings of Dr. Martin Luther King, Jr. and Contract Theory: An Intriguing Comparison*, 50 ALA. L. REV. 63 (1998).

25. Eric A. Posner, *Altruism, Status, and Trust in the Law of Gifts and Gratuitous Promises*, 1997 WIS. L. REV. 567, 567.

In the words of Eisenberg, "An important general principle of contract law is that a donative promise—a promise to make a gift—is not legally enforceable simply because it is a promise, although certain kinds of donative promises are enforceable under special principles, like reliance." Eisenberg, *supra* note 20, at 821–22.

Although his point is well taken, Eric Posner's language is unfortunately colloquial for a law review article in that he distinguishes between donees and purchasers. Although a lay person uses the terms "purchaser" and "buyer" interchangeably, the law does not. "Purchaser" is a broad term of art that includes anyone who takes title in a voluntary transaction. *See, e.g.*, U.C.C. 1–201(32)–(33) (1999), 11 U.S.C. 101 (43) (West 1998).

Consequently, a more accurate statement of the law of fraudulent transfers and conveyances is that in some circumstances creditors may void a transfer of debtor property when the purchaser has not paid fair consideration. Of course, a person who receives something for nothing is normally considered the donee of a gift, but many fraudulent transfers and conveyances are in the form of sales in which the "buyer" pays something but not enough. Other forms of economic relations that do not fall within the usual rubric of gifts (such as dividends paid to stockholders of an insolvent corporation) can also be fraudulent conveyances.

26. As Baron states, "Thus, with respect to gifts, where the primary legal goal is to effectuate donative intent, formalities are said to be required to put that intent beyond question. In contrast, with regard to contracts, where the primary legal goal is protection of expectations and security of transactions, consideration is said to be required to mark off those promises customarily understood, in a market economy, to be binding." Baron, *Gifts, supra* note 21, at 156.

I argue that this apparent disjunction between society's stated values and legal norms is not an aporia, but a reflection of gift's fundamentally ambiguous nature. Gift may pass as the generous act of the donor, but it always also includes an implicitly aggressive moment whereby the donor achieves dominance over the donee. In contrast, contract, not gift, reflects the true love relationship in its most rudimentary and primitive form. Indeed, as I discuss, contract is *hysterically* erotic in the technical sense.

Moreover, contract does not necessarily repress altruism. Contract helps to establish the conditions of equality and mutuality that are necessary for the particular altruism necessary for the companionable family, as well as the general altruism necessary for the constitutional state. If gift is a necessary human relationship, it is not despite but because of its ambiguity.

In this chapter, I first introduce the polar extremes of the legal analysis of gift.[27] For convenience, I call these the "utilitarian" and the "romantic" views. I am well aware that relatively few scholars, if any, are purists. Most fall somewhere in between. Nevertheless, despite the fact that actual theoretical positions tend to form a continuum between them, identifying the possible extremes serves a valid analytical purpose. In Hegelian terminology, there is a fundamental "qualitative" difference between the utilitarian and romantic positions, even though the distinctions between them are "quantitative" in nature.[28] I shall use Judge Richard Posner and his offspring, Eric Posner, as

---

Of course, to say that the law is suspicious of gratuitous promises is not to say that they are never enforceable. Rather, in form, the default rule tends to be that gratuitous promises are not enforced unless the claimant establishes the appropriate exception to the default rule. Some contemporary analysts have suggested that such exceptions are in fact so frequent that the empirical norm is that gratuitous promises are in fact enforceable. For a critical discussion of this strain of "Third Wave" gift jurisprudence, see Eisenberg, *supra* note 20.

27. Eisenberg has similarly noted a split, which he dubs the "Second" and "Third Waves" of gift scholarship. He describes the history of modern gift scholarship in terms of three waves. *See* Eisenberg, *supra* note 20, at 825–31. "Classical contract law theorists made the mistake of thinking that legal rules could be justified simply on doctrinal grounds." *Id.* at 825.

The "First Wave" of criticism, associated with Lon Fuller, argued that the substantive law of gift could be justified on both formal and substantive grounds. *Id.* at 827 (quoting Lon L. Fuller, *Consideration and Form,* 41 COLUM. L. REV. 799, 815 (1941) (footnote omitted) (citation omitted)).

The "Second Wave" of scholarship, which began in the late 1970s and early 1980s was loosely linked by an analysis of the relative costs and benefits to both the parties and society of enforcement. The "law-and-economics," or what I call the "utilitarian," position would fall within Eisenberg's Second Wave.

The "Third Wave" of scholarship, which began in the late 1980s, "argues that simple donative promises should be enforceable." *Id.* at 831. What I call the "romantic" view generally falls within this last wave.

28. I introduced the relation between quality and quantity in Jeanne L. Schroeder, *Never Jam To-day: On the Impossibility of Takings Jurisprudence,* 84 GEORGETOWN L. J. 1531 (1996) [hereafter, Schroeder, *Never Jam To-day*] and discuss it in more detail in Chapter 4.

proxies for the utilitarian position, and Lewis Hyde and Margaret Jane Radin as spokespersons for the romantic position.[29]

The legal utilitarian, who views all human relations in terms of individual self-interest,[30] analyzes gift as a primitive, incomplete, imperfect, and inferior form of contract, in the sense that both are essentially economic transactions intended to increase the utility or wealth of the donor.[31] The legal system should therefore concentrate on facilitating the more complete and efficient form of contract rather than encouraging and protecting gifts.[32]

In contrast, the romantic, who believes that human relations can and should be based on altruism, sees gift as being not merely different from, but superior to, the market regime of contract.[33] Consequently, the law should

29. In this chapter, when I use the family name "Posner" standing alone I refer to the father (Richard). No doubt both Posner and Radin will object to my terminology. As I discuss briefly in this chapter, Posner has traditionally characterized himself as a "wealth maximizer," although he has more recently called himself a "pragmatist." POSNER, OVERCOMING LAW 4–21 (1995) [hereinafter, POSNER, OVERCOMING LAW]. Radin also self-styles herself a "pragmatist." *See, e.g.*, Margaret Jane Radin, *Market-Inalienability*, 100 HARV. L. REV. 1849, 1856, 1883 (1987) [hereinafter, Radin, *Market-Inalienability*]. Nevertheless, I hold to my characterization of their theories as "utilitarian" and "romantic," within the sense of those terms used in this chapter. I discuss Posner's distinction between wealth maximization and utilitarianism in Chapter 4.

30. This is the assumption usually made within the law-and-economics movement, although, as discussed in Chapter 4, a true utilitarian must in fact be radically communitarian.

31. For example, Allan Farnsworth asserts that today "those who make them [i.e., the most significant gifts] are not motivated solely or even primarily by altruism." E. Allan Farnsworth, *Promises to Make Gifts*, 43 AM. J. COMP. L. 359, 359 (1995). Some legal scholars who do not take a hard-line utilitarian position have come to recognize this aspect of gift. For example, Melanie Leslie states, "Even when promises are not part of an express bargain, they are seldom purely gratuitous." Melanie Leslie, *Enforcing Family Promises: Reliance, Reciprocity, and Relational Contract*, 77 N.C. L. REV. 551, 554 (1999).

Despite this, many law-and-economics scholars do not have the courage of their wealth-maximization convictions. For example, Eric Posner asserts that "law and economics literature, almost exclusively, assumes that altruism is the sole motive of gift-giving." E. Posner, *supra* note 25, at 567–68.

32. For example, Eric Posner states, "Taken together, the arguments in their strongest form suggest that courts should not enforce gratuitous promises as routinely as they enforce commercial promises. This conclusion is based on the following propositions: (1) that status-enhancing and 'exchange gift' promises should not be enforced, even if altruistic and 'signaling' promises should sometimes (but not always) be enforced; (2) that altruistic and signaling promises, when they are enforced, should result in lower levels of damages than should non-gratuitous promises; (3) that courts cannot reliably distinguish the different kinds of gratuitous promises; (4) that given a set of commercial promises and gratuitous promises that do not violate standard policy restrictions, such as the policy against price-fixing or against coercion, the commercial promises are likely to be more socially valuable than are the gratuitous promises." *Id.* at 608.

33. As Eisenberg states, a gift is "made[]for affective reasons like love, affection, friendship, comradeship, or gratitude, or to satisfy moral duties or aspirations like benevolence or generos-

give special solicitude to gifts and discourage or prohibit contracts concerning at least some forms of property.[34]

Because proponents of both the utilitarian and romantic positions rely to some extent on anthropological studies of "archaic" societies that are organized around systems of "gift exchange," as opposed to our norm of contract, I turn briefly to these studies. I will show that neither school of thought accurately describes these institutions. Rather, they choose to discuss only those aspects of these societies that superficially support their presuppositions and suppress those that are inconvenient. I suggest that the institution of potlatch—gift as war—is not a perversion of gift, but rather its epitome.

I then present in detail a Hegelian-Lacanian analysis of contract and gift to show that both the utilitarian and romantic views are partially correct and partially incorrect, but in precisely opposite ways. Indeed, utilitarianism and romanticism are mirror images of each other.

Both utilitarians and romantics start from the same misconceptions of the nature of contract and commodification. They agree that contract is based on coldly rational considerations of narrow self-interest. They further agree that contract leads to the commodification of goods in the market and that commodification makes objects indistinguishable and subjects indifferent. The two schools merely disagree on valorization. The utilitarian, who cham-

---

ity, and which is not expressly conditioned on a reciprocal exchange." Eisenberg, *supra* note 20, at 823.

34. For example, Radin would place a variety of restraints on contractual (i.e., market) alienation of those objects that she identifies as "personal property" on the grounds that such "commodification" of "personal property" is destructive of personhood. In contrast, she would continue to permit gratuitous transfers of such objects on the grounds that gifts are conducive to constructive human relations.

As I have said, many, or most, scholars fall between these two poles. For example, Eisenberg and Baron share the romantic view of gift, but come to strikingly different legal conclusions. As a contract scholar, Eisenberg defends the (utilitarian) conclusion that the law's differential treatment of contract and gift is justified, but rejects the utilitarian premise that gift is an imperfect form of contract. Rather, he maintains that the gift relation is not merely morally superior to contract specifically, but also to law generally. Submitting gift to law, therefore, would have a deleterious affect on gift. Eisenberg, *supra* note 20, at 823.

In contrast, Baron takes the romantic position that gratuitous promises are morally superior to contract and therefore should be at least as enforceable as contract. To justify this, however, she feels she must agree with the utilitarian position that there is no essential difference between gift and contract. She therefore straddles the uncomfortable fence between arguing that gifts should be enforced because they are different from contract, and that gifts should be enforced because they cannot be distinguished from contract. For example, Baron criticizes society's refusal to grant blanket enforcement of gratuitous promises as a denigration of the virtue of generosity, while simultaneously arguing that gift, like contract, is a matter of exchange. *See* Baron, *Generosity, supra* note 21.

pions rationality and indifference, reduces gift to contract—a form of commodification. The romantic, who cherishes intuition and difference, distinguishes gift from contract.[35]

In contrast, I argue that, far from being characterized solely by the cold calculation of self-interest, markets are erotic in the Hegelian-Lacanian sense that they are driven by the desire for recognition.[36] Contract, being mutual, reflects the true love relation in which recognition is freely granted and received by equals.[37] Gift, being unilateral, reflects the failed attempt at a forced relation between unequals, which Hegel describes in his famed lord and bondsman dialectic. In gift, recognition is demanded but not granted. Gift is not free, but imposes obligations on the donee without her consent. In other words, if the romantic is correct that gift relations are erotic, it is not the shared, voluntary eroticism of love, but a combination

35. Baron is an exception in that she tries to defend gift in part by arguing that the traditional distinction between gift and contract is incoherent: gift as well as contract is often implicitly reciprocal, and, as an empirical matter, one cannot draw a bright-line distinction between actual gratuitous and gift relations. Baron, *Gifts, supra* note 21, at 157.

To a Hegelian, the fact that the differences between two concepts are quantitative in nature (i.e., actual, concrete examples of the categories fall within a continuum) does not mean that the concepts are not qualitatively different. Baron, in fact, implicitly recognizes this. After arguing that the law's distinction between contract and gift cannot be rationally maintained, she nevertheless asserts the uniqueness, and perhaps moral superiority, of some form of gift relations.

36. Rose is one of the few writers on gift and contract who show any recognition of the affective aspect of contract, albeit from a different theoretical perspective than mine. In support of her argument that the categories of gift and contract tend to "leak" into each other, Rose does not merely make the usual assertion that gifts, like contract, involve exchange and selfishness. *See* Rose, *supra* note 21, at 302–08. She also maintains that contract behavior cannot be totally explained by the utilitarian assumptions of atomistic self-interest. Contract, like gift, necessarily requires an element of trust and altruism. *See id.* at 308–13.

37. As Michel Rosenfeld writes, contrasting, as I do, the more full recognition achieved in contract and the partial recognition achieved in the lord-bondsman dialectic:

> Self-consciousness' desire for recognition can only be satisfied by another self-consciousness, through mutual recognition. Moreover, an optimal way to bring about genuine mutual recognition is through love. Indeed, in love each self-consciousness recognizes the other without attempting to reduce it to being a mere reflection of itself. In other words, in love both self-consciousnesses are united in mutual recognition, but each is able to preserve its individuality and freedom in the course of its union with the other.

Michel Rosenfeld, *Hegel and the Dialectics of Contract,* 10 CARDOZO L. REV. 1199, 1221 (1989). Rosenfeld differs slightly from me in that he sees contract as a more abstract form of mutual recognition among strangers necessitated because "in a large society all social relationships cannot be founded on love." *Id.* In contradistinction, I concentrate on the shared moment of mutuality in love and contract, as well as a Lacanian understanding of the eroticism of recognition, to argue that the recognition of contract should be seen as a primitive form of love.

of the solipsistic eroticism of masturbation and the violent, forced eroticism of rape.

Consequently, the utilitarian is correct in recognizing that gift relations are driven by the self-interest of the donor and that gift imposes reciprocal obligations on the donee, but incorrect in thinking that gift can be analyzed in terms of contract. In contradistinction, the romantic is correct in recognizing that gift and contract are fundamentally different, but incorrect in thinking that gift relations are characterized by the altruism of the donor and the freedom of the donee.

I then turn to the misconception of the nature of contract and commodification shared by utilitarians and romantics. They both assume that commodification is the suppression of difference. In fact, it is only in contract that subjects can first recognize each other as unique, but equal, individuals. In contradistinction, although gift also establishes a degree of distinction between persons, this distinction is that of status and not individuality. Gift establishes relations of superiority and inferiority, envy and fear, not equality and love.

I next offer a Lacanian analysis of the romantic position, which fears contract and markets as the cause of alienation. Finally, I conclude with a brief consideration of the necessary role of imperfection and difference, not only in human relations but also in the structure of the world.

Utilitarianism

Probably the best known proponent of what I call the "utilitarian" analysis of gift is Richard Posner.[38] Posnerian utilitarianism analyzes all human relationships in the same way it analyzes contracts and markets. In Posner's terms, the "economist's basic analytical tool for studying markets"[39] can be used to study other behavior. "That tool is the assumption that people are rational maximizers of their satisfactions."[40] Posner rhetorically asks, "Is it plausible to suppose that people are rational only or mainly when they are transacting in markets, and not when they are engaged in other activities of

38. Posner considers himself a proponent of "wealth maximization" and tries to separate himself from utilitarianism. RICHARD A. POSNER, THE ECONOMICS OF JUSTICE 61 (1981) [hereinafter, POSNER, ECONOMICS OF JUSTICE]. The differences that Posner identifies between utilitarianism and wealth maximization do not relate to the analysis of gift. For an excellent critique of Posner's attempt to distinguish wealth maximization from utilitarianism, *see* Robin Grant, *Judge Richard Posner's Wealth Maximization Principle: Another Form of Utilitarianism?*, 10 CARDOZO L. REV. 815 (1989). I take Posner's distinctions seriously in Chapter 4.

39. POSNER, ECONOMICS OF JUSTICE, *supra* note 38, at 1.

40. *Id.*

life, such as marriage and litigation and crime and discrimination and concealment of personal information?"[41]

Consequently, people make gifts for the same reason they enter into contracts. Gift "creates utility for the promisor over and above the utility to him of the . . . performance."[42] Accordingly, a utilitarian would apply the same standard for the enforcement of gratuitous promises as he would contracts. "Promises should not be enforced where the enforcement cost—to the extent not borne by the promisor—exceeds the gain from enforcement."[43]

Posner thinks that this rationality justifies the current legal regime. Gratuitous promises are generally unenforceable because of society's "empirical hunch that gratuitous promises tend both to involve small stakes and to be made in family settings where there are economically superior alternatives to legal enforcement."[44] Exceptions to this rule are appropriate when society determines that the utility to be gained by enforcing the gift promise is likely to exceed costs.[45]

Posner bases his analysis of gifts in part on an examination of the gift-exchange institutions that characterize many archaic[46] societies, both historic and contemporary. His goal is to show that gifts are a more "primitive" and therefore inferior form of economic exchange. Thus, he needs to explain gifts in terms of wealth (or utility) maximization.

Not surprisingly, Posner insists that archaic gift should not be thought of in terms of the modern (romantic) notion of altruism. From a Posnerian standpoint, the word "gift" is a misnomer insofar as that term carries with it altruistic baggage.[47] Rather, "the gift system is plainly a form of trade in that

41. *Id.*

42. Richard A. Posner, *Gratuitous Promises in Economics and Law,* 6 J. LEGAL STUD. 411, 412 (1977) [hereinafter, Posner, *Gratuitous Promises*]. In his article, Posner concentrates his analysis on gratuitous promises rather than present gifts. This difference is not relevant to my analysis.

43. *Id.* at 414.

44. *Id.* at 417. Of course, this suggests that the rule should be changed if empirical evidence indicates that this hunch is unfounded.

45. The examples discussed by Posner include past consideration, promises under seal, charitable pledges, and contract modification. *See id.* at 418–24. I do not discuss Posner's specific arguments because only one of these exceptions (promises under seal) is likely to arise in the limited class of gratuitous transactions that I include in my definition of gift. Posner thinks that the legislative abolition of this rule in many states is "a mysterious development from the standpoint of efficiency." *Id.* at 420. This is because the seal requirement "eliminates the major administrative costs associated with the enforcement of unilateral promises. The formalities and written character of the promise reduce both the costs of determining the content of the promise and the probability that the promise was not made or was not intended to be binding." *Id.* at 419–20.

46. Posner does not limit his examination to the contemporary archaic societies studied by anthropologists. He also considers ancient Hellenic society, as described in the Homeric epics.

47. *See* POSNER, ECONOMICS OF JUSTICE, *supra* note 38, at 160.

it is explicitly reciprocal."[48] Certain surface differences between modern markets and archaic gift exchange merely mask a shared essence.

In modern markets, the trading partners exchange different objects,[49] contract exchange is simultaneous,[50] and prices are usually set by negotiation. Sales contracts are enforced by a highly developed legal system.

In archaic gift exchange, the parties frequently exchange the same or similar objects,[51] such as ornamental or ceremonial objects. Typically, the reciprocal countergift will not be given until some time in the future. Indeed, this future date may be uncertain, to be determined at the discretion of the donee/counterdonor or by the demand of the donor/counterdonee.

Gift exchange often lacks explicit pricing. Nevertheless, both the appropriate amount and the timing of the return gift are frequently well established either by custom or indirect negotiation. Because archaic societies lack effective government and laws, other mechanisms are used to establish the countergift obligation, such as social pressure, desire for prestige, fear of revenge, and so on.

Nevertheless, according to Posner, both contract and gift are essentially the same, because they are forms of exchange through which the participants seek to maximize their utility or wealth. The specific difference between modern contract and archaic gift can be explained by the precise functions they serve in two very different types of economies. Modern people engage in contract in order to recognize the productive advantages of division of labor and specialization.[52] Archaic societies do not have the political or economic organization to permit this degree of specialization.

Consequently, Posner proposes two general functions for gift exchange in primitive or archaic societies: information gathering and insurance.[53] He discusses the former in detail in the context of the archaic society described in the Homeric epics and the latter in terms of contemporary archaic societies. Households have four basic needs: food, shelter, reproduction, and

48. *Id.* at 136 (citations omitted). This statement is made specifically in his analysis of Homeric Greek culture, but this concept underlies Posner's more general analysis of primitive cultures in subsequent chapters of *The Economics of Justice.*

49. *See id.* at 136, 170.

50. This is true even of executory contracts, in the sense that both parties simultaneously exchange binding promises.

51. *See id.*

52. *See id.* at 136, 160.

53. Posner makes five assumptions about the typical characteristics of archaic economies. First, there is no effective government. *See id.* at 151. Second, lack of technical knowledge limits the variety of types and qualities of consumption goods. *See id.* Third, goods are generally consumed by the group that produces them rather than being traded. *See id.* at 151–52. Fourth, consumption goods are perishable and must be consumed quickly. *See id.* at 152. Fifth, various structural reasons prevent individuals from being able to capture any gains or savings from innovation. *See id.*

protection against other households.[54] In Homeric Greece, each household was relatively self-sufficient with respect to the first two. Gift exchange, according to Posner, was designed to fulfill the last two. The incest taboo required that members of the household's ruling family marry its children into distant families.[55] In a warrior culture, a household could enhance its security if it installed some of its members into other households through marriage or otherwise.[56] One of the problems of ancient societies was lack of communication technology and the resulting lack of knowledge about those who are not members of one's immediate kinship group. Gift exchange was a means of gathering information about strangers in order to judge the candidacy of potential familial and defensive partners.

> If I give you a gold tripod and receive in exchange a coarse blanket, I learn something about your suitability as an ally or as a father-in-law: if that is all you have to give me, it probably means you are not a very good fighter, for you have not been able to collect a store of booty from which to give me a good present.[57]

In contemporary archaic societies, according to Posner, gift exchange is more likely to act as a way of fulfilling the first two types of needs that Posner identifies (i.e., food and shelter). Because consumption goods are perishable in these societies, and because there is no effective contractual insurance, as in modern cultures, archaic peoples set up gift-exchange relations as a form of "hunger insurance."[58] When consumer goods "are limited in variety and durability, giving away one's surplus . . . may be the most useful thing to do with it."[59] A wealthy man who does not share his excess has "no use to the other members of the society"[60] and might be killed, whereas one who does engage in this mutually beneficial regime of exchange is held in high regard.

Both systems of gift exchange are therefore means of wealth or utility maximization just like contract. The donor makes a gift today in order to receive beneficial goods or services in the future. In Homeric Greece, the donors used gift as a means of acquiring wives, as well as familial and military alliances. In contemporary archaic societies, gifts made in times of plenty are means of securing support in times of hardship.[61] That is, if we moderns

54. *See id.* at 137.

55. *See id.*

56. *See id.*

57. *Id.*

58. *Id.* at 153. The most basic insurance institution in Posner's scheme is the elaborate kinship relations that characterize primitive societies.

59. *Id.* at 158.

60. *Id.*

61. *See id.* at 160.

exchange in order to vary present consumption, archaic man exchanges in order to even out his consumption over time. This is supposed to explain why the timing of exchange is not simultaneous in archaic societies.

Eric Posner also offers a utilitarian analysis of the treatment of gift.[62] Posner *fils* rejects what he thinks of as the more common approach, even among economists, of assuming that all gifts are altruistic in nature.[63] He recognizes that many so-called "gift" transactions

> do call for a return transfer, if only implicitly or by convention: a gift to a friend often calls for a return gift on a future occasion, or at least expressions of gratitude; a gift to a business associate frequently creates the expectation of future dealings; and a gift to a politician generally requires the politician to show some favoritism to the donor in return.[64]

Although he claims to "resist [the] impulse" to "collapse the categories of gift and exchange,"[65] he does analyze gift, like contract, as being primarily a means of increasing the utility of the donor. Eric Posner proposes three possible reasons people engage in gifts: to "(1) enhance the well-being of the donee, (2) increase the status of the donor, or (3) enter or enhance an exchange relationship."[66]

I discuss only his first and third rationales because his second rationale relates to charity, not personal gifts.[67] At first blush, Eric Posner's first rationale seems to reflect a romantic belief in community rather than utilitarianism. This is incorrect. Like Posner *père,*[68] Posner *fils* claims not to believe that the hypothesis of utility or wealth maximization requires that people be narrowly self-interested. A person might feel pleasure in the well-being of her

62. Eric Posner uses the term "gift" more broadly than I do to include a wider variety of gratuitous transfers. He defines "gift" "as a transfer of goods or services by a "donor to a 'donee,' where the donee is not required by agreement or convention to transfer something specific back to the donor in exchange." E. Posner, *supra* note 25, at 569. His definition would sweep in testamentary and charitable transfers.

63. *See id.* at 567.

64. *Id.* at 569.

65. *Id.*

66. *Id.* at 567.

67. *See id.* at 588–91. One reason why socialites give extravagant gifts to universities and other public charities is to gain social prestige. Consequently, these gifts are typically publicly acknowledged by the recipient by naming buildings and so forth after the donor, honoring the donor in testimonials, or at least permitting the donor to attend exclusive charity balls. Although I argue that personal gifts establish the hierarchical relation of status, my point is slightly different. Eric Posner is speaking about the donor's position in society generally. I am arguing that in gift the donor's status is increased vis-à-vis the donee specifically.

68. Who believes that a self-interested person may have a "preference" for altruism. *See* POSNER, OVERCOMING LAW, *supra* note 29, at 16.

family and loved ones (or society generally).[69] If so, it can be possible for someone to increase her own personal utility by increasing the utility of others. Although utilitarianism claims to preserve a place for altruism, it does so only at the expense of redefining altruism from its traditional sense of selflessness to a form of self-interest.[70]

In other words, "through gift-giving, one increases one's utility by increasing the well-being of someone one cares about (altruism) . . . or by signaling one's desire to enter an exchange relationship or by benefitting the other pursuant to that relationship in anticipation that others will reciprocate."[71] Consequently, gift, like contract, is a form of utility maximization. The problem is that gift, which lacks explicit bargaining and specificity, is particularly subject to bargaining failure for a number of reasons.[72] The donor may miscalculate the desires of the donee, so that the gift's cost to the donor may outweigh the combined utility to the donee and the donor.[73] In "impure altruistic" gifts, the donor gives the donee what the donor thinks is good for the donee (such as nutritious food or a college education), rather than what would really make the donee happy (such as recreational drugs or an expensive sports car), resulting in a decrease in utility for the donee.[74] Some "altruistic" promises rashly made in an unconsidered, emotional moment may result in a net decrease in aggregate long-term utility if one considers the subsequent regrets of the rueful donor, or the potential harm to creditors and dependents of the donor—as when a prodigal father gives extravagant gifts to his mistress, thereby reducing his children's birthright.[75] In the case of gifts intended to enhance relationships, the donee may not understand why the donor is making the gift and what is expected in return.[76] Moreover, an unscrupulous, opportunistic person may solicit and obtain trust-enhancing gifts by falsely signaling that she wishes to cooperate and form a mutually satisfactory relationship with the donor.[77]

69. Posner, *Gratuitous Promises, supra* note 42, at 412.

70. E. Posner, *supra* note 25, at 586.

71. *Id.* at 582.

72. *See id.* at 586.

73. Consequently, Joel Waldfogel (perhaps facetiously) estimates that Christmas gifts alone result in billions of dollars of deadweight lost every year. *See* Joel Waldfogel, *The Deadweight Loss of Christmas,* 83 AM. ECON. REV. 1328, 1336 (1993).

74. *See* E. Posner, *supra* note 25, at 586. The only standard of utilitarianism is supposed to be the aggregate subjective happiness of society, which is most accurately measured by each member's idiosyncratic feelings. Society is not to impose its judgment as to what its members should want.

75. *See id.* at 588.

76. "Recipients are never quite sure whether a gift is intended for altruistic or for trust-enhancing reasons." *Id.* at 586.

77. *See id.* at 586–87.

Eric Posner argues that, on the one hand, gifts are less likely than contracts to result in an increase in aggregate utility. On the other hand, the failure to enforce gratuitous contracts should be expected to result in less damages than a failure to enforce contracts. This is because, given the signaling uncertainties surrounding gifts, the parties to gratuitous promises are less likely to incur substantial costs in reliance than the parties to contracts.[78]

The implication drawn from this is that if the primary goal of law is wealth or utility maximization, then gift has an ambiguous role to play in our modern economy. Because economic efficiency is the goal (or at least one of the most important goals) of private law, law should offer relatively little support to gift relations that might interfere with contract relations. Consequently, Eric Posner argues that executory contracts to make gifts should be relatively disfavored. Indeed, insofar as gift continues to serve valuable functions in modern society, these functions are primarily personal and social rather than economic or legal.[79]

Romanticism

Perhaps the most sustained, and influential, expression of the romantic position is Hyde's *The Gift: Imagination and the Erotic Life of Property.*[80] Although Hyde presents his analysis as part of a theory of literary interpretation, his work is a standard citation for legal scholars undertaking a romantic defense of gift.

Hyde maintains that gift is erotic in nature.[81] Gift is to be contrasted with contract, which is the expression of reason or logos.[82] By this he means that gift builds lasting relations. It binds people together,[83] whereas contract separates and alienates people.[84] If people in market economies are free, this is so only in the negative sense that they lack bonds to others.[85]

Gift and contract treat objects differently. In gift exchange, people develop a unique relation to individual objects, whereas in contract, objects are commodities.

78. *See id.* at 596–99.

79. If so, efforts to regulate these gifts by law may actually reduce the value of gifts. *See id.* at 567. Surprisingly (or perhaps not so surprisingly, given my analysis that romanticism and utilitarianism are mirror images), Eisenberg comes to precisely the same conclusion. *See* Eisenberg, *supra* note 20, at 847–49.

80. HYDE, *supra* note 23.

81. *See id.* at xiv n.*, 22.

82. *See id.* at xiv n.*.

83. *See id.* at xiv, 66.

84. *See id.* at 67.

85. *See id.*

> I would begin the analysis by saying that a commodity has value and a gift does not. A gift has worth. . . . I mean "worth" to refer to those things we prize and yet say "you can't put a price on it." We derive value, on the other hand, from the comparison of one thing with another.[86]

In order for gift to be effective, it is necessary that the donee not retain the gift. The gift must be kept "in circulation" by one means or another. The actual object of the gift must either be further gifted to another person, increasing the circle of relationships,[87] or consumed or destroyed.[88] Like Posner, Hyde seeks empirical support for his theory in archaic gift-exchange institutions. According to Hyde, gifts are dynamic and contract is static. "A market exchange has an equilibrium or stasis: you pay to balance the scale. But when you give a gift there is momentum, and the weight shifts from body to body."[89]

Reciprocity is an essential aspect of gift. Gift creates an obligation on the part of the donee to respond in kind, thereby establishing a continued relationship between donor and donee.[90] The reciprocity of gift differs from contractual exchange in that the former is relational, whereas the latter is obligatory. For example, Radin, a leading romantic in contemporary legal scholarship, describes the reasoning implicit in Richard Titmuss's well-known proposal that the American mixed system of blood donations (whereby blood is both sold and donated) be replaced with a completely donative system because "donation fosters altruism."[91]

> The possibility of reciprocity is also a part of this cementing process, because a donor's sense of obligation could be partially founded on the recognition that she could be a recipient someday. From the recipient's perspective, it is said that knowing one is dependent on others' altruism rather than on one's own wealth creates solidarity and interdependence, and that this knowledge of dependence better preserves and expresses the ideal of sanctity of life.[92]

Even though gift objects gain value through circulation, they have no exchange value in the modern sense in that there can be no preset standard

86. *Id.* at 60.

87. *See id.* at xiv, 11–19.

88. *See id.* at 9.

89. *Id.*

90. *See id.* at 15–16.

91. *See* MARGARET JANE RADIN, CONTESTED COMMODITIES 96 (1996) [hereinafter, RADIN, CONTESTED COMMODITIES]. I only discuss Richard Titmuss in passing in this book because he concentrates on public charity rather than on personal gift. I question whether the personal relation of gift can be compared to the public altruism of charity. Kenneth Arrow similarly chides Titmuss for unreflectively assuming that the two are related. Kenneth J. Arrow, *Gifts and Exchanges,* 1 PHIL. & PUB. AFF. 341, 360 (1972).

92. RADIN, CONTESTED COMMODITIES, *supra* note 91, at 96.

for the return object. "The equivalence of the counter-gift is left to the giver."[93] Consequently, there is no express bargaining between donor and donee over the countergift and " 'it cannot be enforced by any kind of coercion.' If a man gives a second-rate [ritual gift] in return for a fine [ritual gift], people may talk, but there is nothing anyone can do about it."[94] That is, if contract is "free" in the negative sense that people are free from bonds to others, gift is "free" in the positive sense that people are free to enter into it and free to respond or not respond, as they see fit.

Finally, according to Hyde, gift relations are altruistic and egalitarian; cultures based on gift exchange do not have organized governments and are nonhierarchical.[95] Contract leads to social stratification and laws that protect the dominant group.[96]

Indeed, Radin believes that contract and market rhetoric is itself alienating.

> The critique of market rhetoric tells us that the way we conceive of things matters to who we are. To conceive of something personal as fungible assumes that the person and attribute, right, or thing, are separate. This view imposes the subject/object dichotomy to create two kinds of alienation, depending upon whether or not the bearer of the attribute, right, or thing internalizes the commodified conception.
>
> If the discourse of commodification is partially made one's own, it creates disorientation of the self that experiences the distortion of its own personhood. . . .
>
> To conceive of something personal as fungible also assumes that persons cannot freely give of themselves to others. At best they can bestow commodities.[97]

The romantic conceives of persons as being originally or essentially connected. The presence of alienation in the world, therefore, must have been caused by something external. Markets and contract are identified as the source of this alienation. Gifts are seen as means of continuing or restoring our essential, primal relationality.

The utilitarian vision of human nature and gift is considered uniquely

93. BRONISLAW MALINOWSKI, ARGONAUTS OF THE WESTERN PACIFIC: AN ACCOUNT OF NATIVE ENTERPRISE AND ADVENTURE IN THE ARCHIPELAGOS OF MELANESIA NEW GUINEA (Waveland Press, Inc. 1984) (1922), quoted in HYDE, *supra* note 23, at 15.

94. *Id.*

95. *See* Thomas D. Barton, *Legal Anthropology and Economic Analysis,* 80 NW. U. L. REV. 476, 478 (1985) (reviewing KATHERINE NEWMAN, LAW AND ECONOMIC ORGANIZATION: A COMPARATIVE STUDY OF PREINDUSTRIAL SOCIETIES [1983] and RICHARD POSNER, A THEORY OF PRIMITIVE SOCIETIES IN THE ECONOMICS OF JUSTICE, *supra* note 38).

96. *See* HYDE, *supra* note 23, at 15.

97. RADIN, CONTESTED COMMODITIES, *supra* note 91, at 93.

repugnant. "At worst—in universal commodification—the gift is conceived of as a bargain. . . . Conceiving of gifts as bargains not only conceives of what is personal as fungible; it also endorses the picture of persons as profit-maximizers."[98] In contrast, gifts are "expressions of the interrelationships between the self and others. A gift takes place within a personal relationship with the recipient, or else it creates one."[99] This vision reflects a "better view of personhood" than the narrow utilitarian one.[100] If contracts cause fungibility, alienation, and separation, "gifts diminish separateness."[101]

Unfortunately, the romantic analysis fails for the same reasons as the utilitarian—both are theoretically inadequate and empirically inaccurate.

GIFT AS POTLATCH

Looting and Pillaging Anthropological Data

Both utilitarians and romantics claim to find support for their positions in anthropological studies of archaic societies organized around complex gift institutions. Even a brief review of the literature indicates, however, that neither school attempts a serious examination of these data to determine the true nature of gift-exchange institutions, let alone to consider whether they are similar or even relevant to modern gift customs. Rather, they loot and pillage anthropology for whatever snippets of information might appear to support their preexisting presuppositions, and they ignore or minimize the significance of any evidence that does not fit their theories. Moreover, both the utilitarian and romantic positions unreflectively assume, without analysis, that there is an essential similarity or relation between the complex, highly ritualistic, and public institutions of archaic societies and the modern customs of personal gift giving and public charity.

As most modern professional anthropologists recognize, one must be extremely careful in trying to reinterpret vastly different forms of society in light of modern Western concepts and vernacular. The data are extremely complex and ambiguous. Anthropologists do not themselves agree as to how to interpret them. Nonanthropologists must be even more careful.[102]

Consequently, I do not purport to offer a "correct" interpretation of these societies specifically or gift-exchange institutions generally. What I do is to

98. *Id.*

99. *Id.*

100. *Id.*

101. *Id.* at 94

102. For an impassioned protest against the promiscuous exploitation of anthropological studies of "exotic" cultures in gift scholarship, see Mary Louise Fellows, *His to Give; His to Receive; Hers to Trust: A Response to Carol M. Rose,* 44 FLA. L. REV. 329, 345–46 (1992).

argue that the data suggest profound differences between gift exchange and the modern market relations favored by the utilitarians on the one hand, and the ideal erotic interrelations hypothesized by the romantics on the other. Archaic gift lacks the equivalence, mutuality, and individualistic freedom of market relations, as well as the warmth and interrelationality of erotic relations. I also very tentatively suggest that the data may be more consistent with the Hegelian account of gift—aggressive agonistic institutions in which participants attempt to attain recognition of status and prestige at the expense of others.

Gift Exchanges

In his ground-breaking book, *The Gift: The Form and Reason for Exchange in Archaic Societies,*[103] published in 1925, Marcel Mauss argued that "gift exchange," as practiced by many, if not most, "archaic" societies is not merely an important social institution, but a premarket economic system as well. Mauss not only revealed a fundamental similarity between such apparently different institutions as *kula,*[104] potlatch,[105] and the practices of certain

103. MARCEL MAUSS, THE GIFT: THE FORM AND REASON FOR EXCHANGE IN ARCHAIC SOCIETIES (W. D. Halls trans., Routledge 1990) (1950).

104. *Kula* is practiced in the Trobriand Islands, a small archipelago in Micronesia. In *kula,* members of the chief class of one island sail clockwise with their retinue in ceremonial ships to the nearest island in order to give gifts of shell bracelets to the chiefs of that island identified as their partners. At other times, donors sail counterclockwise in order to give gifts of shell necklaces to partners on the next island. Over the years, the same bracelets could theoretically make a complete clockwise circle, and the necklaces a complete counterclockwise circle, until they return to their island of origin, or even their original owners. These gifts of bracelets and necklaces are not two separate, parallel institutions. Rather, it is understood that each gift of bracelets obligates the donee to make a return gift of necklaces having the appropriate value, and vice versa.

Kula was introduced to the West in Bronislaw Malinowski's famous study, *Argonauts of the Western Pacific* (*see supra* note 93), and has been the subject of numerous anthropological studies since. As Mauss explains, there are many types of *kula,* as well as other forms of gift and market exchange practiced by the Trobrianders. He and others merely concentrate on "the most solemn, lofty and competitive form." MAUSS, *supra* note 103, at 22.

The word "class" is somewhat misleading in the sense that the Trobriands apparently do not have a rigid political system. As I explain, however, *kula* is a means of establishing prestige and status, and is only practiced by the highest strata of Trobriand society. For convenience, I follow custom and use the words "chiefs" and "class" to refer to those who are permitted to engage in *kula.*

105. Potlatch was a gift-exchange institution formerly practiced among the nations of the Pacific Northwest that has since been largely suppressed by the Canadian government. In potlatch, wealthy men would make what looks to Westerners like absurdly large gifts in elaborate ceremonies.

other contemporary archaic cultures. In an attempt to demonstrate the universality of gift exchange among premarket economies, he also argued that a number of other apparently diverse societies, such as ancient India, prerepublican Rome, and the Germanic tribes of the early middle ages, were characterized by similar institutions.

Although Mauss's observations are rich and complex,[106] I will limit my discussion to two points. This is because utilitarians and romantics have each seized on one of these points to the exclusion of the other and, therefore, have both misinterpreted the data. In contrast, I argue that if one takes both of these two Maussian hypotheses seriously and applies a Hegelian-Lacanian analysis, one sees that both the utilitarian and romantic positions are both wrong, but for opposite reasons. Contract and gift are indeed essentially different, as the romantics maintain. But it is gift that is a failure of eroticism. Gift establishes relation, but this relation is that of status, not love.

Mauss's first point is that no gift is ever given or received freely. "Exchanges and contracts take place in the form of presents; in theory these are voluntary, in reality they are given and reciprocated obligatorily."[107] Donors give not out of altruism but out of social obligation. "To refuse to give, to fail to invite, just as to refuse to accept, is tantamount to declaring war; it is to reject the bond of alliance and commonality. . . . One gives because one is compelled to do so. . . . "[108] Every gift obligates the donee to give a return gift of equal or greater value. "Almost always such services have taken the form of the gift, the present generously given even when, in the gesture accompanying the transaction, there is only a polite fiction, for-

---

In a single potlatch, literally scores of thousands of trade goods, such as blankets and pots, might have been given, as well as purely ceremonial objects, such as engraved metal shields known as "coppers." Sometimes the "gifts" were not physically delivered to the recipients at all, but were destroyed as a sacrifice to the recipients' ancestors or guardian spirits. Recipients of potlatch were expected to give an even larger gift to the donor at a return potlatch. This return obligation was so great that many participants literally impoverished themselves rather than bear the shame of ingratitude. Consequently, some Western observers have compared potlatch to war. *See* MAUSS, *supra* note 103, at 37.

106. The primary point of Mauss's work might be summarized thus: gift is an extremely complicated and ambiguous relation that cannot be pigeonholed easily into simple categories. The very etymology of the English word "gift" reveals its Janus-faced nature—it comes from a Germanic root that means both present and poison. *See* Marcel Mauss, *Gift, Gift,* in THE LOGIC OF THE GIFT: TOWARD AN ETHIC OF GENEROSITY 28–31 (Alan D. Schrift ed., 1997) [hereinafter THE LOGIC OF THE GIFT].

107. MAUSS, *supra* note 103, at 3. Mauss is specifically referring to medieval Scandinavian civilization, as revealed in a quoted Edda. He is using this as an introduction, however, to what he believes is a universal characteristic of gift exchange.

108. *Id.* at 13 (endnotes omitted).

malism, and social deceit, and when really there is obligation and economic self-interest."[109] A potential donee cannot avoid the obligation to give a countergift by refusing a gift because gift-exchange societies also impose strict obligations on their members to accept gifts.[110] Consequently, potlatch—gift as war—is not an aberration, but rather the exemplar of archaic gift exchange. The utilitarian relies primarily on this exchange aspect of gift.

Mauss's second point is that, although it may be a necessary aspect of archaic economies at a certain level of development, gift exchange cannot be reduced to a simple economic function. Gift exchange also serves social functions such as the establishment of relationships (both friendly and hostile) among and the relative status of tribal or family groups or members engaged in the exchange. Indeed, a central part of Mauss's theory is that archaic societies have not yet distinguished the economic realm from other aspects of social intercourse. Consequently, gifts in general, and gift exchange in particular, can be explained neither in terms of gratuitous or personal relations nor in terms of the market. They are a hybrid. They are "at the same time juridical, economic, religious, and even aesthetic and morphological, etc."[111] The romantic relies primarily on this relational aspect of gift.

The utilitarian analysis of gift as contract fails on two closely related grounds. First, it confuses the reciprocal nature of gift with the principle of the equivalence of exchange value in contract; by concentrating on the shared exchange aspect of contract and gift, it represses the nonbargain aspect of gift. Second, it assumes that one engages in gift (like contract) primarily to obtain utility or wealth in the form of future goods or services. In

109. *Id.* at 3. Since Mauss, some anthropologists and sociologists have suggested that archaic gift-exchange systems should technically be called "prestation," defined as " 'the action of paying, in money or services, what is due by law or custom, or feudally,' . . . [when there is implied] a fairly clear obligation on the part of an individual to render something specific, the obligation being enforced by law or at least strong public pressure." CYRIL S. BELSHAW, TRADITIONAL EXCHANGE AND MODERN MARKETS 47 (1965) (citation omitted). As Cyril Belshaw points out, "Gifts in our society are given personally, to be retained by the recipient." *Id.* Nevertheless, the more careful anthropologists are fully aware that even though we tend to deny it, "it may be questioned whether any gift is free of equivalence in the Oxford Dictionary sense." *Id.* at 46. In contrast, in archaic gift-exchange societies, "the gift is much more of an abstract symbol." *Id.* at 47. Of course, this is precisely my point.

110. That is, gift exchange comprises three distinct obligations: a duty to give gifts, a duty to accept gifts tendered, and a duty to give a return gift. *See* MAUSS, *supra* note 103, at 13.

111. *Id.* at 79. He continues, "They are juridical because they concern private and public law, and morality. . . . They are political and domestic at the same time, relating to social classes . . . clans and families. They are religious. . . . They are economic. Moreover, these institutions have an important aesthetic aspect. . . . Finally , the phenomena are clearly structural." *Id.* (citations omitted).

fact, these errors may more accurately be seen as different aspects of one common error: the application of modern liberal assumptions about the free, atomistic nature of man to people and institutions in archaic societies.

Gift exchange is selfish, as the utilitarian presupposes. But archaic man does not define himself as a separate, atomistic individual. Rather, being bound in complex webs of family, clan, and tribe, he is defined by others in terms of status. As Mauss states, "It is not individuals but collectivities that impose obligations of exchange and contract upon each other."[112] That is, archaic gift exchange relates to the individual's familial, social, political, and religious position, as well as his economic standing, in the society. In archaic societies, therefore, the greatest benefits do not take the form of things or services to be consumed by the individual and his children, but rather relate to one's position. Archaic gift exchange is a strategy whereby participants seek to increase their prestige and debase their enemies within a given static hierarchy.

The utilitarian point of view also displays a fundamental misunderstanding of reciprocity, as first elaborated by Mauss. The utilitarian infers from the fact that there is an obligation to return a gift that the returned gift is equivalent to the original gift, and that the gift exchange is a form of pseudocontract characterized by mutuality. This interpretation is perhaps not surprising among economists and lawyers, who do not do anthropological field research themselves, but merely read popularized accounts through the lens of their own preconceptions about economic relations.[113] It is surprising, however, that many prominent anthropologists seem to make the same mistake, often ignoring or distorting their own data to fit their economic prejudices about the nature of reciprocity.[114]

According to Annette Weiner, mainstream anthropologists (and, I would add, utilitarians) misinterpret Mauss's hypotheses as to the economic function served by the reciprocity of gifts. They assume that gift exchange is literally just a simple, albeit imperfect, form of market. Accordingly, their analysis is based on modern markets. This inappropriate analogy to contract obligations results in the misperception that the reciprocity of gift exchange is characterized by mutuality and equality.[115]

112. MAUSS, *supra* note 103, at 5 (citation omitted).

113. Of course, if this is a sin, as a lawyer, I am equally guilty.

114. *See* ANNETTE B. WEINER, INALIENABLE POSSESSIONS: THE PARADOX OF KEEPING-WHILE-GIVING 17–18, 28–33 (1992).

115. *See* WEINER, *supra* note 114, at 17. As I explain in the text, Weiner (as well as the scholars she criticizes) assumes that "reciprocity" must always imply equivalent (or close) counter-obligations. In fact, the term more generally implies that the actions by the donee obligate the donee to reciprocate in some way.

Nothing could be further from Mauss's point. Mauss intended his essay to be a critique of utilitarianism.[116] Although he proposed that gift exchange has an essential economic aspect, he insisted that it is essentially and radically different from modern markets. According to Mauss, archaic peoples enter into gift exchange as a customary way of establishing and maintaining certain ritualized relationships and status with respect to other tribes, clans, and individuals. I return to this later in this chapter.

The inequality and hostility of potlatch has long been recognized. Westerners have characterized it as a form of war disguised as gift, but have at least implicitly considered it an anomaly, the exception that proved the rule of altruism. In potlatch, not only could gifts not be refused, they had to be repaid upon demand, with interest—that is, the return gift had to exceed the original gift by a customary amount.[117] This was readily apparent; by the later nineteenth century the gift cycle had so accelerated that the parties were exchanging literally scores of thousands of blankets and other objects.[118]

Yet, it is precisely Mauss's point that potlatch is not an exception, but rather the epitome of an institution virtually universal among societies at a certain level of social development. Weiner interprets the empirical evidence as suggesting that gift exchange is always unequal. The purpose of gift exchange is, as Mauss hypothesized, the creation of status and hierarchy. One institutes a gift exchange in order to increase one's status (or the status of one's clan or tribe) in comparison to the donee and other participants in the gift ritual.

A donor institutes a gift relationship to increase his prestige in two ways. The fact that he gives establishes his reputation as a wealthy and generous man, brave and crafty enough to risk the competition of gift. As Mauss says in connection with potlatch, "To give is to show one's superiority, to be more, to be higher in rank. . . . "[119] The position of the donee is ambiguous at this point. To the extent that he receives a particularly prestigious object as a gift, his status is enhanced. To the extent that he is viewed as the passive recipient of the generosity of another, it is diminished. "To accept without giving

116. *See* Mary Douglas, *Foreword: No Free Gifts,* in MAUSS, *supra* note 103, at vii–viii.

117. *See* BELSHAW, *supra* note 109, at 24–25. Belshaw explains how this mandatory aspect of *potlatch* enabled it to serve as a sort of credit system for young men trying to enter into society. By making a number of small strategic gifts and receiving bigger gifts as "interest," the youth could eventually accumulate sufficient "capital" to engage in a proper potlatch.

118. *Id.* at 29. The return obligation imposed by potlatch was so great that no one wanted to be the original recipient in a potlatch exchange. The potlatch would continue until one of the parties had given away all he had, could no longer play, and was disgraced.

119. MAUSS, *supra* note 103, at 74.

in return, or without giving more back, is to become client and servant, to become small, to fall lower."[120] The donee needs to reciprocate the gift for several reasons. Partly it is to avoid revenge. More importantly, he must reestablish his reputation for generosity to avoid being considered a miser and losing face. The return gift must be greater than the original for two reasons. First, by giving a bigger gift, the donee seeks public recognition that he is a greater man than the donor. Second, by giving a larger gift, the original donee in turn obligates the original donor to give back another yet larger gift. In this way, he seeks to best or even ruin his "partner" by eventually forcing him to give away all of his most valuable gift objects.

Consequently, Weiner hypothesizes that gift exchange is a strategy by which participants plot to obtain and keep the most prestigious objects for themselves while simultaneously depriving rival participants of their prestigious objects in order to establish higher status and dominance over the latter.[121] This system is not merely aggressive. It is also unstable and unproductive because prestige is established by two mutually inconsistent tests: by being known as the most generous giver and by being known as the recipient of the most prestigious gift objects. As I suggest below, Weiner's empirical observation is more consistent with the Hegelian analysis of gifts.

The utilitarian assumes that gift exchange is a means of obtaining commodities or services in the future. In contrast to the untested assumptions of utilitarians and anthropologists, empirical observation suggests that many archaic property and economic relations do not serve the function of allocating and supplying needed material goods. Nor do they serve to establish long-term military or family alliances with their gift-exchange partners, as Posner suggests. Gift exchange tends to exist in societies characterized by subsistence economies, in which social groups (such as families, matrilineages, clans, and tribes) typically produce substantially all of their own food and necessities.[122] Market exchange is not unknown, but is relatively unimportant. The objects of desire given as gifts are generally symbolic objects produced purely for the sake of exchange, with little or no economic use.[123]

120. *Id.*

121. *See* WEINER, *supra* note 114, at 8. Weiner more fully develops her theory of "keeping-while-giving" in her account of *kula*. *See id.* at 131–48.

122. By subsistence, I am not implying hand-to-mouth scarcity. Exchange economies flourish in locations where food and other resources are relatively plentiful, such as the tropical islands inhabited by the Trobrianders and the salmon-rich rivers fished by the peoples of the Pacific Northwest.

123. According to Mauss, "What they exchange is not solely property and wealth, movable and immovable goods, and things economically useful. In particular, such exchanges are acts of politeness: banquets, rituals, military services, women, children, dances, festivals, and fairs,

For example, in *kula* the objects exchanged are bracelets and necklaces made of shells. Although these are theoretically useful objects of adornment, they are often so large and heavily decorated that they are impracticable to wear and are displayed only at ceremonial occasions.[124] Moreover, the Trobriands set the value of these objects based not on their beauty or craftsmanship, but on their genealogy—how many times they have been given and by whom. The genealogies of the exchanged gift objects establish the prestige of the participants who possess the most frequently exchanged objects.[125] The *kula* objects take on a personal, even sacred, character.[126]

Potlatch might at first blush seem different in that it often involved the exchange of apparently useful objects, such as blankets, pots, and cooking oil. By the time the institution was suppressed, however, participants were giving away such absurdly large numbers of these objects—literally scores of thousands at a time—that it seems obvious that they could not have been intended for use. Consequently, romantics such as Hyde,[127] who bemoan the fact that cheap blankets sold by the Hudson Bay Company eventually replaced the beautiful traditional handmade blankets in potlatch, miss the point of the institution. The object given in gift exchange has no intrinsic value. It exists only to be exchanged. The introduction of cheap trade goods in the Northwest, therefore, may not have resulted in a corruption of potlatch but rather enabled it to expand to its logical conclusion.

This hypothesis is further supported by the aspect of potlatch that seems most peculiar to Western eyes—the destruction of "gifts." This practice supports the hypothesis that the purpose of potlatch was neither the exchange of useful goods nor altruism, but rather the increase of the donor's prestige and the abasement of the donee. In potlatch the donor had the option of destroying the gift objects rather than actually conveying them to the

---

in which economic transaction is only one element, and in which the passing on of wealth is only one feature." MAUSS, *supra* note 103, at 5.

124. Mauss (who did not personally do field work in the Trobriands but relied on Malinowski's account) speaks of the bracelets being worn by men and the necklaces by women. *See* MAUSS, *supra* note 103, at 23. Weiner, who did field work, maintains otherwise (and illustrates this assertion with photographs). *See* WEINER, *supra* note 114, at fig. 24.

125. *See* WEINER, *supra* note 114, at 134–35.

126. As Mauss states: "The institution [of *kula*] has also its mythical, religious, and magical aspect. . . . Each [object of exchange] . . . , at least the dearest and the most sought after—and other objects enjoy the same prestige—each one has its name, a personality, a history, and even a tale attached to it. So much is this so that certain individuals even take their own name from them. . . . To possess one is 'exhilarating, strengthening, and calming in itself.' Their owners fondle and look at them for hours. Mere contact with them passes on their virtues. [The objects] are placed on the forehead, on the chest of a dying person. . . . They are his supreme comfort." MAUSS, *supra* note 103, at 24 (citations omitted).

127. *See* HYDE, *supra* note 23, at 29–30.

donee.[128] This is perceived of as a "gift" because the "donor" ostensibly sacrificed the objects to the spirits for the sake of the donee.[129] The "donee" is then put in the unenviable position of having to return an even greater gift even though he received nothing material. Obviously, the destructive potlatch is an extremely effective way for the potlatcher to demonstrate his great wealth[130] without also enriching his rival.[131] I return to destructive potlatch in my critique of the romantic theory of gift later in this chapter.

Weiner persuasively argues that even what seem like obviously useful exchanges have been misunderstood by those anthropologists and utilitarians who start from the assumption that gift exchange is merely an imperfect form of market exchange—or, in Posner's formulation, insurance contract. For example, in the Trobriand Archipelago, it is the custom for maternal uncles to maintain ritual gardens in order to give gifts of yams to their sisters' children.[132] This looks, of course, like an arrangement whereby the chil-

128. As Georges Bataille explains:

> Gift-giving is not the only form of *potlatch*: A rival is challenged by a solemn destruction of riches. . . . As recently as the nineteenth century a Tlingit chieftain would sometimes go before a rival and cut the throats of slaves in his presence. At the proper time, the destruction was repaid by the killing of a large number of slaves. The Chukchee of the Siberian Northeast have related institutions. They slaughter highly valuable dog teams, for it is necessary for them to startle, to stifle the rival group. The Indians of the Northwest Coast would set fire to their villages or break their canoes to pieces. They have emblazoned copper bars possessing a fictive value (depending on how famous or how old the coppers are): Sometimes these bars are worth a fortune. They throw them into the sea or shatter them.

Georges Bataille, The Accursed Share: An Essay on General Economy 68 (Robert Hurley trans., 1988).

129. *Id.*

130. He obviously proves his wealth through such ostentatious demonstrations of indifference, reminiscent of the familiar caricature in our society of the billionaire who lights his cigar with a hundred-dollar bill. Bataille suggests that the effect is even more profound: "But if he destroys the object in front of another person or if he gives it away, the one who gives has actually acquired, in the other's eyes, the power of giving or destroying. He is now rich for having made use of wealth in the manner its essence would require: He is rich for having ostensibly consumed what is wealth only if it is consumed. But the wealth that is actualized in the *potlatch,* in consumption for others, has no real existence except insofar as the other is changed by the consumption." *Id.* at 69–71.

131. In Mauss's words: "In a certain number of cases, it is not even a question of giving and returning gifts, but of destroying, so as not to give the slightest hint of desiring your gift to be reciprocated. Whole boxes of olachen (candlefish) oil or whale oil are burnt, as are houses and thousands of blankets. The most valuable copper objects are broken and thrown into the water, in order to put down and to 'flatten' one's rival. In this way one not only promotes oneself, but also one's family, up the social scale." Mauss, *supra* note 103, at 37 (endnotes omitted).

132. Such avuncular obligations (from the Latin *avunculus,* mother's brother, as opposed to *patruus,* father's brother) are common among archaic societies, including that of the European high middle ages. *See* Jeanne L. Schroeder, *Feminism Historicized: Medieval Misogynist Stereo-*

dren are provided with food—an important economic necessity in a subsistence economy. In fact, the avuncular yams used in this ritual are virtually inedible and have little nutritional value.[133] The gifted yams are frequently piled up outside the family's house and ostentatiously left to rot, apparently as a symbol of the family's wealth.[134] The yams only exist for the sake of gift and the resulting creation of prestige.

To say that gift objects are valuable only insofar as they are exchanged implies that they serve as units of exchange. Nevertheless, archaic gift objects are not merely primitive forms of money. Rather, the objects are symbols of the exchange, reflecting the prestige of previous winners of the exchange game. In *kula* the highest ranking shells, as determined by their genealogy of ownership, are even given individual names.[135] Each time the object is exchanged it becomes more valuable. It increases more if it passes through the hands of a higher status participant rather than a lower status one. Conversely, one gains prestige by becoming the recipient of a valuable (high status) shell rather than a lower one.[136]

As Mauss explains, gift exchange is a complex web of relations. The objects exchanged "are living beings";[137] they bear the spirits of the persons engaged in the exchange relation.[138] "Each one of these precious things possesses, moreover, productive power itself."[139] "Yet it is also because by giving one is giving oneself, and if one gives oneself, it is because one " 'owes' oneself—one's person and one's goods—to others."[140]

The romantic correctly recognizes Mauss's point that gift institutions precede the development of contractual institutions as a historical matter, and therefore are essentially different. The romantic also embraces Mauss's hypothesis that gift exchange is a means of establishing relationships. In the Maussian view, "[a] gift that does nothing to enhance solidarity is a contradiction."[141]

But the romantic makes the opposite error from that of the utilitarian. The romantic misapplies Mauss's hypothesis to unexamined and unproven assumptions about the market economy. Observing both alienation and contract in modern society, the romantic leaps to the conclusion that contract

---

types in Contemporary Feminist Jurisprudence, 75 IOWA L. REV. 1135, 1205 n.271 (1990) [hereinafter, Schroeder, *Feminism Historicized*].

133. *See* WEINER, *supra* note 114, at 31–32.

134. *See id.* at 31.

135. *See id.* at 134.

136. *See id.* at 134–48.

137. MAUSS, *supra* note 103, at 44.

138. *See id.*

139. *Id.*

140. *Id.* at 46.

141. Douglas, *supra* note 116, at vii.

is a major cause of alienation. Because gift in our society tends to be limited to the intimate realm of family and friends, the romantic assumes that gift supports (or creates) relationships, as opposed to alienation.

The empirical data presented by the romantics themselves are at best deeply ambiguous and at worst at odds with their hypothesis. The romantic presumes that, in contrast to contract, gifts are free acts of altruism that do not impose any specifically articulated return obligation and that result in the formation of lasting beneficial relations based on interdependence and mutuality. In fact, in archaic societies, gifts are made, accepted, and returned out of strict obligation according to standards rigidly set both by custom and by implicit negotiation that result in unstable relations based on hierarchy and status.

The romantic insists that gifts are free—given out of generosity, affection, or relation—to be distinguished from the compulsory and enforceable obligation of contract. In support of this, Hyde points to the lack of formal sanctions enforcing the countergift obligation. Despite his protests to the contrary, however, this argument suggests that the romantic is so imbued with the ethos of modern American culture that he can imagine compulsion only in terms of legal sanction. Consequently, he ignores or minimizes the effect of other forms of compulsion and sanctions employed in premodern cultures.

In contradistinction, Posner, as a lawyer and judge, is fully aware that legal sanctions are not necessarily the only possible, let alone the most effective, type of enforcement mechanism. In archaic societies in which there is little mobility, other forms of social control (exclusion, shunning, revenge, etc.) are probably more effective. If one is not able to skip town, if one is dependent on one's social group for food and protection, and if there is no government to protect one from violence, one had better live up to the expectations of one's family, friends, and neighbors. In a tribal society, the threat of war with neighboring peoples is a great deterrent against the breach of customary obligations. To an animist, the possibility that a disgruntled donor might resort to sorcery may be the greatest danger of all.

In other words, archaic gift may look free in form, but it is bound in substance. As Mauss stated, in gift-exchange societies obligations "are committed to in a somewhat voluntary form by presents and gifts, although in the final analysis they are strictly compulsory, on pain of private or public warfare."[142] That is, "to refuse to give, to fail to invite, just as to refuse to accept, is tantamount to declaring war; it is to reject the bond of alliance and commonality."[143]

142. Mauss, *supra* note 103, at 5.

143. *Id.* at 13 (citations omitted). Consistent with the fact that, at the time Mauss was writing, anthropologists had not yet concentrated on the reciprocal nature of gift institutions is

Status also plays a crucial coercive role in archaic societies. In potlatch, a chief can only maintain his rank by showing through gift that he is favored by the spirits.[144] Chiefs who do not give are said to have a "rotten face," which has an even stronger connotation than the familiar Asian notion of face: it is the right or ability to wear the sacred masks, incarnate the spirits, and have a "persona."[145] Acceptance of gifts is also obligatory. Failure to accept is evidence that one is afraid that one cannot reciprocate, that one will be "flattened," " 'lose the weight' attached to one's name."[146] The greatest chiefs can refuse to receive a potlatch, but only on the acceptance of the obligation to return an even greater potlatch.[147]

"The obligation to reciprocate constitutes the essence of the *potlatch,* in so far as it does not consist of pure destruction."[148] Moreover, the return obligation must be accompanied by interest at 30 percent to 100 percent per year.[149] One does not merely lose face for failing to reciprocate potlatch. "The punishment for failure to reciprocate is slavery for debt."[150]

> The greatest *potlatchers* of all are those who not only give fantastic amounts, making it well-nigh impossible for their rivals to repay in a future *potlatch* at the appropriate interest, but who also demonstrate how rich and magnificent they are by actually destroying their most valued items: canoes, coppers, blankets, even stocks of fish grease and oil. The destruction of property is the most dramatic and characteristic feature of the *potlatch.*[151]

Once again, Mauss did not think that the compulsory nature of potlatch was the exception that proved the rule of freedom. He demonstrates this with the terminology of *kula.* Bronislaw Malinowski translated the Trobriand term of the return gift as the "clinching gift" that seals the transaction.[152] However, Mauss points out that an alternate name is "the tooth that bites, that really cuts, bites through, and liberates."[153] Its return is not truly left to the donee's discretion. If an appropriate return gift is not made within the customary time frame, it may be "seized by force or by surprise."[154] If the return gift is

---

Mauss's observation that anthropologists just did not then know the true sanctions for breach of this obligation. Are they moral or magical, or does the breacher lose his rank or prestige?

144. *See id.* at 39.
145. *See id.*
146. *Id.* at 41.
147. *See id.*
148. *Id.* (endnote omitted).
149. *See id.* at 42.
150. *Id.*
151. BELSHAW, *supra* note 109, at 26.
152. *See* MAUSS, *supra* note 103, at 26.
153. *Id.*
154. *Id.* (endnote omitted).

not deemed equivalent, "revenge may be taken by magic, or at least by insult and a display of resentment."[155] Consequently, if the donee cannot immediately reciprocate as required, he will at least offer a smaller gift as a sort of down payment. This gift "merely 'pierces' the skin, does not bite, and does not conclude the affair."[156] Rather than freeing the donee, gift binds him as a debtor.[157]

Probably the most telling example of Hyde's blindness towards the obligatory nature of gift is his discussion of Biblical sacrifice. He describes sacrifice as a gift from man to God.[158] The passages cited, however, expressly state the opposite. Hyde asserts that "in the Pentateuch the first fruits always belong to the Lord. In Exodus the Lord tells Moses: 'Consecrate to me all the first-born; whatever is the first to open the womb among the people of Israel, both of man and of beast, is mine.' "[159] Moreover, as Hyde notes, those who refuse God's unequivocal demand that sacrifice be made are punished. For example, Hyde asserts that the reason Pharaoh was plagued by toads was because he interrupted the divine circle of gifts.[160] If this is freedom, what could compulsion be?

And so, Hyde is incorrect in stating that archaic gift is free in the sense that the decisions as to whether, when, and how much to reciprocate are left to the discretion of the donee. The return obligations are, in fact, well established by custom and practice and are enforceable through a variety of traditional devices. This raises the suspicion that Hyde is also wrong in maintaining that gift does not entail negotiation. Indeed, the evidence suggests that far from unknown, negotiation is common, although it may not meet Hyde's stereotypical image of how modern lawyers and businessmen act. In the words of Cyril Belshaw,

> These matters are regulated through the judgment of the partners as to whether the ornaments exchanged are indeed appropriately equivalent, and any hesitancy is dealt with through the intermediary exchanges or by prolonging the exchanges until both partners are satisfied. This is not the rough haggling of the bazaar. But it certainly is delicately negotiated price adjustment of the same kind. The difference is not in the principles of valuation, but in the etiquette of negotiation.[161]

Weiner insists that *kula* is a strategic enterprise whereby the parties engage in complex, multilayered plots lasting ten years or more to force rivals to

155. *Id.* (endnotes omitted).
156. *Id.*
157. *See id.*
158. *See* HYDE, *supra* note 23, at 19–20.
159. *Id.* at 19.
160. *See id.* at 20.
161. BELSHAW, *supra* note 109, at 17.

give up their valuable objects.[162] Even face-to-face negotiation is not unknown.

Hyde himself gives an example of express negotiation. He quotes at length the conversations of two chiefs in a potlatch who propose and reject counter-offers.[163] As a deal lawyer, I can testify that this conversation typifies the dickering that accompanies the negotiation of a corporate acquisition agreement. Each party argues as to why she deserves more in the transaction than originally offered. The only difference is that, in the traditional culture of potlatch, desert is discussed in terms of personal and familial prestige, whereas in modern cultures other standards are used.

Despite the existence of implicit (and sometimes express) negotiation, however, there is an essential difference between modern contractual exchange and archaic gift exchange. In the former, no party is obligated to enter into a contract and no conveyance is made until the parties reach a bargain. Obligations must be mutually assumed. In the latter, the transaction begins when one party unilaterally imposes an obligation on the other by conveying property. The donee is obligated both to accept the gift and to make a return gift. Only subsequently do the parties haggle over the return duties. In other words, in contract, negotiation precedes obligation, whereas in gifts, negotiation succeeds obligation.

Gift exchanges, as the romantics suggest, establish or reinforce relations between individuals, clans, and tribes in "archaic" cultures. For example, *kula* arguably keeps hostilities from breaking out between neighboring islands in the Trobriand Archipelago.[164] The temporary peace established during *kula* ceremonies enables the participants (and their colleagues) to engage in market-trade as well.[165]

162. As Weiner explains:

> It takes years of work to convince the player to release the shell and this necessitates having many other shells to move along this particular path. . . .
>
> *Kula* as a topic of conversation with nonpartners abounds with accounts about the lost chances, the broken promises, the things given to someone in an attempt to get a shell only to be faced with an empty return. . . . But as one *kula* player told me, all *kula* talk is dangerous because most of it is lies, specious rhetoric set forth to serve one's own ends.
>
> . . . . Instead of perceiving *kula* transactions simply as gifts and counter-gifts, it is essential to visualize the maze of plays and strategies as layers of exchanges which one must constantly build up over time and then keep track of.

WEINER, *supra* note 114, at 141; footnotes omitted.

163. *See* HYDE, *supra* note 23, at 31.

164. *See* BELSHAW, *supra* note 109, at 14.

165. *See id.* at 16. Also: "The exchange of gifts creates or reinforces relationships of alliance between individuals and the groups of which they are representative. They open the way for the exchange of other acts of duty and support, both material and nonmaterial. In the *kula* ring, the partnership establishes an alliance with political overtones, in that law and order is guar-

But gift exchanges can hardly be described in terms of altruism, generosity, or freedom. They are strictly circumscribed by custom. The relations established are not what we would call friendship or love, but rather status. They may, in fact, lead to relations of hostility rather than peace. In the words of Belshaw, gift exchanges are "dynamic competition for sociopolitical status based upon the use of wealth to control social relationships."[166]

> Although the details vary considerably from culture to culture, the main variables are remarkably consistent. These include emphases on relationships between individuals which are also seen as relationships between groups, and upon gaining advantages which can be expressed as prestige as well as in material ways, and with greater or lesser degrees of competition and rivalry.[167]

As we have seen, Hyde draws from the fact that archaic societies frequently lack modern governments and formal feudal social hierarchies, such as class and caste, that archaic gift exchange fosters egalitarian relationships. Weiner argues precisely the opposite. The lack of a formal political hierarchy increases, rather than decreases, the status-forming role of gift exchange.

> The Trobriands also represent the most complex ranking system . . . *Kula* activity provides a context for chiefly authority where actual ranking and chiefs do not exist. In these situations, ranking is sustained briefly yet ultimately defeated because the shells are inalienable only for a limited time. But within that time period, exchange is subverted, keeping is paramount and difference is politically flaunted. . . .
>
> Out of this difference negotiated in exchange over what is not exchanged, power is generated and, under certain circumstances . . . transforms difference into hierarchy.[168]

Similarly, the purpose of potlatch was the establishment of rank and status among men. For example, Kwakiutl society is organized around social groups structured by "a complex system of titles which indicate a man's position and prerogatives."[169] Although some of these titles are determined by familial descent, others may be acquired by various means, including potlatch.[170] Accordingly,

---

anteed between the communities involved. It opens channels of substantial trade and social intercourse." *Id.* at 19.

166. *Id.* at 18.

167. *Id.* at 35.

168. WEINER, *supra* note 114, at 19.

169. BELSHAW, *supra* note 109, at 22.

170. *See id.* at 22–23.

> a more persistent theme in the *potlatch* is the validation of social position, symbolized in the acquisition and holding of a title and improving its status. . . . Status competition and distribution competition go hand in hand. . . . It contains the component of challenging one's rival to do better. . . . It also includes a strong element of denigration, or deriding the other fellow, and this carries over into a show of contemptuous and arrogant hostility.[171]

Potlatch has been described as a "kind of love-hate relationship with some other social group."[172]

As mentioned, "gifts" were destroyed as well as given in potlatch. Hyde, trying to fit this within his romantic preconceptions, argues that so far as the donor is concerned, the gift object is always in some sense "destroyed" in that it is forever lost to him.[173] He compares this to the potlatch practice with respect to one of the most valuable types of desired objects in Northwestern societies—metal objects called "coppers." The donor frequently broke the copper before giving it away.[174] Strangely, Hyde sees this practice—by which the donor insures that the "gift" is less valuable in the hands of the donee—as proof of the generous, altruistic nature of gift. By contrast, Mauss points out that the sumptuary destruction of potlatch is "not without egotism."[175] "Through such [destructive] gifts, a hierarchy is established."[176]

Weiner argues that acts that seem like the destruction of gifts are not a net loss to the donor at all, but yet another strategy whereby the donor seeks to increase his wealth and status. Indeed, in some cases, the apparently destructive act invests the object with increased prestige that eventually redounds to the donor. The donor breaks off a piece of the copper so that it will not be whole (and as valuable) in the hands of the donee. The donor schemes to engage in future *potlatches* in order to force the original donee to return the broken copper. The broken shard is then welded back onto the returned copper.[177] Such repaired coppers are more valuable than whole coppers precisely because they are visible proof that the original donor won the exchange and vanquished the donee.[178]

171. *Id.* at 26.

172. *Id.* at 25. Also: "Everything is based upon the principles of antagonism and rivalry. The political status of individuals in the brotherhoods and clans, and ranks of all kinds, are gained in a 'war of property' [*sic*], just as they are in real war, or through chance, inheritance, alliance, and marriage. Yet everything is conceived of as if it were a 'struggle of wealth.' " (MAUSS, *supra* note 103, at 37 (endnotes omitted).

173. *See* HYDE, *supra* note 23, at 9. Hyde is, of course, repressing the fact that the gift is not always destroyed so far as the donee is concerned.

174. *See id.* at 30–31.

175. MAUSS, *supra* note 103, at 74.

176. *Id.*

177. *See* WEINER, *supra* note 114, at 41.

178. *See id.*

Gift exchange does not, therefore, lead to equality and mutuality, as Radin hopes, but differentiation and inequality.[179] Hyde is so inculcated with modern Western culture (and its immediate historical past) that he can only recognize hierarchy when it takes the form of modern or feudal structures. Weiner, the anthropologist, shows that gift exchange is a form that hierarchy takes in archaic cultures.

THE EROTICISM OF THE MARKET

The Hegelian approach differs from both the utilitarian and the romantic traditions. In Hegelian philosophy, the essence of human nature is radical freedom and rationality, as in classical liberal philosophy. To the Hegelian, however, this freedom can never become actual in the lonely, atomistic state of nature posited by liberalism. Freedom is actualized only in human relationships, as the romantic understands. Being rational, humans seek to maximize what they desire—just as utilitarians predict. However, because humans rationally seek to actualize their essential freedom, what they desire is human relationship. To Hegel, rationality does not lead to cold, calculating behavior, as the utilitarian and the romantic implicitly assume. The actualization of rationality is eroticism—the passionate, unquenchable desire for the desire of the Other.[180] Contract, in which two parities recognize each other as the bearers of legal rights, is a moment in mankind's struggle for the actualization of freedom. Contract is therefore a form of eroticism, albeit a primitive and imperfect one.

Consequently, on the one hand, the utilitarian is correct that gift attempts to achieve the type of relationship achieved by contract, but is wrong in saying that gift and contract are the same. On the other hand, the romantic is

179. As Weiner maintains, "Exchange does not produce a homogeneous totality, but rather an arena where heterogeneity is determined. Although individuals or groups negotiate with each other on many levels in each exchange encounter, the ownership of an inalienable possession establishes and signifies marked differences between the parties to the exchange." WEINER, *supra* note 114, at 10.

This means that gift exchange is not based on generous giving to others. It has often been pointed out that gift exchange is not altruistic in the way that ordinary gift transactions might arguably be. The food given as ceremonial gifts is given not to feed the recipient, but to symbolize the relation between the parties. See notes 132–34 and accompanying text. *See* also BELSHAW, *supra* note 109, at 15–16.

180. Indeed, to Hegel self-consciousness is nothing but desire. G. W. F. HEGEL, HEGEL'S PHENOMENOLOGY OF SPIRIT ¶ 167 (A. V. Miller trans., Oxford Univ. Press 5th ed. 1977) (1952) [hereinafter, HEGEL, THE PHENOMENOLOGY OF SPIRIT]. *See also* DANIEL BERTHOLD-BOND, HEGEL'S THEORY OF MADNESS 46–47 (1995).

correct in thinking that gift is fundamentally different from contract, but wrong in thinking that gift is superior to contract. Rather, when analyzed as a legal relation, gift appears as a failed attempt to achieve the erotic recognition of contract. Contract enables us to recognize each other as unique individual subjects, creating relations of equality. Gift tends to produce a differentiation of type; it creates hierarchical relations of status.

To understand this argument requires a more detailed account of the Hegelian dialectic of "abstract right" and how it relates to the Lacanian dialectic of desire.

Freedom, Recognition, Subjectivity

Hegel's *Philosophy of Right* is the bildungsroman of personality.[181] It explains the logic by which the abstract atomistic person in the hypothetical state of nature posited by liberal philosophy leads to the concrete social individual in the modern constitutional state. The first stage in this process is "subjectivity"—the state of being a speaking, legal subject capable of bearing legal rights and duties.[182] From a Lacanian point of view, subjectivity also includes the capability of bearing sexual identity. Subjectivity is created in the regime Hegel called "abstract right"—property and contract, the so-called "private law" of the capitalist market. Law is located in the psychological order that Lacan called the "symbolic." The subject is therefore artificial rather than natural—a creature, not a being.

According to Hegel, we seek property and engage in market transactions out of unfulfillable desire. But this desire is not, as economists pretend, a desire for material things, utility, or wealth. To Hegel, each abstract person (i.e., the individual in the state of nature posited by Enlightenment political philosophy) seeks to actualize his potential freedom through recognition by others. Although Hegel does not use the term, in Lacanian psychoanalysis this desire to understand oneself through recognition is eroticism generally and hysteria specifically. We desire things derivatively as a means of achieving our true desire—the desire of the Other.[183] When we repress this deriva-

181. *See* Arthur J. Jacobson, *Hegel's Legal Plenum*, in HEGEL AND LEGAL THEORY 115 (Drucilla Cornell, David Gray Carlson & Michel Rosenfeld eds., 1991).

182. In this chapter I use the term "subject" slightly differently from Hegel's in that in the *Philosophy of Right* the abstract person only becomes a subject at the point when abstract right is internalized and sublated by morality.

183. JACQUES LACAN, ÉCRITS: A SELECTION 264 (Alan Sheridan trans., 1977) [hereinafter LACAN, ÉCRITS]. A full explication of Lacan's complex and paradoxical notion of the Other (with a capital "O") is beyond the scope of this book. It includes, but is not limited to, the concepts of other concrete people as well as the symbolic order generally. *See* generally BICE BEN-

tive aspect of our desire for objects, we treat them as substitutes for our true object of desire.[184]

Hegel began his analysis of human nature by tentatively accepting the presuppositions of classical liberalism.[185] Specifically, Hegel adopted the liberal assumption that freedom is the essence of human nature.[186] He also tentatively agreed with the assertion that the radically free person would have to begin (as a logical, not historical or biographical, matter) as atomistic and separate from others. Hegel then argued that these liberal presuppositions contain internal contradictions. This does not mean that they are false: the liberal construct is one true and essential moment of human nature. But it is not a full or adequate account of human nature. It must, therefore, give way to more complex and developed forms of personality that incorporate other elements.

Specifically, Hegel argued that the liberal conception of freedom, which is supposedly the essence of the abstract person, can be a mere potential in the state of nature.[187] To oversimplify, John Locke believed that the liberty of man took the form of natural rights (most importantly, the right to property) in the state of nature. Immanuel Kant expressed the essence of man in terms of duties. By their very definition, however, the concepts of rights and duties are intersubjective rather than atomistic. As Wesley Newcomb Hohfeld argued, rights and duties can only be thought of in terms of relationships

---

EVENUTO & ROGER KENNEDY, THE WORKS OF JACQUES LACAN: AN INTRODUCTION (1986). *See also* BRUCE FINK, THE LACANIAN SUBJECT: BETWEEN LANGUAGE AND JOUISSANCE 13 (1995).

184. These objects serve as "*objets petit a*," which I discuss in more detail later in this chapter.

185. Hegel thought that one of the flaws of liberal philosophy was its inability to examine its own presuppositions. Of course, Hegel understood that it is logically impossible to develop any theory without presuppositions or hypotheses as a starting place. He believed, however, that the circular nature of the dialectic method enabled one to return and test these presuppositions. To oversimplify, Hegel's is a holistic theory in which the explanatory power of the whole is deemed evidence of the validity of its component parts. "Generally, according to this methodology, nothing which is a part of a larger whole can be understood except in terms of that whole, and conversely, the whole cannot be fully grasped except in terms of the full panoply of determinate relationships that exist among its various constituent parts." Rosenfeld, *supra* note 37, at 1203; *see also* JEANNE LORRAINE SCHROEDER, THE VESTAL AND THE FASCES: HEGEL, LACAN, PROPERTY AND THE FEMININE 25–27, 273–74 (1998) [hereinafter, SCHROEDER, THE VESTAL AND THE FASCES].

186. *See* HEGEL, THE PHILOSOPHY OF RIGHT, *supra* note 19, at 35–37. Hegel, like Kant, abstracted from his observations of actual persons to form the minimal conception of personality.

187. The most primitive conception of what a person could be is self-consciousness as free will. *Id.* at 67–68. *See also id.* at 35. Such a conception of personality is not only totally abstract; it is radically negative. To be truly free and beyond constraints is to have no positive characteristics at all. *Id.* at 37–40, 48–49. Right is the actualization of freedom. *See id.* at 35.

between and among human beings.[188] A person's claim to rights and duties is, in fact, a call to the other to recognize this claim. Therefore, the actualization of freedom, as understood by liberalism, requires recognition.

Although agreeing that freedom is essential to human nature, Hegel thought that freedom was merely potential in the "state of nature" of autonomous individuality. Freedom can only become actualized through love.[189] Hegel adopted the liberal Kantian conception of freedom as radical negativity[190]—the total absence of constraints. This abstract concept becomes concrete in social relations.[191] By this I mean that Hegel posited that the abstract person can only achieve legal subjectivity (and therefore more complex stages of personality) by being recognized as a subject by a person whom one in turn recognizes as a subject.[192] We are, therefore, driven to help others fulfill and exceed their highest potential, in the hope that once they do so they will then turn around and recognize us as their equals. That is, man's desire is the desire of the Other in both senses of the expression—we want to have the other but, more importantly, we want the other to desire (recognize) us.

In our search for recognition we create legal and other rights, not to claim them for ourselves but in order to bestow them on others in order to increase their dignity. The regime of abstract right—property, contract, and market relations—is the simplest and most primitive manifestation of this dialectic of desire.

As freedom is the essence of personality, the abstract person rationally seeks to actualize her freedom. Freedom can be actualized through intersubjective relationship. The abstract person, therefore, actively seeks to be recognized by another person: she desires to be desired by another.

The proposition that rights can only be actualized through relations with and recognition by others causes another contradiction. The liberal purely autonomous person is not recognizable. Kant showed that to be truly, radically free, the atomistic individual must be totally abstract, lacking all patho-

188. *See* WESLEY NEWCOMB HOHFELD, FUNDAMENTAL LEGAL CONCEPTIONS AS APPLIED IN LEGAL REASONING (Walter Wheeler Cook ed., 1919).

189. Arthur J. Jacobson, *Taking Revelation Seriously* (unpublished manuscript 1998).

190. HEGEL, THE PHILOSOPHY OF RIGHT, *supra* note 19, at 37–39.

191. *See e.g.*, "The system of right is the realm of actualized freedom." *Id.* at 35. I discuss the Hegelian concepts of potentiality and actuality in SCHROEDER, THE VESTAL AND THE FASCES, *supra* note 185, at 32–33, 311–12; Schroeder, *Never Jam To-Day, supra* note 28, at 1559–61.

192. *See* Rosenfeld, *supra* note 37, at 1199, 1220–21. Similarly: "Property is . . . for Hegel a moment in man's struggle for recognition." AVINERI, *supra* note 19, at 89.

Hegel's complex reasoning leading to this conclusion is beyond the limited scope of this book. I present an exegesis of Hegel's argument in SCHROEDER, THE VESTAL AND THE FASCES, *supra* note 185.

logical characteristics.[193] Freedom requires that one's actions not be compelled, but freely chosen. Pure freedom is therefore arbitrary.[194] If one's actions are compelled by heteronomy or to fulfill a need, one is not truly free.

The abstract person in the state of nature has only her potential freedom—her negativity. Lacking individuating pathological characteristics, each abstract person is identical to every other and therefore unrecognizable.[195] To be recognized by other subjects and have interrelationships, therefore, persons must form object relations (i.e., take on specific recognizable characteristics). To Hegel, the regime of abstract right—property, contract, and the capitalist market—is the most primitive form of interrelationship from a *logical* standpoint.[196] Note, I did not say historical or biographical—modern property rights and capitalistic markets are relatively modern inventions.[197] Although the market is logically the simplest and most primitive form of erotic relationship, it was one of the last to develop.

The most rewarding recognition is, of course, recognition by the most noble. The admiration of the base, the vulgar, and the servile is less than worthless and is to be despised. We therefore wish to make ourselves worthy in the eyes of those individuals we consider worthy. The goal of recognition therefore requires that we find worthy others in our world.[198]

This reveals yet another side of this contradiction of abstract personality. The abstract personality seeks to be recognized by a person she recognizes as worthy (i.e., someone whose opinion counts). But, in the state of nature, not only the person seeking recognition, but *all* persons lack distinguishing (pathological) characteristics. Consequently, Hegel argued that no abstract

193. *See* HEGEL, THE PHILOSOPHY OF RIGHT, *supra* note 21, at 70–71.

194. *See id.* at 48–49.

195. *See id.* at 42, 44, 54–57, 70. The problem is that the concept of "absolutely free will" is empty, abstract, arbitrary and negative: it is, by definition, totally stripped of all distinguishing characteristics. *Id.* at 27.

196. Hegel's dialectic purports to be a circular form of reasoning in the sense that theoretically one should be able to start from any point in the analysis and derive the entire system. Nevertheless, for practical reasons, Hegel starts each of his books with a consideration of the simplest, most primitive conception of the topic to be analyzed. As THE PHILOSOPHY OF RIGHT is a consideration of personality and society, he starts with the Kantian construct as the bare minimum concept of what it could mean to have personality. Alan Ryan, *Hegel on Work, Ownership and Citizenship* in THE STATE & CIVIL SOCIETY: HEGEL'S POLITICAL PHILOSOPHY 178, 185 (Z. Pelczynski ed., 1984).

197. I repeat this because it is an important point frequently missed by critics of Hegel. For example, as I discuss in Jeanne L. Schroeder, *Virgin Territory: Margaret Radin's Imagery of Personal Property as the Inviolate Feminine Body,* 79 MINN. L. REV. 55 (1994) [hereinafter, Schroeder, *Virgin Territory*], Radin misinterprets Hegel's dialectic of property, as though he was trying to describe the empirical process by which human beings become mature adults through object relations.

198. For a discussion of the logic of multiplicity in the *Philosophy of Right, see* David Gray Carlson, *How to Do Things with Hegel,* 78 TEX. L. REV. 1377 (2000).

person can merely search for preexisting worthy others. She must go out and affirmatively help others to achieve worth and nobility. She cannot merely seek to be recognizable herself. She must learn to recognize others.

The Hegelian dialectic of right is, therefore, a primitive form of the relationship that Lacan calls love.[199] According to Lacan's understanding of love, the lover sees in his beloved more than she is. When love is requited, the beloved finds that she must live up to her lover's expectations and achieves the ability to give back more than she had. She thereby turns the lover into a beloved, making him into more than he once was.[200] Similarly, in the dialectic of abstract right, the abstract person grants to another person rights that the second person did not originally have, i.e., he recognizes her as a legal subject. If this person responds, she in turn will recognize that the first person should also be entitled to the same rights, thereby making him into a subject. The moment of the creation of abstract right (law) is the moment of the creation of subjectivity—law and subjectivity are mutually constituted.[201]

In other words, right and love are forms of alchemy whereby persons intersubjectively recreate each other out of nothing. The person engaged in the dialectic of right feels herself inexorably driven in the same way as the lover. This is a paradox. Although both rights and love must be free (by definition that which is imposed is neither a right nor love), they are experienced by the abstract person and the lover as inexorable. One can no more refuse the desire to actualize one's freedom than one can prevent oneself from falling in love. Love requires choice, but it is love that chooses us.

The reader should feel uncomfortable with the seeming perfection of this system. You should be asking yourself, how can this dialectic ever get started? Doesn't the recognition that satisfies the Hegelian ideal need to be simultaneous? How does one leap from the not-yet-recognizable of abstract personhood to the always-already-recognized of subjectivity? How can love

199. Hegel famously stated that the subsumption of marriage under the concept of contract "can only be described as disgraceful." HEGEL, THE PHILOSOPHY OF RIGHT, *supra* note 21, at 105. This does not contradict my statement. Hegel locates marriage within the regime of *Sittlicheit* (ethical life), which is much more highly developed than the regime of abstract right, in which contract is located. Of course, it is incorrect to reduce the complex relationships of ethics to the simplistic ones of abstract rights. I am certainly not proposing that romantic and marital love are identical to legal contract, but am merely asserting that contract is an extremely primitive form of eroticism that takes a more complex form in other relationships. Hegel's analyses of marriage and sexuality are problematic on other grounds beyond the scope of this book.

200. *See* SCHROEDER, THE VESTAL AND THE FASCES, *supra* note 185, at 49. "It is only at this point that true love emerges, love as a metaphor in the precise Lacanian sense: we witness the moment when *eromenos* (the loved one) changes into *erastes* (the loving one) by stretching out her hand and 'returning love.' " SLAVOJ ŽIŽEK, THE METASTASIS OF ENJOYMENT: SIX ESSAYS ON WOMAN AND CAUSALITY 103 (1994) [hereinafter, ŽIŽEK, METASTASIS]; see also Miran Božovič, *The Bonds of Love: Lacan and Spinoza,* 23 NEW FORMATIONS 69 (1994).

201. *See* SCHROEDER, THE VESTAL AND THE FASCES, *supra* note 185, at 50.

be the actualization of freedom when nothing binds our hearts more securely than the chains of love? As I discuss at the close of this chapter, the Hegelian-Lacanian analysis is not merely aware of this "impossibility" and "imperfection." Rather, they are posited as fundamental aspects, not only of Hegelian and Lacanian theory, but of the human condition and, indeed, the universe. The dialectic functions, not despite, but just because of its necessary imperfection.

Contract vs. Gift

Let me explain the eroticism of contract in more detail. Hegel's theory of the function of property anticipates Lacan's understanding of human nature. Indeed, Hegel's dialectic of right is hysterical in the technical sense that Lacan gave the term. Hysteria is not, however, an aberration. It is the very form of human desire.[202] According to Lacan, the desire of the hysteric is the desire of the Other.[203] The multiple, ambiguous meanings of this expression are the same in the original French as they are in English. The hysteric desires the Other, he desires to be desired by the Other, and his desire is imposed upon him by the Other. The hysteric's very consciousness depends on recognition by others.

To reiterate, Hegel posited that whatever is potential must be actualized. This is one of the meanings of his famous slogan: "What is rational is actual; and what is actual is rational."[204] If human freedom is only potential in the state of nature, logic dictates that this freedom be made actual. Because the necessity that human freedom be actualized is logical and because persons are essentially rational creatures, we are rationally driven to engage in this dialectic of recognition and right.

Economists have accustomed us to speak of markets in terms of "rationality." The Hegelian analysis agrees on the rational and logical nature of the dialectic of right, and therefore markets. But it also reveals it to be essentially erotic—driven by unquenchable desire. Hegel disagreed with the assumed irresolvable dichotomy between reason and passion that is accepted by both utilitarians and romantics. In contrast, Hegel believed that the two are necessarily and inextricably linked—each generates and requires the other. To

202. As Slavoj Žižek points out, although Lacan's assertion that "man's desire is the desire of the Other" is frequently quoted, few recognize that Lacan is speaking about the nature of hysteria. Lacan's point, however, is precisely that hysteria is the characteristic human condition. *See* SLAVOJ ŽIŽEK, THE INDIVISIBLE REMAINDER: AN ESSAY ON SCHELLING AND RELATED MATTERS 167 (1996) [hereinafter, ŽIŽEK, THE INDIVISIBLE REMAINDER].

203. *See id.*

204. HEGEL, THE PHILOSOPHY OF RIGHT, *supra* note 21, at 20. For an excellent discussion of this phrase, *see* AVINERI, *supra* note 19, at 126–27.

put it another way, rationality is the potentiality of desire, and desire is the actuality of rationality. "The concretely rational human [being's] . . . rationality is essentially expressed in and through passion. . . . "[205] The abstract person does not merely prefer to enter market relations and become a subject. Rather, she feels inexorably compelled to do so by the very logic of personhood. This follows from the proposition that freedom, which is the essence of human nature, is only potential in the state of nature and can be actualized only through human relations in subjectivity.

This, in turn, relates to the retroactive nature of Hegel and Lacan's theories and their understanding of possibility and necessity. According to Hegel, one can only retroactively determine what was potential once we consider what has in fact become actual.[206] The logical proposition that man is essentially free can therefore only be proved by establishing the actual freedom of empirical human beings. Hegel thought that the rights citizens were obtaining in the new liberal constitutional and early capitalist economies of the early nineteenth century were evidence of the truth of his political philosophy.

To put this another way, the abstract person seeks confirmation of her freedom. In the state of nature, her freedom is merely potential. She can only confirm the potentiality of freedom retroactively, after she has actualized it. In the liberal state, freedom is actualized through the recognition of rights,[207]

205. CLARK BUTLER, HEGEL'S LOGIC: BETWEEN DIALECTIC AND HISTORY 162 (1996). In this specific passage, Clark Butler is discussing not the dialectic of abstract right, but Hegel's concept of "ground" as explicated in Hegel's *Science of Logic*. *See* G. W. F. HEGEL, HEGEL'S SCIENCE OF LOGIC (A. V. Miller trans., 1969) [hereinafter, HEGEL, THE GREATER LOGIC].

206. The fundamental retroactivity of Hegel's dialectic is reflected in his famous metaphor in the preface to the *Philosophy of Right*: "When philosophy paints its grey in grey, a shape of life has grown old, and it cannot be rejuvenated, but only recognized, by the grey in grey of philosophy; the owl of Minerva begins its flight only with the onset of dusk." HEGEL, THE PHILOSOPHY OF RIGHT, *supra* note 21, at 23; see also SCHROEDER, THE VESTAL AND THE FASCES, *supra* note 185, at 31–32, 311–12; SLAVOJ ŽIŽEK, FOR THEY KNOW NOT WHAT THEY DO: ENJOYMENT AS A POLITICAL FACTOR 130 (1991) [hereinafter, ŽIŽEK, FOR THEY KNOW NOT WHAT THEY DO]; Schroeder, *Never Jam To-day*, *supra* note 28, at 1561.

207. It is not clear to me whether or not Hegel thought that recognition through rights was the only way to reconcile the contradictions of abstract personhood. As I have emphasized elsewhere, Hegel's analysis is retroactive. *See* SCHROEDER, THE VESTAL AND THE FASCES, *supra* note 185, at 13–14, 31–32, 311–32; Schroeder, *Never Jam To-day*, *supra* note 28, at 1536 n.21, 1560–62. In the *Philosophy of Right* he sought to explain not only the logical foundations of the concrete relational individual in the modern constitutional state, but also how they relate to the seemingly contradictory liberal presuppositions of the atomistic abstract person in the state of nature. He purported to show that the former can be understood when one realizes that they solve the inherent contradictions of the latter. The essence of the abstract person is, however, freedom. Consequently, this process could not be deterministic. *See* HEGEL, THE PHILOSOPHY OF RIGHT, *supra* note 21. That is, Hegel did not argue that, when viewed from the position of the abstract person, it was preordained that the abstract person must develop into the concrete

but rights only exist insofar as they are recognized by others. The confirmation of freedom, therefore, can only come through the mutual recognition by another. The abstract person, therefore, rationally seeks out the recognition of others. Her hysterical desire to be desired is perfectly logical.

Because love requires mutuality[208] and equality, unilateral unrequited love is only potential love. At best, in its solipsistic form, it is sterile, lonely autoeroticism. At worst, in its aggressive form, it is destructive, violent rape. Potential love is not actualized until the consummation of the union whereby lover and beloved exchange places. If one can only retroactively determine what was truly potential after it is actualized, then failed attempts at love that do not achieve consummation are eventually, and sadly, revealed as no love at all.

Persons must, therefore, develop a system that embodies at least a fleeting moment of mutuality and equality—a meeting of minds. For the dialectic to work, neither party can dominate the other. Because the purpose of recognition is the actualization of freedom, the meeting of minds must be such that it does not impinge upon either party's freedom. To be free is to be one's own end and not the means to the ends of another.[209] Consequently, the meeting of minds cannot directly define or constrain either party's personhood because that would treat that party as the means to an end, denying the freedom of that person. Rather, an external third, an object, must be found as a means of mediating between the two parties.[210]

The abstract person in the state of nature is not recognizable because she (or more accurately "it") lacks all idiosyncratic pathological characteristics. To be recognizable one needs to become concrete, not abstract.[211] To become concrete, one must take on individuating characteristics external to abstract personality. In this philosophical tradition, anything external to this abstraction is defined as an "object."[212] From the standpoint of philosophy (as well as in law), the concept of "object" cannot be limited to physical things, but rather includes intangibles and even personal characteristics,

---

individual. Rather, he suggested that, when viewed from the position of the concrete individual, the dialectic suggests that this is what must have happened.

208. "Love, of course, constitutes a sign [*fait signe*] and is always mutual." JACQUES LACAN, THE SEMINAR OF JACQUES LACAN. BOOK XX: ENCORE, ON FEMININE SEXUALITY, THE LIMITS OF LOVE AND KNOWLEDGE, 1972–73 4 (Jacques-Alain Miller ed. & Bruce Fink trans., 1998) [hereinafter, LACAN, SEMINAR XX].

209. HEGEL, THE PHILOSOPHY OF RIGHT, *supra* note 21, at 38.

210. *Id.* at 102–103.

211. The free abstract person, as pure negativity, can only be defined in terms of what it is not. *See id.* It can only give itself determinative existence by objectifying itself (i.e., by establishing object relations that will make it recognizable). *See id.* at 70; *see also* ALAN BRUDNER, THE UNITY OF THE COMMON LAW: STUDIES IN HEGELIAN JURISPRUDENCE 42–43 (1995).

212. *See* HEGEL, THE PHILOSOPHY OF RIGHT, *supra* note 21, at 73.

such as our body and personality.[213] In order to become recognizable, therefore, one must form object relations. The primitive object relations of abstract right are called "property" and "contract."

Hegel posited that the object relations of property consist of the elements of possession, enjoyment, and alienation, understood in the most general and abstract sense.[214] I have explicated the Hegelian conception of possession[215] and enjoyment[216] extensively elsewhere. In the rest of this chapter, I will concentrate on alienation in its most developed form of exchange, which is the ability to enter into contracts.

It is sufficient at this point to state that "possession" cannot be limited to the physical custody of tangible objects. This follows from the fact that the concept of "objects" cannot be limited to tangible things. Possession is, instead, the more general concept of identifying an object to a specific person.[217] This serves the function of individuating the owning person—making her potentially recognizable. Enjoyment is the owner's assertion of her mastery over the object owned.[218] It is an expression of the owner's freedom that distinguishes the owner from the owned object and therefore establishes the owner not merely as a recognizable thing, but as a recognizable person. Consequently, possession and enjoyment establish the conditions of recogniz-

213. See id. at 40–41; Peter Benson, *Abstract Right and the Possibility of a Nondistributive Conception of Contract: Hegel and Contemporary Contract Theory,* 10 CARDOZO L. REV. 1077, 1164 (1989). Indeed, in his *Philosophy of Mind,* Hegel argued that the most fundamental object is one's own self. In other words, the moment one asks "Who am I?," one is experiencing a distance from oneself. The subject-object distinction is not, therefore, as is often thought, a separation of self from other. Rather, it is an internal self-alienation. See G. W. F. HEGEL, HEGEL'S PHILOSOPHY OF MIND 153 (William Wallace & A. V. Miller trans., 1971). This anticipates Lacan's concept of the split, castrated subject.

214. As I have discussed in detail elsewhere, it is a common modern error to conclude from the observation that property comes in many different forms, as an empirical matter, that there is either no essential core of property as a logical or jurisprudential matter, or that property consists of an arbitrary bundle of a number of rights picked from a long laundry list. *See* Schroeder, *Never Jam To-day, supra* note 28, at 1547–50. A Hegelian position argues that one can identify a minimum definition of property so long as one stays at the appropriate level of abstraction.

215. *See* SCHROEDER, THE VESTAL AND THE FASCES, *supra* note 185, at 38–43, 145–56; Jeanne L. Schroeder, *Chix Nix Bundle-O-Stix: A Feminist Critique of the Disaggregation of Property,* 93 MICH. L. REV. 239, 310–12, 317 (1994); Jeanne L. Schroeder, *Some Realism About Legal Surrealism,* 37 WM. & MARY L. REV. 455, 512–16 (1996)

216. *See* SCHROEDER, THE VESTAL AND THE FASCES, *supra* note 185, at 43–44, 239–46; Schroeder, *Virgin Territory, supra* note 211, at 88–93, 136–37. I return to a consideration of the enjoyment of property in Chapter 2.

217. *See* HEGEL, THE PHILOSOPHY OF RIGHT, *supra* note 21, at 76–88; Benson, *supra* note 213, at 1177 n.140, 1179; Alan Brudner, *The Unity of Property Law,* 4 CAN. J. L. & JURIS. 3, 24 (1991).

218. *See* HEGEL, THE PHILOSOPHY OF RIGHT, *supra* note 21, at 59. The form of enjoyment depends on the particular object enjoyed: food may be eaten, a picture admired, an account receivable collected, etc.

ability. Standing alone, however, possession and enjoyment are inadequate. Through the final element of alienation (contract exchange), the potentiality of recognition is actualized and interrelations are consummated.

The first two elements of property, possession and enjoyment, are necessary but insufficient for the purpose of the actualization of freedom because only their subject-object aspect is explicit—the essential subject-subject interrelational aspect of property still remains merely latent. Possession—the assignment of a specific object to a specific subject—is implicitly intersubjective because assigning an object to one subject is necessarily not to assign it to others. But this means the relation between the owning subject and the non-owning subject is the negative relation of exclusion. Enjoyment is also implicitly intersubjective, not merely because one's enjoyment of one's object often necessarily precludes another rival subject from enjoying the same object, but also because one subject's enjoyment of her object often necessarily interferes with the ability of another subject to enjoy his object.[219] A classic example (that I explore in Chapter 3) is the environmental nuisance in which a factory owner's ability to enjoy his factory in production interferes with a neighboring consumer's ability to drink her water. Consequently, the relation of enjoyment is once again negative—it is exclusion plus interference.

Because possession and enjoyment are negatively intersubjective, they threaten to become solipsistic—they exclude all others. Solipsism is the opposite of the desired goal of mutual recognition. Only recognition by a self-certain end-unto-itself (i.e., another subject) can provide lasting confirmation that freedom is actual. Moreover, in possession and enjoyment, the subject depends on the object for her self-confirmation, and therefore risks becoming dependent on the object in the same way that an addict is dependent on her drug.[220] As dependency is the opposite of freedom, this not only defeats the purpose of property; it also betrays human nature.

The person therefore needs to find a way of disencumbering herself from any specific object while still maintaining the object relations necessary for recognizability. The logic of property suggests that the vast majority of objects should be alienable by the owners. Hegel discussed three possible modes of alienation: abandonment, gift, and contract. Abandonment, which destroys any relationship between the owner and the object, is inadequate for the goal of recognizability[221] and shall not be discussed here. In the *Philosophy of Right,* Hegel first explains the problems posed by gift and then

219. *See* SCHROEDER, THE VESTAL AND THE FASCES, *supra* note 185, at 44–45.
220. *See* Brudner, *supra* note 217, at 31; Schroeder, *Virgin Territory, supra* note 197, at 138.
221. *See* Brudner, *supra* note 217, at 34.

shows how they are solved by contract. In this chapter, I proceed in the opposite direction. I first explicate the eroticism of the contract relationship. I then show that gift does not merely compare unfavorably with contract in accomplishing the goal of mutual recognition and freedom. It can actually be destructive of this goal, causing domination and restriction.

Subjectivity—the capability of being a legal actor—is constituted by mutual recognition. This occurs in the bilateral relationship of contract. Contract is therefore the minimum condition of law. Gift, in contrast, is a failed, one-sided attempt at recognition that falls short of abstract right. Gift is therefore only quasi legal in nature. This may explain why contemporary American law only grudgingly gives limited recognition to gratuitous promises.

To reiterate, in order for the abstract person to achieve her goal of obtaining subjectivity, she must help others achieve their subjectivity. The circularity of this is obvious. For this fiction to work, neither party can go first. The two parties must simultaneously recognize each other so that the very moment of recognition is the mutually constitutive moment of intersubjectivity. The necessity of simultaneity means that a successful recognition that creates subjectivity must have a moment of mutuality and equality.

Accordingly, Hegel argues that the object-relations of property, contract, and market serve two functions. First, as we have already discussed, they make abstract persons recognizable. Second, they also serve as mediators—means by which persons can achieve their ends and be recognized by others while remaining free, neither dominating nor being dominated by the other. Property sets us apart so that we can come together. As I have stated, Kant and Hegel defined "objects" as those things that are external to the abstract person understood as free will—i.e., anything that is not another human being. Because objects are not free (i.e., are not ends in themselves), they can rightfully serve as means.[222]

In contract, one person exchanges one of his objects for another object owned by another person.[223] In contract, each party recognizes the other as a unique person—the owner of a specific identifiable object. The fact that

222. This is why slavery is essentially and abstractly wrong (not just wrong as a matter of convention, morality, or ethics). Slavery treats the slave as a means to the master's ends, rather than a person who is an end in and for himself. *See* HEGEL, THE PHILOSOPHY OF RIGHT, *supra* note 21, at 97; Jeanne L. Schroeder, *Hegel's Slaves, Blackstone's Objects, and Hohfeld's Ghosts: A Comment on Thomas Russell's Imagery of Slave Auctions,* 18 CARDOZO L. REV. 525, 531–33 (1996).

223. Note that because Hegel defined object as anything external to subjectivity, contracts for services are as much an exchange of objects, as so defined, as contracts for the sale of goods, i.e., despite the fact that we might identify with the fruits of our labors, they are external to our minimal personality.

the party is willing to exchange her object demonstrates to the other party that the first party is not dependent on that specific object but remains a free person.[224] The fact that each person obtains a new object in the exchange means that each party will remain recognizable as a person after the transaction is finished. Because contract is a voluntary transaction, both parties' actions must have a moment of freedom and mutuality. Because each party agrees that she is obtaining an object that is the equivalent of the object she is giving up, each party perceives the relationship as one of equality.

In other words, at the moment of the meeting of minds in contract, neither party is subject to the will of the other. Rather, they are for a fleeting second joined in a common will.[225] For a brief shining moment, each party recognizes the other as a free, equal legal subject, and therefore achieves her goal of becoming a subject. It is a moment of love. No doubt this is why the consummation of the deal is traditionally symbolized by the physical union of the two negotiators in the joining of hands—a gesture reminiscent of the more complete joining of lovers.

This is not to imply that, in an empirical sense, all contracts are perfectly mutual, lacking in domination, or characterized by total equality and meeting of minds. Even from a theoretical viewpoint, in order for contract to be successful it must simultaneously contain the seed of its own failure. If the parties to a contract truly merged in a perfect meeting of minds, they would become indistinguishable and unrecognizable. If the objects exchanged in contract were perfectly equivalent, exchange would never occur. For the mutuality of contract to occur, each party must, paradoxically at some level, think that she is getting the better deal, and therefore exploiting the other party.

This is a contradiction. But, in Hegel's philosophy, contradiction is a necessary and inevitable aspect of reality.[226] Moreover, as contradiction is unstable, it is the engine of movement and change in the system.[227] Contradiction is the pain or lack that creates desire. Without contradiction, not only

224. *See* HEGEL, THE PHILOSOPHY OF RIGHT, *supra* note 21, at 95; Brudner, *supra* note 217, at 34.

225. "A person, in distinguishing himself from himself, relates himself to another person, and indeed it is only as owners of property that the two [persons] have existence . . . for each other. Their identity in themselves acquires existence . . . through the transference of the property of the one to the other by common will and with due respect of the rights of both that is by contract." HEGEL, THE PHILOSOPHY OF RIGHT, *supra* note 21, at 70; *see also id.* at 102.

226. Contradiction "is not to be taken merely as an abnormality which only occurs here and there, but is rather the negative as determined in the sphere of essence, the principle of all self-movement. . . . " HEGEL, THE GREATER LOGIC, *supra* note 205, at 440. Hegel was particularly hard on those philosophers who try to deny or do away with contradiction. *See id.* at 237–38.

227. *See* Schroeder, *Never Jam To-day*, *supra* note 28, at 1560.

would no exchange occur; the universe would be totally static.[228] This world of no contradiction is, of course, the deathly order that Lacan called the "real," which I discuss in the last section of this chapter.

The myth of Pandora teaches us that we can obtain hope only by first accepting the ills of this world. Similarly, it is only the existence of imperfection, impossibility, and loss that makes desire not only necessary but also possible. The negativity that characterized the abstract person posited by Kant and Hegel continues in all human relations—including contract. But this space between and within people is the condition precedent of freedom in that it gives us the space to move and create. It is precisely because human relations are always to some extent unsuccessful, no one is ever satisfied, and everyone desires greater love and recognition that we are driven continuously to engage in new relations. This understanding of the radical negativity of freedom reflects the Lacanian concept of the "feminine."

Consequently, it is essential to the Lacanian-Hegelian system that not all aspects of human relationality can be circumscribed within the symbolic order of law.

Like all sexual relations,[229] contract is always a partial failure—the relationship of intersubjectivity is always mediated by objectivity; we externalize and feel alienated from a part of our essential nature. But contract is also always a partial success—it enables us to create our subjectivity as intersubjectivity, albeit mediated by objectivity. True, the Lacanian subject is split, negative, and empty, and the erotic relation is a failed encounter. But the erotic encounter is a failure only if one envisions success as the obliteration of all difference and the achievement of immediate relationship or merger with the other. In Lacanian terms, this would be an impossible reversal of "castration" and reabsorption into the order he called the "real." Such a reabsorption is the destruction not only of subjectivity, but also of the possibility of freedom, which is man's essence. Consequently, the negativity that

228. As F. W. J. Von Schelling stated: "Although men—in both living and knowing—seem to shy away from nothing so much as contradiction, they still must confront it, because life itself is in contradiction. Without contradiction there would be no life, no movement, no progress; a deadly slumber of all forces. Only contradiction drives us—indeed forces us—to action. Contradiction is in fact the venom of all life, and all vital motion is nothing but the attempt to overcome this poisoning." F. W. J. Von Schelling, *Ages of the World* (Judith Norman trans.), in SLAVOJ ŽIŽEK, THE ABYSS OF FREEDOM / AGES OF THE WORLD 105, 124 (1997) [hereinafter, ŽIŽEK, THE ABYSS OF FREEDOM].

229. Lacan notoriously asserted that there are no sexual relations. *See* LACAN, SEMINAR XX, *supra* note 208, at 9; ELIZABETH GROSZ, JACQUES LACAN: A FEMINIST INTRODUCTION 137 (1990); Ellie Ragland-Sullivan, *The Sexual Masquerade: A Lacanian Theory of Sexual Difference,* in LACAN AND THE SUBJECT OF LANGUAGE 49, 67 (E. Ragland-Sullivan & M. Bracher eds., 1991).

remains at the heart of subjectivity is the necessary feminine moment of radical freedom. The separation and distinction between subjects that remains after contract is, therefore, the distinction of individuality. Individuality enables us not only to love but also to actualize the freedom that is our potential. The "failure" of contract is therefore creative and dynamic.

Gift is a wholly different form of failure. In contradistinction to the romantic position, therefore, the distinction and recognition created by gift is not the individuality that allows for the unique and creative relation of love. Rather, it is the distinction of status—the static, oppressive relation of domination and subordination. If contract is the mutual eroticism of intercourse, gift is autoeroticism—masturbation or rape. If market relations are the characteristic economic activity of modern liberal constitutional states that to some extent or another organized around rights and the individual, it is also true that "gift exchange" is the characteristic economic activity of "archaic" traditional, hierarchical societies that are based on status and clan. In other words, gifts are a failed attempt to achieve the mutual, equal recognition of abstract right (law). Consequently, there is a moment of truth in the utilitarian position that law cannot adequately account for gift.

Hegel only made passing reference to gift in the *Philosophy of Right.*[230] To completely understand this failure, however, one must also reflect on the failed relationship of lordship discussed by Hegel in the *Phenomenology of Spirit.*[231]

The function of property relations is the actualization of freedom through mutual recognition. In gift, the donor seeks recognition from a donee by giving an object to him. "What is wrong with this?" one might interpose. "Don't we all enjoy gifts? Isn't it a way for us to express our affection for the donee?" asks the romantic. The utilitarian suggests: "Isn't the donee better off because he received something for nothing?" Moreover, the utilitarian adds, "The donor would not have made the gift unless she anticipated that she would receive something in return that would afford her at least as much utility as the gift—such as personal gratitude of the donee or the general esteem of society." The only problem with gift, according to the utilitarian, is that it is subject to bargain failure and therefore is more likely than contract to result in inefficient transfers. Society cannot, therefore, assume that the benefits of enforcing gratuitous promises justify the expense of doing so. The romantic might chide the utilitarian for being so narrow-minded and

230. Hegel, The Philosophy of Right, *supra* note 21, at 106; *see also* Brudner, *supra* note 217, at 34.

231. Hegel, The Phenomenology of Spirit, *supra* note 180, at 111–19. For an excellent discussion of the interrelationship between the dialectics of recognition in the *Philosophy of Right* and the *Phenomenology, see* Rosenfeld, *supra* note 37.

crass, but would nevertheless agree that the donor, as well as the donee, is benefited by gift in the sense that we often feel even greater pleasure in giving than receiving gifts.

The Hegelian replies: The problem is that gift is a unilateral action foisted by the donor onto the donee, not a choice mutually made by both parties. Freedom necessitates that a person act out of choice, not out of compulsion. For a gift to be a gift, by definition, it cannot be a matter of express prior bargain between the donor and the donee. The donor chooses to give a gift. But the donee does not choose to initiate the relationship. The only freedom reserved to the donee is the minimal reactive power to refuse the gift.[232] In actual social situations, however, the donee may have little or no practical ability to refuse the gift. At best, refusals of gift would make the donee appear ungrateful, petty, and despicable in the eyes of others. The efficacy of gift in establishing status in archaic gift-exchange societies is based on the fact that it is deemed impossible as a practical matter to refuse a ritual gift.

More importantly, in gift, the donor does not recognize the donee as a free subject. As we have seen, the Hegelian definition of freedom is to be one's own end and not the means to the ends of another.[233] In gift, however, the donor treats the donee as a means to the donor's own end—he gives a gift in order to be recognized.[234] He *demands* recognition from the donee. In contradistinction, in contract one party makes an offer to another and the transaction does not proceed unless and until the two parties come to mutual agreement. Mutual agreement indicates that each party has determined that the contract will serve her own ends.[235] Because in gift the donor is treating the donee as a means rather than an end in himself, the donor is not recognizing the donee in his capacity to become a subject. Consequently, any recognition given back by the donee is ineffectual in respect to the goal of achieving subjectivity.

Moreover, as we have seen, abstract persons create the institution of property because they need to take on specific object relations in order to become recognizable. In gift, the donor ostensibly gives up one object and receives no object in return. This is not fatal in any specific transaction because the donor may continue to own enough other objects to remain recognizable. An economy based totally on true gifts, however, would be

232. Consequently, Hegel did recognize that gift does have an imperfect contractual element. *See* HEGEL, THE PHILOSOPHY OF RIGHT, *supra* note 21 at 106–107.

233. *See id.* at 67.

234. *See* Brudner, *supra* note 217, at 34.

235. This is true in theory. In practice, however, contracting parties may be constrained in ways that limit their ability to negotiate beneficial contractual terms.

untenable because of the possibility that some donors eventually become bereft of objects. Any gift economy must, therefore, be based on the presumption of the donors that they will eventually receive new objects to compensate for the donated objects.

On the one hand, this expectation of future gain keeps actual gift relations from being the free, generous relations celebrated by romantics.[236] Gifts always reflect a fundamental moment of selfishness. On the other hand, the lack of bargaining and promise and the inability to bind future compensating givers precisely keep actual gift relations from being the free, mutual contract-like exchanges described by utilitarians.

This suggests that gift is unsuccessful as a means of establishing relations of mutuality—the purpose of law as abstract right. It may, however, have positive roles to play once relations of mutuality are established. As I have said, Hegel believed that the particular selfishness of the state of nature and the universal selfishness of civil society (i.e., the market) require the particular altruism of the family and the universal altruism of the liberal constitutional state. Gift, in the form of the selfless love and altruism within family and friendships and the self-sacrifice of loyalty and charity within the state, may be not only appropriate but a necessary complement to contract. It is a category mistake, however, to try to reduce the realms of family and state to that of the market. This may explain why our society intuitively resists submitting gratuitous promises to the market regime of abstract right.

Probably the best-known aspect of the Hegelian dialectic is the analysis of slavery in the *Phenomenology of Spirit*. If the *Philosophy of Right* is the dialectic of the actualization of human freedom in individual persons, the *Phenomenology of Spirit* is the dialectic of the actualization of *Geist* (spirit, intellect). Famously, in the *Phenomenology*, Hegel purports to show how the potentiality of *Geist* becomes actualized in human history starting from simple consciousness of objects. As my colleague Michel Rosenfeld has argued before,

236. As sociologist Peter Blau has written:

> A person who fails to reciprocate favors is accused of ingratitude. This very accusation indicates that reciprocation is expected, and it serves as a social sanction that discourages individuals from forgetting their obligations to associates. Generally, people are grateful for favors and repay their social debts, and both their gratitude and their repayment are social rewards for the associate who has done them favors. The fact that furnishing benefits to others tends to produce these social rewards is, of course, a major reason why people often go to great trouble to help their associates and enjoy doing so. . . . There are, to be sure, some individuals who selflessly work for others without any thought of reward and even without expecting gratitude, but these are virtually saints, and saints are rare. The rest of us also act unselfishly sometimes, but we require some incentive for doing so, if it is only the social acknowledgement that we are unselfish.

Peter M. Blau, EXCHANGE AND POWER IN SOCIAL LIFE 16–17 (1964) (footnotes omitted).

Hegel's analysis of the failed recognition in the lord-bondsman dialectic is closely related to his analysis of the more successful recognition of contract.[237]

As we saw in the case of the creation of subjectivity and the actualization of freedom, one moment in the actualization of *Geist* is self-certainty through recognition.[238] When consciousness becomes self-consciousness, self-certainty means the satisfaction of desire: attraction to and consumption of objects.[239] This precipitates a crisis when one self-consciousness confronts another. "Each is indeed certain of its own self, but not of the other, and therefore its own self-certainty still has no truth."[240] Truth requires that each self-consciousness compare itself to an independent object that is itself self-certain.[241]

To understand oneself as self-consciousness, however, one needs to abstract one's understanding of oneself from one's mere accidental existence: that is to say, in order to understand one's own subjectivity, one needs to negate objectivity. Because each self-consciousness confronts the other as an "object" (i.e., that which is external to his own subjectivity), the desire to negate the other has been actualized in the fight to the death between warriors. In this way, not only does each self-consciousness try to negate the other's consciousness, but also each is willing to stake his own life in order to achieve the certainty of truth.[242] It is by staking his life that the self-consciousness seeks to achieve freedom.[243] He who does not risk his life may be a person, but not yet a self-consciousness. The self-consciousness not only stakes his own life, however; he also tries to kill the other, who seems to be a rival to his claims to immediacy.

This strategy is necessarily a failure. To kill the other is not to achieve truth, but to destroy it. This is because the only way we can achieve confirmation of our claims of self-consciousness is through recognition.[244] Obviously, one cannot be recognized if the other is dead. Moreover, death is merely the natural negation of a single empirical other, not the intellectual negation of otherness.

237. *See* Rosenfeld, *supra* note 37, at 1221–25.

238. "Self-consciousness exists in and for itself when, and by the fact that, it so exists for another; that is, it exists only in being acknowledged." HEGEL, THE PHENOMENOLOGY OF SPIRIT, *supra* note 180, at 111.

239. JOSEPH C. FLAY, HEGEL'S QUEST FOR CERTAINTY, 81–87 (1984).

240. HEGEL, THE PHENOMENOLOGY OF SPIRIT, *supra* note 180, at 113.

241. "But according to the Notion of recognition this is possible only when each is for the other what the other is for it, only when each in its own self through its own action, and again through the action of the other, achieves this pure abstraction of being-for-self." *Id.*

242. *See id.* at 112–14.

243. *See id.* at 114.

244. *See id.*

Consequently, the self now realizes that life is as important as death.[245] And so, two moments of self-consciousness have now been created: the moment of self-consciousness that realizes itself in the willingness to risk its own life—lordship—and the moment of self-consciousness that clings to life—servility.[246] Hegel hypothesized that this was empirically played out in the warrior culture of classical Greece (i.e., Posner's archetypical ancient gift culture), where the warrior who surrendered rather than being killed became the slave of the one who was willing to continue to fight.[247]

In the lord-bondsman dialectic, the lord relates to the bondsman as the thinghood (objectivity) from which the lord is independent.[248] The lord's understanding of himself is now mediated by the thinghood of the bondsman. What he could not achieve through desire, he tries to achieve through action—by enjoying the thinghood of the bondsman.[249] The lord, by dominating the bondsman, forces the recognition of the bondsman, who is a separate consciousness.[250] But, as in gift, "the outcome is a recognition that is one-sided and unequal."[251]

True, the lord achieved his goal of recognition by another consciousness, but by treating the bondsman as an object—a means to the lord's ends, the object of his enjoyment—he made the other into a thing "quite different from an independent self-consciousness."[252] The lord seeks to achieve the truth of his own independent self-consciousness through recognition, but the only truth he confronts is the "servile consciousness of the bondsman."[253]

The nature of the lord becomes the reverse of his claim.[254] He seeks to experience himself as essentially free, but it is he who is dependent on the slave. This is because it is only through the slave's recognition that the lord can achieve self-understanding—he is only a master insofar as the slave bows before him. The lord now knows himself only as the reflection of slavery. Ironically, it is the lord's claim of nobility that debases him. Forced recogni-

245. *See id.* at 115.

246. *See id.*

247. This is why the Latin word for slave, *servus,* is derived from *servo, servare*—to save. The slave is he who is saved from death.

248. As Hegel stated, "For it is just this which holds the bondsman in bondage; it is his chain from which he could not break free in the struggle, thus proving himself to be dependent, to possess his independence in thinghood. But the lord is the power over this thing, for he proved in the struggle that it is something merely negative; since he is the power over the thing and this again is the power over the other [the bondsman], it follows that he holds the other in subjection." *Id.* at 115.

249. *See id.* at 116.

250. *See id.*

251. *Id.*

252. *Id.* at 117.

253. *Id.*

254. *See id.*

tion, therefore, has the opposite effect from free recognition—it turns freedom into dependence.

Similarly, in gift, the donor seeks his own self-understanding as a free, generous, loving person by imposing himself on the donee. If the donee, like the slave, fails to resist but surrenders to the wishes of the donor, she subordinates herself to the donor's desire. The donor objectifies the donee by treating her as the means to his ends, in the same way as the lord objectified the bondsman. The donor "enjoys" the donee in the same way the lord "enjoys" a slave. The donee-bondsman is not granted the subjectivity that would allow her desire to be recognized. The donee, as a means to the donor's ends, is literally the object of the donor's desire in both the colloquial and the technical Hegelian-Lacanian senses of the term. The gift relationship can be seen as erotic in the sense that it involves desire and enjoyment. But it is one-sided and autoerotic, as the donor-lord is only concerned with his own desire and enjoyment. Gift is not, therefore, social intercourse, but rather masturbation. Worse, because the donor exploits the donee as his masturbatory object, it is a form of rape.

It is true that in gift, as in bondage, the donee recognizes the donor, but not in freely chosen mutuality. Rather, it is in the servile relation of gratitude. Although the word "gratitude," etymologically related to grace, implies freedom from constraint, it is always in fact compelled. If there is freedom in the gift transaction, it is entirely on the side of the donor.[255] Society demands that the donee graciously accept the gift experience, or at least demonstrate gratitude, or be condemned as "ungrateful," one of the most despised, base, and "unnatural" attributes of a scoundrel beyond ordinary human feelings.[256] As Mauss concluded, "The unreciprocated gift still makes the person who has accepted it inferior, particularly when it has been accepted with no thought of returning it."[257]

As sociologist Peter Blau has recognized, it is an observable fact of cultural organization that the person who cannot return a gift in kind is placed in a subservient role. If one who receives a gift needs to have a continuing relationship with the donor, he can adopt one of three strategies:

255. It is not even clear that the donor is free. In traditional gift-exchange societies, giving is an express obligation.

256. Consequently, as Jacques Derrida suggests, the paradox of gift is that for a gift to be truly a gift—in the sense of an altruistic act that confers no benefit on the donor and imposes no obligation on the donee—it must immediately be erased by being forgotten. *See* Jacques Derrida, *The Time of the King*, in THE LOGIC OF THE GIFT: TOWARD AN ETHIC OF GENEROSITY 128–32 (Alan D. Schrift ed., 1997). To paraphrase Derrida, the only way for a giver to be forgiven for giving a gift is for the getter to forget what he got. *See id.* at 132–33. The relation between the words "give" and "forgive" is not a pun. The same relationship exists between the French equivalents pardon and don.

257. MAUSS, *supra* note 103, at 65.

> First, he may force the other to give him help. Second, he may obtain the help he needs from another source. Third, he may find ways to get along without such help. If he is unable or unwilling to choose any of these alternatives, however, there is only one other course of action left for him; he must subordinate himself to the other and comply with his wishes, thereby rewarding the other with power over himself as an inducement for furnishing the needed help.[258]

And so, as in the lord-bondsman dialectic, the donor now knows herself through her donee, but the knowledge is hollow. He sees only the reflection of dependency. The donor, like the lord, enjoys the donee. But as I have discussed, although enjoyment is a necessary aspect of a property relation, it degenerates into dependency and addiction. The donor is dependent on the donee in the same way that the lord is dependent on his bondsman. Dependency is precisely the reverse of the freedom both claim.[259]

Consequently, neither the dialectic of lordship nor that of gift can stop at this point. Each is a continuing source of struggle. This struggle is not, however, dynamic; rather, it is a vicious, static circle.

The bondsman, albeit negated and debased, is nevertheless a self-consciousness (in the vocabulary of the *Phenomenology of Spirit*), just as the donee remains a person with the potential for freedom (in the vocabulary of the *Philosophy of Right*).

Gift implicitly demands the recognition of gratitude. It would seem at first blush that gratitude could, at least theoretically, be expressed by words, gesture, and/or affection. This is frequently not the case. The donor is not satisfied without a more material form of gratitude, namely a return "gift" of equal or greater value. For example, even though one generally feels self-satisfied and generous when one invites guests over for dinner, it quickly changes to dissatisfaction and resentment if the guest does not reciprocate with a timely, matching act of hospitality. As Blau notes:

> Power differences not only are an imbalance by definition but also are actually experienced as such, as indicated by the tendency of men to escape from domination if they can. Indeed, a major impetus for the eagerness of individuals to discharge their obligations and reciprocate for services they receive, by providing services in return, is the threat of becoming otherwise subject to the power of the supplier of the services. While reciprocal services create an interdependence that balances power, unilateral dependence on services maintains an imbalance of power.[260]

258. Blau, *supra* note 238, at 21–22 (footnote omitted).

259. Blau similarly argues that the imbalance of power is not merely accidental but is typical of the gift relation. *See id.* at 26.

260. *Id.* at 29.

More importantly, the donee, as a self-consciousness and a free person, also desires recognition. The failure to achieve worthy recognition as donee only increases her ardor. The donee is driven, therefore, to try to reverse the process by giving a return gift. By doing so, she not only attempts to undo the subordination forced upon her by the donee; by giving a new gift of greater value than the first gift, the original donee also attempts to win recognition from, and thereby dominate, the original donor. Consequently, gift begets gift, but not mutual gift. This is, of course, the logic of potlatch.

Because this transaction is not mutual and is implicitly aggressive, it does not resolve the search for recognition. As Georges Bataille states (discussing potlatch specifically):

> Not only does [the donor] have the power over the recipient that the gift has bestowed on him, but the recipient is obligated to nullify that power by repaying the gift. The rivalry even entails the return of a greater gift: In order to get even the giver must not only redeem himself, but he must also impose the "power of the gift" on his rival in turn. In a sense the presents are repaid with interest. Thus the gift is the opposite of what it seemed to be: To give is obviously to lose, but the loss apparently brings a profit to the one who sustains it.
>
> In reality, this absurdly contradictory aspect of *potlatch* is misleading. The first giver suffers the apparent gain resulting from the difference between his presents and those given to him in return. The one who repays only has the feeling of acquiring—a power—and of outdoing. . . . Receiving prompts one—and obliges one—to give more, for it is necessary to remove the resulting obligation.[261]

This gift exchange achieves only a partial and inferior mode of recognition. The parties to the gift exchange are differentiated, but not as individuals who are simultaneously recognized as unique and different as well as equal and the same. Rather, this is the difference of dominance and subordination—status. Consequently, gift exchange can only continue in a sterile iteration until one party is defeated.

This is not to suggest that a gift relationship (or a gift-exchange or bondage economy) cannot, in fact, come to an end, empirically speaking. To Hegel, each person retains a moment of essential freedom that can enable him to transcend his particular circumstances. One party can eventually defeat the other. Similarly, like a Ponzi scheme, the sterile circle of any specific gift-exchange regime might come to an end as an empirical matter, although there is no *logical* reason why it must.[262] The end of a gift-exchange institution would require a radical change in the culture that supported the regime and would be tantamount to the creation of a new political-economic

261. BATAILLE, *supra* note 128, at 70–71.

262. *See* David Gray Carlson, *Secured Lending as a Zero-Sum Game,* 19 CARDOZO L. REV. 1635, 1660–62 (1998).

(i.e., symbolic) order. For example, in the modern European world, the market regime of abstract right has replaced a prior regime of gift, fealty, dominance, and subordination called feudalism. There are, however, many "archaic" societies that are still organized around gift exchange. Indeed, it was Mauss's hypothesis that gift exchange characterizes a specific level of development of societies. There is no necessary reason for these cultures to break out of these circles. Within these cultures, individuals can only break out of the circle through defeat. From a Maussian point of view, for a society to break the circle of gift exchange is precisely to change the very structure of a society. That is, the society ceases to be "archaic" and becomes "modern." American law's suspicion of gratuitous promises may reflect an intuitive understanding of gift's essential ambiguity.

COMMODIFICATION AND RELATIONSHIP

One of the flaws at the heart of the romantic position is a misperception of the role of commodification in interrelationship. Once again, utilitarianism shares this basic conceptual error but, as romanticism's mirror image, reaches the opposite normative evaluation.

The romantic goes beyond the conclusions that gift is desirable and can further intimate relations. She also asserts that contract threatens the very existence of the intimate relations furthered by gift. Contract leads to commodification—the treatment of objects as commodities to be exchanged. The romantic asserts that because in commodification all objects can be reduced to their exchange value, all objects become completely fungible, commensurable, and equivalent.[263] The romantic fears that commodification's suppression of difference among objects will inevitably lead to the suppression of difference between subjects. This suppression of individual differences will impede human relations because (as Hegel argued) relationship requires recognition, which in turn requires individuation. The romantic therefore fears that commodification may turn people into undifferentiated cogs in a wheel.[264] Consequently, the romantic finds the very rhetoric of alienation to be alienating.

263. *See, e.g.*, RADIN, CONTESTED COMMODITIES, *supra* note 91, at 1–15. In the words of Eisenberg: "A bargain is about commodities . . . and a bargain focuses on the amount of money or the monetary value of the commodity that each party transfers. In contrast, gifts are, or must at least purport to be, about either affective relationships or the expression of moral duties or aspirations." Eisenberg, *supra* note 20, at 844. He continues, "Cash is a cold, market commodity, while objects are often invested with warmth." *Id.* at 845.

264. *See* Radin, Market-Inalienability, *supra* note 29, at 1877–87; *see also* RADIN, CONTESTED COMMODITIES, *supra* note 91, at 79–101; Margaret Jane Radin, *Justice and the Market Domain, in* MARKETS AND JUSTICE: NOMOS XXXI 165, 167–68 (John W. Chapman & J. Roland Pennock eds., 1989) [hereinafter, Radin, *Justice*].

The utilitarian's ideal is not the idealized community of the romantic, but the perfect market. The perfect market is defined as those conditions that guarantee utility (or wealth) maximization. As I show in Chapters 2 and 4, one of the conditions of the perfect market is perfect commodification. In a perfect market, trade would occur until each participant became indifferent with respect to all objects, in the sense that no further trade could increase her utility (or wealth).[265]

In other words, both the romantic and the utilitarian think that markets lead to commodification and commodification is the suppression of difference. The romantic fears this vision as a perversion of human freedom, while the utilitarian embraces it as the fulfillment of human freedom.

Moreover, both view markets as an inexorable march towards commodification. The romantic, therefore, wishes to save gift from the oncoming juggernaut,[266] whereas the utilitarian suspects that gift could be a roadblock impeding its progress. In this section, I first provide a brief account of the romantic fear of commodification and suggest a psychoanalytic account of romanticism's intuitive appeal. I then turn to Hegelian-Lacanian theory to introduce the basic analytical flaw in the account of commodification shared by romanticism and utilitarianism.

Romanticism

An excellent example of the romantic fear of commodification and belief that gift and markets are incompatible can be seen in Titmuss's famous book, *The Gift Relationship: From Human Blood to Social Policy*.[267] As is well known, Titmuss compares the blood supply system in the United States and the United Kingdom. He argues not merely that voluntary blood contributions are morally superior to paid ones or that a voluntarily contributed blood supply is likely to be relatively safer than a purchased one. He also hypothesizes a sort of Gresham's law of blood. Paying for blood is affirmatively bad because it drives out voluntary contributions. Titmuss argues that "private market systems . . . deprive men of their freedom to choose to give or not to give."[268] As Kenneth Arrow suggests, "Evidently Titmuss must feel that attaching a

265. *See* PAUL A. SAMUELSON & WILLIAM D. NORDHAUS, ECONOMICS 264 (15th ed. 1995).

266. For example, Radin asserts, "At worst—in universal commodification—the gift is conceived of as a bargain. . . . A better view of personhood should conceive of gifts not as disguised sales. . . . A gift takes place within a personal relationship with the recipient, or else it creates one. Commodification stresses separateness both between ourselves and our things, and between ourselves and other people. . . . Seen this way, gifts diminish separateness." RADIN, CONTESTED COMMODITIES, *supra* note 91, at 93–94 (endnote omitted).

267. RICHARD M. TITMUSS, THE GIFT RELATIONSHIP: FROM HUMAN BLOOD TO SOCIAL POLICY (1971).

268. *Id.* at 249.

price tag to this activity anywhere in the system depreciates its value as a symbolic expression of faith in others. But note that this is really an empirical question, not a matter of first principles."[269]

Radin is probably the legal scholar who comes closest to taking this position. She is concerned that the commodification of those privileged objects that she calls "personal property" could lead to the commodification and alienation of people from themselves.[270] Melvin Eisenberg, relying on Radin, argues that "commodifying the gift relationship"[271] would impoverish "the world of gift [that] is driven by affective considerations like love, affection, friendship, gratitude, and comradeship."[272]

As Arrow has so accurately stated in his critique of Titmuss, the romantic fear of market is the mirror image of the right-wing fear of socialism. Both the utilitarian and the romantic fear that mixed economies are inherently unstable and can be pushed over the edge by the slightest touch. This might be called the "disease" theory of economic organization. The right-winger morbidly fears that the smallest drop of socialism in the bloodstream of the body politic might infect and kill off the entire capitalistic economic system as we know it. Similarly, the romantic fears that the slightest drop of commodification negates the possibility of relationship and intimacy.[273] Although the competing schools both insist on the vigor of their relative institutions (market and individuality on the one hand, gift and altruism on the other), they simultaneously treat them as sickly invalids unable to withstand exposure to even the mildest infection.

Neither Radin nor Titmuss, however, explains the mechanism of this economic Gresham's law by which the bad form of alienation (market) will drive out the good (gift), although Titmuss does at least assert that his comparison of the U.K (all voluntary) and U.S. (mixed) blood supply systems supports his hypothesis. I will not repeat Arrow's critique of Titmuss's empirical argument here. I argue, however, that Radin merely asserts her hypothesis

269. Arrow, *supra* note 91, at 351.

270. *See* MARGARET JANE RADIN, REINTERPRETING PROPERTY 198–99 (1993) [hereinafter, RADIN, REINTERPRETING PROPERTY] (discussing, specifically, the commodification of female sexuality); Radin, *Market-Inalienability, supra* note 29, at 1857, 1870–74, 1888, 1904, 1921–22; Margaret Jane Radin, *Reflections on Objectification,* 65 S. CAL. L. REV. 341, 345–46 (1991).

271. Eisenberg, *supra* note 20, at 848.

272. *Id.* at 847. In contrast to many other romantics, the conclusion that Eisenberg draws from this is that the simple gratuitous promise should not be legally enforceable. "That world [i.e., of gift] would be impoverished if it were to be collapsed into the world of contract." *Id.* He continues, "In short, legal enforcement of simple, affective donative promises would move the commodity rather than the relationship to the forefront, would essentially convert the gift promise into a cash equivalent, and would submerge the affective relationship that the gift was intended to totemize." *Id.* at 848.

273. *See* Arrow, *supra* note 91, at 360.

that commodification drives out intimacy without demonstrating it by logical argument or empirical evidence. She feels alienated and senses alienation in others. She has the false memory experienced by most persons in our society that she once was not alienated. She sees property as a mediator of human relation in our society. She draws the non sequitur that property, and specifically commodification, caused our alienation. She concludes that further commodification would inevitably cause more alienation and that we might be able to reduce alienation if we could only eliminate (or at least reduce) commodification.

Radin, to her credit, fights against the simplistic view that any commodification of any class of objects inevitably leads to universal commodification of human subjects. She calls what I term the "disease theory" the "domino theory."[274] She suggests that such a domino theory unconsciously echoes the utilitarian argument. In other words, she recognizes that the theory that any commodification will lead to complete commodification implicitly accepts either that all human relations tend to be market in nature or that human relationality is extremely fragile. "For the domino theory to hold, we must 'naturally' tend to commodify."[275] She claims that it is possible to have a mixed system of incomplete commodification for a wide range of objects.

Unfortunately, Radin addresses her accusers not with reasoned refutation, but with mere denial. Nevertheless, despite her denials, Radin does in fact implicitly adopt a disease or domino theory of commodification for a limited class of objects. To simplify Radin's theory of "property for personhood," human beings form relationships with certain objects and these relationships are a necessary part of the development of their personhood.[276] Indeed, she posits that certain property relations can be so intimate that one cannot distinguish between oneself and one's possessions.[277] Intimate object relations are only healthy with respect to a limited class of objects she calls "personal property."[278] They can be destructive or fetishistic with respect to most objects, which she calls "fungible property."[279] As I have written extensively elsewhere,[280] Radin's examples of personal property are those objects that literally constitute the female body and those that are traditionally iden-

274. *See* RADIN, CONTESTED COMMODITIES, *supra* note 91, at 96–101.

275. *Id.* at 97.

276. *See* RADIN, REINTERPRETING PROPERTY, *supra* note 270, at 38; Margaret Jane Radin, *Property and Personhood,* 34 STAN. L. REV. 957, 961–62 (1982) [hereinafter, Radin, *Property and Personhood*].

277. *See* RADIN, CONTESTED COMMODITIES, *supra* note 91, at 57; Radin, *Property and Personhood, supra* note 276, at 966.

278. *Id.* at 959–60.

279. *Id.* at 960.

280. *See* SCHROEDER, THE VESTAL AND THE FASCES, *supra* note 185; Schroeder, *Virgin Territory, supra* note 197 at 62–66.

tified with the female body by metaphor (such as home, car, and wedding ring).[281]

Believing that "personal" property relations are necessary for personhood, Radin argues that the law should prevent or discourage the separation of persons from their personal property through market relations.[282] *Gifts* of personal property, in contradistinction, might be permitted.[283] By imposing rules of market inalienability, the law should act paternalistically to prevent those who are misguided or weak from making inappropriate decisions. This should be done not merely in order to protect these owners, who are tempted to market-alienate their own personal property; it is also necessary to protect society at large, because the market-alienation of a type of object by one person risks the commodification of the entire class of objects involved. This commodification would prevent other persons from being able to develop appropriately intimate relations with this class of objects in the future, thereby interfering with the proper development of personality. This stunting of personality would, in turn, impede the person's ability to form relations with other persons.

For example, the commodification of women's bodies in prostitution threatens to commodify women, preventing them from having a healthy relationship to their own bodies and objectifying women so that men cannot relate to women as free and equal subjects.[284] She states, "If sex were openly commodified [i.e., through legalized prostitution] . . . its commodification would be reflected in everyone's discourse about sex, and in particular about women's sexuality."[285] Therefore, law could properly prohibit or regulate prostitution, not for the sake of the prostitute but for the sake of her more "virtuous" sisters.[286] This is precisely the kind of domino argument that Radin criticizes in others: if we allow any commodification of a category of objects, then all such objects will inevitably become completely commodified.

Eisenberg, another romantic, makes a similar disease or domino argu-

281. *See* Radin, *Property and Personhood, supra* note 276, at 959, 996–1002. Radin begins her analysis with the sale of feminine sexuality in prostitution and surrogate motherhood. She expands it to consider the sale of body parts and blood. She then analogizes this to the home and the automobile. She uses the wedding ring as an example of the other type of objects that might properly become personal property.

282. Radin, styling herself a pragmatist and a pluralist, does not adopt a radical Marxian condemnation of all commodification, just the commodification of "personal" property.

283. "A gift takes place within a personal relationship with the recipient, or else it creates one. . . . Seen in this way, gifts diminish separateness." RADIN, CONTESTED COMMODITIES, *supra* note 91, at 93–94; see also Radin, *Justice, supra* note 264, at 168–75; Radin, *Market-Inalienability, supra* note 29, at 1907–09.

284. *See* RADIN, CONTESTED COMMODITIES, *supra* note 91, at 132–34; Radin, *Market-Inalienability, supra* note 28, at 1922–23.

285. RADIN, CONTESTED COMMODITIES, *supra* note 91, at 133.

286. *See* Radin, *Market-Inalienability, supra* note 29, at 1916.

ment in his analysis of gift. He thinks that the implications of the disease theory are that gratuitous promises should generally not be legally enforceable. He argues:

> Making simple, affective donative promises enforceable would have the effect of commodifying the gift relationship. Under an enforceability regime, it could never be clear to the promisee, or even to the promisor, whether a donative promise that was made in a spirit of love, friendship, affection, or the like, was also performed for those reasons, or instead was performed to discharge a legal obligation or avoid a lawsuit.[287]

That is, to enforce a gratuitous promise would be to treat it as a contract. Contracts are performed out of legal obligation, not love. Consequently, the enforcement of a gratuitous contract threatens to infect the relationship, changing it from love to calculation and obligation.

Even if prostitution is degrading to women generally, Radin's theory of how commodification prevents intimacy breaks down when one considers examples that are only metaphorically identified with the female body. Anecdotal evidence suggests that the disease theory of commodification is inaccurate. Psychoanalysis suggests why it might nevertheless seem intuitively true.

Radin supports residential rent control and mandatory renewal rights for tenants of residential leases.[288] She recognizes that both of these are forms of market-inalienability in that they are limitations on the ability of tenants and landlords to contract concerning certain real estate.[289] She justifies this on the grounds that one's primary residence falls into her category of personal property.

Most jurisdictions in the United States do not have the two tenant protection rules that Radin proposes. Indeed, free alienability of residential real estate is a treasured ideal in this country.[290] I seriously doubt that most Americans are radical libertarians who believe that property is the most fundamental natural right. Nevertheless, it is probably true that many, if not most, Americans do believe that it is an important right, as evidenced by its protection under the Fifth Amendment. Alienability, as one of property's three basic elements, should therefore be respected, if not totally unlimited. Moreover, relative freedom of alienability not only helps to maintain property values, but also enables Americans to be mobile.

287. Eisenberg, *supra* note 20, at 848.

288. *See* Radin, *Property and Personhood, supra* note 276, at 992–96.

289. *See* Radin, Reinterpreting Property, *supra* note 270, at 57–59.

290. This is not to suggest that there are not many restraints on alienation. In addition to the types of servitudes, covenants, etc., covered in first-year law school property classes, antidiscrimination, pollution, and other rules restrain alienation.

Despite this, I am sympathetic to Radin's intuition that Americans become attached to their homes, often fanatically so. It would seem, therefore, that market-alienability of homes has not interfered with the status of homes as personal property as an empirical matter. Indeed, one could argue the opposite: Our solicitude for property and contract rights—including the right of market-alienation that, as Hegel suggested, allows the owner to have full mastery over the object—encourages this.[291]

Moreover, there are many relationships that are both affective and legally enforceable. For example, the obligation of a parent to support her child is legally enforceable in both theory and practice.[292] Despite this, the vast majority of parents continue to support their children out of love, and our society continues to view the family relationship as primarily affective in nature. "Mother love" remains our ideal of the most pure and unselfish form of human relationship.

Radin implicitly recognizes that commodification does not interfere with the ability of subjects to form object relations. For example, she tries to justify the extension of Fourth Amendment restrictions on searches and seizures of individually owned automobiles on the grounds that they are "personal property."[293] Indeed, Americans are notoriously sentimental about their cars. Nevertheless, our society does not place any meaningful limitation on the right of individuals to alienate their cars, whether by sale, hypothecation, or whatever. Nor does Radin suggest that such limitation would be either appropriate or desirable.

Probably the most striking failed example of Radin's commodification hypothesis can be seen in one of her favorite, and most romantic, examples of personal property—the wedding ring.[294] She states that if a wedding ring is stolen, insurance can cover the monetary value, but probably no amount of money could recompense the bride for her emotional loss.[295] If one accepts this morbidly sentimental proposition (which I don't), it would seem to be evidence against, not for, her theory.

What object is more commodified than gold? It has traditionally been one of the most common forms of money. And yet, this has not prevented the bride from becoming sentimentally attached to her wedding ring. Much

291. This is not to say that we should not be concerned with tenants or even that we should not on other grounds adopt paternalistic laws limiting freedom of contract in leases.

292. Of course, extreme utilitarians such as Posner suggest that even mother love is "selfish." *See* RICHARD A. POSNER, SEX AND REASON 189, 201, 259 (1992).

293. *See* RADIN, REINTERPRETING PROPERTY, *supra* note 270, at 59–63.

294. *See* Radin, *Property and Personhood, supra* note 276, at 959–61.

295. *See id.* at 959. The example of the wedding ring is a striking example of Radin's implicit identification of personal property with female sexuality and how her argument for market-inalienability echoes the traditional masculine concern for feminine virginity—mandatory chastity for women.

more importantly, it has not led to the commodification of spouses, nor to the breakdown of marital love.

As Radin herself recognizes, it is not the object itself that causes the feeling of attachment in the owner.[296] It is the owner and other persons who invest the object with signification. In the case of the wedding ring, the bride does not care for the gold per se (in the sense that she does not value the gold in the wedding ring any more than she values her other gold jewelry or other items of wealth and beauty); she values the ring because it is a visible symbol of her love for her husband and her status as a married woman. The fact that gold, or any class of objects, is commodified does not interfere with our ability to instill a specific object with symbolism.

I go even further. It is precisely the commodification of objects—the stripping away of extrinsic meaning from objects generally—that enables us to instill our idiosyncratic symbolism onto specific objects without becoming slaves to the objects. That is, by objectifying *things,* commodification deobjectifies *persons,* enabling them to achieve subjectivity.

This is the distinction between objects in markets and in gift exchange. In archaic gift exchange, specific objects gain value through exchange. Their value derives from their genealogy—how many times they have been exchanged and by whom. The objects themselves thereby obtain specific identities, even souls. They are treated as though they were subjects, not objects. The exchange partners gain distinction by becoming identified with the most valuable objects. This distinction is one of status—superiority over other trading partners—not individuality. The trading partner's status is dependent on his continued possession of the unique object, not his own intrinsic personal characteristics. He is not free, but dependent on the object. He is an object addict. Indeed, not only are the objects given names; sometimes the owner changes his own name to that of the object. As Weiner argues, the owner vainly tries to make the gift object inalienable when the only thing that made the useless object valuable in the first place was the fact that it was the object of ritual exchange.

This epitomizes Radin's concept of personal property: such an identification of owner with object that the owner's identity cannot be separated from the object. Rather than achieving subjectivity, the owner becomes objectified. The owner has an intimate relationship with his object, but his relationship with other persons is one of domination and subordination. This is hardly the ideal of relationality and freedom from alienation that Radin imagines. And yet, tellingly, the objects that Radin identifies as "personal property" are precisely those that are the primary status symbols in our

296. *See* Radin, *Market-Inalienability, supra* note 29, 1904, 1915–21; Radin, *Property and Personhood, supra* note 276, at 959–62, 1005.

society: the house, the car, and jewelry.[297] Indeed, the hideously accurate slang term "trophy wife" reveals the nature of Radin's preeminent ideal of "personal property." The objectified nubile female body is the ultimate status symbol.

Radin's terminology gives her away: she says that people become "bound up" with personal property.[298] Similarly, Radin's discussion of the relationship of gift immediately degenerates into a discussion of the relationship of the parties to the object, rather than the relationship between the subjects. The Hegelian subject, by contrast, seeks to be free of objects, so that she can embrace other subjects.[299] She desires objects only derivatively, as a means of achieving her true love—the desire of the Other.

Eisenberg is therefore correct in saying that in gift the object takes on the role of a totem, and that commodification would interfere with the totemic nature of the object.[300] He believes that such totemism is positive because the "gift reflects or manifests the relationship with the donee."[301] A Hegelian would challenge this normative judgment precisely because it represses the derivative aspect of the desire for the object. As Radin says, the parties are bound—indeed, spellbound—by the object rather than by the relationship with each other. The object is therefore not so much a totem as a fetish, in both the colloquial and the psychoanalytical sense of that term.

In psychoanalysis, a pervert, as generally understood, is a person who seeks to be not a subject, but the object of the *jouissance* of the Other.[302] The specific perversion of fetishism in effect reverses the "normal" subject-object

297. *See* RADIN, REINTERPRETING PROPERTY, *supra* note 270, at 59–63; Radin, *Property and Personhood, supra* note 276, at 959.

298. This is the essence of my critique of Radin, which I develop extensively in SCHROEDER, THE VESTAL AND THE FASCES, *supra* note 185, and Schroeder, *Virgin Territory, supra* note 197. From a Lacanian perspective, "enjoyment" and identification are the feminine moments of property. As I have argued, Radin's image of personal property is figured by the female body. Consequently, Radin's obsession with the identification with, and the enjoyment and protection of, personal property can be identified with the masculine sex's morbid preoccupation with feminine chastity.

299. Romantics often confuse this relationship. For example, Eisenberg states that "in bargains, commodities are an end in themselves; in gifts, commodities are a means to an end. In bargains, the nexus is the commodity; in gifts of objects, the nexus is the relationship or the embedded moral values." Eisenberg, *supra* note 20, at 844. However, Eisenberg's discussion implicitly reveals how the parties to the gift become entrapped by the object, in what he calls the "totemic aspect of gifted objects." *Id.*

300. *See id.* at 844.

301. *Id.*

302. The pervert "identifies himself with the imaginary object of this desire." LACAN, ÉCRITS, *supra* note 183, at 198. *See also* SLAVOJ ŽIŽEK, THE PLAGUE OF FANTASIES 33 (1997) [hereinafter, ŽIŽEK, PLAGUE OF FANTASIES]; SLAVOJ ŽIŽEK, TARRYING WITH THE NEGATIVE: KANT, HEGEL, AND THE CRITIQUE OF IDEOLOGY 194 (1994); ŽIŽEK, FOR THEY KNOW NOT WHAT THEY DO, *supra* note 206, at 234, 271.

distinction: the person takes the position of object and treats the fetish-object as a subject.[303] This dynamic may be seen in *kula*. The relationship of subject to object (as opposed to subject to subject) is so intense that not only do the objects acquire names, but the owners' social and political rank is determined by their relationship with prestigious objects.[304] I am not, of course, saying that Radin is herself a pervert, but merely that Radin's attempt to submerge her personhood in her privileged objects of personal property betrays a fetishistic tendency.

Indeed, the real harm that the romantic should fear is not commodification, but what I would call "consumerism." Consumerism does not treat objects as fungible. Rather, the consumer feels she desperately needs specified individual objects identified by changing fashion.

In Lacanian terms, the consumer good becomes an *objet petit a*—an imaginary object retroactively erected as a substitute for the consumer's true desire so that it can serve as the object cause of desire.[305] What the subject truly desires is the desire of the Other in the symbolic and the impossible, immediate relationality of the real. Because such perfect relationality is unattainable, the subject imagines that it is some other, attainable object that is the cause of his desire. He tries to tell himself that his desire will be fulfilled if he can just obtain the *objet petit a*. This strategy is always a failure. As soon as the subject obtains any specific object, he realizes that he still desires. He must therefore locate yet another object to serve this role. Consequently, the consumer becomes stuck in an increasingly frustrating spiral of acquisition.

The Hegelian person seeks subjectivity through recognition by other subjects. The Radinian person, however, becomes objectified through her identification with objects.

Commodification in market relations allows the subject to free herself from any preexisting relation with objects. She can acquire objects and invest them with personal signification or not, as she sees fit. Subjects are thereby freed to use objects as the means to establish particularized intersubjective relations with specific other subjects that go beyond the sterility of status relations. Hegelian philosophy explains why this is so. I show in the next section that Lacanian psychoanalysis suggests why we are drawn to the romantic fear of commodification.

303. That is, to the fetishist, unlike the phallic object of desire that serves as the symbolization of subjectivity precisely because it has no positive content, the fetish is given actual, positive status "fill[ing] in the lack of the (maternal) phallus." ŽIŽEK, FOR THEY KNOW NOT WHAT THEY DO, *supra* note 206, at 249. As such, fetishism is an attempt to disavow castration. In commodity fetishism, relations between things take the place of relations between people. ŽIŽEK, PLAGUE OF FANTASIES, *supra* note 302, at 102.

304. *See* WEINER, *supra* note 114, at 135–37.

305. The *objet petit a* is one of the most complex and important concepts in Lacanian theory. I discuss the *objet petit a* in somewhat greater detail in Chapters 2 and 4.

Nevertheless, as I discuss in Chapter 4, even if the romantic analysis of universal commodification were correct, she would still have no reason to fear it. The universal commodification desired by the utilitarianism is impossible to achieve, not merely empirically, but logically as well.

Separation and Interrelation

The romantic fears that market relations will result in the repression of difference, leading to the commodification and alienation of market participants. Commodified persons are indistinguishable. They are, therefore, unrecognizable and incapable of having relationships because relationship requires the mutual recognition by two distinct persons. But this is an incomplete, one-sided analysis of the dialectic, based on the misconception that persons start out interrelated. The romantic must, then, explain the fact of alienation and separation in our market economy. They assume that separation must be caused by the market.

By contrast, Hegel showed that, if one starts from the philosophical understanding of the atomistic, undifferentiated, separated person of liberalism, then market relations are the means by which these initially separate persons come together. In other words, the market is the point of junction between the individual understood as an atomistic, abstract person and as an interrelational, concrete subject. The romantic assumes that this is because the market is a wall erected between persons, alienating each from the others. Hegel turns this analysis on its head and argues that the market is instead a bridge that allows separate persons to come together, have relations, and become subjects.

Or, more accurately, it is both. Property is a wall in the sense that it enables us to become separate, individuated, and thereby recognizable. This separation creates the potential for love. Simultaneously, property is a bridge that allows us to cross over and recognize each other. This recognition is the condition for the actualization of love.

Property can be both wall and bridge because the Hegelian logic is holistic and circular.[306] Hegel believed that the abstract person in the state of nature was only one true moment of humanity. The subject engaged in the relationship of contract, the empirical person enmeshed in the ties of family, and the individual integrated as a citizen in the modern liberal state are equally true moments of human nature. Moreover, not one of these moments is complete in and of itself, but rather each logically requires and generates the others in the complete system of a modern society. One could,

306. Hegel explains the circular aspect of his method in the first chapter of his greater logic. *See* HEGEL, THE GREATER LOGIC, *supra* note 205, at 71.

theoretically, start at any point of the dialectic and generate every other point.

Nevertheless, there are substantial advantages to be gained by starting an analysis with the simplest, most abstract moment in a concept and then working up to more and more complex ones. The simplest understanding of personality is the abstract, atomistic person as free will that is posited by liberalism. In the *Philosophy of Right,* Hegel showed that, contrary to what liberalism argues, the concept of the abstract person necessarily implies the development of the more complex, interrelational subject, family member, and citizen. Theoretically, however, he could have started with the interrelational subject in order to show how it necessarily includes the abstract, atomistic person as a more primitive element.

This is because interrelation requires recognition. In order for me to recognize you as a unique human being to whom I can interrelate, I must first recognize you as a unique person separate and alienated from me.[307] I must respect your otherness. Property is the mediator—the third term—that stands at the crossroads between these two aspects of personality. This is why, when viewed from the starting place of interrelationality, property appears as a separating wall, but when examined from the other side of individuality, it is revealed as a bridge.

To put this yet another way, the alchemy of contract is a manifestation of the fundamental Hegelian doctrine of the identity of identity and difference.[308] At the moment of contract, on the one hand, the parties recognize themselves as essentially identical in the sense that they share a common will. In contract, the two parties mutually recognize themselves as "we who agree." On the other hand, the parties simultaneously recognize each other as essentially different. The contract only comes about because each party is supplying the other with something the other desires but lacks. To restate this more concretely, if I enter into a contract to buy a widget, I understand myself as "she who has cash but lacks and desires a widget" in relation to my counterparty, understood as "he who has a widget but lacks and desires cash." In other words, in contract I define my counterparty not only as "he who is the same as me," but also as "he who is different from me—my opposite or negation." He is my mirror image, by which I define myself in this transaction. As described by Rosenfeld, contract is the particularization of the abstract and the abstraction of the particular.[309]

Consequently, if property and contract create equality and therefore

307. *See* SCHROEDER, THE VESTAL AND THE FASCES, *supra* note 185, at 34, 290, 328–29; Schroeder, *Virgin Territory, supra* note 197, at 133–34, 170.

308. *See* HEGEL, THE GREATER LOGIC, *supra* note 205, at 419.

309. *See* Michel Rosenfeld, *Contract and Justice: The Relation Between Classical Contract Law and Social Contract Theory,* 70 IOWA L. REV. 769, 807–08, 814–16, 824, 835–36, 840–41 (1985).

equivalence between people, they simultaneously create the difference of individuality. Contract is the first step in the development of the individual who can serve as a citizen of a modern constitutional state. This is why political liberalism as a theory, and constitutionalism as an institution, could not come about until a market economy began to replace the premodern feudal economy in the eighteenth century. Or, more accurately, the market economy, the liberal state, and the free individual are mutually constituting—giving birth to each other. One might also argue that it is only now, when the legal and economic equality of women is first being recognized, that the possibility of true love relations and a truly just state have a chance of finally becoming actualized.

Commodification

We can now understand why the utilitarian-romantic account of commodification is flawed. Both the romantic and the utilitarian assume that commodification is the repression of difference—the treatment of everything as the same. This is a grave mistake. Commodification is, like contract, another example of the identity of identity and difference.

By agreeing to an exchange, the parties recognize the objects exchanged as equivalent in the sense of having the same exchange value. But exchange occurs only because the parties recognize an essential difference between the objects, to which they are not indifferent. In other words, when I enter into the widget contract, I am simultaneously recognizing that my money and your widget are essentially equivalent and demonstrating that my money is fundamentally different from widgets in that I prefer the latter over the former. The establishment of identity in commodification and contract is not, therefore, the suppression of difference, but rather the actualization of difference.

Both the utilitarian and the romantic go astray because they forget that the economic concept of indifference is not an empirical description of any conceivable actual market. Rather, it is a hypothetical result of the ideal of the perfect market. Classical price theory posits the truism that exchange will occur among market participants until they are indifferent between the market basket of objects that each one of them owns and all available objects potentially on the market at the given price ratio.[310] As Ronald Coase has correctly stated, and as I discuss in Chapter 2, if the hypothetical perfect market were ever achieved, all actual market exchange would immediately stop.[311] Actual markets exist because market participants are not indifferent

310. *See* SAMUELSON & NORDHAUS, *supra* note 265, at 88.
311. *See* R. N. COASE, THE FIRM, THE MARKET, AND THE LAW 7–8 (1988).

between the objects they have and the objects offered in the market. By definition, exchange occurs only because each participant believes that she would rather have the latter than the former. Consequently, as I explain in Chapter 4, commodification can never be perfect and universal—commensuration always necessarily implies a moment of noncommensurability.

The Necessary Imperfection of Perfection

As I explore in the next chapter, the perfect market is the ideal or end of actual markets. This means that the actual market would end if it reached perfection. For actual markets to function they must be imperfect.[312] This reflects the Hegelian-Lacanian insight that the ideal of perfection is only generated by imperfection.

To state that contract is driven by an erotic desire is to say that the mutuality of contract is always an aspiration. Contract, like all sexual relations, is both theoretically and empirically always a partially failed encounter.[313] The moment of union in even the most perfect contract or ecstatic sexual joining is impossible, and therefore miraculous.

Nevertheless, the existence of the market regime not only enables us to create the concept of the free, interrelational individual, it allows us occasionally to actualize it and exercise our freedom. We experience ecstasy, albeit fleetingly. The fact that our freedom is not perfect, that exploitation too often occurs, that alienation is a universal experience of modern man, does not mean that the market regime does not also establish the conditions under which we occasionally glimpse and exercise freedom, attain equality, and experience love. For the dialectic of right to function, it necessarily always fails. Indeed, its success requires its partial failure. We interrelate because we desire to end our separation, but in order for us to interrelate we must continue to recognize ourselves as separate. If we did not feel restrained, we would not fight for and actualize our freedom. If we did not understand domination, we would not insist on our equality or, more importantly, insist on the equality of others. If we were not alienated, we would not desire and would have no ability to love.

Indeed, Hegelian-Lacanian philosophy argues that perfection necessarily requires imperfection as its ground. This is even true for the Absolute—*Geist* or God itself.[314] We are God's imperfection—His subjectivity. It is precisely

312. *See generally* David Gray Carlson, *On the Margins of Microeconomics,* 14 CARDOZO L. REV. 1867 (1993).

313. *See* ŽIŽEK, METASTASIS, *supra* note 200, at 188–89.

314. As Žižek explains: "This distinction between God's Existence and its Ground, between the Absolute insofar as it fully exists, insofar as it is posited as such, illuminated by the Light of Reason, and the Absolute qua obscure longing (Sehnsucht) that strives for something outside

this imperfection that allows us a moment of radical freedom in an otherwise determinate universe.

Castration and the Real

Why does the romantic insist that the true essence of human nature is relationship, despite the persistence of alienation as an empirical matter and the necessity for mediation and imperfection as a theoretical one? Why does the romantic see alienation as an external condition imposed upon us? To repeat my metaphor, why does he see contract as the wall that separates us but fail to see that it is simultaneously the bridge that brings us together?

The one-sided romantic position can be explained by Lacanian psychoanalysis. The romantic's account of alienation reflects the false autobiography that each "normal" Lacanian subject writes to explain her feeling of dislocation in society.

The Hegelian dialectic of legal subjectivity parallels and reflects the Lacanian dialectic of sexual subjectivity. In both, subjectivity can only be achieved by mutual recognition in a regime of possession, enjoyment, and exchange of an object of desire. The Hegelian object is property. The Lacanian object is the fictional concept known as "the phallus."

Hegelian theory maintains that abstract right simultaneously creates both separateness and relation—contract actualizes the identity of identity and difference. One way to explain this is that, in contract, what is most ourselves—our subjectivity, our freedom, our rationality—can only be actualized through that which is outside of ourselves: through objects, other subjects, and the law. Consequently, the relation of contract requires us to externalize and alienate part of our essential selves. The exact same dynamic happens in Lacan's analysis.

The Lacanian subject can only be actualized through recognition in language and sexuality.[315] Consequently, Lacan places language and sexuality in the same order of the consciousness as law—the symbolic.[316] Whether or not human beings have an inherent capacity for language (as the Chomskyites

---

itself without a clear notion of what it strives for, means that God is not fully 'himself'—that there is something in God that isn't God." ŽIŽEK, ABYSS OF FREEDOM, *supra* note 228, at 5–6. In this passage, Žižek, a Lacanian, is specifically describing the theory of Hegel's contemporary, F. W. J. Von Schelling. But in the context of the essay, he is describing how Schelling's theory fits into the Hegelian-Lacanian system.

315. *See* SCHROEDER, THE VESTAL AND THE FASCES, *supra* note 185, at 52–54.

316. *See, e.g.*, Jacques Lacan, *Introduction to the Names-of-the-Father Seminar*, in JACQUES LACAN, TELEVISION: A CHALLENGE TO THE PSYCHOANALYTIC ESTABLISHMENT 81, 88–89 (Joan Copjec ed. & Denis Hollier et al. trans., W.W. Norton & Co. 1990) (1974).

insist),[317] any specific language must be learned. What is most ourselves, therefore (our subjectivity and our sexuality), can only be actualized through that which is outside of ourselves—through the phallus, other subjects, and language. Consequently, the relation of sexuality requires us to externalize and alienate part of our essential selves.

It is this universal feeling of essential alienation that Lacan calls "castration."[318] Sexuality is our retroactive hypothetical account of how castration came to be and our response to castration. As expressed by Jane Gallop, in her description of the "feminine" reaction to castration (called "penis envy" by Freud, but more accurately renamed "nostalgia" by Lacan):

> There is no moment of loss, but loss is inferred on the basis of a retrospective view that sees the past as fuller than the present. Something must have been lost. . . . Somehow . . . the mother as mother is lost forever. . . . The mother as womb, homeland, source, and grounding for the subject is irretrievably past. The subject is hence in a foreign land, alienated.[319]

Lacan adopts the conventional view that the newborn has little conscious awareness of himself, but only develops awareness of his literal physical separation from other human beings (starting with Mother) over time.[320] As the infant acquires language, he further experiences alienation. Because his awareness of separation and feelings of alienation are gained over time, the infant feels as though there must have been a time when he was not separated or alienated from that which would make him whole. The infant then concludes that he must have once been whole—he must once have had a perfect, immediate relationship with his mother. Because he cannot remember any moment when he lost it, he hypothesizes that this loss was imposed on him from the outside. Lacan uses the masculine metaphor of mutilation and says the infant feels "castrated." In other words, he feels that he is not whole because a piece of him—and the most valuable piece at that, the one that

317. Many Lacanians believe that their theory is necessarily antagonistic to that of natural language scientists. *See, e.g.*, ELLIE RAGLAND, ESSAYS ON THE PLEASURES OF DEATH: FROM FREUD TO LACAN 193 (1995). I have challenged this assumption elsewhere. *See* SCHROEDER, THE VESTAL AND THE FASCES, *supra* note 185, at 59–60.

318. "That is to say: what, precisely, is symbolic castration? It is the . . . sense of the loss of something which the subject never possessed in the first place." ŽIŽEK, PLAGUE OF FANTASY, *supra* note 302, at 15; *see also* SCHROEDER, THE VESTAL AND THE FASCES, *supra* note 185, at 87–88.

319. JANE GALLOP, READING LACAN 148 (1985).

320. The term "Mother" refers to a role in society. The term reflects the fact that in our society this role is usually filled empirically by the infant's actual mother. When this role is played by another, our society considers that person to be a mother-substitute. It is, however, at least theoretically possible that in another hypothetical society this role would not be associated with the biologically female person. Sexuality—indeed subjectivity—would be radically different in such a subjunctive universe.

would enable him to join with his mother—has been taken away. Accordingly, this "lost" object of desire is called the "phallus." This reflects the fact that the "subjective" position of having the phallus is identified with the masculine position. We conflate this lost object of desire with that which biologically male persons have—the male organ. I discuss the concept of castration and how it relates to the formation of sexuality in subsequent chapters.

Romanticism reflects the Lacanian autobiography. We see alienation and mediated relationship. We desire connection and immediate relationship. We therefore hypothesize that the reason we desire connection and immediate relationship is because we once experienced it (or had the inherent capacity for it). Because we once had this capacity, we hypothesize that it must have been taken away from us. Someone or something is keeping us from immediate relationship. That which keeps us from immediacy is, of course, mediation. The mediator of relationship—that which enables us to be separated—is the symbolic order. The romantic, therefore, concludes that it is the symbolic order—law in the sense of abstract right and the market—that is the cause of our separation.[321] We have been castrated and violated by the market, which denies our claim to subjectivity and threatens to turn us into objects through commodification.

The Lacanian autobiography is, of course, fictional. We were never one with the universe—even in the womb we were separated from our mother by the placenta. The infant did not even become a human subject capable of imagining and desiring such perfection until he was initiated into the symbolic—law, language, and sexuality. It is precisely the feeling of alienation caused by the mediated relationship of language and law that enables us retroactively to imagine and desire the ideal of perfect, immediate relationality. The ability to desire is not, therefore, created by the loss of immediate relationship. Rather, it is the existence of mediation that enables us to imagine what immediate relationship might be, and therefore to desire it. In other words, we imagine that immediate relationship is something we once had—the always-already-lost—when, in fact, it is an ideal or aspiration—the not-yet-found.

321. An interesting variation on the romantic position has been proposed by Robin West. *See* Robin West, *Jurisprudence and Gender*, 55 U. CHI. L. REV. 1 (1988). She posits an essential empirical difference between men and women that, in my analysis, reflects not the two Lacanian sexuated positions, but two moments in the Hegelian dialectic of personality.

In her view, men are literally the atomistic individuals posited by liberalism generally and utilitarianism specifically. Having started as separate, they can only seek community and relationship. Women, however, are like the fictional infant of Lacanian theory. We start connected and must seek separation and individuation through law. I criticize West's theory of "different voice" feminism in SCHROEDER, THE VESTAL AND THE FASCES, *supra* note 185, at 70–71, 92–94; Jeanne L. Schroeder, *Abduction from the Seraglio: Feminist Methodologies and the Logic of Imagination*, 70 TEX. L. REV. 109, 120–47 (1991); Schroeder, *Feminism Historicized, supra* note 131.

The ideal of immediacy is in the order of consciousness that Lacan calls the "real." It is a common misconception that Lacan thought that the real was that which was left behind, or lost, when we entered the symbolic order (i.e., when we learned to speak, took on sexual identity, and became the subject of legal relations).[322] This hypothesis only replicates the subject's autobiography, which Lacan insists is fictional. Rather, Lacan insists that the three orders of the symbolic, imaginary, and the real are created simultaneously. The real is our sense that there is something that cannot be captured in words or images—such as God, death, the physical world, and perfect, immediate relationships—which we only retroactively believe must exist because we experience the limits of language and imagery.

The romantic vision of gift and contract is fictional. It is not contract that prevents us from achieving more complete and satisfying relationships. It is precisely the imperfection of contract that enables us to want more complete and satisfying relationships. Moreover, insofar as contract creates a minimal degree of recognizability and equality between subjects, it creates the minimum conditions for the achievement of more satisfying relationships, such as the loving relationship sometimes achieved in the modern companionable family, characterized by particular altruism, and the loyal relationship of citizenship sometimes achieved in the modern constitutional state, characterized by universal altruism. Both of these institutions are based on equality—sexual equality in the former, political equality in the latter. If they are far from perfect in practice, it is because they have yet fully to actualize the equality that is their essence. The imperfect mutuality and equality of contract is an imperfect step in this process. Gift, in contrast, is not merely the failure to achieve perfect mutuality and equality in practice, it is one-sided and hierarchical by its very nature. Consequently, insofar as the modern rule of law in the constitutional state is based on an ideal of equality and autonomy, there is an inherent logic in the law's privileging of contractual relations and its suspicion of gift.

EPILOGUE: PANDORA'S GIFT

Hesiod insists that hope is a divine gift. And yet, he admits that Pandora never saw hope. Hesiod suggests that this was because she resealed the amphora so quickly that she trapped hope inside. Hegel and Lacan reveal the true meaning of this myth.

Hope was never among the gifts that the gods placed in the amphora. Rather, hope was Pandora's gift to herself—bought and paid for with blind-

322. For a succinct explanation of why this common misinterpretation is incorrect, *see* Žižek, The Indivisible Remainder, *supra* note 202, at 101–02, 110.

ing tears. It was only her release of the ills that made hope necessary that caused her retroactively to imagine that she had captured the hope she now needed. It is the hope that hope exists that calls hope into being. Hope, like love, is alchemy—it makes something out of nothing. Before she opened the amphora, Pandora was merely an object, a living doll manufactured by the gods as a passive instrument of destruction. By creating hope, she recreated herself as an active subject.

This is why the myth insists that Pandora is the mother of us all. Feminine negativity is the center of both Hegelian philosophy and Lacanian psychoanalysis. Negativity is the womb of subjectivity. It is the empty, and therefore potentially fertile, space in the deterministic universe that makes freedom possible and enables us to give birth to ourselves.

The Bible warns us that "in sorrow [the Woman] shalt bring forth."[323] But, as Lacan consoles us, without tears the eye is blind.[324] Hope is created by suffering, desire by castration, love by loneliness, subjectivity by objectivity, law by injustice, the ideal of perfection by the fact of imperfection—and God by woman.

323. *Genesis* 3:16 (King James).

324. *See* LACAN, SEMINAR XX, *supra* note 208, at 109.

Chapter 2

Orpheus's Desire

The End of the Market[1]

PROLOGUE: ORPHEUS AND EURYDICE, EROS AND THANATOS

Orpheus, the most creative of all living beings, sang so beautifully that he charmed wild beasts; trees and rocks moved on their own in order to follow him.[2] He exceeded his mother, Calliope, the muse of music, as well as divine Apollo himself. Mortality was the source of Orpheus's art: he sang in a vain attempt to fill the void left by the death of his beloved Eurydice. The gods, being immortal, perfect, and complete, have no desire, and therefore no ability to create anything truly new.[3]

Orpheus desired Eurydice because he never had her: he was bridegroom and widower, but never husband. Eurydice was bitten by a snake and died at their wedding. Orpheus poured his grief into song. Although Orpheus had lost Eurydice once through death, he could not accept that she was forever lost. He persisted in the impossible fantasy that he might again embrace her. And so Orpheus, still alive, traveled to the land of the dead.

His song protected him from the horrors of hell. Charon the ferryman waived his fee. Cerberus the hellhound crouched at his feet. The demons stopped tormenting the damned so that they could listen. Pale Hecate, mistress of sorcery, was herself enchanted. The implacable Furies, witnesses to

1. An earlier version of this chapter was published as Jeanne L. Schroeder, *The End of the Market: A Psychoanalysis of Law and Economics,* 112 HARV. L. REV. 483 (1998).

2. There are many versions of the Orpheus myth. This is my idiosyncratic synthesis from Ovid's METAMORPHOSIS and a variety of other sources.

3. As Kant stated, if we were perfect like the gods and could know the thing-in-itself, we would lose our freedom and be as lifeless puppets. IMMANUEL KANT, THE CRITIQUE OF PRACTICAL REASON 95–96 (T. K. Abbott trans., 1996).

all sin from time immemorial, wept as Orpheus described a virginal innocence they had never known.

Orpheus arrived at the throne of Persephone, paradoxically both queen and prisoner of death. Goddess that she was, Persephone could not escape the curse that kept her locked in the icy embrace of Hades for two-thirds of the year. Orpheus's song gave her the power to grant him a gift that she could not grant herself—release from death.

Persephone promised Orpheus that his fantasy would come true. He would have Eurydice, but not yet. Eurydice was to follow Orpheus when he left the land of the dead. But he was forbidden to turn back and look at her until he reached the land of the living.

As Orpheus began his long climb out of the pit of Tartarus, his desire was whetted by anxiety. He couldn't quite tell whether or not he heard the muffled sound of her footsteps following him. Could that warm breeze on the back of his neck be her breath, or was it just the receding fires of hell? He finally gave way to his desire and whirled around to embrace his beloved. Nothing. Eurydice was twice lost. But was she always already gone, or had she not yet come? Did Persephone lie or tell the truth? Orpheus could only speculate that Eurydice might have been there from what could be traces of her loss—the mark on the trail that could be her footprint; the fading sound that might be the echo of her farewell.

The myth of Orpheus and Eurydice reflects the Lacanian concept of Eros. Eros is the masculine form of desire[4]—an attempt to fill the emptiness that is the center of human experience by fantasizing a perfect, immediate sexual relationship. This fantasy or "imaginary" dream of "femininity" is erected to take the place of the "real" concept of "the feminine." Sustaining the fantasy allows us to act and create. But the moment we confront the reality that lies beneath the fantasy of femininity, we find nothing there. This leaves us more bereft than before and more in need of fantasy. If we give in to the masculine desire of Eros and look back at the lost feminine, we lose her. We can only keep her by not having her. This is because the feminine is, in fact, the radical negativity of "the real," which is the heart and soul of human freedom and subjectivity.[5] Any attempt to give the feminine positive content is a mas-

4. Jeanne L. Schroeder, The Vestal and the Fasces: Hegel, Lacan, Property and the Feminine (1998) [hereinafter, Schroeder, The Vestal and the Fasces].

5. In the words of Slavoj Žižek: "In short, by playing upon the somewhat worn-out Hegelian formula, we can say that the 'enigma of woman' ultimately conceals the fact that there is nothing to conceal. . . . [The] Hegelian reflexive reversal [recognizes] *in this 'nothing' the very negativity that defines the notion of the subject.* . . . [T]his nothingness behind the mask is the very absolute negativity on account of which the woman is the subject *par excellence,* not a limited object opposed to the force of subjectivity!" Slavoj Žižek, The Metastases of Enjoyment: Six Essays on Woman and Causality 143 (1994) (footnotes omitted).

culine fantasy[6]—a vain attempt to have and to hold that which, by definition, can be neither captured nor tamed.

Eros always threatens to turn into its feminine twin, Thanatos, the death wish. Thanatos is the realization that Eros is always unsuccessful and the only way to achieve wholeness is by regressing to the time before loss. If Eros is the fantasy that one can capture the feminine, Thanatos is the desire to merge back into, and thereby become, the feminine. But the feminine is "Eurydice twice lost."[7] She is our sense that there is something which we have always-already-lost and have not-yet-found. She is yesterday and tomorrow, but never today. As Lacan said, Woman—that is, the feminine per se—does not exist.[8] She was and shall be, but never is.[9] To merge with her now is to achieve oblivion.

And so Orpheus's desire evolved from Eros to Thanatos. He continued to mourn his fantasy image of Eurydice and to dream of joining with the feminine until his desire was fulfilled, but not in a way he expected. He poured his grief into songs in memories of his lost love, and avoided all actual female contact. One day, however, when wandering in the countryside, he encountered a band of Maenads—female worshipers of Dionysus, god of ecstasy, who expressed their devotion in orgiastic, and often violent, revels. Their frenzy reflects feminine *jouissance,* or enjoyment: the momentary achievement of the impossible fulfillment of Thanatos—union with the feminine in the sense of perfect wholeness, the breakdown of the subject-object distinction, the achievement of the Lacanian "real." The Maenads demanded that Orpheus join in their worship. When he hesitated, they tore Orpheus limb from limb in their divine *jouissance.* As Lacan predicted, the masculine claim to personality could not survive an encounter with the feminine. To give way to one's desire is to lose everything.

6. *Id.* at 151.

7. JACQUES LACAN, THE FOUR FUNDAMENTAL CONCEPTS OF PSYCHO-ANALYSIS 25 (J. Miller ed. & A. Sheridan trans., 1981) [hereinafter LACAN, THE FOUR FUNDAMENTAL CONCEPTS]. Lacan uses this beautiful metaphor to describe the unconscious specifically, but it can be generalized to everything in the real, including the feminine.

8. Lacan is speaking not about female human beings, but about the radical negativity of "the feminine." JACQUES LACAN, THE SEMINAR OF JACQUES LACAN. BOOK XX: ENCORE, ON FEMININE SEXUALITY, THE LIMITS OF LOVE AND KNOWLEDGE, 1972–1973 72–73 (Jacques-Alain Miller ed. & Bruce Fink trans., 1998) [hereinafter, LACAN, SEMINAR XX]. (This has also been translated as The Woman does not exist. Jacques Lacan, *God and the Jouissance* of The Woman in JACQUES LACAN AND THE ÉCOLE FREUDIENNE, FEMININE SEXUALITY 137, 144 (Juliet Mitchell & Jacqueline Rose eds. & Jacqueline Rose trans., 1985) [hereinafter, FEMININE SEXUALITY].)

9. I explore this concept of the feminine as the past and the future in Jeanne L. Schroeder, *Never Jam To-day: On the Impossibility of Takings Jurisprudence,* 84 GEORGETOWN L. J. 1531 (1996) [hereinafter, Schroeder, *Never Jam To-day*]; *See also* SCHROEDER, THE VESTAL AND THE FASCES, *supra* note 4.

THE DESIRE OF ECONOMICS

If the world then were as it ought to be, the actions of Will would be at an end. The Will itself therefore requires that its End should not be realized.

G. W. F HEGEL[10]

In this chapter I explore the repressed desire underlying the economic ideal of the perfect market. This desire is Thanatos, the death wish.

The perfect market is the end of all actual markets—it is their ideal form. In normative economics, actual markets are the means of achieving the end or ideal of the perfect market. But this means that to achieve a perfect market would result in the end or cessation of all actual market transactions. This is not a pun, but the necessary implication of the single meaning of the word "end." One acts until one achieves one's goal, upon which action stops. We desire to achieve our ends even as we fear to end. Upon the achievement of perfection there can be no improvement, so one is frozen in crystalline ideality.

As I have already suggested, when viewed from the perspective of Hegelian political philosophy and Lacanian psychoanalysis, law, property, and the market economy are revealed to be essentially erotic[11]—indeed, hysterically so, in the technical sense of that term.[12] As is well known, some legal economists, most notably, Richard Posner, try to analyze sexuality in terms of the market.[13] A Hegelian-Lacanian analysis shows why this seems plausible: markets and sexuality share an essential eroticism. But they are wrong in thinking that the former can be reduced to the latter. It is not that sexuality is an economic relation. Rather, markets and sexuality are both subsets of a more general category of eroticism.

Eroticism is *not* the physical mating urge. Rather, it is the desire for recognition by others and for wholeness. As such, desire can only be played out in legal, linguistic, and other "symbolic" relations. From a Hegelian perspective, the symbolic relations that arise when desire is combined with the mating urge (such as in marriage) are more complex and less "primitive" than that of markets (abstract right).

To understand my thesis, we need to consider in more detail the concepts

10. G. W. F. HEGEL, HEGEL'S LOGIC 291 (William Wallace trans., 1975) [hereinafter, HEGEL, THE LESSER LOGIC].

11. I develop the complex connection between Lacanian sexuality and Hegelian property jurisprudence in my book SCHROEDER, THE VESTAL AND THE FASCES, *supra* note 4, and cannot recapitulate the argument in full here.

12. The desire of the abstract person passionately to achieve subjectivity through intersubjective recognition characterizes hysteria—the paradigmatic mode of desire. SLAVOJ ŽIŽEK, THE INDIVISIBLE REMAINDER: AN ESSAY ON SCHELLING AND RELATED MATTERS 167 (1996) [hereinafter, ŽIŽEK, THE INDIVISIBLE REMAINDER].

13. *See e.g.*, RICHARD POSNER, SEX AND REASON (1992).

of desire and the perfect market. In the first section of this chapter, I relate Hegel's dialectic of market relations to Lacan's concept of the psychic realms of the symbolic, imaginary, and real. I show how Hegel's theory is an economics of desire and explain the nature of the desire which Hegel implicitly identifies in the market.

Desire is the response to castration, which is experienced as loss of the feminine into the realm of the real. Eros and Thanatos are the masculine and feminine versions of the desire to achieve "the feminine" and the real: the former is the longing to have her, the latter the longing to be her. The real stands for the dream of perfection, of perfect, immediate sexual relations beyond all alienating distinctions of time, space, and personality. The real, being perfect, is not mere death; it is a death that is beyond death—Nirvana, oblivion. Castration is the cut that forever walls off the real from the symbolic. The resulting gap between the real and the symbolic creates desire and thereby allows freedom, subjectivity, and the intersubjectivity of sexual relations to function. Our fantasies in the imaginary order are the vain attempt to cross this gap.

I then turn to a consideration of the ideal of the perfect market and its bane, transaction costs. By parsing the scant literature on the ideal, I will bring out and make explicit that which is repressed and implicit. I explore in detail the economic theory of Ronald Coase and contrast it to the misinterpretation that prevails in American law-and-economics literature. I show that the so-called Coase Theorem is not, as is often thought, a statement about the conditions of a perfect market without transaction costs, but rather a proposed radical break or "paradigm shift" in the way economics should think about markets and costs. A true Coasean analysis of markets has startling affinities with Hegelian and Lacanian thought.

In the final section, I show that the ideal of the perfect market is immediate market relations beyond all alienating distinctions of time, space, and personality. It is where all market participants achieve perfect indifference and all economic intercourse stops. The perfect market is therefore the real, Nirvana, oblivion. The desire of the perfect market is Thanatos—the desire for escape into total oblivion. Actual markets, in contrast, are within the symbolic order, which includes such human creations as law, speech, and sexuality. Coase's concept of "transaction costs" serves the same function in economics as castration serves in psychoanalysis. Transaction costs are the cut that forever walls off the real of the perfect market from the symbolic of the actual market. The resulting gap between perfect and actual markets creates desire and thereby allows freedom, subjectivity, and the intersubjectivity of market relations to function.

The law-and-economics movement is located in the imaginary order. It neither concerns itself with actual markets in the symbolic nor directly confronts its ideal of the perfect market in the real. Rather, law-and-economics erects a fantasy structure in a vain attempt to bridge the impossible gap between the symbolic and real orders.

The Hegelian Economics of Desire

The desire of the Hegelian marketplace is Eros. It is an attempt to achieve perfection through a relation with another—the perfect mate.[14] As the myth of Orpheus shows us, Eros is creative, but only insofar as desire remains unfulfilled. To achieve one's desire is death—Eros always threatens to become Thanatos.[15] Hegel always remains true to the Lacanian ethical law that one must never give ground relative to one's desire.[16] Hegel understands, however, that the paradox of desire is that to be true to one's desire, one must at least temporarily postpone its consummation in order to prolong desire. Indeed, postponement creates desire. To immediately give way to one's desire, therefore, is to betray one's desire.

Note that when I speak of Thanatos, I mean the desire—the longing for wholeness—that can only be satisfied through escape into death.[17] I am not using it in the more common sense of Thanatos as the death drive—the living death that is *"the very opposite of dying."*[18] Drive is an alternate mode of confronting the fact that desire as Eros can never be satisfied. Thanatos in my usage is the substitution of one goal of desire (wholeness through merger with the real) for another (wholeness through acquisition of the object of desire), whereas drive is the abandonment of desire and its goal of *jouissance* entirely.

This Hegelian-Lacanian ethic of desire must be contrasted with traditional ethics: "As far as desires are concerned, come back later. Make them wait."[19] This is a "morality of power"[20] that does not seek to temporarily postpone the consummation of desire, but attempts to permanently delay desire in an attempt to destroy it.

When I say that Hegel postpones the consummation of desire, I mean that

14. According to Lacan, "Eros is defined as the fusion that makes one from two"—an impossible goal. LACAN, SEMINAR XX, *supra* note 8, at 66.

15. "Thanatos wishes to return to a state preceding life itself, one that therefore totally undoes the organism." JANE GALLOP, READING LACAN 98 (1985).

16. JACQUES LACAN, THE SEMINAR OF JACQUES LACAN. BOOK VII: THE ETHICS OF PSYCHOANALYSIS, 1959–1960 319 (Jacques-Alain Miller ed. & Dennis Porter trans., 1986) [hereinafter, LACAN, SEMINAR VII].

17. This is the desire experienced by those heroes of Richard Wagner's operas who long for release in death. *See* SLAVOJ ŽIŽEK, THE TICKLISH SUBJECT: THE ABSENT CENTER OF POLITICAL ONTOLOGY 291–92 (1999).

18. *Id.* at 292.

19. *Id.* at 315.

20. *Id.*

in order to insure that both parties to the dialectic of recognition remain free and that neither party subsumes the other, Hegel insists that relationships be mediated—that the lovers be kept apart. As discussed in the previous chapter, in the regime of abstract right, this mediator is property.[21] That is, persons seek subjectivity through mutual recognition in a regime of possession, enjoyment, and exchange of external objects.

Similarly, Lacan insisted that psychic subjectivity can be achieved only through recognition by others.[22] In sexuality, abstract persons seek subjectivity through mutual recognition in a regime of possession, enjoyment, and exchange of an object of desire—the "phallus."[23] This necessity for mediation is one of the meanings of Lacan's famous slogan: There are no [direct and unmediated] sexual relationships.[24]

In other words, although Hegel and Lacan might seem like radically different thinkers at first blush, closer examination shows that their theories are linked by the recognition that subjectivity is intersubjectivity mediated by objectivity.[25] They agree that the freedom at the center of human subjectivity is radical negativity.[26] Hegel emphasizes the comic side of this dialectic. In comedy, conflicts are resolved in a happy ending (traditionally including the marriage of one or more pairs of the protagonists). The Hegelian dialec-

21. This relates to Hegel's concept of "sublation," or the reconciliation of opposites. As is well known, Hegel's dialectic proceeds from the identification of an initial concept, the recognition that the negation of the initial concept is always necessarily implied and followed by the reconciliation of the contradiction between these two concepts. It is a common misperception to think that this reconciliation—this sublation—totally supersedes the original concepts and their contradiction. As the German term for sublation *(Aufhebung)* implies, not only the independence of the two original concepts but their fundamental distinction remain as necessary building blocks of their reconciliation. That is, the doctrine of "the identity of identity and difference" posits that at one moment the two concepts are essentially distinct, and at another moment they are revealed to be essentially identical. Consequently, sublation is not a trilateral relationship, but a quadrilateral one consisting of the thesis, the antithesis, the synthesis, and the irreducible remainder, the hard kernel of *differance,* which resists compromise. To translate this into Lacanian terms, the wound of castration cannot be cured, only overcome.

22. *See, e.g.,* Elizabeth Grosz's description of Lacan's concept of desire: "Desire is a fundamental lack, a hole in being that can be satisfied only by one "thing"—another('s) desire. Each self-conscious subject desires the desire of the other as its object. *Its* desire is to be desired by the other, its counterpart." ELIZABETH GROSZ, JACQUES LACAN: A FEMINIST INTRODUCTION 64 (1990).

23. SCHROEDER, THE VESTAL AND THE FASCES, *supra* note 4.

24. GROSZ, *supra* note 22, at 136; Ellie Ragland-Sullivan, *The Sexual Masquerade: A Lacanian Theory of Sexual Difference,* in LACAN AND THE SUBJECT OF LANGUAGE 49, 67 (E. Ragland-Sullivan & M. Bracher eds., 1991).

25. SCHROEDER, THE VESTAL AND THE FASCES, *supra* note 4, at 14; Jeanne L. Schroeder, *Virgin Territory: Margaret Radin's Imagery of Personal Property as the Inviolative Feminine Body,* 79 MINN. L. REV. 55, 58 (1994).

26. G.. W. F. HEGEL, ELEMENTS OF THE PHILOSOPHY OF RIGHT 37–39 (Allen W. Wood ed. & H. B. Nisbet trans., 1991) [hereinafter, HEGEL, THE PHILOSOPHY OF RIGHT].

tic shows how the contradictions of the abstract person in the state of nature are contingently resolved in social relations, including the market and the family. Moreover, the negativity at the center of the human soul is seen optimistically as the absence of constraints that makes freedom possible, and the space that permits growth and creativity.

Lacan, on the other hand, emphasizes the tragic side of this dialectic. In tragedy, conflicts prove to be irresolvable and result in the death of one or more of the protagonists. The negativity or "split" that lies at the center of our psyche is seen pessimistically. If Hegel emphasizes that relationships occur, Lacan emphasizes that these relationships are always imperfect and mediated, desire is always postponed, and man is in a constant state of yearning.

Despite its ostensible optimism, however, Hegelian analysis never loses sight of negativity. As I have shown in the previous chapter, Hegel always recognizes the necessity of imperfection. It is precisely the failure of abstract right perfectly to achieve its goals that enables markets to function.

We can only bear the pain caused by mediation (castration) by adopting one of a number of delusions that Lacan identified with sexual identity. The contradictions of personality cannot be permanently resolved. The dialectic of desire ultimately can only be solved by death. Eros can only be postponed so long. Postponement eventually turns into procrastination. The ethics of psychoanalysis demand that we never give ground with respect to our desire. And so we must eventually give way to Thanatos.

Hegel provides the link between psychoanalysis on the one hand and law and markets on the other. Lacan's initial theory of the development of subjectivity derives in large part from Hegel. The Hegelian analysis of property as intersubjective relations mediated by object relations prefigures perhaps the greatest insight of late Lacanian thought: even though personality is created through the intersubjective relationships of the symbolic (language, law, and sexuality), we experience ourselves in terms of a hypothesized lost object of desire. Subjectivity as intersubjectivity is mediated by objectivity, in the sense that the subjects claim to possess and exchange or identify with and enjoy the object of desire. In other words, object relations take the place of intersubjective relations.[27] Because the true object of desire—the phallus—is lost in the real, we try to find other objects that might be obtainable in the symbolic and the imaginary to take its place. In other words, we try to make object relations that seem possible stand in for impossible intersubjective

27. As accurately described by Žižek, this is an understanding that Lacan only developed over time. In his early seminars, Lacan tended to concentrate on the role of intersubjective relationships in the formation of personality. As the years went on, he shifted his emphasis more and more to the object relations we form in response to the failure of intersubjectivity. Slavoj Žižek, The Plague of Fantasies 8 (1997) [hereinafter, Žižek, Plague of Fantasies].

relations. This leads to the concept of the *objet petit a,* which I briefly introduced in the previous chapter.[28]

Although subjectivity (which can only be created through recognition in intersubjective relations) is created in the symbolic, human beings are not satisfied with the symbolic. The symbolic is, by definition, not only artificial but incomplete. We long for the impossible wholeness of the real. In an attempt to achieve that which cannot be achieved in the symbolic, we turn to the imaginary. In the imaginary, we erect seemingly attainable fantasy images to stand in for our true object of desire. These fantasy objects of desire—*objets petit a*—are invented retroactively to serve as the cause of our desire.[29] The term *objet petit a* means that this object should be spelled with an "a" because it sits in the place of the other *(autre),* which is our true desire.[30] In truth, we desire because we do not feel whole and the hypothesized object that would satisfy our desire does not exist. To realize this would be the feminine acceptance of castration. In order for our masculine selves to avoid this, we pretend that what we really desire is some identifiable actual object.

We lie to ourselves: if I could just (fill in the blank—possess that beautiful woman's body; have a man's organ or, lacking that, his baby; make partner, get tenure, get a job at a more prestigious law school or firm, etc.,), I would be happy. Any "object" can take on this role. The *objet petit a* can be a conventionally pleasurable object, such as a woman's body (or a part object such as her breasts), or Proust's madeleine, but it can just as easily be a completely abstract concept, such as the voice or the gaze.[31] The point is that this external "object" serves as an explanation for our feelings. One result of this operation is the conflation of the psychic desire for recognition with the biological urge to mate. It is these fantasy identifications that create sexuality and enable markets to operate.

28. Lacan spent the latter part of his career explicating his theory of the *objet petit a.* My discussion here necessarily touches only on one limited aspect of this very complex idea. For an unusually succinct account of the function of the *objet petit a* as the object cause of desire, *see* BRUCE FINK, THE LACANIAN SUBJECT: BETWEEN LANGUAGE AND JOUISSANCE 83–94 (1995).

29. In fantasy, the *objet petit a* "is the object of desire only by virtue of being the end-term of the fantasy. The object takes the place, I would say, of what the subject is—symbolically—deprived of. . . . What is it that the subject is deprived of? The phallus." Jacques Lacan, *Desire and the Interpretation of Desire in Hamlet* (Jacques-Alain Miller ed. & James Hulbert trans.), 55–56 YALE FRENCH STUDIES 11, 15 (1977) [hereinafter, Lacan, *Hamlet*].

30. SCHROEDER, THE VESTAL AND THE FASCES, *supra* note 4, at 108 n.1.

31. Paradoxically, it can also be an object of fear or disgust. This is because we identify an *objet petit a* to serve as an cause of the gap within our subjectivity and the symbolic order. This gap could be caused either by the absence of a wonderful thing or by the presence of a horrible, destructive thing. *See, e.g.,* SLAVOJ ŽIŽEK, DID SOMEBODY SAY TOTALITARIANISM? FIVE INTERVENTIONS IN THE (MIS)USE OF A NOTION 253–55 (2001).

The Lacanian Desire of Economics

To understand the dialectic of desire, it is necessary to consider in more detail Lacan's theory of consciousness and sexuality.

There are three orders of the psyche: the real, the imaginary, and the symbolic.[32] The symbolic is the cultural order of law and language, of signification and sexuality. The imaginary is the realm of imagery, fantasy, meaning, and complementarity. The real is our intuition that there is something beyond or prior to the other two. The real is not the same as the natural world.[33] The real is as much an aspect of human consciousness as the symbolic and the imaginary; it is that part of our thoughts that cannot be expressed in words or depicted in images.[34] Yet for many purposes it functions as though it were the natural world. This is because the real includes *our sense* that there is a natural world external to our thoughts and dreams, something more permanent than our pathetic, fleeting human lives. The real, however, also includes such concepts as death, the thing-in-itself, God (in the sense of *Geist,* or the Absolute), and everything else that is beyond ourselves.[35] It is reminiscent of Kant's concept of "the sublime."[36]

The real is therefore the impossible—not just in the sense that it is impossible for us to have direct access to the real in our conscious minds, but also because it necessarily includes logical paradoxes that are beyond ordinary intuitions of what is possible.[37] We experience the real as though it were

32. *See also* Jacqueline Rose, *Introduction II,* in FEMININE SEXUALITY, *supra* note 8, 31. JACQUES LACAN, THE SEMINAR OF JACQUES LACAN. BOOK I: FREUD'S PAPERS ON TECHNIQUE 80 (J-A. Miller ed. & J. Forrester trans., 1988) [hereinafter, LACAN, SEMINAR I]; *See also generally,* GROSZ, *supra* note 22, at 10.

33. In Grosz's words: "The Real is not however the same as reality; reality is lived as and known through imaginary and symbolic representations." GROSS, *supra* note 22, at 34.

34. "The Real cannot be experienced a such: it is capable of representation or conceptualization only through the reconstructive or inferential work of the imaginary and symbolic orders. Lacan himself refers to the Real as 'the lack of a 'lack.' " *Id.*

35. *See, e.g.,* "The gods belong to the field of the real." LACAN, THE FOUR FUNDAMENTALS, *supra* note 7, at 45. *See also* STUART SCHNEIDERMAN, JACQUES LACAN: THE DEATH OF AN INTELLECTUAL HERO 76 (1983). As discussed in Lacan's seminar on feminine sexuality, the mystic's experience of God is feminine *jouissance.* Of course, this means that any attempt to give affirmative content to the idea of God (as in religion) is imaginary, not in the sense that such a God does not exist, but that our understanding of such a God is located in the imaginary order.

36. IMMANUEL KANT, THE CRITIQUE OF JUDGMENT §§-23–29 (J. H. Bernhard, trans., 1951).

37. "The Real cannot be experienced a such: it is capable of representation or conceptualization only through the reconstructive or inferential work of the imaginary and symbolic orders. Kant's discussion of what he identifies as the four antinomies reflects this idea. IMMANUEL KANT, CRITIQUE OF PURE REASON 230–87 (J. M. V. Meickeljohn trans., 1990). Hegel (and Lacan) went a step further, generalizing Kant's insight into a recognition that contradiction is inherent in all concepts, not merely the four identified by Kant. To oversimplify,

something we had lost. It functions as the "hard kernel"[38] of reality that was left behind when we entered the orders of imagery and speech. This is not really true, however. The real is created simultaneously with the imaginary and the symbolic through castration.[39]

Lacan declared that the subject is split.[40] Lacan, like Hegel, believed that subjectivity—the ability to be a legal actor, capable of bearing rights and engaging in legal relations, and a speaking, sexed person, capable of engaging in social relations, is social.

As we have seen, classical liberal philosophy and jurisprudence are internally inconsistent with respect to the concepts of individuality and rights. Liberalism's autonomous individual located in the state of nature cannot be the subject of law because legal rights can only be understood as relationships between and among people. Similarly, language can be understood only in terms of society. Consequently, the autonomous individual in the state of nature can neither speak nor bear legal rights, as liberalism claims. The freedom that is human potential can become actual only through social relationships.

Hegel argued that the abstract person posited by liberalism is driven to

---

Kant thought one could not resolve the antinomies because even transcendental logic could not have direct access to the thing-in-itself (i.e., the real is impossible to know). Hegel (and Lacan) instead argued that a fundamental split lies at the heart of the thing-in-itself(i.e., the real is impossibility per se). Žižek, The Indivisible Remainder, *supra* note 12, at 110; Hegel, The Lesser Logic, *supra* note 10, at 78.

38. Although we experience it in this way, "the Real is not a hard external kernel which resists symbolization, but the *product* of a deadlock in the process of symbolization." Žižek, The Indivisible Remainder, *supra* note 12, at 110.

39. The real is the sense that there is something on the other side of the boundaries to the symbolic and the imaginary. Slavoj Žižek, Tarrying With the Negative: Kant, Hegel, and the Critique of Ideology 35–39 (1994) [hereinafter Žižek, Tarrying With the Negative]; Jacques-Alain Miller, *Microscopia: An Introduction to the Reading of Television*, in Jacques Lacan, Television: A Challenge to the Psychoanalytic Establishment xi, xxiv (Joan Copjec ed. & Dennis Hollier et al. trans., 1990) (1974). The realm of the real is, therefore, only established by the erection of the boundaries at the moment of the creation of the imaginary and the symbolic. We only retroactively posit the existence of the "lost" real by examining what seem to be clues, traces, stains left in the symbolic by its retreat (Žižek, Tarrying With the Negative, *supra*, at 36–37), just as Orpheus guessed that Eurydice must have followed him from signs that he interpreted as her footprints.

40. *See, e.g.*, Grosz, *supra* note 22, at 137. In his excellent book, Bruce Fink, one of the current translators of Lacan's seminars into English, gives an unusually clear description of Lacan's notion of the split subject. The metaphor of the split subject inevitably suggests a positive content (subjectivity) albeit with a rupture in the center. Lacan's point (which I believe exactly reflects Hegel's understanding of both human personality and *Geist*) is more extreme than this. The split *is* subjectivity. Fink, *supra* note 28, at 45. Perhaps the expression "split subject" would be better written "the split = the subject." Subjectivity is precisely that part of our mind (and of the universe) that is revealed as absence.

make his potential freedom actual; thus each person passionately desires to enter into social relations and achieve first subjectivity and then higher states of human consciousness. As I have already stated, one attains subjectivity when another free subject recognizes one as a subject.

The proposition that subjectivity can only be achieved through the social (i.e., through law and language) creates a paradox. That which is most ourselves—our subjectivity, our freedom, our speech, our sexuality—is simultaneously that which is not ourselves, in the sense that it comes to us from the outside. When understood in this sense, the symbolic order takes on the role known as the Other. As we mature and are initiated into language and law, and achieve sexuality, we experience the sense that we have lost something that we can no longer explain in words or images. Not only our subjectivity but the relations with others that create our subjectivity are mediated. We feel castrated not merely because our subjectivity is dependent on others, but because we can never have a perfectly satisfying relationship with the others on whom we depend. Immediacy is therefore in the real. As a result, perfect, immediate relationships are not just an ideal; they are our desire.

To put this yet another way, to describe or picture our experiences is to interpret them. Consequently, in our capacity *as conscious subjects* we never have direct access to our experiences. To give an example, when we are having a physical sensation such as pain, we are not yet conscious of the fact—we just feel it. Charles Sanders Peirce called this pure unmediated quality "firstness."[41] Firstness can be thought of as the purely reflexive reaction of recoiling, and perhaps letting out an inarticulate screech. The moment we realize that we are experiencing pain, however, we are already interpreting it in the orders of the imaginary and the symbolic. The simplest interpretation—the imaginary—is the awareness of oneself and one's pain. Peirce called this simple negation or opposition "secondness."[42] Secondness is the simple realization, "That hurts!" In the symbolic, we are aware of ourselves, our pain, and our understanding of the pain—what Peirce calls "thirdness."[43] Thirdness is being able to say to another, "I am in pain." In other words, when we picture our experience (the imaginary) or try to explain it (the symbolic), we lose the immediacy of the experience. We either anticipate or dread it in the future, or remember or mourn it in the past. Our direct, immediate experience now seems to be exiled into the real beyond imagination and discourse. Once again, our true self seems divorced from our understanding of ourself. We seem to have lost something—immediacy.

As I introduced in the previous chapter, Lacan calls this operation "cas-

41. Charles S. Peirce, *The Monad, in* Collected Papers of Charles Sanders Peirce, Principles of Philosophy 7 (Charles Hartshore & Paul Weiss eds., 1960).

42. *Id.* at 7.

43. *Id.* at 164.

tration" because we feel not merely that our wholeness is lost, but also that this loss has been imposed upon us by something outside of us.[44] We feel (incorrectly) that we must have once been whole and inviolate, that there was once an object, which is now lost because "someone" has taken it away. This hypothesized object, which we feel must have been lost in castration, Lacan calls the "phallus." This intentionally confusing and apparently masculinist terminology is designed to reflect the conflation of anatomy and psyche in our misogynist society.[45] The phallus has no affirmative content. We feel lack, and the phallus is that which would eliminate the lack. It is the lack of lack, and as such it does not exist. It is the radical negativity of the feminine and the real.

Lacan's castration terminology reflects the masculine position. This terminology can initially seem troublesome to feminists. I have suggested elsewhere,[46] however, that if there are two sexuated positions, there should also be a metaphor that expresses the universal sense of loss from the feminine side. I suggest that this concept, when filtered through the feminine position, should not be translated in terms of the female genitalia and genital mutilation. The feminine, in her acceptance of castration, does not feel the pain of castration as the loss of a part that could theoretically be remedied through an exchange resulting in the acquisition of a new part. Castration is, instead, experienced as a fundamental, irreversible change of condition in the person herself, which can never be cured, but only mourned. Consequently, what the feminine loses in castration is not a part like the penis, but the integrity of the female body as a whole. She feels that she lost her virginity, her girlish innocence, when she was brutally violated by the Other. By teaching the maiden to speak and obey law, the Other forcibly "made a woman out of her." As such, she is no longer self-sufficient, but is now defined only by the intersubjective (sexual) relationships of the symbolic. Because these defining sexual relations are always failures, she experiences herself as incomplete.

The order of the real is conceptualized as that which is beyond the symbolic and the imaginary. As discussed in the previous chapter, because adult subjects speaking in the order of the symbolic and fantasizing in the order

44. As I will keep emphasizing, castration is a retroactive, fictional autobiography that the subject writes: "That is to say: What precisely is symbolic castration? It is . . . the sense of the loss of something which the subject never possessed in the first place." ŽIŽEK, THE PLAGUE OF FANTASIES, *supra* note 27, at 15.

45. Lacan's point was precisely that *despite the fact* that the concept of the phallus is a purely abstract concept devoid of biological content, we nevertheless conflate it with anatomy. We conflate the erotic desire for recognition with the mating urge. We associate the phallus, as symbol of subjectivity and desire, with the penis. This is a conflation—it is a fiction—but it is the fiction that governs our lives. To say that the phallus is the penis is consequently both false and true.

46. SCHROEDER, THE VESTAL AND THE FASCES, *supra* note 4.

of the imaginary feel we have lost something that we can no longer express, we conclude, wrongly, that whatever once made us whole must now be located in the real. This is reflected in our personal histories.[47] From the fact that we were not aware of our separation from our mothers until we entered the imaginary and the symbolic, we retroduce the false hypothesis that we must in fact have been one with our mothers prior to that time. As a result, we feel that the phallus (the wholeness that was lost through castration) must have been unity with the ideal of the feminine. This is why this ideal of the feminine is sometimes known as the all-powerful Phallic Mother.[48] The feminine as the Phallic Mother is, therefore, that which is located in the real.

As discussed, persons theoretically take on object relations in property and contract as a means of achieving their true desire—the actualization of freedom through intersubjective recognition. The market is a means to the end of intersubjectivity. However, this dialectic can never be fully satisfying because our desire must always be postponed and relationships must always be mediated. Consequently, when we engage in actual market relations, we often repress our true desire *for* market relations and act as though we desired *the objects of* market relations as such. We imagine that our intersubjective relations are the means to the end of object relations, rather than the other way around.[49]

How does this relate to sexuality? Sexuality consists of various strategies that subjects can take with respect to castration. For reasons that are beyond the scope of this chapter, the masculine is the position of having and exchanging the phallus, while the feminine is that of being and enjoying the phallus. This is, of course, not literally true. Castration is universal. No one, masculine or feminine, has the phallus. Consequently, masculinity is not superior to femininity. Rather, the masculine can be seen as the cowardly position of denial and fantasy—falsely claiming or pretending that he has "it" when he doesn't. This corresponds to desire as Eros—the fantasy that one can remain a subject in the symbolic order yet attain wholeness by acquiring a perfect mate who will take the place of the lost phallus. In the order of the imaginary, we erect fantasy substitutes to stand in the place of the actual real object of desire (the phallus, the feminine, wholeness, perfect sexual relationship).

47. As I discuss in Chapter 1, romanticism can be seen as the extension of this fictional autobiography to an account of society at large.

48. "The man has the illusion of having the phallus, in the sense of the potency to keep her. The woman 'is' for him as the phallus, as his projected desire." DRUCILLA CORNELL, BEYOND ACCOMMODATION: ETHICAL FEMINISM, DECONSTRUCTION AND THE LAW 38 (1991).

49. I discuss this conflation in markets and law extensively in Jeanne L. Schroeder, *Chix Nix Bundle-O-Stix: A Feminist Critique of the Disaggregation of Property*, 95 MICH. L. REV. 239 (1994) [hereinafter, Schroeder, *Chix*]; *and* SCHROEDER, THE VESTAL AND THE FASCES, *supra* note 4.

In the imaginary, we try to find natural (i.e., seemingly real) analogs to stand in the place of the symbolic concepts of sexuality. That is, in the imaginary, we conflate sexuality with anatomy.[50] Consequently, we look for things that anatomic males have or can attain, and that anatomic females can be, to serve as metaphors for the phallus. Specifically, the phallus is conflated with the male organ (hence Lacan's terminology) and the female body. By wielding the penis and subordinating women, those who are in the masculine position vainly pretend not to be castrated. The subordination of women has often taken a literal form in traditional societies, in which women are exchanged among men in marriage.[51] It also takes the more subtle form of an imaginary ideal of an affirmative "femininity," which can be tamed and captured in order to take the place of the radical negativity of the real feminine, which cannot be tamed or captured.

50. This does not mean that anatomy is not crucial to sexual identity: "Anatomy is what figures in the account: for me 'anatomy is not destiny,' but that does not mean that anatomy does not 'figure' . . . , but it only figures *(it is a sham).*" Rose, *supra* note 32, at 44 (quoting M. SAFOUAN, LA SEXUALITÉ FÉMININE DANS LA DOCTRINE FREUDIENNE 131 [1976]). These positions are only generally associated with the biological sexes.

> This account of sexual desire led Lacan, as it led Freud, to his adamant rejection of any theory of the difference between the sexes in terms of pre-given male or female entities which complete and satisfy each other. Sexual difference can only be the consequence of a division; without this division it would cease to exist. But it must exist because no human being can become a subject outside the division into sexes. One must take up a position as either a man or a woman. Such a position is by no means identical with one's biological sexual characteristics, nor is it a position of which one can be very confident—as the psychoanalytical experience demonstrates.

Juliet Mitchell, *Introduction I,* in FEMININE SEXUALITY, *supra* note 8, 1, 6. That is:

> For Lacan, men and women are only ever in language ('Men and women are signifiers bound to the common usage of language', . . .). All speaking beings must line themselves up on one side or the other of this division, but anyone can cross over and inscribe themselves on the opposite side from that to which they are anatomically destined.

Rose, *supra,* at 49.

To say that Lacan sought to destroy any lingering biological determinism in Freud's theories while explaining how gender difference becomes mapped upon biological sexual difference is not to imply that biological sexual difference does not exist or is not important. Lacan's point is that our experience of sexuality as speaking, conscious subjects can never be simply reduced to our biological sex for the same reason that property cannot be reduced to our sensuous relationship with physical things. Sexuality is artificial, and therefore authentic to man the artist. The sexual status quo is neither natural nor inevitable in the sense that anatomy is destiny. Nevertheless, Lacan hypothesizes a mechanism by which a sexual status quo—once in place—is able to reproduce itself.

51. Lacan was initially influenced by the structuralist anthropology of Claude Lévi-Strauss, who held that societies are formed through arrangements by which men of different clans exchange women. Over time, Lacan moved farther and farther away from claims that his theory was an empirical account of individual or societal development. Rather, like Hegel's, it is a speculative account, which often plays itself out in our empirical lives.

The feminine sexuated position, in contradistinction, is the acceptance of castration—the understanding that this loss cannot be cured. The feminine, therefore, is identified with castration, with lack.[52] She is identified with that which is lost in the real. The feminine position with respect to castration corresponds to desire as Thanatos. This is the understanding that no external object of desire can heal the wound of castration. It is a belief that wholeness could be achieved if one could somehow retreat back to the precastrated state. To do so would be to lose individuality and subjectivity. It would be as though one were never born; it is to be dead.

This concept of sexuality as the result of castration can be seen in the Biblical creation myth. According to the first chapter of Genesis, God "created man in his own image . . . male and female created he them."[53] But chapter 2 relates that Lord God created Eve out of Adam's rib.[54] One way theologians have tried to reconcile these two apparently inconsistent creation stories[55] is to propose that the second story is not the story of the creation of woman, but the story of the creation of sexual difference.

In this view, God initially created a single human being, *ha-'adam,*[56] who was, as Genesis 1 relates, both male and female and therefore, bi- (or perhaps more accurately, non-) sexual. Subsequently, as recounted in Genesis 2, God created sexuality by separating this single complete creature into two incomplete ones.[57]

To put this in Lacanian terminology, we posit that the subject was once perfectly whole, and therefore self-sufficient. God castrated *ha-'adam* by taking away a precious part of his/her body—the (phallic) rib—and building it into another being. The resulting subject-who feels that he has lost a part of himself is man. The resulting subject who identifies herself with that which the other has lost is woman.

In other words, through castration, the masculine subject feels that he no longer has what he once *had.* Through violation, the feminine subject feels that she no longer is what she once *was.* The difference between the masculine and the feminine is the difference between having and being, which is reflected in the verb forms found in all Western language.

52. Drucilla Cornell, *The Doubly-Prized World: Myth, Allegory and the Feminine,* 75 CORN. L. REV. 644, 660–61 (1990).

53. *Genesis* 1:27.

54. *Genesis* 2:21–22.

55. Biblical historians, of course, explain this textually by positing that the Pentateuch is a later redaction of a number of earlier texts. This approach does not, of course, explain how one should approach the Bible as a religious text and the fundamental inspirational source of Western civilization. The Bible as it comes down to us is a single work, whether written by Moses or by a redactor.

56. The Hebrew word is not a proper name. It means human being.

57. JONATHAN SAWDAY, THE BODY EMBLAZONED: DISSECTION AND THE HUMAN BODY IN RENAISSANCE CULTURE 185 (1995).

"Desire" is a term of art with a meaning quite diverse from the economic concept of "preference." Desire is specifically the longing to have what is missing in the symbolic—the wholeness lost when the subject was split.[58]

A perfect example of the dream of Eros—the desire to achieve wholeness by finding the perfect mate—can be found in an orthodox Catholic interpretation of the Biblical account of the Fall. According to St. Augustine, it is vulgar and dirty-minded to think that either there was no sex in the Garden of Eden or that sex was the Original Sin.[59] Original Sin consisted of Adam and Eve's pride in wishing to be like God and disobedience in eating the fruit of the Tree of the Knowledge of Good and Evil. Lust is the punishment for, not the cause of, Original Sin.[60]

58. "Desire, for Hegel, is ontologically constitutive of human consciousness: 'Self consciousness *is* desire.' Now desire is essentially a desire for unity, both the unity of the self with the world it inhabits (the desire to overcome the sense of disparity between what the world is and what we wish it to be, and the unity of the self with itself (the desire to overcome the sense of disparity between what we are and what we wish to be)." DANIEL BERTHOLD-BOND, HEGEL'S THEORY OF MADNESS 46 (1995) (quoting Hegel's *Phenomenology of Spirit*). Berthold-Bond's thesis is that Hegel's theories of desire and madness anticipated those of psychoanalysis. *See, e.g.*, "We shall see that Hegel significantly anticipates Lacan's own descriptions of desire as the nostalgic yearning to uncover unconscious origins." *Id.* at 76.

59. PETER BROWN, THE BODY AND SOCIETY: MEN, WOMEN AND SEXUAL RENUNCIATION IN EARLY CHRISTIANITY 400–402 (1988). As man was created as both spirit and flesh, he was intended to experience both mental and physical pleasure: "For neither was it a paradise only physical for the advantage of the body, and not also spiritual for the advantage of the mind; nor was it only spiritual to afford enjoyment to man by his internal sensations, and not also physical to afford him enjoyment through his external senses. But obviously it was for both ends." AUGUSTINE, THE CITY OF GOD 458 (Marcus Dods trans., 1950) [hereinafter, AUGUSTINE, CITY OF GOD]. Thomas Aquinas agreed about the existence of sexual pleasure in the Garden. See ŽIŽEK, PLAGUE OF FANTASIES, *supra* note 27, at 15.

60. "For the corruption of the body, which weighs down the soul, is not the cause but the punishment of the first sin; and it was not the corruptible flesh that made the soul sinful, but the sinful soul that made the flesh corruptible." AUGUSTINE, CITY OF GOD, *supra* note 59, at 444. The Garden was a place of perfect, albeit hierarchical, harmony between God and man, man and woman, and soul and body. When Adam and Eve turned away from God, they destroyed this harmony:

> The twisted human will, not marriage, not even the sexual drive, was what was new in the human condition after Adam's Fall. The fallen will subjected the original, God-given bonds of human society—friendship, marriage, and paternal command—to sickening shocks of willfulness, that caused these to sway, to fissure, and to change their nature.

BROWN, *supra* note 59, at 404. As I shall discuss shortly, before the Fall, the body followed the dictates of the soul. *Id.* at 405. After the Fall, the body gained a mind of its own, and now rebels against the soul through uncalled-for lust and embarrassing impotence. AUGUSTINE, CITY OF GOD, *supra* note 59, at 465, 422. *See also* BROWN, *supra* note 59, at 417.

> Sexuality and death are linked because they are the two ways in which the rift between spirit and flesh (symbolizing as well the rift between God and man, and between man and woman) are physically manifest: in death the spirit is involuntarily deprived of its beloved spouse, flesh; in sex, the spirit loses its harmonious governance over the rebel

Eve was created as the perfect mate to make Adam whole[61]—to replace the piece (the rib) that God took away from him. Because God created two sexes and commanded Adam and Eve to be fruitful and multiply, sexual intercourse must have been part of the plan.[62] Consequently, Adam and Eve did have sexual intercourse in the Garden.[63] Moreover, since the Garden was the land of perfect relationships, prelapsarian sexual relations would have been infinitely more pleasurable than they are now in our postlapsarian world.[64] The difference, however, is that sex was not ecstatic—there was no *jouissance* in the Garden. During orgasm Adam and Eve retained perfect control and distance.[65] They felt completion without losing their separate consciousness.

The Fall was a form of castration whereby the subject became split and

---

lious flesh. Death comes to us at the end of our lives and we can try not to think about it. Sexuality, on the other hand, is always with us.

Jeanne L. Schroeder, The Taming of the Shrew: The Liberal Attempt to Mainstream Radical Feminist Theory, 5 YALE J.L. & FEMINISM 123, 170 (1992) [hereinafter, Schroeder, Taming of the Shrew] (citations omitted).

61. AUGUSTINE, *The Good of Marriage, in* SAINT AUGUSTINE: TREATISES ON MARRIAGE AND OTHER SUBJECTS, *in* THE FATHERS OF THE CHURCH 9 (Charles T. Wilcox et. al. trans. & Roy J. Deferrari ed., 1955). "This [the good of marriage] does not seem to me to be a good solely because of the procreation of children, but also because of the natural companionship between the two sexes." *Id.* at 12 (citations omitted).

62. "But it is quite clear that they were created male and female with bodies of different sexes for the very purpose of begetting offspring . . . and it is great folly to oppose so plain a fact." AUGUSTINE, CITY OF GOD, *supra* note 59, at 469. "And it is by this original example, which God Himself instituted, that the apostle admonishes all husbands to love their own wives in particular. *Id.* at 470.

63. ŽIŽEK, PLAGUE OF FANTASIES, *supra* note 27, at 15. Or, as St. Augustine suggests, they would have if they had not been expelled so rapidly. Apparently, Eve ate of the Tree of the Knowledge of Good and Evil shortly after she was created. BROWN, *supra* note 59, at 402, 404.

64. "The married intercourse of Adam and Eve . . . would have been an object lesson in the balanced rapture with which human beings might have used the physical joys showered up upon them by their creator." BROWN, *supra* note 59, at 407. ŽIŽEK, PLAGUE OF FANTASIES, *supra* note 27, at 15.

65. "As happy, then, as were these our first parents, who were agitated by no mental perturbations and annoyed by no bodily discomforts, so happy should the whole human race have been . . . this original blessedness continuing until, in virtue of that benediction which said, "Increase and multiply," . . . there would then have been bestowed that higher felicity which is enjoyed by the most blessed angels." AUGUSTINE, CITY OF GOD, *supra* note 59, at 457. "The man, then, would have sown the seed, and the woman received it, as need required, the generative organs being moved by the will, not excited by lust." *Id.* at 472.

Also: "In such happy circumstances and general human well-being we should be far from suspecting that offspring could not have been begotten without the disease of lust, but those parts, like all the rest, would be set in motion at the command of the will; and without the seductive stimulus of passion, with calmness and with no corrupting of the integrity of the body, the husband would lie upon the bosom of his wife." *Id.* at 475. *See also* BROWN, *supra* note 59, at 402, 407–08; Schroeder, *Taming of the Shrew, supra* note 60, at 169–70.

perfect relationships impossible. As Augustine lamented in his *Confessions,* "Surely I have not ceased to be my own self . . . and yet there is still a great gap between myself and myself. . . . Oh that my soul might follow my own self . . . that it might not be a rebel to itself."[66]

The cold, nonecstatic union that Augustine imagines occurred in the Garden is the imaginary relationship of Eros. It cannot occur precisely because castration is a lie. Woman is not man's lost phallus. There never was, nor will there ever be, a piece that was taken away from the subject that would make him whole. Eros fantasizes the two sexes to be complementary—that the feminine can complete the masculine. The two sexes are, by contrast, symbolic. They do not form two halves of a single subject, but are each a split subject.[67]

Moreover, the masculine fantasy of Eros presumes that one can be both separate and complete at the same time, like Adam and Eve in the Garden of Eden. Indeed, the fantasy of the Garden of Eden is perverse, in the technical sense of the term.[68] One cannot heal castration—the split that is subjectivity—without destroying subjectivity and the symbolic realm of speech, law, and sexuality. To achieve wholeness is to lose oneself, to rejoin the primordial unity of the real. This is the feminine acceptance of castration. To be a subject is to be castrated, to not be castrated is to lose one's subjectivity.

Indeed, to return to my earlier exegesis of the creation myth, by the logic of Genesis itself, if Adam and Eve were to achieve perfect sexual relations, they would merge back into the single bisexual creature of the initial creation prior to the creation of sexual difference. As the Bible suggests, God created sexual difference precisely to enable humans to love—"It is not good that the man should be alone; I shall make him an helpmeet for him."[69] As a result, "A man shall leave his father and his mother, and shall cleave to his wife: and they shall be one flesh."[70] Love requires not only that there be two

66. AUGUSTINE, CONFESSIONS 10.30.41–42 (R. Pine-Coffin trans., 1961). As I have discussed elsewhere, Lacan was following Augustine when he declared that the phallus was the symbol of loss. SCHROEDER, THE VESTAL AND THE FASCES, *supra* note 4, at 90.

67. "Lacan thus moves as far as possible from the notion of sexual difference as the relationship of two opposite poles which complement each other, together forming the whole of 'Man.' 'Masculine' and 'feminine' are not the two species of the genus Man but rather the two modes of the subject's failure to achieve the full identity of Man. 'Man' and 'Woman' together do not form a whole, since each of them is already in itself a failed whole." Renata Salecl, *The Spoils of Freedom: Psychoanalysis and Feminism After the Fall of Socialism,* 116 (1994).

68. "[Adam and Eve's] pleasure was even greater than ours (i.e., the pleasure of having sex after the Fall), the only and crucial difference being that, while copulating, they maintained proper measure and distance, and never lost self-control—this assertion unknowingly reveals the secret of Paradise: it was the kingdom of *perversity.* That is to say: does not the fundamental paradox of perversion reside it he fact that the pervert successfully avoids the deadlock of the 'states which are essentially by-products.' " ŽIŽEK, PLAGUE OF FANTASIES, *supra* note 27, at 15.

69. *Genesis* 2:18.

70. *Genesis* 2:24.

separate persons, but that they each lack something, and therefore desire each other. Sexual relations must therefore be impossible, in the sense that lovers always fail to achieve their goal of achieving union.

Nevertheless, all subjects continue nostalgically to long for our hypothesized precastrated, previolated integrity, wholeness, and satisfaction. Eros is related to masculine phallic *jouissance,* and therefore requires the denial of castration so that the subject can retain the hope that he could achieve wholeness if he could have sexual relations with the perfect mate. Thanatos, in contrast, is related to the supplemental *jouissance* that Lacan identified with the feminine, which gives the feminine subject a different additional access to the real. As the masculine desire of Eros is based on denial, it must eventually give way to Thanatos, either in the sense used in this chapter—as the feminine desire of Thanatos, which is based on acceptance if castration—or in the sense of the death drive, which is the abandonment of phallic *jouissance* and desire. The ultimate desire is the death wish—the desire to merge with the real.

Similarly, in the symbolic realm of law, we lose sight of the purely intersubjective nature of legal relationships and concentrate on the object relations that are only the mediators of intersubjectivity. In the masculine phallic metaphor for property that dominates American legal doctrine and theory, property is seen archetypically as the sensuous grasp of a tangible thing.[71] This metaphor comes in a positive and negative version. In the positive version, only relations that can be reduced to sensuous grasp are considered true property interests, and other forms of "property" are enforceable insofar as they can be analogized to the tangible archetype.[72] In the negative version, the legal analyst correctly realizes that such a tangible notion of property is untenable in our modern society but, assuming that sensuous grasp is the only possible way of explaining property, incorrectly concludes that property does not or should not continue to exist as a coherent legal category.[73] Both masculine approaches attempt to reduce the mediated trilateral relationship of property (subject-object-subject) to a bilateral one (either subject-object or subject-subject). The positive masculine metaphor tries to analyze property as a simple relationship between an owning subject and an object, and emphasizes the single masculine element of possession. The negative masculine metaphor tries to analyze property as a contractual relationship between two subjects that does not require an

71. I present my analysis of the masculine metaphor for property in Schroeder, *Chix, supra* note 49, at 95; SCHROEDER, THE VESTAL AND THE FASCES, *supra* note 4, at 107–228.

72. This approach can be seen in the commercial law doctrine of "ostensible ownership." SCHROEDER, THE VESTAL AND THE FASCES, *supra* note 4, at 130–43.

73. Wesley Newcomb Hohfeld and Thomas Gray are probably the two most prominent proponents of this position. *Id.* at 156–79.

object, emphasizing the single masculine element of exchange. In both, loss of property, as illustrated in the language of the U.S. Constitution, is conceptualized as "takings" (castration). This reflects the masculine desire of Eros—the attempt to achieve wholeness while retaining distinct, separate subjectivity by finding the missing piece—whether imagined as the object of desire or perfect helpmate—lost through castration.

Expressions of the feminine phallic metaphor for property are less common in law, but arise frequently in colloquial conversation. Radin's theory of property for personhood, briefly introduced in the previous chapter, is probably the most widely known example.[74] Reflecting the feminine desire of Thanatos, the feminine moment of property is an attempt to regress to the perfect, virginal integrity that supposedly existed before castration-violation. It is an attempt to reduce the trilateral relationship of property not to a binary relationship but to a simple unity of subject merged with and into object. One's property becomes so necessary to one's personhood and one's identification with it is so complete that one cannot distinguish personhood from property. In other words, in contrast to the masculine imagery of property as a bilateral relationship of subject possessing object, the feminine imagery of property as identification of subject with object is not based on the proposition that the subject will remain separate; there is no relationship between subjects, only union with the object. The feminine approach emphasizes the single feminine element of enjoyment of property. Property is that which one identifies with, enters, enjoys, and protects from others. Possession is acknowledged only insofar as it is necessary for enjoyment. Exchange in the form of market alienation is to be discouraged to the extent practicable, as alienating to personhood. Within the feminine metaphor, losses of property are described not in terms of taking that can be cured through damages, but as rape, pollution, a permanent loss of self.

This brief explanation helps us to understand why we desire, but cannot bear to confront, the real. The masculine desire of Eros is built on fantasy—the lie that desire is caused by an obtainable imaginary object. It is the delusion that we can remain located in the symbolic order without being castrated. Since that which is lost in castration—the feminine—by definition is the real, she cannot be captured in words (the symbolic) and images (the imaginary). Thus any and all positive conceptions of the feminine must, by necessity, be fantasy images that stand in for the feminine.[75]

74. I set forth my analysis of Radin's use of the feminine metaphor for property in Schroeder, *Virgin Territory*, *supra* note 25; SCHROEDER, THE VESTAL AND THE FASCES, *supra* note 4, at 229–92.

75. "As negative to the man, woman becomes a total object of fantasy (or an object of total fantasy) elevated into the place of the Other and made to stand for its truth. Since the place of the Other is also the place of God, this is the ultimate form of mystification." Rose, *supra* note 32, at 50. *See also* ŽIŽEK, THE INDIVISIBLE REMAINDER, *supra* note 12, 158–61.

In market relations, we substitute actual, seemingly real, objects for the object lost in castration, in the dream that if we can just obtain that desired object, we will be complete.[76] And so we act as though it is really that wedding ring, big new house, fancy sports car, or whatever that will make us happy. This is a fantasy that cannot bear close scrutiny. The wedding ring is only a phantasm, not our true desire. If we were to turn around to look directly at our fantasy, as Orpheus turned to look at Eurydice, the fantasy would come to an end. We can only see the real if "eyed awry." [77] Eros functions only so long as we keep up pretenses.

In contrast, when we take on the feminine sexuated position, we are sometimes able to glimpse the real in an experience Lacan calls feminine *jouissance*—an enjoyment supplemental to masculine phallic *jouissance*[78] Despite the name, however, enjoyment is not enjoyable in the conventional sense of the word, because to achieve the real is to leave the symbolic, and therefore to lose one's own personality. *Jouissance* is the hope of wholeness in ecstatic union with the feminine as Phallic Mother. But when we actually confront the real, we see that it results in the obliteration of self. Consequently, *jouissance* is also the gut-wrenching horror of staring into the abyss.[79] This is

76. I explore this process at length in Schroeder, *Chix, supra* note 49. This is not to imply that human beings do not have certain biological (i.e., real) requirements (such as food and shelter) that are also satisfied through market relations. Indeed, Lacan recognized that "need" is the real equivalent to the symbolic longing of desire (and the imaginary form of longing called "demand"). Rather the Lacanian position is to hypothesize that property cannot be reduced to such "real" concerns and that market relations are not entered primarily to meet "needs." SALECL, *supra* note 67, at 124.

77. SLAVOJ ŽIŽEK, LOOKING AWRY: AN INTRODUCTION TO JACQUES LACAN THROUGH POPULAR CULTURE 9–12 (quoting William Shakespeare, *Richard II*) (1992) [hereinafter ŽIŽEK, LOOKING AWRY].

78. There is no precise English cognate for the French word "*jouissance*" used by Lacan. Literally, it refers to enjoyment or joyfulness generally. It includes the legal right of "enjoyment" of property, but is also a slang term for sexual orgasm specifically. BICE BENEVENUTO & ROGER KENNEDY, THE WORKS OF JACQUES LACAN: AN INTRODUCTION 179 (1986). Lacan's term is not perfectly translatable because it is defined as that which is beyond the masculine, symbolic order of language. What I will generally refer to as *jouissance* is in fact one aspect of the concept more precisely called "feminine" *jouissance*. Jacques-Alain Miller, Lacan's son-in-law and editor of Lacan's seminars, has identified at least six different "paradigms" of *jouissance* adopted by Lacan over time. Jacques-Alain Miller, *Address* at SYMPOSIUM. THE SUBJECT—ENCORE: THE FORMATION OF THE AMERICAN LACANIAN LINK March 6, 1999, University of California at Los Angeles. Also: "If, as Lacan taught, unconscious drives do not always wish one's good, feminist theories that have equated *jouissance* with pleasure and the erotic pleasure of sexual freedom to gender liberation, have missed the meaning of Lacan's rethinking of the links between repetition, the death *beyond* the pleasure principle, and *jouissance*." Ragland-Sullivan, *supra* note 24, at 70.

79. *See generally* ŽIŽEK, LOOKING AWRY, *supra* note 77; ŽIŽEK, PLAGUE OF FANTASIES, *supra* note 27.

uniquely horrible because the abyss is simultaneously revealed to be the very center of our soul.

As in the masculine desire of Eros, the feminine desire of Thanatos must always be postponed, but for a different reason. To achieve the real is to be torn limb from limb by the ecstatic feminine of the Maenads. As with Eros, we must avoid looking too closely at Thanatos, but for a different reason. We are afraid to look at Eros because he is imaginary; he is not real enough. We are terrified to look at Thanatos because she is all too real. The ultimate reality is death.

But we are like children at a scary movie: although we cover our eyes, we can never resist the guilty pleasure of peeking through our fingers. As Slavoj Žižek says, "The trouble with *jouissance* is not that it is unattainable, that it always eludes our grasp, but, rather, that *one can never get rid of it.* . . . "[80]

Similarly, the law-and-economics movement, which neither describes actual markets nor adequately comes to grips with the its own ideal of the perfect market, is located in the imaginary. It is the weaving of a series of fantasy images in a vain attempt to reconcile the symbolic with the real. But law-and-economics cannot stand to look past the fantasy into the abyss of the perfect market.

What are contours of the real? By definition, we cannot explain the real in words (the symbolic) or depict it in pictures (the imaginary). The real is entirely negative. We must describe it in terms of what it is not.

We, as subjects, now feel separate from other persons. We imagine that once we must have been complete in ourselves and one with the other in order to love the other and be loved in return. The real is the universe before the big bang that created subjectivity (i.e., before castration). It is the ideal of perfect union with no mediation or alienating distinctions of any type which could separate us from the ideal mother. There is, therefore, no time in the real, since time separates yesterday from today and today from tomorrow. As is the case with the physical universe, time only began with the big bang of castration. The real is therefore an event, simultaneously both an instant and eternity. There can be no space in the real, since space separates here from there.[81] There are no objects in the real. Objects can only be understood in terms of that which is other than—different from—a subject.[82] But this requires that subject and object be separated. There can be

80. Žižek, The Indivisible Remainder, *supra* note 12, at 93.

81. Subjectivity itself is the birth of time and space—the conditions of possible experience. Kant, *supra* note 37, at 28–33.

82. "What is immediately different form the free spirit is, for the latter and in itself, the external in general—a *thing* [*Sache*], something unfree, impersonal and without rights." Hegel, The Philosophy of Right, *supra* note 26, at 73. *See also generally* Schroeder, *Chix, supra* note 49.

no desire in the real. Desire is the longing for wholeness. Since the real is that which is already perfect and whole, there is nothing left to desire. In the real we are totally indifferent to everything, because nothing is different from anything else.

That is, in the symbolic we are castrated and violated. In the real we are intact, yet impotent; virgin, yet sterile.

Most importantly, there is no subjectivity, no personality, no individuality in the real. As discussed in the previous chapter, to become a subject, I must be recognized by others. To be recognized, I must have distinguishing characteristics. But distinguishing characteristics, by definition, distinguish and thereby separate me from others. To restate this from the other side, to claim to be a subject, I must understand myself as being at least minimally different from someone or something else. This requires me to withdraw from and expel the other. In Lacan's terms, there are no sexual relations in the sense that all inter*subjective* relations are mediated. I must put space between me and the other. To have perfect union, I must give up all distinctions. I must give up myself.

Without individuality and without desire, not only is there no need for speech, but speech is impossible: there is no one to speak, no one to speak to, and nothing to speak about. As the Bible tells us: "In the beginning, the world was without form and void."

This is why the real—the *jouissance* of Thanatos—is not merely death (which might hold out the possibility of an afterlife, transmigration, or rebirth), but death beyond death, obliteration, Nirvana. We can only achieve subjectivity in the social realm of law, in the symbolic. Subjectivity includes the ability to speak, to have sexuality, and to attain consciousness. To leave the symbolic and (re)enter the real would be to lose one's subjectivity, one's individual personality.

Once again this is illustrated in myth. The Bible tells us that when God decided to destroy Sodom and Gomorrah, He told Lot and his family to leave but warned them not to turn around and look back at their homes and loved ones. Lot's wife heard the sounds of destruction behind her and gave way to her desire. In her *jouissance* she doubly turned—around and into a pillar of salt.[83] When Orpheus turned, he was driven by Eros. He sought to embrace the perfect fantasy wife. When he faced the image he constructed to serve as the object of desire, he merely lost this specific fantasy. His desire and his subjectivity remained. When Lot's wife turned, however, she was driven by Thanatos. She yearned to confront and return to her origins; she wanted to go home. By fulfilling her desire, she lost not merely her life but her self. She

83. *Genesis* 19: 26.

literally lost her subjectivity and became an inanimate object. Her very name, her individuality, was lost forever.[84] All we know about her is that she had been married to Lot.[85]

THE PERFECT MARKET

The Ideal of the Perfect Market

Mainstream economics is driven by a number of closely related ideals that I shall call collectively the "perfect market." Achieving the efficiency[86] of the perfect market is the object of the economist's desire and the end towards which all actual markets aspire. According to legal economists, efficiency would be achieved if the ideal of the perfect market were implemented. We should, therefore, modify our legal and political institutions so as to make the actual market as nearly perfect as we can or, if that is impossible, to replicate the results of the perfect market as closely as possible.[87]

Given the centrality of the ideal of the perfect market, one would expect that there would be a substantial economic literature delineating its characteristics. Yet there is remarkable silence among both lawyers and economists on the issue. I started this project largely because over the years I had heard numerous critics of law-and-economics movement assert that the concept of

84. She is not merely lost to man, but, given the tradition that Genesis was written by Moses under inspiration of the Holy Spirit, lost to God as well.

85. SCHROEDER, THE VESTAL AND THE FASCES, *supra* note 4.

86. There are several standard versions of efficiency, but they all revolve around achieving a proper allocation of resources in society. The two most common formulations of efficiency are based on the maximization of an aggregate valued quality. Utility maximizers argue, as the name implies, that society should maximize the aggregate utility (roughly, happiness) in society. For a brief discussion of utilitarian economics, see GEORGE J. STIGLER, ESSAYS IN THE HISTORY OF ECONOMICS 66–155 (1965) [hereinafter, STIGLER, ESSAYS]. Others, most notably Posner, champion wealth maximization. *See, e.g.*, Richard Posner, *Utilitarianism, Economics, and Legal Theory*, 8 J. LEG. STUD. 103, 110–111 (1979). I discuss the distinction between these two desiderata in Chapter 4.

87. For example, the Calabresi-Melamed trichotomy of environmental nuisance remedial regimes, which is the subject of Chapter 3, was developed as a tool for studying whether there were ways of variously lowering transaction costs, mimicking the results that would result absent transaction costs, or stimulating bargaining despite the existence of transaction costs. Guido Calabresi & A. Douglas Melamed, *Property Rules, Liability Rules, and Inalienability: One View of the Cathedral*, 85 HARV. L. REV. 1089 (1972). Alternatively, Ian Ayres and Eric Talley suggest legal rules that do not mimic the efficient result, but which are supposed to cause parties to act in such a way that would make the market more efficient (by, for example, incentivizing the parties to reveal information). *See generally* Ian Ayres & Eric Talley, *Solomonic Bargaining: Dividing a Legal Entitlement to Facilitate Coasean Trade*, 104 YALE L. J. 1027 (1995) [hereinafter, Ayres & Talley, *Solomonic Bargaining*].

perfect markets was surprisingly not worked out, considering its importance. As a former student of economics, I replied, "That's nonsense. Every introductory economics text book contains a discussion of the perfect market." Indeed, I thought I remembered reading such discussions, albeit almost thirty years ago when I was a college student. "Show me," my interlocutors would challenge. In an attempt to prove them wrong I searched for such a discussion. To my surprise, the discussions I found were sketchy and conclusory. This chapter reflects the result on my search for a coherent analysis of the perfect market. This led me to try to understand the underlying logic of the perfect market, as it is so imperfectly described in the literature, as well as why economists and lawyers (including myself) not only fail to attempt such an analysis, but repress the fact that they do so.

For example, Richard Posner's standard introduction to law-and-economics, *Economic Analysis of Law*,[88] nowhere defines the concept of the perfect market. Classically trained economists, such as Ronald Coase and George Stigler, are scarcely braver.[89] Paul Samuelson and William Nordhaus's introductory economic textbook on classic price theory[90] only contains a few passing sentences as to the parameters of this founding ideal. In other works, if discussed at all, selected conditions of the perfect market are alluded to in an incomplete and unsystematic way. Frequently, if not usually, the author assumes that its characteristics are generally known, and therefore need not be explicated.

Compare this phenomenon with William Blackstone's famous observation that we desire property yet are afraid to confront its origins, which I quote at the head of this book. We are now in a position to understand my suggestion that this embarrassed reticence shown by law-and-economics

88. Richard Posner, Economic Analysis of Law (5th ed. 1998) [hereinafter, Posner, Economic Analysis of Law].

89. George Stigler has probably written most extensively about perfect markets and the related concept of perfect competition, and even he is, at best, parsimonious. He admits that its contours are not clear: "The minimum assumptions for a theoretical model [of the perfect market] can be stated with precision only when the complete theory of that model is known. The complete theory of competition cannot be known because it is an open-ended theory; it is always possible that a new range of problems will be posed in this framework, and then, no matter how well developed the theory was with respect to the earlier range of problems, it may require extensive elaboration in respects which previously it glossed over or ignored." George J. Stigler, *Perfect Competition, Historically Contemplated, in* Microeconomics: Selected Readings 183 (Edward Mansfield ed., 1971). *See also* David Gray Carlson, *On the Margins of Microeconomics* 14 Cardozo L. Rev. 1867, 1880 (1993) [hereinafter, Carlson, *Margins of Microeconomics*]. Nevertheless, Stigler has attempted a description: "A perfect market is one characterized by perfect knowledge on the part of the traders. Or, stated differently, in a perfect market no buyer ever pays more than any seller will accept, and no seller accepts less than any buyer will pay." George J. Stigler, The Theory of Price 82 (1987) [hereinafter, Stigler, Price].

90. Paul A. Samuelson & William D. Nordhaus, Economics (15th ed. 1995).

reflects the essentially erotic nature of markets. Confronting what I have called the erotic origins of market theory causes us to blush with a shame comparable to that which we would feel if forced to consider our own erotic origins. In both cases, we fear to gaze into the abyss. Why?

I believe that the reason is the psychoanalytic nature of the perfect market. The perfect market is in the impossible order of the real. Actual markets are in the legal, intersubjective order of the symbolic. As such, the perfect market is the death of the actual market. The perfect market is an extraordinary world with no differentiation, no time, no space, no desire, no exchange, no objects—no subjectivity. We cannot bear to contemplate directly the ideal of the perfect market, just as we cannot resist our desire for it. Being real and neither imaginary nor symbolic, the perfect market is not merely impossible, it is literally unimaginable and unspeakable. Consequently, in the legal imaginary, we erect unthreatening fantasy images of the market that seem more satisfying than actual markets yet less terrifying than perfect markets.

In order to continue to create, we must follow our desire. Yet we will lose the object of desire if we try to confront the fantasies we erect to stand in its place, as Orpheus found out when he tried to embrace Eurydice. Moreover, if we were to actually achieve our desire, we would lose not merely our desire, but our very existence as free subjects, as Orpheus and Lot's wife learned when they achieved *jouissance.*

Consequently, for the ideal of the perfect market to function, two things are necessary. First, its contours must be repressed and replaced with a fantasy image. Second, desire must always be postponed. The perfect market can never be achieved, because to do so would destroy the actual market and our freedom. We dare not give way to our desire.

One might suggest that the fact that the perfect market is impossible is irrelevant to economic analysis. All ideals, this argument would say, are impossible. This does not mean that we shouldn't strive to be as close to the ideal as possible. This specific simplistic analysis is inept, although a more sophisticated analysis may be of some interest.

First and foremost, I agree that one should not necessarily give up an ideal one has adopted for philosophical, religious, or other reasons—such as freedom, justice, grace, or whatever—just because it is empirically impossible. Ideals serve as inspiration even if they are not a reasonable aspiration. My complaint is not, therefore, the impossibility of the ideal, but rather the failure of economics to consider the implications of having an impossible ideal. This can lead to the incorrect conclusion (and resultant complacency) that the goal has been already reached or is within sight, or that one's policy recommendations will result in the achievement of something close to the ideal.

Those legal economists who formulate legal rules designed to mimic the results that would have been achieved if the market were perfect must first describe the contours of the perfect market they wish to emulate. This task is not merely impracticable; it is logically impossible. To pretend to describe what would happen in the perfect market is a fantasy in the technical sense of the term: it is an attempt to erect a seemingly attainable imaginary substitute for the unattainable, indescribable, and unimaginable real. Those legal economists who seek to make the actual market more efficient run up against the logical problem of the "second best."[91]

A fundamental concept of classical economics—and one of Coase's primary points—is that *if* one has a market with numerous imperfections, *then* one cannot assume a priori that correction of any one imperfection in the market will move one any closer to achieving the perfect market. That is, even if one accepts that the perfect market is only an asymptote that one approaches but never reaches, the theory of the second best states that if one cannot remove *all* imperfections, then one can never predict *as a logical matter* what one can do to get closer to that goal. In other words, one cannot deduce the second best alternative from a hypothesized first best one.[92]

What the economist *can* do is to make empirical studies of the practical effects of certain changes in certain contexts under certain conditions, and then make pragmatic, contextualized, and contingent recommendations. This is an economic corollary to Hegel's fundamental principle that while philosophical logic may generate abstract, generalized principles, it cannot be used to make day-to-day pragmatic decisions or to legislate specific positive law. This is not to say that many economists have not heard Coase's call to engage in such empirical research and pragmatic reasoning. It is to note, however, that such a pragmatic approach, while not unknown, is still relatively unusual in *legal* scholarship.

Let us proceed to the literature. The usual way the perfect market is described, in good Hegelian-Lacanian fashion, is by reference to what it is not.[93] Consequently, in this chapter I develop a definition of the perfect mar-

91. Richard G. Lipsey & Kelvin J. Lancaster, *The General Theory of the Second Best,* 24 REV. ECON. STUD. 11 (1956).

92. Although there are many discussions of the theory of the second best in law reviews, they tend to be by critics, not practitioners, of standard law and economics. For suggested explanations of this phenomena, *see* Richard S. Markovits, *Second Best Theory and the Standard Analysis of Monopoly Rent-Seeking: Generalizable Critique, a "Sociological" Account, and Some Illustrative Stories,* 78 IOWA L. REV. 327 (1993); Richard S. Markovits, *Monopoly and Allocative Efficiency of First-Best-Allocatively-Efficient Tort Law in Our Worse-than-Second-Best World: The Whys and Some Therefores,* 46 CASE W. RES. L. REV. 313 (1996); *and* David Gray Carlson, *On the Efficiency of Secured Lending,* 80 VA. L. REV. 2179 (1994).

93. For example, in their classic economics textbook, Paul Samuelson and William Nordhaus call the conditions that prevent a market from achieving perfection "market failure," defined as "an imperfection in a price system that prevents an efficient allocation of resources. Important examples are *externalities* and *imperfect competition.*" SAMUELSON & NORDHAUS, *supra* note 90, at 909.

ket by identifying what it lacks. By definition, the perfect market lacks imperfections, and imperfections are called "transaction costs."

Perfect Competition

A brief aside before turning my vulture eye upon transaction costs: It is often assumed that a perfect market is characterized by perfect competition. I will not include perfect competition as a necessary component of the perfect market for a number or reasons.

First, competition is only a *means* to achieve the *end* of a perfect market. Classical price theory argues that perfect competition will lead to this efficient pricing.[94] It does not follow from the proposition that perfect competition can lead to the pricing necessary for a perfect market, that perfect competition is the *only* possible means to this end. Coase himself argues that markets (and therefore the subset of perfectly competitive markets) are only one of a variety of institutions that a society could develop in order to reduce transaction costs; another institution is the firm.[95] Which alternative is superior depends on the specific fact situation. Indeed, Stigler goes further to suggest that "it was unfortunate that a perfect market was made a subsidiary characteristic of competition, for in realistic cases a perfect market may also exist under monopoly, since complete knowledge is easier to achieve under monopoly."[96]

Second, once efficiency is reached, the distinction between many market

94. A perfect market requires a specific pricing structure, which makes all consumers and producers indifferent among all commodities in the market place. Consequently, if the Samuelson and Nordhaus definition is examined more closely we can see that they merely see imperfect competition as a factor that can lead to imperfect pricing, and therefore inefficient allocation of resources. *Id.* at 264.

95. R. H. Coase, The Firm, The Market, and the Law 5–10 (1988) [hereinafter, Coase, The Firm, The Market, and the Law].

96. Stigler, Essays, *supra* note 86, at 262. As Stigler notes, it is wrong to think that the only efficient markets are those with unlimited numbers of participants and perfect competition:

> The merging of the concepts of competition and the market was unfortunate, for each deserved a full and separate treatment. A market is an institution for the consummation of transactions. It performs this function efficiently when every buyer who will pay more than the minimum realized price for any class of commodities succeeds in buying the commodity, and every seller who will sell for less than the maximum realized prices succeeds in selling the commodity. A market performs these tasks more efficiently if the commodities are well specified and if buyers and sellers are fully informed of their properties and prices. Possibly also a perfect market allows buyers and sellers to act on different expectations of future prices. A market may be perfect and monopolistic or imperfect and competitive.

Id. at 245.

participants and one participant—between competitive markets and monopoly—disappears. All participants lose individuality, so no one has market power.

Finally, and most importantly, it is my fundamental thesis that if the perfect efficiency of the perfect market were to be achieved, all actual markets—and therefore all competition—would end. As Coase himself has stated: "Markets are institutions that exist to facilitate exchange, that is, they exist in order to reduce the cost of carrying out exchange transactions. In an economic theory which assumes that transaction costs are nonexistent, markets have no function to perform."[97]

The Coase Theorem

The concept of transaction costs as discussed in legal scholarship purports to derive primarily from the Coase Theorem. Ironically, the oft-misinterpreted Coase[98] is one of the few economists who has come close to internalizing the psychoanalytic and philosophic implications of the perfect market ideal.

It has often been noted that Coase did not expressly set forth his famous theorem in *The Theory of Social Cost,*[99] but merely alluded to it indirectly. I would go further. In context, Coase's allusion to what has become known in legal literature as the Coase Theorem was only a relatively minor corollary of his larger actual theorem.

First and foremost, Coase was not, as is usually thought, making any claim

97. COASE, THE FIRM, THE MARKET, AND THE LAW, *supra* note 95, at 7–8. Stigler implicitly agrees. He restates the Coase Theorem as "under perfect competition private and social costs will be equal." GEORGE J. STIGLER, THE THEORY OF PRICE 113 (3d. ed. 1966) (quoted in COASE, THE FIRM THE MARKET AND THE LAW, *supra* note 95, at 158). But, Stigler also asserts that in a world of zero transaction costs "monopolies would be induced to 'act like competitors.' " COASE, THE FIRM THE MARKET AND THE LAW, *supra* note 95, at 158 (quoting George J. Stigler, *The Law and Economics of Public Policy: A Plea to the Scholars,* 1 J. OF LEG. STUD. 1, 12 [1972]). Consequently, as Coase realizes, Stigler's proposition should be reduced to "with zero transaction costs, private and social costs will be equal" deleting the requirement of perfect competition as redundant. COASE, THE FIRM THE MARKET AND THE LAW, *supra* note 95, at 158. To put this in another way, in the perfect market all prices are set so that *all* parties are price takers.

98. In a recent article, Daniel Farber also argued that Coase has been misunderstood, leaving "what became known as the Coase Theorem almost as a kind of parody of reductionist theory." Daniel A. Farber, *Parody Lost / Pragmatism Regained: The Ironic History of the Coase Theorem,* 83 VIR. L. REV. 397, 398 (1997). I agree. Farber alleges, however, that "despite the fact that his message was misunderstood, the article sparked a debate that ultimately helped foster the kind of pragmatist scholarship he actually advocated in law and economics." *Id.* Not only do I disagree with this statement, but I believe that Farber himself does not fully internalize many of Coase's most important points.

99. R. H. Coase, *The Problem of Social Cost,* 3 J.L. & ECON. 1 (1960) [hereinafter, Coase, *The Problem of Social Cost*].

about the contours of a hypothetical world without transaction costs. Coase was instead trying to develop a new paradigm for defining and identifying economic costs in actual markets.

It is in this context that he throws out in passing what is frequently called the "Coase Theorem": in a perfect world without transaction costs, it doesn't matter how the law allocates legal rights because people will always contract to reallocate such entitlements in an economically efficient manner. But this is not, as is so frequently thought, a hypothesis about what would happen if certain identifiable costs were eliminated or reduced. Rather it is an assertion that the conditions of a perfect market are impossible.[100] As Coase states, "But the whole discussion [of ideal worlds] is largely irrelevant for questions of economic policy since whatever we may have in mind as our ideal world, it is clear that we have not yet discovered how to get to it from where we are."[101] It is not adequate for economists to propose policies to reduce specific costs, because of the theory of the second best: if we cannot eliminate *all* imperfections, we cannot predict a priori whether the elimination of any one cost will have a positive or negative effect. As Coase says, "But in choosing between social arrangements within the context of which individual decisions are made, we have to bear in mind that a change in the existing system which will lead to an improvement in some decisions may well lead to a wors-

100. This is impossible by definition. Thoughtful economists realize that there can be no perfect markets in the real world. They argue that the perfect market nevertheless is a useful ideal model to serve as a starting point for analysis. For example, the perfect market is sometimes metaphorically described as a world without friction. *See, e.g.*, Calabresi & Melamed, *supra* note 87, at 1095 (1972). The fact that friction cannot be eliminated entirely in the real world does not prevent classical Newtonian mechanics—which posits such a frictionless world—from being true or useful.

Coase disputes the policy implications that he believes economists have drawn from this analogy. To state Coase's point within the terminology of the metaphor, although engineers are trained in the physics of mechanics, they do not make the mistake of designing machines as though friction did not exist. Rather, their entire skill consists of understanding and compensating the practical implications of friction, inertia, and the other empirical limitations on theory. In contrast, when economists propose policies, they do not give sufficient consideration to the friction of economics—transaction costs. Instead they design their economic machines based on the frictionless market (i.e., what would theoretically happen if the markets were perfect), and then after the fact try to compensate for friction. Alternatively, they incorrectly assume that if they minimize one source of friction (one type of transaction cost), the machine will work more nearly as though friction did not exist. This does not necessarily follow, as different sources of friction might counterbalance each other. Consequently, eliminating *one* source of friction without simultaneously addressing other sources might in fact result in even more inefficient activity.

I discuss Posner's and Milton Friedman's misuse of the friction metaphor in Jeanne L. Schroeder, *Just So Stories: Posnerian Methodology*, 22 CARDOZO L. REV. 351 (2001) [hereinafter, Schroeder, *Just So Stories*].

101. Coase, *The Problem of Social Cost*, *supra* note 99, at 43.

ening of others."[102] Coase was asserting that since transaction costs *always* exist, economists should concentrate on the real world of costs, not a hypothetical perfect, costless world. This requires that economics adopt an appropriate definition of costs.

> A better approach would seem to be to start our analysis with a situation approximating that which actually exists, to examine the effects of a proposed policy change and to attempt to decide whether the new situation would be, in total, better or worse than the original one. In this way, conclusions for policy would have some relevance to the actual situation.[103]

Or, to put it more strongly: Coase thought that mainstream economists were mystics. The economists' dream of a perfect world without costs is a vision of Heaven. There can be no heavenly economics because, in Heaven, all our desires are always already fulfilled. Economists are wrong in assuming that they can learn about the sublunar world by studying the celestial. Economics is a failure precisely because it has failed to get down to earth and study real markets characterized by real costs and real choices.[104]

To repeat this point in Lacanian terminology, the perfect market (where all desires are fulfilled) is in the order of the real. Actual markets are creatures of law and communication, and are therefore located in the flawed, incomplete, artificial realm of the symbolic. Symbolic markets function because they are walled off from the real by the barrier of castration. Coase proposes that we think of costs as whatever keeps actual markets from being perfect markets. Transaction costs are, therefore, the economic analog to the psychoanalytic concept of castration. Despite the fact that (or more accurately, because) castration makes the real and the symbolic structurally incompatible, we are unsatisfied by the symbolic and we desire the real. It is this very gap, this desire, that serves as the engine that makes actual markets function. Nevertheless, we vainly attempt the impossible task of bridging this gap through fantasy images generated in the imaginary.

Similarly, mainstream economics, when it purports to deduce something

102. *Id.* at 44. As far as I know, Coase does not use Lipsey and Lancaster's second-best terminology (apparently coined in their article published four years earlier than *The Problem of Social Cost*), but his proposition is consistent with their theory.

103. *Id.* at 43.

104. No doubt Coase's complaint was an exaggeration, even at the time he was writing. I would note, however, that whether or not economists in academia, government, and business are doing more of the type of empirical work for which Coase called, the vast majority of legal writing that invokes economic theory continues to rely on the type of speculative armchair arguments Coase criticizes.

about actual markets by analyzing ideal ones, is engaged in the imaginary act of fantasy. This is why, despite Coase's express language to the contrary, legal economists persist in purporting to study the "world of zero transaction costs, to which the Coase Theorem [supposedly] applies,"[105] even though it is "remote from the real world."[106] In a stinging reproach to the law-and-economics movement, Coase suggests: "The reason for this movement of economic theory into neighboring fields is certainly not that we have solved the problems of the economic system; it would perhaps be more plausible to argue that economists are looking for fields in which they can have some success."[107]

In *The Theory of Social Cost,* Coase critiqued the Pigouvian tax. In context, however, it is clear that this was intended as a specific example of the dominant paradigm of *costs.*

Pigou analyzed pollution and other "externalities" as the failure of producers to internalize all costs of production, thereby resulting in misallocation of resources. He proposed that government could force producers to internalize costs by taxing them in an amount equal to the costs otherwise exported to third parties.

Coase thought that Pigou's reasoning was faulty because Pigou, like most economists, unwittingly adopted an implicit natural law view of costs and causation. This conflates the legal status quo with economic reality. Pigou assumed that all losses suffered by any individual from changes in the legal status quo were *economic* costs. Assuming that a person who suffered the change in the status also incurred an economic cost led to the unwarranted conclusion that the party who made the change in the status quo caused an economic loss.[108]

For example, if one were to start from the assumption that a consumer has a property right in the clean water in the well on her property, then if the neighboring producer were to pour pollutants into the aquifer, the producer would be interfering with the consumer's property rights. Pigou assumed from the fact that the consumer suffered a legal harm (interference with a property right), society thereby incurred an economic cost. Moreover,

105. Coase, *The Problem of Social Cost, supra* note 99, at 15.

106. *Id.*

107. Ronald Coase, *Economics and Contiguous Disciplines,* 7 J. LEG. STUD. 201, 203 (1978). This is in part because Coase himself does not always have the fortitude to heed his own warning and postpone his desire. He frequently falls off the wagon, enters the imaginary, and tries to describe the unknowable perfect market.

108. For simplicity, in this discussion I am assuming a two-party transaction in a two-party world. I sharply criticize this approach in Chapter 3 but believe that it is sufficient for the very limited purpose of introducing the Coasean analysis.

Pigou assumed that if the producer interfered with the consumer's right as a matter of law, then the producer was the sole cause of an economic loss experienced by the consumer.

Coase, in contrast, rejected the existing paradigm of costs, with its implicit natural law jurisprudence. Coase's paradigm is based on a radical positivist view of law with an implicit Hohfeldian turn. Hohfeld is the most eloquent exponent of the position that legal rights can only be understood in terms of relationships between or among legal subjects.[109] Similarly, Coase thought that costs could only be understood relationally—or, in his language, costs are always reciprocal.[110]

From a legal viewpoint, I suffer a *legally cognizable* loss only if there is a change in the status quo— i.e., interference with a pre-existing legal rights or imposition of a new legal obligation.[111] But, according to Coase, since all rights and obligations are interrelational, both parties are always *but-for* causes of all losses. That is, when a producer pours pollutants into the water supply, the fact that a consumer claims the right to drink clean water is as much a but-for cause of any "loss" by the consumer as the producer's pollution of the water.[112] A legal decision in favor of the consumer is precisely a decision as to how we will assign *legal* (i.e., symbolic) causality, not *natural* (i.e., real) causality.[113] Consequently, Coase himself eschews the term

109. Wesley Newcomb Hohfeld, Fundamental Legal Conceptions as Applied in Legal Reasoning (W. Cook ed., 1919). This idea was hardly original to Hohfeld. *See generally* Schroeder, *Chix, supra* note 49. Nevertheless, he so convincingly illustrated it in his magisterial theory of jural correlatives and opposites that the recognition of the relational nature of legal rights is justifiably tied to his name.

110. As I discuss in Chapter 3, opponents have misinterpreted Coase's insistence on the reciprocity of costs as an assertion that all economic entitlements are equal and mirror images of one another.

111. For simplicity, in this chapter I am using the term "right" not in the narrow Hohfeldian sense, but rather, for lack of a more convenient term, as a catchall phrase for any or all of the four Hohfeldian desirables. I am using the term "obligation" as a catchall for any or all of the four Hohfeldian undesirables.

112. For example, Coase asserts: "The answer seems fairly clear. The smoke nuisance was caused both by the man who built the wall *and* by the man who lit the fires. Given the fires, there would have been no smoke nuisance without the wall; given the wall, there would have been no smoke nuisance without the fire. Eliminate the wall *or* the fires and the smoke nuisance would disappear." Coase, *The Problem of Social Cost, supra* note 99, at 13. Coase does not use the specific example of water pollution but draws his illustration from a number of English common law cases. I explicate the Coasean-inspired water pollution example in Chapter 3.

113. Even some of his admirers miss this point. For example, Farber states that whereas Pigou thought that "cost allocations should track physical causation," Coase thought that we should "design institutions that will maximize the overall well-being of society." Farber, *supra* note 99, at 420. But as we have seen, Coase is denying the naturalness of Pigou's causation assumptions. Pigou's concept of cause follows not physical but legal rules—it is not real, but symbolic. From a physical viewpoint the presence of the consumer who wants to drink water is every

"externality" because it begs the question, *presupposing* the solution to the economic problem that should be explored. That is, it assumes a specific causal relationship and allocation of entitlements and liabilities. Coase instead prefers the more neutral "harmful effects."[114]

Under the traditional paradigm, economists uncritically imported a definition of costs from law. Economics, however, should adopt its own paradigm of costs. Economics, according to Coase, is concerned with the goal of efficiency, in the sense of maximization of the value of production as measured by the market.[115] Law, in contradistinction, has other goals, which Coase refers to generally as "aesthetics and morals."[116] If law tries to assign rights and obligations in accordance with the goals of law, there is no reason to think that legal costs and causality (dependent on the legal status quo) will be identical to economic costs and causality.[117] Economists should, therefore, develop their own concept of costs and causality to serve economic goals.[118] In Lacanian terms, the fact that law and markets are both located in the symbolic does not mean that they are the same. Legal losses, therefore, are not necessarily the same as economic costs.

Consequently, Coase chided his fellow economists for ignoring the significance of legal rules. Like natural lawyers, economists implicitly assumed the existence of a pregiven law without realizing that laws are written by soci-

---

bit as much a but-for cause as the production of widgets for the harm caused when water is polluted.

114. COASE, THE FIRM, THE MARKET, AND THE LAW, *supra* note 95, at 26–27. *See also* Stewart Schwab, *Coase Defends Coase: Why Lawyers Listen and Economists Do Not,* 87 MICH. L. REV. 1171, 1184–85 n.37 (1989).

115. Coase, *Problem of Social Cost, supra* note 99, at 43.

116. *Id.*

117. In Coase's words, "Judges have to decide on legal liability but this should not confuse economists about the nature of the economic problem involved." *Id.* at 13. He continues:

> The reasoning employed by the courts in determining legal rights will often seem strange to an economist because many of the factors on which the decision turns are, to an economist, irrelevant. Because of this, situations which are, from an economic point of view, identical will be treated quite differently by the courts. The economic problem in all cases of harmful effects is how to maximize the value of production. . . . But it has to be remembered that the immediate question faced by the courts is *not* what shall be done by whom *but* who has the legal right to do what.

Id. at 15.

118. Interestingly, Stigler seems to believe that lawyers agree that the goal of economics (like law) should be justice, whereas economists have given up purporting to know what society's goals should be. George J. Stigler, *The Law and Economics of Public Policy: A Plea to the Scholars,* 1 J. OF LEG. STUD. 1, 2 (1972) [hereinafter, Stigler, *Plea to Scholars*]. This is ironic, because one reason why law-and-economics has become so trendy is precisely because many law professors find the goals of our own discipline to be controversial and assume that economics provides certainty.

ety. In the world in which we live, he argued, the choice of legal rules that assign legal entitlements is not merely significant; it can be outcome determinative because it is costly to change the initial allocation.[119] It is at this juncture of the argument that Coase throws out the statement that would later be known as the Coase Theorem:

> It is always possible to modify by transactions on the market the initial legal delimitation of rights. And, of course, if such market transactions are costless, such a rearrangement of rights will always take place if it would lead to an increase in the value of production.[120]

Only in a perfect world, where there are no costs to changing legal entitlements, is the initial allocation of legal entitlements irrelevant. As Coasean enthusiast Calabresi puts it: "If one assumes rationality, no transaction costs, and no legal impediments to bargaining, *all* mis-allocations of resources would be fully cured in the market by bargains."[121]

Many legal economists try to deny Coase's tautologous definition of transaction costs.[122] Daniel Farber goes so far as to assert that Coase would not have

119. According to Coase:

> In these conditions [i.e., when transaction costs exist] the initial delimitation of legal rights does have an effect on the efficiency with which the economic system operates. One arrangement of rights may bring about a greater value of production than any other. But unless this is the arrangement of rights established by the legal system, the costs of reaching the same result by altering and combining rights through the market may be so great that this optimal arrangement of rights, and the greater value of production which it would bring, may never be achieved.

Coase, *The Problem of Social Cost,* supra note 99, at 16.

120. *Id.* at 15.

121. Guido Calabresi, *Transaction Costs, Resource Allocation and Liability Rules—A Comment,* 11 J. OF L. & ECON 67, 68 (1968) [hereinafter, Calabresi, *Transaction Costs*].

122. For example, Daniel Farber states that "the best interpretation of Coase, then, would seem to be that a 'transaction cost' is something more than a label for failure to reach a bargain." Farber critiques this as an "abstract definition" (Farber, *supra* note 98, at 405) and rejects an "unbounded ('anything that prevents a bargain')" definition of transaction costs. *Id.* Stewart Schwab makes similar arguments in Schwab, *supra* note 114.

Robert Cooter tries to make a distinction between a tautology and a theorem: "A tautology is true by virtue of the definition of words. A theorem is true by virtue of its deduction from the assumptions or a theory. Tautologies are based upon linguistic conventions and theorems are based upon theoretical assumptions. The power of Coase's Theorem is explained by the fact that it is treated as if it were an economic theorem, that is, a proposition deduced from standard economic assumptions." Robert Cooter, *The Cost of Coase,* 11 J. OF LEG. STUD. 1, 14 (1982).

From this, Cooter draws the non sequitur that in order to treat the Coasean observation as a "theorem" one must read it as an empirical prediction—that is, as the hypothesis that under certain identifiable empirical conditions legal rules can be shown to be irrelevant to efficiency. *Id.* We should then be able to test this hypothesis through falsification by identifying a test cases

received a Nobel Prize for suggesting a mere truism.[123] Consequently, he argues that the term "transaction costs" should be interpreted "as measurable costs of entering into transactions."[124] Of course, as Coase offers no statistical or experimental evidence to support any statement about any specific "measurable cost," Farber is suggesting, in effect, that the Nobel committee awards prizes for unsupported empirical claims—surely a dim view of the Nobel Prize.

These views reflect a basic misunderstanding of the difference between a *theorem* and a *theory*.[125] All scientific theorems, as opposed to theories, are tautologies: they are necessarily true given the acceptance of both definitions and assumptions. In contradistinction, theories are hypotheses that need to be empirically tested. To say that theorems are tautologous is not, however, to imply that they are empty.[126]

Theorems are paradigms—ways of organizing and interpreting the world. A theorem, or paradigm, is not itself empirically tested. Rather, it generates a set of subsidiary hypotheses or theories that might be tested.[127] Coase proposed a paradigm shift: a revolutionary new way of defining the problem of

---

in which these conditions exist and then determining whether or not the legal rules made a difference.

123. "On the tautologous interpretation, Coase's theory of the firm would reduce to: 'Market transactions are used to structure production except when they aren't.' This is hardly the stuff of which Nobel prizes are made." Farber, *supra* note 98, at 405.

124. *Id.*

125. For example, in the passage quoted *supra* in note 122, Cooter offers a definition of a theorem similar to mine, but then incorrectly assumes that theorems are falsifiable.

An extreme example of this misunderstanding of the nature of the Coase Theorems is the attempt of Elizabeth Hoffman to "test" the theorem through laboratory experiments. *See* Elizabeth Hoffman & Matthew L. Spitzer, *Experimental Law and Economics*, 85 COLUM. L. REV. 991, 1009–21 (1995); and Elizabeth Hoffman & Matthew L. Spitzer, *The Coase Theorem: Some Experimental Tests*, 25 J.L & ECON. 73 (1982).

126. Philosophers of science since at least Immanuel Kant have recognized that one can study the object world only from a specific subjective perspective. *See generally* KANT, *supra* note 37. For example, it is impossible to perceive the object world as a whole. One must consciously choose what to look at and how to organize it. Consequently, even Karl Popper, the arch-defender of the possibility of "objective" scientific knowledge, insisted that all scientific investigation begins with an inevitable and necessary subjective, irrational moment. KARL R. POPPER, THE LOGIC OF SCIENTIFIC DISCOVERY 31–32 (Karl R. Popper et al. trans., 2d. ed. 1968). To Popper, scientific objectivity is more accurately intersubjectivity—the consensus of a self-selected elite community of scientists reached after the application of an agreed-on methodology. *Id.* at 44. Jeanne L. Schroeder, *Abduction From the Seraglio: Feminist Methodologies and the Logic of Imagination*, 70 TEX. L. REV. 109, 161–64 (1991), Schroeder, *Just So Stories*, *supra* note 100, at 407–10. Thomas Kuhn called Popper's concept of perspectivity and intersubjectivity "paradigms." THOMAS KUHN, THE STRUCTURE OF SCIENTIFIC REVOLUTIONS 43–51 (2d. ed. 1970).

127. The falsification of any specific subsidiary hypothesis does not in and of itself necessarily disprove the overarching theorem. Kuhn argues that one accepts or rejects a paradigm not because it is logically or empirically proven (which is impossible), but for "good reasons,"

costs. Arguably, it is precisely this tautologous nature of Coase's theorem that warranted a Nobel Prize.[128]

Coase has famously claimed that his theories are little followed by his fellow economists. Schwab suggests that the reason why Coase is more followed by law professors than economists is that lawyers are used to examining and questioning the legal status quo. "Economists, on the other hand, are more apt to take the initial distribution of rights or entitlements as given and examine how parties will trade or respond to them."[129]

This, of course, is *precisely* Coase's critique. Most economists, who tend to act like normal scientists, fail to grasp that Coase is engaging in revolutionary science.[130] Unfortunately, despite Schwab's claims to the contrary, most

---

such as "accuracy, scope, simplicity, fruitfulness, and the like." KUHN, *supra* note 126, at 166. Although Popper considered himself an opponent of Kuhn, Kuhn himself believed that he was merely bringing Popper's theory of "sophisticated" falsification to its logical conclusion. According to Lakatos's reading of Popper, the sophisticated scientist does not reject a hypothesis merely because he observes seemingly inconsistent empirical evidence. Rather, he first tries to develop alternative explanations or auxiliary hypotheses to account for the apparent anomaly. Imre Lakatos, *Falsification and the Methodology of Scientific Research Programmes,* in CRITICISM AND THE GROWTH OF KNOWLEDGE, 91, 119 (Imre Lakatos & Alan Musgrave eds., 1970); Schroeder, *Abduction From the Seraglio, supra* note 126, at 168–69.

128. Consequently, some of Coase's most enthusiastic supporters, such as the early Calabresi, admit that the Coase theorem is a truism. "Far from being surprising, this statement is tautological, at least if one accepts any of the various classic definitions of mis-allocation." Calabresi, *Transaction Costs, supra* note 120, at 68 (1968).

Nevertheless, "most discussions of the Coase Theorem do not treat it as an empty tautology; rather, it is taken to suggest a definite approach to policy and legislation—use the law to lubricate private bargaining." Cooter, *supra* note 120, at 14.

Of course, this discussion of whether or not the Coase Theorem was or was not deserving of the Nobel Prize is not merely moot; it might be inept. He did, in fact, win the prize after all. But, perhaps more importantly, the Nobel Committee did not purport to bestow the prize on Coase for the Coase Theorem alone. Rather, it was rewarded for his entire body of work, including, most importantly, his theory of the firm.

129. Schwab, *supra* note 114, at 1191.

130. In contrast, Farber, Cooter, and the like shrink from the radicalism of Coase's proposal and try to render him into the safe and comfortable world of normal science. They would have Coase merely propose a theory, or hypothesis, about the effects of a limited number of identifiable actual costs without which markets would be perfect. Consequently, Farber is correct that Coase thought that transaction costs were measurable, but he is wrong in assuming that this means that Coase was trying at this stage to definitively identify those costs that do in fact hinder efficient bargains, or that he was proposing that we could ever replicate in the actual world the ideal conditions of the Coase Theorem.

Robert Ellickson cleverly suggests why legal economists who cite Coase persist in studying cloud-cuckoo lands without transaction costs: "Transaction costs themselves . . . help explain why there has been little empirical work on transaction costs." Robert C. Ellickson, *The Case for Coase and Against "Coaseanism,"* 99 YALE L. J. 611, 613 (1989).

legal scholars have been similarly uncritical of the existing economic paradigm.[131]

Coase's new paradigm of economic costs can be stated as "anything that prevents an economically efficient result."[132] This, in turn, allowed him to identify an important subcategory of economic costs that would eventually be named "transaction costs." Transaction costs are whatever would prevent an efficient reallocation of resources. This new paradigm enabled economists and lawyers to recognize that things that impede efficient transactions are just as much economic costs as, for instance, costs of production, and are just as much in need of study. One unfortunate result of the identification of transaction costs seems to be, however, that law-and-economics has become obsessed with transaction costs to the exclusion of costs generally. Coase's startling insight allowed legal economists to identify a wide variety of things which were heretofore invisible—such as time, asymmetric information, etc.—as costs. Coase's point, however, is not that these "transaction costs" are unique, but that they are *just like any other costs.*

Specific Transaction Costs

What are some examples of transaction costs? Undoubtedly, they are infinite in faculty. Their serial elimination is therefore an infinite progress that can never be completed, keeping us forever in the realm of the symbolic and outside the realm of the real. I do not speculate as to what transaction costs *might* be. Rather, I discuss some of the examples of transaction costs that are most

131. Despite claims to the contrary by his self-professed followers, Coase does not draw the conclusion from his theorem that society should seek to reduce transaction costs, so that misallocations of resources would be remedied and the economy made more efficient. Coase thought that we did not yet know enough about actual economic institutions to know where the elimination or reduction of any one transaction cost would result in a net increase or decrease in efficiency. Nor does he suggest that society should reallocate entitlements in such a way as to mimic the efficient allocation that would hypothetically result if transaction costs were eliminated. As Calabresi suggests, "The resource allocation aim is to approximate, both closely and cheaply, the result the market would bring about if bargaining actually were costless." Calabresi, *Transaction Costs, supra* note 119, at 69. Rather, Coase suggests that, since transaction costs can never be eliminated, the efficiency effect of changes in the legal regime is unknowable: "The answers to all these questions [i.e., whether laissez-faire or government intervention is to be preferred in an imperfect world] are shrouded in mystery and every man is free to draw whatever conclusions he likes." Coase, *The Problem of Social Cost, supra* note 99, at 43.

Consequently, economists have nothing to recommend to lawyers on questions of allocations of legal rights because "problems of welfare economics must ultimately dissolve into a study of aesthetics and morals." *Id.* at 43.

132. In Stigler's words, "Costs are the obstacles that cause us to fulfill less than our full desires. " STIGLER, PRICE, *supra* note 89, at 111.

frequently discussed in the literature. I take each of these costs to its logical extreme to suggest the paradoxes that would occur if one really could eliminate them. Each identified transaction cost has the peculiar property of generating the perfect market by its own singular elimination. This suggests that there is but one abstract concept of transaction costs, which can be actualized in any number of concrete manifestations. In the succeeding section, I will show that this single transaction cost is the existence of mediation—that which makes perfect, immediate relations impossible. Transaction costs are, therefore, castration, in the sense of a barrier that separates the symbolic of actual markets from the real of perfect markets.

Most scholars recognize that "the concept of 'perfect' information—meaning free, complete, instantaneous, and universally available—[is] one of the defining features of the perfect market."[133] Indeed, one can argue that most of the specific examples of empirical "transaction costs" identified by Coase in *The Theory of Social Cost* can be seen as subsets of the more general category of information costs.[134]

In order to develop a Coasean definition of perfect information, one

133. James Boyle, *A Theory of Law and Information: Copyright, Spleens, Blackmail, and Insider Trading,* 80 CAL. L. REV. 1414, 1443 (1992). Boyle calls the fact that the concept of perfect information in an ideal market is a tool invented for analysis of actual markets which are characterized, by definition, by imperfect information a "basic theoretical *aporia*" of economic analysis. *Id.*

According to Stigler, "A perfect market is one characterized by perfect knowledge on the part of the traders." STIGLER, PRICE, *supra* note 89, at 82 (1987). Similarly, Ellickson believes that information costs are the "broadest" category of transaction costs. Ellickson, *supra* note 130, at 615. Ian Ayres and Eric Talley agree that "private information is a particularly pernicious form of transaction cost," and therefore propose legal structures which, they believe, would encourage parties to reveal information. Ayres & Talley, *Solomonic Bargaining, supra* note 87, at 1030.

134. First, Coase mentions the need for a market participant to identify other market participants (Coase, *The Problem of Social Costs, supra* note 99, at 13)—a matter of gathering information. Second, the participant must inform the others of her desire to deal and on what terms (*Id.*)—a matter of insuring that others have the necessary information. Monitoring the performance of the contract, another cost identified by Coase (*Id.*), is also an information-gathering activity. As a contract lawyer, I can attest that one of the primary reasons for another of Coase's costs—drawing up a written contract (*Id.*)—also relates to information. Parties negotiate extensive contracts, partly in order to establish their deal in the sense of insuring that both parties understand the implications of the deal and have a true meeting of minds.

This is a point that is frequently passed over in academic literature. For example, Ellickson recognizes that bargaining can itself be a form of information investigation, but seems to think that it is only strategic behavior in bargaining that generates information. Ellickson, *supra* note 130, at 616. This is true, but it is only one aspect of the dynamics of contract formation.

Ellickson identifies other types of information costs in addition to those information costs specifically mentioned by Coase. For example, if property is to be transferred in the proposed bargain, the parties need information about specifications, quality, and title. If services or future obligations are anticipated, the parties need information about their respective skill and trustworthiness, as well as information about the legal regime that will govern the contract. *See id.* at

must keep in mind the definition of transaction costs. In a perfect market, information is not merely perfect; it must be complete and symmetrical.[135] Each participant in the market must have perfect information, not merely "about the market generally" but about "each party's position within it."[136] That is, everyone must know not only what everyone else knows, but what everyone else is thinking as well.[137]

Viewed in this context, it becomes apparent that each party must have perfect information not only about her own preferences, but also about the preferences of every other market participant, so as to preclude forms of strategic behavior and moral hazard that might otherwise impede an efficient bargain.[138] As Herbert Hovenkamp has accurately stated, bluffing and

---

615 for a useful list of typical information costs. With a little thought, the reader can easily add to this list.

135. That is, information asymmetries are defined as a transaction cost. Elizabeth Warren, *Bankruptcy Policymaking in an Imperfect World,* 92 MICH. L. REV. 336, 379 (1993); Eric Talley, *Liability-Based Fee-Shifting Rules and Settlement Mechanisms Under Incomplete Information* 71 CHI-KENT L. REV. 461, 464 (1995); Ian Ayres & Eric Talley, *Distinguishing Between Consensual and Nonconsensual Advantages of Liability Rules,* 105 YALE L. J. 235, 237 (1995) [hereinafter, Ayres & Talley, *Liability Rules*].

136. Warren, *supra* note 135, at 379.

137. Edith Stokey and Richard Zeckhauser include the condition that "information in the market must be fully shared" as the first of "the most crucial of the ideal conditions that guarantee the efficiency of competitive markets." EDITH STOKEY & RICHARD ZECKHAUSER, A PRIMER FOR POLICY ANALYSIS 293 (1978). They describe this requirement as follows:

> For the price system to perform its signaling function perfectly, information must be costlessly shared among all individuals, including information on the prices charged by various suppliers. Uncertainties will of course remain. No one predicts the weather with complete accuracy; no one knows for sure what technologies will be relied on in the next century. But there can be no asymmetries in the availability of whatever information exists. . . . Obviously, perfection is rarely achieved. The critical issue will be how consequential the asymmetries in information are.
>
> The unhindered flow of information is essential to the market system to ensure that all participants are trading the same goods. . . . In short, the free flow of information and the ability of people to use it is essential if the trading of commodities on competitive markets is to lead to an efficient outcome.

Id. at 298.

As Cooter notes: "Perfect information requires not only the declaration of intentions, it also requires the certification of their truthfulness. Certifying an intention is an act which destroys a player's freedom." Cooter, *supra* note 122, at 17.

138. For example, according to Cooter: "The transaction costs of bargaining refer to the cost of communicating among the parties (including the value of time used up in sending messages), making side payments (the cost of the transaction, not the value of what is exchanged), and the cost of excluding people from sharing in the benefits exchanged by the parties. In the case of contingent commodities, the cost of obtaining information on the actions of the players is also treated as a transaction cost, so the inefficiencies from moral hazard and adverse selection are swept under the blanket of transaction costs." *Id.* at 16.

similar "strategic behavior is inconsistent with the assumption of perfect information."[139] That is, in the perfect market there is no room for strategy. This means that game theory is inapplicable in the perfect market.[140] I shall return to this.[141]

Even this does not go far enough to capture the Coasean ideal. As both Stigler and Calabresi have stated, the Coasean definition of transaction costs is *literally* anything that keeps us from our desire, including the fact that impossible desired events—such as manna raining from heaven—do not occur. Our inability to predict future events, such as the weather, natural disasters, the development of new technologies, or most importantly, the day of our death, are, therefore, information failures and transaction costs. The perfect market can only exist either when the future is perfectly predictable or when there is no future because there is no time.

Such perfect information about ourselves and others, the future and the past, breaks down all distinctions between persons and eliminates the possibility of unforeseen acts. It is, therefore, the destruction of subjectivity and freedom—the real.

One of the most surprising aspects of the Coasean analysis is the identification of time and space as transaction costs. These are rarely expressly discussed, but they are implicit in all discussions of imperfection.[142] I only dis-

139. Herbert Hovenkamp, *Marginal Utility and the Coase Theorem,* 75 CORNELL L. REV. 783, 290 (1990).

140. "The obstacles to cooperation are portrayed as the cost of communicating, the time spent negotiating, the cost of enforcing agreements, etc. These obstacles can all be described as transaction costs of bargaining." *Id.* at 17. Game theory is designed to predict behavior when information is incomplete creating opportunities for strategic behavior—i.e., like in actual markets. Consequently, it may be more in keeping with Coase's project than traditional price theory economics.

141. Few writers fully grasp the radical nature of the Coasean concept of perfect information and communication. For example, Cooter tries to argue that the possibility of strategic behavior disproves the Coase Theorem because this behavior can prevent efficient bargains despite the absence of transaction costs: "The error in the bargaining version of the Coase Theorem is to suppose that the obstacle to cooperation is the cost of communicating, rather than the strategic nature of the situation. Bargainers remain uncertain about what their opponents will do, not because it costs too much to broadcast one's intentions, but because strategy requires that true intentions be disguised." Cooter, *supra* note 122, at 23.

142. Ellickson, for example, correctly notes that one important category of transaction costs are what he calls "get-together costs": "Get-together costs are the burdens of arranging physical and electronic connections among transacting parties. They include the costs of establishing lines of communication, setting up meetings, and transporting parties and goods." Ellickson, *supra* note 130, at 615. He does not, however, follow through on this analysis, which would imply that distance itself is a transaction cost. I should not be harsh on Ellickson, however. He does not explicate the contours of zero-transaction costs precisely because he wishes to emphasize Coase's (and my) point that such an ideal world is impossible and should not be the focus of economic analysis.

cuss them briefly at this point because they relate more precisely to the unacknowledged necessary but impossible implications of the perfect market idea.

From an economic standpoint, one of the most important costs is time itself, because "time spent" is a "major factor"[143] in price differentiation, and price differentiation is, by definition, a market imperfection. The first thing one learns in any finance course is the "time value of money" and the corresponding "money value of time." A dollar tomorrow is worth less than a dollar today. All delays in time must, therefore, be compensated. We call this the "discount rate" or "interest." One of the major costs of dealing with a lot of people is, of course, time. It is more time-consuming to negotiate with many people than it is to negotiate with one. Indeed, even identifying the people affected, with whom one must negotiate, is time-consuming.

Consequently, according to classical price theory, in the perfect market all actions happen "instantaneously and simultaneously."[144] "Goods are instantly produced, distributed, and consumed. . . . Sales do not occur sequentially."[145] In addition, "Time is frozen in the form of a *rate* of production. . . . Although a rate is supposed to subsume a time, it effectively banishes it by sublating it into a fixed quantity."[146] These assumptions are required in order for the requirement that there be no price dispersion (or no dispersion in the marginal utility to price ratio). That is, time is a cost that must be included in the price of a commodity.[147]

To put this another way, markets exist in order to fulfill human desires, whether defined in terms of wealth, utility, or otherwise. Although capitalism has allowed us to increase many of the good things of the world, the one thing we will never be able to change is "time." "The welfare of people cannot be improved in a utopia in which everyone's needs are fully satisfied, but the constant flow of time makes such a utopia impossible."[148] The existence of time makes it impossible to fulfill our desires. Both its limitations and passage make it impossible for to us have everything we want at the same time. This is reflected in the hoary cliché, "you can't have your cake and eat it too."

143. MICHA GISSER & PETER S. BARTH, BASIC ECONOMICS 41 (1970).

144. Carlson, *Margins of Mircroeconomics, supra* note 89, at 1893.

145. *Id.* at 1892.

146. *Id.* at 1893.

147. As Stigler noted. In the former Soviet Union prices of basic commodities like bread and meat were kept nominally low. As a result, there was excess demand at the official prices. Consequently, people were required to stand in long queues or to pay higher prices in the black market in order to buy these products. It is obvious that the real cost to consumers cannot be reduced to the nominal price. Rather, "the cost of a good is its price *plus* the value of the time spent in the queue." STIGLER, PRICE, *supra* note 89, at 103.

148. Gary S. Becker, *Nobel Lecture: The Economic Way of Looking at Behavior,* 101 J. OF POL. ECON. 385, 386 (1993).

As soon as we consume the object of desire, it is gone and we desire it again. Fulfillment can only happen in utopia, Heaven, Nirvana (i.e., the real). Since the real is unity before and beyond all distinctions, there is no time in the real. Like the feminine, the fulfillment of desire is always in the past or the future. One can only obtain one's desire by collapsing yesterday and tomorrow into today.

Coase himself understood the temporal implications of perfect market assumptions. He noted that the "consequence of the assumption of zero transaction costs, not usually noticed, is that, when there are no costs of making transactions, it costs nothing to speed them up, so that eternity can be experienced in a split second."[149] Indeed, as Schwab points out, "Coase's argument does not work in a world with a time dimension."[150]

It follows from the fact that there is no time in the perfect market that there can also be no space and no movement—or that if there is space, movement is instantaneous. In the words of Frank Knight, the perfect market assumes "complete absence of physical obstacles to the making, execution, and changing of plans at will; that is, there must be 'perfect mobility' in all economic adjustments, no cost involved in movements or changes."[151] In the perfect market, all differences in geography must be done away with because distance not only entails transportation costs, but necessarily results in differentiation between different producers and their products.[152]

Following Immanuel Kant, the abolition of time and space from the market is the abolition of human subjectivity, as well as objectivity, from the market. The consumer blends with the commodity and the producer in the perfect market. No concept can be distinguished from any other. The perfect market is a Kantian thing-in-itself, and hence belongs in the real.

A perfect market requires that all participants be economically rational. Irrationality in market transactions is therefore a market imperfection or a transaction cost.[153] One should not caricature the requirement as the sim-

149. COASE, THE FIRM, THE MARKET, AND THE LAW, *supra* note 99, at 15.

150. Schwab, *supra* note 114, at 1180.

151. Quoted in STIGLER, ESSAYS, *supra* note 86, at 257.

152. GISSER & BARTH, *supra* note 143, at 40.

153. I believe that one of the biggest obstacles to coherent discussions of the concept of economic rationality is unfortunate terminology. *See generally* Jeanne L. Schroeder, *Rationality in Law and Economics Scholarship*, 79 OREGON L. REV. 147 (2000) [hereinafter, Schroeder, *Rationality*]. Some colloquial meanings of "rationality" have strong positive connotations, such as sane as opposed to insane. Others have arguably negative ones (depending on one's theoretical position), such as rigidly and coldly logical in the sense of resistant to intuition, spirituality, and other nonlogical sources of knowledge.

Moreover, I believe that despite claims to the contrary, the term "rationality" is often used inconsistently by economist. On the one hand, some legal economists, such as Posner, claim to

plistic proposition that people act like the radically autonomous individuals of classical liberalism, who care about nothing but their own narrow self-interest. Many proponents of classic economics claim that their concept of economic rationality only assumes "that individuals maximize welfare *as they conceive* it, whether they be selfish, altruistic, loyal, spiteful, or masochistic."[154] In other words, this concept of "self-interest" is so highly stylized that it can encompass any conceivable behavior, and therefore is arguably of little (or no) predictive value, let alone normative purchase. What characterizes economic rationality is, therefore, not necessarily selfishness as narrowly defined, but the ability to know what one wants and how to get it. As put by Knight, economically rational persons are supposed to 'know what they want' and to seek it 'intelligently.' . . . They are supposed to know absolutely the consequence for their acts when they are performed, and to perform them in the light of the consequences."[155]

Stigler explains the three characteristics of an economically rational person: "1. His tastes are consistent; 2. His cost calculations are correct; 3. He makes those decisions that maximize utility."[156] Consistency does not imply that the participant have any principled criteria for making choices.[157]

---

use it as a descriptive term about the way people in the aggregate tend to act with enough regularity to serve as a reasonable predictive model of behavior. *See, e.g.,* POSNER, ECONOMIC ANALYSIS OF LAW, *supra* note 88, at 17–19; RICHARD A. POSNER, OVERCOMING LAW 15–21 (1995) [hereinafter, POSNER, OVERCOMING LAW].

In contrast, Coase's paradigm of transaction costs necessarily leads to an implicit normative, rather than descriptive, definition of rationality. That is, "rationality" must be defined as whatever behavior market participants need to manifest so that the goal of economic efficiency is achieved. Of course, by saying this is a normative definition, I do not wish to imply that Coase believes that people should act in this way in all circumstances.

154. Becker, *supra* note 148, at 386. Utility maximization arguably does not need such a narrow definition of rationality. This is because we can posit that individuals have a "preference" for altruistic behavior, egalitarian income, or wealth distribution, etc. POSNER, OVERCOMING LAW, *supra* note 153, at 16. *See* POSNER, ECONOMIC ANALYSIS OF LAW, *supra* note 88, at 4; *and* Becker, *supra* note 148, at 385. In other words, if helping others makes one happy, one can maximize one's utility by acting unselfishly. Of course, if watching other people suffer makes one happy, one can maximize one's utility by acting sadistically.

155. FRANK KNIGHT, RISK, UNCERTAINTY AND PROFIT (1921), quoted in STIGLER, ESSAYS, *supra* note 86, at 257.

156. STIGLER, PRICE, *supra* note 89, at 52.

157. My husband reports that he was once chided by a high school guidance counselor for not taking a job aptitude test seriously on the grounds that his preferences did not meet her criteria for consistency. When asked whether he would rather go to a baseball game or the ballet, he chose baseball, but when asked whether he would rather go to a football game or the opera, he chose the opera. She was convinced that one must either prefer sports or classical music at all times and refused to accept the fact that my husband is a baseball fanatic who hates all other sports, and an aficionado of most forms of classical music who just happens to be lukewarm towards ballet.

In this limited sense, economics believes that there is no accounting for tastes. Consistency merely means well ordered and transitive—if one prefers A to B and B to C, then one will also prefer A over C.[158] Critics of classical economics question the accuracy of this assumption as an empirical matter.[159]

158. *Id.* at 52.

159. First, Arrow's voting paradox shows that transitivity may not characterize group preferences. KENNETH J. ARROW, SOCIAL CHOICE AND INDIVIDUAL VALUES (2d ed. 1963). Second, even at the individual level, it may not describe how people actually act. Third, and most importantly, it assumes that people know what their preferences are and that these preferences remain stable, at least in the short run. In Becker's words, economists believe that "behavior is forward-looking, and it is also assumed to be consistent over time." Becker, *supra* note 148, at 386.

The psychoanalytic theory of the unconscious, of course, challenges the presumption that people know their preferences and always act in their own self-interest. People engaged in fashion, advertisement, and public relations base their professions on the hope that tastes are much more malleable than this would suggest.

Amartya Sen discusses many interesting problems of economic theories of rational behavior and choice as revealed preferences in AMARTYA SEN, CHOICE, WELFARE AND MEASUREMENT (1982). For example, should economists consider it "rational" to include sympathy/antipathy and commitment towards others in market decision-making? That is, do we deem it rational for one to choose X over Y, despite the fact that one prefers Y over X, because one believes that by doing so one will bestow a benefit or detriment on others? *Id.* at 7–8, 91–92. One's answer might depend on whether or not one is a wealth or utility maximizer because, in the latter case, one's subjective pleasure in giving pleasure and pain to others has the same status as the pleasure one receives from any other source. However, to do so comes close to defining all human activities as rational. Another question is how to accommodate a taste for variety with the requirement for consistency. After all, we probably don't want to argue that if one generally prefers steak to fish, then it is irrational ever to choose fish for dinner. *Id.* at 3. Indeed, as Sen suggests, it is not even clear whether the economic rationality requirement is an axiom to be assumed or a hypothesis to be falsified. "If today you were to poll economists of different schools, you would almost certainly find the coexistence of beliefs (1) that the rational behavior theory is unfalsifiable, (ii) that it is falsifiable and so far unfalsified, and (ii) [*sic*] that it is falsifiable and indeed patently false." *Id.* at 91.

In a famous article, Stigler and Becker argue that despite the influence of fashion, advertising, and the like, "tastes neither change capriciously nor differ importantly between people." George J. Stigler & Gary S. Becker, *De Gustibus Non Est Disputandum*, 67 AM. ECON. REV. 76 (1977). People's tastes are stable with respect to basic commodities—such as social status—as opposed to specific objects. People are perfectly rational when they buy a new wardrobe every year and rely on professionals (such as fashion editors) for information as to the latest style. *Id.* at 83–88. Other arguments they make include the proposition that investments in human capital may change one's ability to enjoy pre-existing tastes (i.e., it is possible that everyone starts with the same inherent taste in classical music, but one's ability to enjoy classical music can be enhanced by exposure and education) (*id.* at 77–81); and that following custom and habit rather than one's personal implication may be a rational decision to save the costs of investigation by relying on the collective experience of society (*id.* at 81–83). The question is whether these arguments are at such a high level of generality that they are not useful in making predictions in specific markets.

Posner takes a different approach and does not try to show that behavior that falls within the colloquial understanding irrationality is, in fact, rational. This is probably necessary because he is not a utilitarian who includes all measures of pleasure and pain in his calculus of rationality, but rather a wealth maximizer. He asserts that whether or not individuals act economically

The rationality requirement that a market participant know his preferences combined with the perfect information requirement imply that in the perfect market there is no "false consciousness." One can never say in the perfect market that a participant *should* prefer A over B, or that she *would* if she only knew better.

In Stigler's words, the requirement of making correct cost calculations is equivalent to stipulating that consumers can do "proper arithmetic," and "is so obvious as to be vulgar."[160] Stigler notes, however, that despite this, it is a well known empirical fact that people are poor at comparing costs that are not monetarized.[161]

The last requirement, which Stigler calls "utility maximization," states merely that when given the choice of two "market baskets," the consumer will choose the one he prefers.[162] To restate this, people will choose to act in such a way as to produce what they believe would be good results and to avoid what they believe would be bad. Once again, there are reasons to doubt the empirical validity of this assumption, in that we observe people (including ourselves) doing stupid and self-destructive things all the time.[163]

---

irrationally from time to time, people in the aggregate act as though they were rational consistently enough to justify the use of the assumption of rationality when making general predictions about the economy. POSNER, OVERCOMING LAW, *supra* note 153, at 16–17. Critics of the rationality requirement implicitly challenge Posner's empirical assertion as unproven or intuitively unlikely. Schroeder, *Rationality, supra* note 153, at 208–25.

160. STIGLER, PRICE, *supra* note 89, at 53.

161. The classic example cited by Stigler is the common practice of making weekly deposits in a non–interest bearing "Christmas Club" rather than buying an interest bearing investment. *Id.* To try to explain this away by reference to individual "preferences" (i.e., the investor just has a "taste" for Christmas Clubs) essentially does away with the requirement by turning it into a truism. *Id.* at 55.

162. That is, given a specific budget, they will choose the market basket that lies on the highest utility curve. *Id.* at 55. Obviously, this same concept can easily be translated into wealth maximization criteria—given two alternatives, he will choose the one that yields the greater wealth or profit.

163. To explain this type of behavior in terms of economic rationality once again reduces utilitarianism to a truism. By definition, when a fool rushes in where angels fear to tread it is because the fool has calculated, based on his own idiosyncratic utilities and whatever information is available to him at the time (which is probably partial), that the immediate pleasure he will experience in engaging in foolish behavior will outweigh the discounted expected future pain of the consequences. This is true even if after the fact he recalculates and decides that the pain he is now feeling outweighs the past pleasure. This is reflected in the common rueful statement "it seemed like a good idea at the time." Of course, critics argue that utilitarianism is a useless philosophy precisely because it logically always dissolves into truism.

A few years on the bench has turned law-and-economics idealogue Posner into a self-proclaimed pragmatist. POSNER, OVERCOMING LAW, *supra* note 153, at 1–29. He has modified his definition of rationality to make it less like the ideal world of the perfect market and more like that actual world of empirical markets. He argues that rationality is pragmatism. *Id.* at 16. The rational or pragmatic person bases his decisions on the costs to be incurred and the bene-

Since rationality is required for the perfect market, irrationality is by definition a market imperfection or a Coasean transaction cost. As stated by Coleman, the Coase Theorem can be seen as a definition of what it is to act rationally.[164] "To act rationally . . . is to promote allocative efficiency [by, in the cases discussed by Coase,] . . . put[ting] resources to their profit-maximizing use."[165]

In other words, the requirement of economic rationality is equivalent to

---

fits to be reaped from alternative causes of action (which, of course, is Stigler's definition of costs as foregone opportunities) and does not accept the sunk costs fallacy. *Id.* Rational persons "respond to incentives—that is, if a person's surroundings change in such a way that he could increase his satisfactions by altering his behavior, he will do so." POSNER, ECONOMIC ANALYSIS OF LAW, *supra* note 88, at 4. Although worded slightly differently, Posner's definition of rationality seems very similar to Stigler's.

164. Jules L. Coleman, *Efficiency, Exchange, and Auction: Philosophic Aspects of the Economic Approach to Law,* 68 CAL. L. REV. 221, 225 (1980).

165. *Id.* Paul Samuelson is one of the most forceful doubters of the empirical validity of the so-called Coase Theorem. Samuelson's disagreement with Coase might result from an implicit but unrecognized difference in their respective definitions of rationality. Samuelson believes that Coase has shown the conditions under which market participants *could or might* reach an efficient bargain, but he has failed to show that they *must* do so. *See, e.g.,* SAMUELSON & NORDHAUS, *supra* note 90, at 353. "Saying that there is room for an efficient, cost-saving bargain does not mean that a deal will always be struck—as the history of war, labor-management disputes, and the theory of games amply demonstrate." *Id.* Samuelson's bases his argument on empirical observations that sometimes "one or both [market participants] is unwilling to discuss the possibility of making a mutually favorable movement for fear that the discussion may imperial the existing tolerable *status quo.*" *Id.* at 1612. But this means that the parties are either acting irrationally (not acting in their own best interests) or with imperfect knowledge (not understanding that the contract will benefit them). Since these characteristics keep an efficient bargain from coming about, they are by definition transaction costs.

The disagreement between Samuelson and Coase might be explained by making express their implicit and unacknowledged differences in the concept of rationality adopted by wealth and utility maximizers. As we have seen (*see supra* text at note 131), Coase believes that the goal of economics is the maximization of production. COASE, THE FIRM, THE MARKET, AND THE LAW, *supra* note 99, at 159. Samuelson, however, implicitly defines rationality in terms of utilitarian values. In the Samuelson example, *if* the pleasure one party experiences in being stubborn or destroying the other party's bargain outweighs the pleasure he would anticipate obtaining if the wealth maximizing efficient bargain was consummated, *then* that party would be rational, from a utility maximizing point of view, if he refused to sign the deal, although he would be irrational from a wealth maximizing point of view. Correspondingly, if the other party correctly estimated that the pain she would experience by risking entering into a feared bargain would outweigh the expected pleasure from any profit she would receive, she would once again be rational from a utility maximizing point of view, but irrational from a wealth maximizing one, if she refused to go forward.

In other words, the Coase Theorem requires that one adopt a definition of rationality that matches one's definition of efficiency. The problem with Samuelson's critique, therefore, is that he is applying a utilitarian definition of rationality, whereas Coase is applying a wealth-maximization definition of efficiency. Samuelson is correct, therefore, that the former will not necessarily lead to the latter, but incorrect in thinking that the Coase Theorem posits that it would.

saying that the requirement of perfect information extends to knowledge of one's own psyche. There is, therefore, no unconscious or repressed desire in the perfect market. This also means that there is no consciousness or subjectivity. Perfect rationality is direct access to the real.[166]

Another of the most commonly identified categories of transaction costs relates to the existence of multiple parties who are affected by and/or participants in an economic transaction.[167] Although the former is frequently placed in a special subset called "externalities," Coase himself rejects this characterization.[168]

Externalities—also called social costs or neighborhood effects—are effects of economic behavior "upon people who are not parties to an agreement."[169] But Coase (like Hohfeld) argued that all legal rights can only be understood in terms of other persons: *all* economic activity affects others. Consequently, as we have seen, Coase thought it pernicious to try to identify only some costs as suprarelational (i.e., externalities).

The issue of whether one party's economic behavior affects one, two, or a large number of other persons is really only a question of how many people

166. To put this into Lacanian terminology, economics assumes that the market participant is an "ego." The ego is in the imaginary. FINK, *supra* note 28, at 84. The ego is only one part of the psyche, however.

167. *See, e.g.,* Ayres & Talley, *Solomonic Bargaining, supra* note 87, at 1029.

168. In Coase's words:

> I never used the word "externality" in "The Problem of Social Cost" but spoke of "harmful effects" without specifying whether decision-makers took them into account or not. Indeed, one of my aims in that article was to show that such "harmful effects" could be treated like any other factor of production, that it was sometimes desirable to eliminate them and sometimes not, and that it was unnecessary to use a concept such as "externality" in the analysis in order to obtain the correct result. However, I was clearly unsuccessful in cutting my argument loose from the dominant approach, since "The Problem of Social Cost" is often described, even by those sympathetic to my point of view, as a study of the problem of "externality."

COASE, THE FIRM, THE MARKET, AND THE LAW, *supra* note 99, at 27.

169. STIGLER, PRICE, *supra* note 89, at 324. Similarly, Coase states that the usual definition of externality is "the effect of one person's decision on someone who is not a party to that decision." COASE, THE FIRM, THE MARKET, AND THE LAW, *supra* note 99, at 24.

In their classic textbooks, Samuelson and Nordhaus formulate the definition slightly differently, as "activities that affect others for better or worse, without those others paying or being compensated for the activity. Externalities exist when private costs or benefits do not equal social costs or benefits." SAMUELSON & NORDHAUS, *supra* note 90, at 751. Samuelson and Nordhaus exclude external effects that have been internalized (by payment or compensation), whereas the definition quoted by Stigler and Coase would consider these to be externalities, albeit internalized ones. Nothing in this book depends on the difference between these two definitions because, according to the Coase Theorem, if transaction costs could be eliminated, then social and private costs would be equal (i.e., there would be externalities, according to Samuelson and Nordhaus's definition, or all externalities would be internalized, according to Stigler's).

must become parties to a transaction. Many commentators in this area emphasize that the problems—i.e., costs—of contracting are greater the larger the number of persons affected.[170]

Some of the problems of multiple parties are subsets of the more general problem of information costs. For example, as I have discussed, identifying counterparties is an information cost which increases with the number of parties. It also presumably takes more time to negotiate X number of separate contracts with X parties than it does to negotiate one contract with one party. But not all costs associated with multiple parties are additive in nature, nor can they be limited to information costs. The mere fact that a class is large can present new opportunities for strategic behavior.[171] Coordination and collective action problems can enable individuals to be " holdouts"[172] and "free-riders."[173]

In the perfect market, all actors must act as one.[174] The breakdown of dis-

170. For example, "Decision costs are likely to be nontrivial, however, when a transacting party is either a nonhierarchical group of two or more persons who must coordinate together or a hierarchical organization with a multi-person decisionmaking structure." Ellickson, *supra* note 130, at 615.

171. Ayres & Talley, *Solomonic Bargaining, supra* note 87, at 1029.

172. *See, e.g.,* A. MITCHELL POLINSKY, AN INTRODUCTION TO LAW AND ECONOMICS 18 (1989); James E. Krier & Stewart J. Schwab, *Property Rules and Liability Rules: The Cathedral in Another Light,* 70 N.Y.U. L. REV. 440, 450 (1995).

173. *See, e.g.,* Calabresi, *Transaction Costs, supra* note 121; Calabresi & Melamed, *supra* note 87; ALLEN BUCHANAN, ETHICS, EFFICIENCY, AND THE MARKET 22–24 (1985); *and* Krier & Schwab, *supra* note 172.

174. This is one area where the law has developed some devices that in fact enable many parties to act "as one." Business organizations are a means for many investors to pool their economic resources. Indeed, insofar as the law recognizes a corporation as a separate legal person, it "literally" collapses the separate shareholders into one personality for certain limited purposes. This relates to Coase's theory of the firm, whereby a business organization serves as an alternative to the market for the purpose of reducing market costs (in this case, the coordination problems of dealing with multiple parties).

Another way that many act as one for limited persons is class action litigation, whereby the claims of the several litigants are represented by one characteristic class representative (or, more accurately as a practical matter, the class action lawyer).

Both of these devices encompass at least a partial repression of the individuality and subjectivity of the many participants. In a public corporation, individual shareholders cannot generally interfere with management, but must rely on their elected representatives. Similarly, class members cannot generally manage the litigation, but must rely on the class representative. In both cases, the effective ability of the small participant to express her subjectivity is, with some exceptions, limited to exit (the ability to sell her stock or opt out of a class), because she has no effective voice. Other forms of cooperative organization (such as partnerships and close corporations, or perhaps the interests of relatively large shareholders or class members who, because of their size, have some meaningful voice) give more voice or subjectivity to the participants, at the expense of more coordination costs.

tinctions among persons and the achievement of immediate relationship is, once again, the destruction of subjectivity and the achievement of the real.

Robert Cooter has suggested that the possibility of strategic behavior disproves the Coase Theorem.[175] This is incorrect. Insofar as strategic behavior prevents efficient bargaining, it would fall within Coase's definition of transaction costs. Consequently, the substantial literature generated by Calabresi and Melamed's property-liability-inalienability analysis of environmental nuisances so treat strategic behavior.[176] A better analysis, however, might be that strategic behavior should *not* be considered a separate category transaction cost, but rather the unfortunate result of, or reaction to, other types of transaction costs, which we have already discussed.

There are two basic categories of "strategic behavior." One set relates to imperfect, asymmetric[177] information. Another relates to market position created by the existence of multiple parties.

Examples of strategic behavior that results from informational failures include "bluffing," underbidding, and threatening to leave the bargaining table. Participants engage in these types of strategies either to hide their own valuations, to force the other participant to reveal her valuations, or both. They can only be used in those situations where the parties have imperfect information.

In a world of imperfect information, these types of strategies are economically rational. They are, however, irrational in a world of perfect information.[178] It would not make any sense to try to bluff in a world where other parties always have perfect information about your desires.

Other forms of strategic behavior, such as "holding out" and "free riding," can only be partially solved by perfect information (i.e., by each party knowing what is in the head of every other relevant party). A holdout might still be able to use her strategic position to "extort" value, even if all the parties have perfect information about how she values the transaction, because of the coordination problems associated with the existence of multiple parties. Consequently, holding out and free riding is dependent on coordination and collective action problems stemming from the existence of multiple parties.[179]

This suggests that strategic behavior could be eliminated if we could cre-

175. Cooter, *supra* note 122, at 16.

176. *See, e.g.*, Calabresi, *Transaction Costs, supra* note 121, at 67; Ayres & Talley, *Solomonic Bargaining, supra* note 87, at 1029; Krier & Schwab, *supra* note 172, at 448 n. 30.

177. *See* Talley, *supra* note 135, at 464; Ayres & Talley, *Liability Rules, supra* note 87, at 237 n. 7.

178. Hovenkamp, *supra* note 139, at 790.

179. Ayres & Talley, *Solomonic Bargaining, supra* note 87, at 1029.

ate the conditions of perfect information or eliminate the practical effect of multiplicity by making many act as one. Consequently, some of the literature dealing with strategic behavior seeks implicitly to limit individuality and differentiation by devising devices to coerce market participants into certain transactions or to incentivize them to not exercise their freedom but enter into bargains.[180] Once again, this limitation of freedom and repression of individualism are characteristic of the real.

In the perfect market, the law must be perfectly clear and justice immediate. That is, even though, according to Coase, the initial allocation of rights is irrelevant, in order to contract, the parties must have information about their relative rights and obligations so that they know what they are contracting for.[181] In a perfect market, therefore, their knowledge of the law would be perfect. This means not only that legal rights must be clear and unambiguous but also that everyone in the market must know not only their own rights and obligations, but the relative rights and obligations of all other market participants.[182] But even this is not enough. Each party must be able

180. This analysis concentrates on formulating legal regimes that would lessen holdout and free-rider opportunities. Although some of these concentrate on the information aspects of these strategic problems, others involve ways either to eliminate the existence of holdout and free-rider opportunities or to incentivize, coerce, or force holdouts and free-riders into bargains. As such, these proposals seek to limit the differentiation between participants or the subjective freedom of the participants in the market to act in their own self interest. An example of methods that would reduce (but not eliminate) the ability to act individuality is the class action law suit. The takings power of the state is an even more extreme example of an institution that prevents such individualistic behavior as holding out.

Ayres and Talley's "Solomonic" division of property rights is designed to reduce the incentives for strategic bargaining by forcing the participants to reveal their preferences. *Id.*

181. At first blush, Ayres and Talley's suggestion that certain allocations of entitlements should be "Solomonic" (uncertain or otherwise divided between claimants) would seem to be an exception to this view. *See* Ayres & Talley, *Solomonic Bargaining, supra* note 87. At further examination, however, this seems not to be the case. The certainty of legal rights would seem to be part and parcel of the requirement of perfect information in the perfect market. Although I criticize Ayres and Talley on other grounds in Chapter 3, they are to be congratulated for avoiding in their article one trap of the perfect market ideal: they purport to deal not with the perfect world but with our world, where there are other information problems. Specifically, parties do not know what is in other people's heads, thus permitting strategic behavior. They also are aware of the problem of the second best: that when there are many market imperfections, one has no way of knowing whether or not one comes closer to the ideal situation if one cures only one problem. Consequently, solving one informational problem—legal certainty—will not necessarily get us to the goal of efficiency when others still exist. Ayres & Talley suggest that under some circumstances, *legal* uncertainty might increase the total amount of useful information generally available to the market.

Ayres & Talley do fall into the second trap of the perfect market ideal, in that they purport to know enough about this impossible ideal to attempt to propose legal rules to mimic it.

182. Warren, *supra* note 135, at 379. Coase does not include legal certainty in his enumeration of specific transaction costs. He states, however, "Of course, if market transactions were

to perfectly monitor and police each other in order to enforce their legal rights.[183]

In order for contracts to take place, there must be a perfect enforcement mechanism. Moreover, there must be no restraint on alienation, or other legal impediments to free contract.

Part of the issue of enforcement is informational: I need to know what my bargain is and whether or not the other party is living up to her end of the bargain. This requires the parties to have a perfect meeting of minds. This in turn requires either that the contract contemplate every conceivable future contingency or that the parties have perfect foreknowledge of the conditions that will arise under the contract in the future. Perfect enforcement also requires perfect government: once I know there is a breach, I must be able to punish it instantaneously, or the threat of punishment must be so certain that there will never be a breach. That is, I will not contract to pay my full valuation for a commodity unless I can be assured of enforceable contract and property rights. Any uncertainty in enforcement, any delay in the enforcement mechanism, will cause me to reduce my bid price. This is the case not merely with voluntary transactions. As we have discussed, the possibility of holdouts and free riders also requires enforcement of entitlement allocations against involuntary parties. In our modern legal system, this takes the form of eminent domain and taxation, respectively.

Most importantly, the requirement of perfect clarity of legal rights means that the legal system must be closed and complete. A rule for every conceivable fact situation that might ever arrive must have always already been promulgated. There can never be any question of statutory interpretation.[184] Every market participant must know the result of every future litigation even before the complaint is filed. The requirement that legal rights be perfectly clear is inconsistent with our dynamic, open-ended common law jurisprudence, in which law is always in the state of being made.[185] More importantly, it would, once again, require that society have perfect foreknowledge of the future. Finally, since time is money, enforcement of legal rights must be not

costless, all that matters (questions of equity apart) is that the rights of the various parties should be well-defined and the rights of legal actions easy to forecast." Coase, *The Problem of Social Cost, supra* note 99, at 19. In my reformulation of Coase's definition of transaction costs, insofar as ill-defined legal rights and difficult legal forecasts would impede efficient market transactions, they would be transaction costs.

183. *Id.*

184. As I discuss in Chapter 5, this is the "masculine" imaginary conception of law—a necessary moment of in the process of judging.

185. This is equally the case with Hegel's open-ended, ever-expanding jurisprudence of right. *See* Arthur J. Jacobson, *Hegel's Legal Plenum,* in HEGEL AND LEGAL THEORY 115 (Drucilla Cornell, Michel Rosenfeld & David Gray Carlson eds., 1991) *and* SCHROEDER, THE VESTAL AND THE FASCES, *supra* note 4.

merely swift, but instantaneous. In other words, such a perfect legal system reiterates the requirement that time be eliminated in the perfect market.

Of course, this closed, timeless world of perfect information and perfect constraint is yet another example of the timeless, deadly order of the real.

The perfect market is the one that leads to efficiency, defined in terms of some preferred allocation of resources. The most common tests of efficiency are Pareto Superiority or Optimality, and Kaldor-Hicks Optimality applied to the appropriate standard of either utility or wealth maximization.[186] This means that when the perfect market is achieved, there is no way of making society better off (whether measured in wealth or utility), given the existing limitations of productive capacity. Thus all parties must be indifferent between the current resources allocated to them and any other possible allocation that could be made, given scarcity. If society would be better off or if total societal production could be increased by a different allocation of resources, trade should occur and the market is not yet perfect. To put it another way, according to Stigler, all costs[187] can be defined as opportunity costs—the existence of a alternative.[188] If society does not become indifferent—if it would prefer an alternative allocation of resources—then there are still net positive costs that could be reduced, and the market is not perfect.

Some analysts believe that this means that in the perfect market all com-

186. *See, e.g.*, Coleman, *supra* note 164, for a concise introduction to the standards of efficiency adopted in law and economics literature. Because nothing in this discussion depends on the difference between the various standards of efficiency and most of the Coasean literature I will discuss seems to adopt some variation of the Pareto standard, purely for convenience I generally refer to that standard. The most significant rival to the Pareto standards of efficiency is Kaldor-Hicks efficiency. Posner is probably the most prominent proponent of this standard. *See generally* POSNER, ECONOMIC ANALYSIS OF LAW, *supra* note 88.

Some critics have suggested that the Coasean standard of maximization and Pareto analysis are, in fact, mutually inconsistent. *See, e.g.*, George Fletcher, *Law and Economics* (unpublished manuscript quoted in Coleman, *supra* note 164, at 227). Posner argues that only the Kaldor-Hicks standard is compatible with wealth maximization. Richard A. Posner, *The Ethical and Political Basis of the Efficiency Norm in Common Law Adjudication*, 8 HOFSTRA L. REV. 487, 489–91, 495–96 (1980); POSNER, ECONOMIC ANALYSIS OF LAW, *supra* note 88, at 14–17. Once again, these debates, although interesting, are beyond the scope of this book.

Yet another debate in which I will not join is whether the Coase Theorem requires invariance (i.e., a unique solution to any economic problem), or whether it permits multiple possible efficient outcomes. *See, e.g.*, Cooter, *supra* note 122, at 15; *and* Hovenkamp, *supra* note 139, at 785.

187. In this sentence Stigler is referring to costs generally, rather than transaction costs specifically. The implication of the Coase Theorem is that transaction costs are just like any other type of cost.

188. "The basic concept of cost is therefore something different: the cost of any productive service in producing *A* is the maximum amount it could produce elsewhere. The foregone alternative is the cost." STIGLER, PRICE, *supra* note 89, at 112.

modities must be homogenous and perfectly divisible.[189] The question is whether such lack of differentiation is the cause or effect of a perfect market.[190]

Stigler believes that it is a cause because "even minor differences . . . might lead some people to pay a slightly higher price for one seller's product than for another's product.[191] Others stress that literal homogeneity is not a requirement of the market. Indeed, this would seem to be necessarily the case. One cannot posit a market—a system of exchange—unless there are two different things to exchange. I will return to this.

Consequently, Samuelson insists that functional identity is a result, not a condition, of the perfect market. In a perfectly competitive market, trade continues until the marginal consumer is indifferent between all commodities in the market. At the market price ratio, each commodity is a perfect substitute for any other.[192] This concept of indifference (perfect substitutability) is an explanation of how actual products can be made to fit the criteria of homogeneity and perfect divisibility.[193]

189. For example, Stigler posits four conditions of a perfectly competitive market. In addition to perfect knowledge and large numbers of participants, there must be:

> 3. *Product homogeneity.* If the product is not homogeneous, it is meaningless to speak of large numbers. Hence, if every unity is essentially unique (as in the market for domestic servants), there cannot be large numbers. Yet if the various units are highly substitutable for one another, the market can easily approach competition.
>
> 4. *Divisibility of the product.*

Id. at 82–83.

190. On the one hand, if one party has "monopoly power" (the ability to affect the price), then there is no "perfect market". On the other hand, if the market is perfect, then all parties will be price takers. I will not dwell on this element because it does not exist in the Coasean problem, which is the primary concern of this book.

191. STIGLER, PRICE, *supra* note 89, at 83. Gisser and Barth agree for similar reasons. GISSER & BARTH, *supra* note 143, at 39–40.

192. SAMUELSON & NORDHAUS, ECONOMICS, *supra* note 90, at 87. That is, the ratio of marginal utility to price is the same for all commodities. The substitutability of commodities at various price combinations given a total expenditure can be graphically plotted as an "indifference curve." In an efficient market, the purchase by each consumer is set by the intersection of her budget curve and her highest indifference curve. *Id.* at 90.

193. This must be the case because if a consumer prefers one commodity over another at any given price, than she can always be made happier (or wealthier) if she trades the one she likes less for the one she likes more. If she can be made happier (or wealthier), the market is not yet at its most efficient point.

> Decisions may thus be simplified by focusing on the marginal rate of substitution (MRS), the rate at which an individual is *willing* to substitute one good or one attribute for another—and the marginal rate of transformation (MRT), the rate at which an individual is *able* to substitute that good or attribute for the other. If these two rates are unequal, then the individual can make a substitution that will move him to a position

As Stigler says, all transaction costs can be thought of as opportunity costs. In the perfect market, there can be no transaction costs, no foregone preferred opportunities, no better alternative, no differentiation.

Moreover, it is not enough that there be no distinction between objects in the perfect market. There can also be no distinction between subjects. The requirement of perfect homogeneity means that market participants are not only indifferent but impotent. All are passive price takers. The existence of differences between market participants, such as in strategic position or knowledge, can lead to strategic behavior. This means that in the perfect market either all differentiations permitting strategic behavior are eliminated or the subjective freedom of participants to engage in such behavior is restrained. The former solution requires uniformity of persons and the letter, conformity of behavior.

As a result, there can be no subjectivity or freedom in the perfect market. Subjectivity is created by recognition and therefore requires distinction. In the perfect market, everyone is, or is forced to act, the same.

CONCLUSION: THE IDEAL OF THE MARKET AS THE END OF THE MARKET

Costs are the obstacles that cause us to fulfill less than our full desires.

GEORGE J. STIGLER[194]

The Thanatos of Economics

In his more recent work Calabresi internalizes the inherent radicalism of the Coase Theorem. First, one should not distinguish transaction costs from

---

that he prefers. Moreover, if he is an efficient maximizer of his own satisfaction, he will do so.

STOKEY & ZECKHAUSER, *supra* note 137, at 171.

It is not merely the case that consumers will be indifferent between commodities: at the property price, producers will be indifferent as well. This is necessitated by the basic law that sets price at the intersection of the supply and demand curves. If producers prefer one unit of input over another at a given market price, they could produce more efficiently if they changed their production ratio. Consequently, the perfect market "will bring the marginal rate of transformation of producers into equality with the marginal rate of substitution of consumers. As long as the MRT differs from the MRS, producers and consumers have every incentive to change their behavior." *Id.* at 303.

Stokey and Zeckhauser, explicating classical price theory, assert that a perfectly competitive market will bring this about. As Stigler reminds us, perfection does not necessarily require competition. They are describing the result, or definition, of a perfect market. But one can hypothesize other institutions that might have the same result.

194. STIGLER, PRICE, *supra* note 89, at 111.

other costs, and, second, the revolutionary Coasean paradigm of costs (transaction or otherwise) is mediation—anything and everything that stands in the way of perfect immediate relations is a cost. According to Calabresi:

> The essence of Coase's insight is that transaction costs are no different form any other costs. . . . As such, to put the matter in technical language, they may at any given moment help define the Pareto possibility frontier, that series of social states that represent the best we can do at the moment without making someone worse off. But so does the fact that we do not have an engine that runs with less friction or that manna does not rain from heaven. Thus, the existence of transactions costs no more keeps us from reaching a frontier that is, in fact, currently available to us than does the fact that today a given degree of friction is a reality of life and that manna does not at the moment rain from heaven. All of these do the same thing. They define what is and what is not currently feasible.[195]

To paraphrase what I believe is Calabresi's point, Coase's new paradigm of economic costs has enabled economists to identify, and thereby study, an important subset of costs that theretofore had received inadequate attention: transaction costs. Until Coase, it was not self-evident that certain things—like time, lack of information, etc.—should be analyzed in terms of costs. This identification of transaction costs as cost has ironically led to the opposite result. Legal economists have become so preoccupied with transaction costs that they have forgotten the more basic point that these are like any other type of costs. Transaction costs may prevent transactions that would lead to desirable reallocation of resources, but, as stated by Stigler in the quote at the head of this section, costs generally are *whatever* keeps us from our desires, however defined. The fact that transactions are expensive may keep us from fulfilling our desires (by impeding desirable transfers), but then so do the expense of manufacturing, lack of funding, and, in Calabresi's terms, the fact that manna no longer rains from Heaven. Desires are only fulfilled in the real. Costs are whatever keeps us from the real. Consequently, the distinction between transaction costs and other costs may be a distinction without meaningful difference for the purpose of economic analysis. Like any other form of costs, transaction costs might be subject to reduction, but not to elimination. As Coase states,

> Indeed, one of my aims in [*The Problem of Social Costs*] was to show that such "harmful effects" could be treated like any other factor of production, that it was sometimes desirable to eliminate them and sometimes not, and that it was

195. Guido Calabresi, *The Pointlessness of Pareto: Carrying Coase Further,* 100 YALE L. J. 1131, 1218–19 (1991).

> unnecessary to use a concept such as "externality" in the analysis in order to obtain the correct result.[196]

In other words, if law-and-economists are going to hypothesize an impossible "perfect market," why stop with the elimination of transaction costs and not go all the way to describing Paradise?

If markets exist as a means to fulfill desire, then markets are erotic. The desire of law-and-economics would seem, at first blush, to be Eros. The various definitions of efficiency all share a belief that utility or wealth could be increased by shifting objects to the highest valuing user. The masculine pretends that the hole of castration could be healed if he could just acquire through exchange the feminine—in the sense of the lost object of desire—with whom he could join in a perfect, immediate relationship. The legal economist believes that the inefficiencies of the economy can be cured if each subject immediately obtains his desired object through exchange. This desire can only be maintained in the imaginary order, through fantasy. Without fantasy, Eros always turns into Thanatos—the desire to achieve wholeness by dissolving back into the real.

If the masculine were ever to achieve his Eros by obtaining an immediate relationship with the feminine, he would lose the separation of castration, which creates and maintains his subjectivity. He would enter the real. The desire to achieve the perfect market is, therefore, Thanatos.

Consequently, there are two ways for the masculine position of mainstream economics to maintain itself. The first is the prolonging of its desire as Eros through fantasy. He can erect a protective fantasy structure in the imaginary. Thus law-and-economists purport to discuss hypothetical markets in which transaction costs (but not all costs) are supposedly eliminated, without considering the logical implications of their stated assumptions. Coase reveals that this is a phantasm and insists that we confront the symbolic nature of actual markets and eschew the impossible end of achieving the real of the perfect market. But, despite his denials, like all other human beings, Coase is driven by the desire for wholeness that eventually leads to Thanatos.

Since costs are what keeps us from desire by walling off the symbolic of actual markets from the real of perfect markets, transaction costs are a form of castration. Human life is a slave to limit—we all die. Only in Heaven, where individual souls are granted their desire, or in Nirvana, where the soul casts off all individuality and desire, can we meet the requirements of a perfect market. The perfect market, the resolution of castration, is the real.

The alternative strategy for masculine economics is to compromise its

196. COASE, THE FIRM, THE MARKET, AND THE LAW, *supra* note 95, at 27. Although in this passage Coase speaks of externalities specifically, in my reading of *The Problem of Social Cost* this should be generalized to transaction costs.

desire and thereby substitute drive for desire—and, as Lacan famously asserted, all drives are death drives. As I discuss in Chapter 4, this is the road taken by Posner, who seeks to avoid the unsatisfied eroticism of actual markets characterized by desire through the creation of a jurisprudence based on a hypothetical market characterized by the deathly drive of wealth maximization. He forswears desire's goal of achieving *jouissance* and imagines a market in which enjoyment (or, in the language of economics, utility) is no longer a goal and market participants endlessly circulate in a closed circuit aimed at the accumulation of wealth.

Let us now dare to gaze into the abyss of the perfect market we would create if we could eliminate transaction costs; let us confront the real we desire to achieve by curing castration. It turns out that each seemingly different transaction cost is merely a different aspect of the same cost. This cost is the mediation, and separation, that permits the creation of subjectivity. It is the space, the radical negativity that enables freedom to function. This radical freedom is, in Hegelian-Lacanian theory, "the feminine." By trying to identify and eliminate transaction costs, therefore, we are like Orpheus and Lot's wife—we seek to capture the moment of feminine *jouissance.* As they learned, the fundamental human condition is ironic. The moment we achieve our desire and join with the feminine, we destroy our self. If we were to capture the feminine moment of transaction costs, understood as the mediation that allows desire, subjectivity, and freedom to function, and achieve the immediate relation of the perfect market, we would destroy not only actual markets, but our subjectivity and freedom. To be true to our desire is to postpone it. To give way to our desire is to end it. If the perfect market is the end of actual markets, achievement of the perfect market would end all actual markets.

In the perfect market, there is no distinction between subjects. Information is not merely perfect, but complete—"free, complete, instantaneous and universally available."[197] *If* the ability to use strategic behavior impedes reallocations, *then* strategic behavior is a transaction cost *by definition* that cannot exist in the perfect market. Consequently, in the perfect market there can be no secrets; there can be no difference in position. Each individual not only has perfect understanding of her own thoughts, dreams, desires, and intentions, but of those of every other person in the market. It is as though there were only one mind, one individual in the universe. There can be no freedom. In the words of Cooter, the type of disclosure and certification of intent required by the perfect market destroys a player's freedom.[198] But without individuality, freedom, and the unconscious, there is no

197. Boyle, *supra* note 133, at 1443.
198. Cooter, *supra* note 122, at 17.

subjectivity. There is no reason to speak, since everything has already been said. But more importantly, there is no one left to speak.

As discussed in the previous chapter, intersubjective relations require a fundamental separation from, and even ignorance of, the other.

> We can recognize the other, acknowledge him as person, only in so far as, in a radical sense, he remains unknown to us—recognition implies the absence of cognition. A neighbor totally transparent and disclosed is no more a "person," we no longer relate to him as to another person: intersubjectivity is founded upon the fact that the other is phenomenologically experienced as an "unknown quantity," as a bottomless abyss which we can never fathom.[199]

But it is precisely this separation and ignorance that cannot exist in the perfect market. Consequently, no one can recognize anyone else as a person in the perfect market. If subjectivity and interrelationship require mutual recognition, there can be no individual subjectivity in the perfect market.

The perfect market is perfectly unfree. Since all legal rights must be clear and unambiguous, there is no room for the creation of legal rights. Since every member of the market polices and monitors every other member, the market is perfectly coercive. All information is public, so not only does the public-private distinction essential to liberalism disappear, but also the private individuality necessary for differentiation among and recognition by persons. If everyone has perfect information about everyone else, then there can be no surprises in the perfect market. In the perfect market, all participants are perfectly rational. This means that each participant must single-mindedly seek her own self-interest. She must use any and all means to achieve her ends and therefore come to her end. In order not to give ground with respect to her desire, she must eventually stop procrastinating, give way to her desire, and achieve *jouissance.* All action must, therefore, be preordained. Similarly, the rigid definition of rationality adopted by the Coase Theorem requires human behavior to be as "rigorously deterministic as a multiplication table."[200] Without freedom, there can be no individuality, no subjectivity.

In the perfect market, there are no distinctions between objects. Product

199. SLAVOJ ŽIŽEK, FOR THEY KNOW NOT WHAT THEY DO: ENJOYMENT AS A POLITICAL FACTOR 198–99 (1991).

200. George J. Stigler, *Two Notes on the Coase Theorem,* 99 YALE L. J. 631 (1989). As is usually the case when the perfect market and zero transaction costs are discussed, Stigler is speaking in the negative. He is asserting that one of the reasons why Coasean bargains are not reached is that human behavior is not deterministic. He continues: "There are people who do not care for wealth, more who do not reason well, and vastly more who are incompletely informed. These people will not necessarily achieve optimal agreements, and especially is this true in new circumstances. We do not believe that such people govern important markets. Others who love wealth, reason precisely, and buy information in optimal quantities will call the tune." *Id.* In

differentiation is an imperfection by definition.[201] At the efficient price, all objects are perfect substitutes for all other objects. This means that the perfect market is the destruction of subjectivity. The fact that there are no differentiated mediating objects for persons to use to individuate themselves implies that there can be no subjectivity in the perfect market. This also turns out to be the case. Since there can be no strategic behavior in the perfect market, all participants must be identically situated.

In a perfect market, there are no transactions, no movement, no market intercourse. According to Coasean analysis, the initial legal regime is irrelevant only if all misallocations (i.e., inefficient allocations) of entitlements can be costlessly corrected. In other words, mistakes must be corrected instantaneously. This means that in the perfect market there are no actual market transactions because all resources will have always already flowed to the highest valuing user. Moreover, actual markets depend on information being imperfect: "costly, partial, and deliberately restricted in its availability."[202] The exchange price of all entitlements equals the use value of all users. The economic theory of marginalism holds that, in the perfect market, exchange will continue until all subjects become perfectly indifferent to all objects. There is, therefore, no desire. Without desire, there is no exchange.

Once the perfect market is achieved, all markets stop. Once again, this was one of Coase's points. Markets only exist as a means of eliminating transaction costs. When transaction costs are eliminated, markets are also necessarily eliminated. "In such a world the institutions which make up the economic system have neither substance nor purpose."[203]

Moreover, the elimination of markets results in the destruction of the legal subjectivity that is necessary for the actualization of our freedom in the modern, liberal, representative democratic state. As I argued in the previous chapter, the most basic erotic interrelationship of mutual recognition necessary for the creation of personality is that of abstract right—property, contract, and the market. These cannot exist without transaction costs. Personality is created through desire, but in the perfect market, all desires are always already fulfilled. Once again, Coase has already intuited this result.

> I showed in "The Nature of the Firm" that in the absence of transaction costs, there is no economic basis for the existence of the firm. . . . it does not matter what the law is. . . . In such a world the institutions which make up the eco-

---

other words, despite the fact that many or most individuals do not meet the strict definition of economic rationality, large markets operate as though their participants were fairly rational.

201. Gisser & Barth, *supra* note 143, at 41.

202. Boyle, *supra* note 133, at 1443.

203. Coase, The Market, the Firm, and the Law, *supra* note 95, at 14.

> nomic system have neither substance nor purpose. . . . [I]f transaction costs are zero, "the assumption of private property rights can be dropped. [204]

Finally, in the perfect market there is no time or space. The universe collapses back to the primordial unity that existed before the big bang. Kant teaches us that once the perfect market is achieved, there can be no thought, no consciousness. According to Kant's science of the transcendental aesthetic, the most basic mental function underlying thought is sensuous intuition.[205] The two pure forms of sensuous intuition are space and time.[206] Space is not a concept that we derive from experience,[207] nor is time an empirical concept;[208] rather, space and time are a priori intuitions that conscious beings need to presuppose in order to understand external objects (space)[209] and change and motion (time).[210] That is, space and time are not properties of objects or things[211] and do not subsist in themselves or inhere in the objective world.[212] "Time is . . . merely a subjective condition of our (human) intuition . . . and in itself, independently of the mind or subject, is nothing."[213] In other words, time and space are the ways human organize their understanding of the world. They are the "two sources of knowledge" that "make synthetical propositions *a priori* possible."[214] They are the "conditions of our sensibility."[215]

204. *Id.* at 14 (quoting Steven N. S. Cheung). As stated by Stokey and Zeckhauser, once Pareto Optimality is achieved, all parties are perfectly indifferent between all commodities so that "no profitable trades between producers, between consumers, or between combinations thereof will be possible." STOKEY & ZECKHAUSER, *supra* note 137, at 294.

205. According to Kant:

> In whatever mode, or by whatsoever means, our knowledge relates to objects, . . . the only manner in which it immediately relates to them is by means of an intuition. . . . But an intuition can take place only in so far as the object is given to us. . . . The capacity for receiving representations (receptivity) through the mode in which we are affected by objects, is called *sensibility*. By means of sensibility, therefore, objects are given to us, and it alone furnishes us with intuitions; by the understanding they are *thought*, and from it arise conceptions. But all thought must directly, or indirectly, by means of certain signs, relate ultimately to intuitions; consequently, with us, to sensibility, because in no other way can an object be given to us.

KANT, *supra* note 40, at 21.

206. *Id.* at 22.

207. *Id.* at 23.

208. *Id.* at 28.

209. *Id.* at 23.

210. *Id.* at 29.

211. *Id.* at 25.

212. *Id.* at 30.

213. *Id.* at 31.

214. *Id.* at 33.

215. *Id.*

From the propositions that sensible intuition is the most basic element of thought and that time and space are the pure forms of sensible intuition, it follows that to do away with time and space is to do away with the possibility of thought. This is, of course, Lacan's conclusion. The real—the elimination of all distinctions, including time and space—is the destruction of subjectivity and consciousness.

And so, if subjectivity is created through castration, then subjectivity also requires the existence of transaction costs. Subjectivity requires that desire be repressed, that the psyche be divided between consciousness and the unconscious—conditions inconsistent with the requirements of perfect information and economic rationality. Subjectivity requires distinction and separation—conditions inconsistent with the requirement of indifference. Subjectivity requires time and space.

Consequently, the perfect market is not merely the destruction of actual markets. It is the destruction of freedom, subjectivity, and consciousness. There is no exchange in the perfect market, not merely because there is nothing left to be exchanged, but also because no one exists who can exchange.

The perfect market is therefore pure, immediate relationship, where all distinctions of time and space, subject and subject, subject and object, desire and fulfillment are merged and obliterated. It is therefore real, not imaginary or symbolic. It is not merely impossible; it is by definition unimaginable and unspeakable.[216]

This is why we cannot bear to confront the perfect market or describe it in law and language. And yet, paradoxically, law-and-economics cannot escape its fixation. It is driven by its desire. Coase, perhaps intuiting that fantasy drives Eros, warns us not to look too closely at the model. He declares that "it would not seem worthwhile to spend much time investigating the properties of such a world."[217] He is particularly upset because his fame lies almost entirely on his formulation of the Coase Theorem, "a world of zero transaction costs . . . remote from the real world."[218] Economists are seduced by the beauty of the perfect market.

But, although Coase tells others to lash themselves to the mast, he him-

216. Richard Epstein is a rare exception, probably because he is not a utilitarian legal economist, but a libertarian who believes in a natural right to property regardless of any efficiency implications. In a critique of the perfect market assumptions underlying the Calabresi and Melamed analysis of environmental nuisances, he notes: "It is an open question, however, whether one can even understand what a world of zero transaction costs means, given the violence it does to our ordinary understanding of the importance of time." Richard A. Epstein, *A Clear View of The Cathedral*: The Dominance of Property Rules, 106 YALE L. J. 2091, 2092 (1997). Ironically, Epstein is repeating Coase's point.

217. COASE, THE MARKET, THE FIRM, AND THE LAW, *supra* note 95, at 14.

218. *Id.*

self cannot resist the sirens' call. He does not let any real or imagined challenge to the Coase Theorem go unanswered.[219] By doing so, he does precisely what he warns others not to do—fantasizes about the feminine perfection of the real.

This is, perhaps, inevitable. It is precisely the feeling of castration that makes us imagine and desire the perfect wholeness of the real. Similarly, the recognition of the concept of transaction costs causes us to speculate and desire the perfect market without cost.

Making the Impossible Possible

> *The postmodernist subject must learn the artifice of surviving the experience of a radical Limit, of circulating around the lethal abyss without being swallowed up by it. . . . Is not Lacan's entire theoretical edifice torn between these two options: between the ethics of desire/Law, or maintaining the gap, and the lethal suicidal immersion in the Thing?*
>
> SLAVOJ ŽIŽEK[220]

Despite the obsession with the perfect market, other than Coase, few if any have been able fully to internalize the logical implications of its assumptions. They cannot bear to gaze into the real. To achieve the perfect market is *jouissance,* the transgression of the market, law, and language. To achieve the perfect market would be to regress to a state before the birth of subjectivity. The perfect market is death.

David Gray Carlson has come to a similar conclusion in deconstructing price theory. The perfect market

> spells the death of price theory *qua* theory, a death foretold in the etymology of the word "economy," derived as it is from *Oikos* (household), which is akin to *Oikesis* (tomb). The real economy in microeconomics, then, is an *economy of*

219. *See, e.g., id.* at 129–163; and R. H. Coase, *The Coase Theorem and the Empty Core: A Comment,* 24 J. OF L. & ECON. 183 (1981). Ellickson makes a similar point: "Coase himself may deserve a bit of blame for the interminable analysis of the zero-transaction-costs world. Although his writings often emphasize the value of studying real situations, he has published but one major empirical study. . . . Coase's recent essay, *Notes on the Problem of Social Cost* . . . for the most part is a response to others' critiques of his analysis of the dynamics of a world without transaction costs. . . . He devotes less space to exploring the implications of the fact that transaction costs exist." Ellickson, *supra* note 130, at 613–14 n. 18 (citations omitted).

For example, as discussed above in his colloquy with Samuelson, rather than taking the opportunity to show the similarities between his and Samuelson's conclusions (that there are many significant barriers to efficient bargains in the real world), he defended his version of what would happen in a world without transaction costs.

220. ŽIŽEK, PLAGUE OF FANTASIES, *supra* note 27, at 239.

> *death* . . . a tomb, incidentally, that is memorialized on the back of every dollar bill turned out by the United States Treasury Department.[221]

Carlson sees price theory as logocentric, a philosophy of presence "whose will to power works to exclude the trace of its origin in death."[222] But Carlson's analysis, based on Derridean philosophy, is only partial.

We do not exclude the trace merely because it stands for death. Psychoanalysis reveals that the perfect market is not merely the death of economics; it is its desire. Only desire makes us human, enables us to love and create, and drives the economy on. Consequently, we repress the object of desire, postpone the moment of consummation in *jouissance* not *because* we desire but *just so we may* desire. Psychoanalysis teaches us that repression does not exclude the object it expels. It preserves it. What is repressed in the symbolic always returns in the real.[223] By repressing the perfect market, we make it serve as the object of desire.[224]

The entire symbolic order, including language, law, and the market, is a fiction—a human creation. Being a fiction, it only works if the fiction is maintained. If we give in to the masculine desire of Eros and confront the fantasy image we have made, we will destroy the fantasy. And the only way to achieve the feminine desire of Thanatos is by dying. Consequently, in order for desire to function, it must be prohibited.

Prohibition is, however, alchemy. The real, and the feminine, are impossible. They don't exist. However, once we forbid them, we create the sense of their possibility.[225] This is because there is no reason to forbid what can't be done. What had been mourned as the always-already-lost is now anticipated as the not-yet-found. We now live our lives not merely in the hope but in the confidence that the real, the feminine, radical freedom, and perfect immediate sexual relationships can yet be attained. In this way, human beings make their own freedom.[226]

Similarly, it is necessary in order for the market economy to function that the economy be a means to an end. The means will end if and when it

221. Carlson, *Margins of Microeconomics, supra* note 89, at 1874–75 (citations omitted).

222. *Id.* at 1875.

223. JACQUES LACAN, THE SEMINAR OF JACQUES LACAN. BOOK III: THE PSYCHOSES, 1955–56 86 (Jacques-Alain Miller ed. & Russell Grigg trans., 1993).

224. We must prohibit our impossible desire in order to make it possible. That is, in contradiction to the platitudes of pop psychology, repression is not a negative force imposed on us by society which destroys our desire and impedes our enjoyment. Repression is an affirmative choice we accept in order to create our desire and enable us to enjoy.

225. ŽIŽEK, TARRYING WITH THE NEGATIVE, *supra* note 39, at 116.

226. Consequently, as I discuss in Chapter 5, the injunction of the superego is not merely, as is usually thought, "Don't enjoy." Rather, it is also "Enjoy!" LACAN, SEMINAR XX, *supra* note 8, at 7.

achieves its ends. This means we must dream the ideal end of the perfect market while repressing and postponing the end of that dream.

We must never give ground relative to our desire, but we are lost as soon as we give way to our desire.

What does this mean for the law-and-economics movement? Although the real (the perfect market) is an ideal necessary to the functioning of the symbolic (the actual market), the symbolic by definition can never be the same as the real. Insofar as legal economists wish to formulate policy recommendations for actual markets, they should therefore heed Coase's call not to give way to their desire by concentrating on the ideal of the real, or on imaginary substitutions for this ideal. Transaction costs can no more be eliminated than any other costs; they are the limits of our mortality. The real is impossible to achieve, and the theory of the second best tells us that one will not necessarily get any closer to the ideal by eliminating or reducing any one transaction cost. Castration cannot be cured bit by bit. Moreover, the real cannot be captured in the symbolic of language or the imaginary of picture thinking. The real is not merely impossible to achieve as a *practical* matter; it is *logically* impossible in the sense that it is the order of intractable paradoxes. The perfect market is an unimaginable and unspeakable world of the living dead, without time, space, or subjectivity. This dooms any attempt to create legal rules that will mimic the perfect market, because we can never know the true contours of the ideal to be mimicked. When legal economists purport to describe what would occur if transaction costs could be eliminated, these can only be fantasies, in the technical sense of that term. They are not descriptions of the real of the perfect market, but rather comforting imaginary substitutes erected to stand in its place.

What we can do, as Coase pleads, is to study actual costs and actual behavior in actual markets on their own terms. Although we can retain the impossible ideal of the perfect market, we must set realistic goals based on contingent, empirical judgments as to the relative efficiency of possible actual market choices.

Chapter 3

Narcissus's Death

The Calabresi-Melamed Trichotomy[1]

PROLOGUE: NARCISSUS AND ECHO

Narcissus was the most beautiful of mortals and he knew it. Loved by both men and women, he was unable to return love.[2] The seer Teresias predicted that Narcissus would live as long as he failed to recognize himself. Although Narcissus dismissed this as nonsense, it was destined to come to pass.

The oread Echo was known for her ability to speak. She would regale others for hours with the latest gossip and clever, but empty, small talk. Zeus thought Echo would make a perfect handmaiden for his wife, Hera, and installed her in the Olympian palace. While Echo diverted Hera, Zeus could slip out for trysts with his many mistresses. When Hera discovered Zeus's ruse, she turned her jealous rage against the silly nymph and punished her with an appropriate curse. Echo would never again initiate a conversation, but would only repeat what others said.

The fates were even crueler than Hera to Echo; they caused her to fall in love with Narcissus. Unable to articulate her love, Echo was spurned by Narcissus. As a result, her desire turned from Eros into Thanatos, and she starved herself. But even this desire was thwarted, because, being a nymph, she was immortal. Consequently, although she wasted away, she lived on as a disembodied voice.

1. An earlier version of this chapter was published as Jeanne L. Schroeder, *Three's a Crowd: A Feminist Critique of Calabresi and Melamed's One View of the Cathedral*, 84 CORNELL L. REV. 394 (1999) [hereinafter, Shroeder, *Three's a Crowd*].

2. My account is based primarily on OVID, THE METAMORPHOSES, and ROBERT GRAVES, THE GREEK MYTHS 286 (1955).

Narcissus's many rejected suitors prayed to Nemesis for revenge.[3] Nemesis decided to use desire to punish Narcissus's rejection of desire; she caused him to fall in love with his own image reflected in a pool. Narcissus did not understand what he saw, but instead thought the image was another youth—the spirit of the spring—who returned his love. When Narcissus gazed at the image with desire, the image returned his gaze. When Narcissus held out his arms, the image tried to return his embrace. When Narcissus bent down to kiss the image, the image drew near and offered his lovely lips. Yet, at the moment when consummation seemed near, his imaginary beloved disappeared into the ripples of the water. As the image seemed to repeat Narcissus's frustration that the two were kept apart, Narcissus concluded that someone had erected a barrier, a mysterious boundary, that kept him from his object of desire. Somebody must have done this to him.

Echo's spirit still loved Narcissus. Her attempts to save Narcissus from his delusion only fed his fantasy. Whenever Narcissus expressed his love to the image, he misinterpreted Echo's repetition as his beloved requiting his love.

Narcissus's desire began as Eros—the hope that he would be fulfilled if he could obtain this perfect fantasy mate of his imaginary. Eventually, of course, Eros became Thanatos, and Teresias's prediction became reality. One day, Narcissus recognized that his beloved was nothing but his own reflection. Realizing that he would never achieve his desire for the image, he now desired death. He leapt into the pool and drowned in his own fantasy.

Narcissus is a myth of male desire. The masculine denies castration; the feminine accepts it. The masculine can never directly recognize the feminine, because to do so would be to confront castration.

Masculine subjectivity is constituted through the myth of a homoerotic regime of possession and exchange of an object of desire between masculine subjects. As discussed in preceding chapters, the masculine subject first tries to deny castration by claiming that he still has the phallus. He does this by conflating the real with reality, and the phallus with that which the community of men has. He claims that the fact that he has a penis is proof that he possesses the phallus.[4] This strategy is inevitably unsatisfactory because the masculine subject continues to feel the universal sense of loss. Indeed, the reason the penis stands in for the phallus is precisely because it is so fragile and at risk of loss.[5] He must, therefore, simultaneously adopt a second, inconsistent and equally unsuccessful, strategy. He claims that he is not castrated, because nothing was *taken* from him. He merely gave his retroactive consent to the loss of his original phallus (the feminine as the phallic mother) in

3. *Id.* at ll. 576–84.

4. Jeanne Lorraine Schroeder, The Vestal and the Fasces: Hegel, Lacan, Property and the Feminine 82 (1998) [hereinafter, Schroeder, The Vestal and the Fasces].

5. *Id.* at 89–90.

exchange for the fantasy that the community will someday be given an even better phallus in the future (the feminine in the form of a perfect mate). In this way, the masculine can pretend he is not castrated. Masculine desire, therefore, takes the form of Eros.[6] This is the fantasy that one could become whole (i.e., cure castration) if one could just find a perfect mate who would fill the hole of castration, like a piece fitting into a jigsaw puzzle. Masculine desire is the dream of immediate sexual relations. Thus it seeks complementarity. Eros is in the imaginary.

Because castration is the loss of immediacy, which makes mediation necessary, the masculine position is a denial of mediation. All relations are fantasized as direct—either immediate bilateral relations between subject and object (possession) or immediate bilateral relations between subject and subject (exchange). Paradoxically, although this relation can take place only because of the presence of a feminine mediatrix (the object of possession and exchange), masculine subjects must repress her existence in order to pretend that their relationship is immediate. In order to maintain this fantasy, the masculine must repress femininity. The masculine inconsistently denies castration while identifying castration with the feminine. Thus it is structurally impossible for the masculine community to recognize feminine speech, because to do so would be to confront castration. In this regime, the speaking subject is the masculine subject. At most, the masculine community can recognize the feminine only as the silent object of masculine desire passively exchanged among male subjects. In order for anatomically female persons to speak, they must temporarily take on or mime the masculine position. Speaking women are always male impersonators. As a result, the so-called different voice championed by Carol Gilligan is really just the same old masculine voice sung in falsetto.[7] Different voice feminism is just another form of the masculine imaginary fantasm of affirmative femininity, of the perfect mate.

Eros, being imaginary, can only be maintained through fantasy. If one were to confront the truth—that desire can never be fulfilled, that castration is inevitable and irreversible—then Eros would turn to Thanatos.

And so, in the myth, the masculine Narcissus could not hear the speech of the feminine Echo. Echo's desire quickly turned to Thanatos and she

6. *Id.* at 333–34. "Eros is defined as the fusion that makes one from two, as what is supposed to gradually tend in the direction of making but one from an immense multitude." JACQUES LACAN, THE SEMINAR OF JACQUES LACAN. BOOK XX: ENCORE, ON FEMININE SEXUALITY, THE LIMITS OF LOVE AND KNOWLEDGE, 1972–1973 41 (Jacques-Alain Miller ed. & Bruce Fink trans., 1998).

7. Although I disagree with her on almost every other point, I gratefully acknowledge Catharine MacKinnon's insightful use of a similar metaphor for different voice feminism. CATHARINE A. MACKINNON, FEMINISM UNMODIFIED 34 (1987).

merged with the real—the death beyond death. Narcissus, in contrast, sustained his Eros through fantasy. He fantasized that he had found a perfect mate with whom he could have a perfect relationship. As the masculine rejects the feminine necessity of mediation, Narcissus's perfect object of desire was the masculine fantasy image of himself: Eros is homoerotic in nature. As Teresias predicted, however, masculine subjectivity can only be maintained so long as its fantasy structure is maintained and the subject does not directly confront his own desire. As soon as Narcissus recognized himself, he realized that the wholeness he sought was impossible in the symbolic order. Perfect immediacy only exists in the real; Thanatos eventually supersedes Eros. Consequently, Narcissus committed suicide by literally trying to merge with the imaginary object of his desire, drowning himself in his own reflection. Yet up to the very moment of his death, he still could not recognize the feminine voice—imagining that Echo's desperate farewell came from the mouth of his imaginary masculine lover.

VIEWING THE CATHEDRAL; SEEING THE FEMININE

I will do the impossible and it will work.

CLAUDE MONET[8]

In his Rouen Cathedral series, Claude Monet attempted the impossible task of capturing the moment.[9] Traditional painting fails because it has an artificial permanence that experience lacks. Life is within time, but painting is outside of time; life is a process, but a painting is an event.[10] In the moment of experience, we lose ourselves in ecstasy. We stand outside ourselves and have no consciousness that we are having the experience because we are one with the experience. The instant we become aware that we are experiencing

8. Michael Brenson, *Monet's Complexity and Grandeur, Through His Series Paintings.*, N.Y. TIMES, Feb. 7, 1990 at C15 (quoting Claude Monet).

9. Monet stated, "One must know how to seize the moment of the landscape on the very instant, for that moment will never return.' " VIRGINIA SPATE, CLAUDE MONET 201 (1992). Sylvie Patin, Chief Curator at the Musée d'Orsay, expressed that the Rouen Cathedral "series offers the most dazzling and convincing demonstration of Monet's determination to capture instantaneousness.' " Alan Riding, *Monet's Fixation on the Rouen Cathedral,* N.Y. TIMES, Aug. 15, 1994, at C9

10. One critic has opined that the Rouen Cathedral series illustrates Claude Monet's "resistance to Academic painting, with its linear precision and fixed structure, and reinforce[s] his argument for the primacy of shifting and timeless nature. In his series paintings, everything seems soft and flowing, and there is no beginning, middle and end. At the same time there is a continuous sense of inevitability and finality. Where Monet found the essence of a fleeting moment, he also found a slice of eternity." Brenson, *supra* note 8. This merger of the moment, inevitability, and eternity perfectly describes the real.

something, we no longer enjoy it in its immediacy. Future enjoyment is always mediated by anticipation, and past enjoyment is always mediated by memory.

This sense of lost immediacy is feminine *jouissance*—enjoyment. Like Eurydice, you anticipate jouissance as she who has not-yet-come, but the instant you turn to try to hold her, she is always-already-gone.

Monet wanted to capture his jouissance of the Rouen Cathedral's facade, but each attempt was frustrated because it changed moment by moment.[11] He devised an ingenious solution. Every day, he brought several canvasses with him to the cathedral. He started at daybreak and painted one canvass until the lighting changed; he then moved on to a second, then to a third, and continued until sunset.[12] This series of views of the cathedral constitutes, in effect, one work of art, reflecting the subtle changes in color of the cathedral's facade over the course of a day.

Monet's works have been reproduced with such frequency that it is hard to reclaim them from the banality of the overly familiar. With this in mind, I refreshed my memory by visiting the two cathedral paintings displayed in the National Gallery of Art in Washington, D.C. What surprised me when viewing the originals is how nearly Manet succeeds despite his failure. Or, more accurately, how he succeeds because he fails. The differences in coloration of even two paintings in the series illustrate that experience is so fleeting that its totality could never be captured, regardless of how many canvasses were used.[13] That was Monet's secret.

11. *See* Spate, *supra* note 9, at 229. "Monet's perception of the motif became more acute as he struggled to embody its transient moments in a form both stable and evanescent." *Id.*

12. *See id.* at 227. Monet started the cathedral series in late winter and early spring 1892, and returned the following year at about the same time in order to recapture the same light. He reworked the paintings over the next year in his studio at Giverny and exhibited twenty paintings from the series in 1895. *See* WILLIAM C. SEITZ, CLAUDE MONET 116 (1982); Spate, *supra* note 9, at 226–27. Monet would paint in front of the cathedral from dawn to dusk and then continue on his canvasses in the evening at his hotel. *See id.* at 227. He started with nine canvasses a day, but found that the light kept changing. He increased the number of canvasses to ten, then twelve, then fourteen. *See id.* at 227–29. Eventually, he would change his canvass every half hour, "expressive of his resolve to capture the specific moment (*instantanéité*) as perceived by his ever more sensitive eye." STEPHAN KOJA, CLAUDE MONET 120 (John Brownjohn trans., 1996). Initially he rented one studio across the street from the cathedral, later renting space in a ladies' apparel shop a few doors down. *See id.* His obsession turned him into such a fixture that women were too embarrassed to enter the shop. Finally, the shopkeeper built a screen around the artist to shield his clientele from Monet's lugubrious presence. *See* Riding, *supra* note 9.

13. *See* SEITZ, *supra* note 12, at 116. Monet eventually completed thirty paintings of the cathedral, including twenty-eight of the facade. *See* Riding, *supra* note 9. As described by Georges Clemenceau, who was so impressed by the inaugural exhibition of twenty of the series that he immediately wrote an editorial on the front page of the Paris journal *La Justice* urging the French government to buy the entire series to keep it intact, *see id.*, "The painter has given us the feeling . . . that he could have . . . made fifty, one hundred, one thousand, as many as the seconds

The series suggests the existence of an enjoyment that can never be captured. Enjoyment of the cathedral is not what we view in the paintings, but our view of the paintings reminds us that an "excess enjoyment" beyond our view must have existed in the past and will again exist in the future.[14] The paintings let us intuit feminine enjoyment, not by depicting its presence, but by suggesting its absence. They are Eurydice's footprints, the fading echo of her voice, the stain of her lost virginity. The paintings mediate between the viewer and the impossibility of immediacy. In Monet's words, he did not attempt to depict the cathedral itself, but rather "to reproduce . . . what exists between the [cathedral] and me."[15]

Monet's understanding of his limitations stands in stark contrast to the claims of a famous law review article that invokes his work. Guido Calabresi and Douglas Melamed published their seminal analysis of environmental

---

in his life.' " SEITZ, *supra* note 12, at 116 (quoting Clemenceau). Clemenceau continued, "Each beat of his pulse he could fix on the canvas as many moments of the model." Spate, *supra* note 9, at 230 (quoting Clemenceau) (alteration in original). The paintings inspired in Clemenceau "a lasting vision not of twenty, but a hundred, a thousand, a million states of the eternal cathedral in the immense cycles of the sun." *Id.* (quoting Clemenceau).

Spate agreed with Clemenceau's interpretation. She believed that Monet chose the cathedral as his subject precisely because he thought its stone architecture would be relatively unchanging, enabling him to capture it in "a work of 'no weather and no season.' " *Id.* at 232 (quoting Monet). As he started to paint, he realized he was wrong and became "totally absorbed in the representation of ephemeral effects." *Id.* Eventually, Monet sought "to embody not only an external reality which was ceaselessly changing, but also a continuous perceptual experience of that reality, and the more intensely he focused on changing light, the more the stable reality of the cathedral disintegrated." *Id.* at 231 (footnote omitted).

It is easy to dismiss Manet as a simple painter who merely reproduced his immediate impressions of pretty scenery. Even his contemporary Paul Cézanne declared that Monet was "only an eye, but what an eye!" John Russell, *Art View: The Poet Who Kick-Started a Stalled Cezanne,* N.Y. TIMES, July 28, 1991, 2, at 27. Nonetheless, Monet understood that immediacy was impossible. The fact that Monet did not complete his Rouen series until he returned to his studio two years after he started indicates that they are "not fleeting impressions," but his "least sketch-like" paintings done with "great consideration." Michael Kimmelman, *Eclectic Monet, Bathed in Chicago's Ballyhoo,* N.Y. TIMES, July 24, 1995, at C9.

Spate accurately stated that Monet's was an "inherently terrifying vision of reality." Spate, *supra* note 9, at 231. This observation is precisely correct. Although we long for the real, our occasional contacts with it are occasions of abject, sickening terror. As discussed in Chapter 2, the real is, after all, the total obliteration of our subjectivity.

14. As E. H. Gombich noted in his classic study, in the painting that depicts the cathedral at noon, Monet suggests "the effect of the midday sun by exploiting the dazzle that results from its glare, and such pictures will even gain in poetry from the artist's determination to achieve the impossible." E. H. GOMBICH, ART AND ILLUSION: A STUDY IN THE PSYCHOLOGY OF PICTORIAL REPRESENTATION 49 (1969).

15. National Gallery of Art, *Rouen Cathedral, West Facade, Sunlight—Notes* (visited Sept. 20, 1998) <http://www.nga.gov/cgi-bin/pinfo?Object = 46371+0-note>.

nuisances,[16] *Property Rules, Liability Rules, and Inalienability: One View of the Cathedral,*[17] almost thirty years ago. Their article has generated virtually endless discussion in the literature.[18]

Their title, an allusion to Monet's cathedral series, supposedly expresses modesty. Calabresi and Melamed claim that their taxonomy is not an attempt to capture all of property or environmental law, but rather only one way of looking at them—useful tools for legal scholars and decision makers. They state that their "article is meant to be only one of Monet's paintings of the Cathedral at Rouen. To understand the Cathedral one must see all of them."[19]

In fact, these protestations of humility are evidence of hubris. Modesty is psychoanalytically feminine, in that it only exists insofar as it slips away. The moment modesty announces herself, she has already been replaced by pride. Unlike Monet, who wished to suggest that which cannot be captured, Calabresi and Melamed claim to capture the immediacy of property. They claim to give one view of the cathedral and insist that we can understand the cathedral if we see all of the views.[20] Monet's point, however, was that we can only understand the cathedral when we realize that the real—excess enjoyment—can never be seen, even in an infinite number of views.

The difference between their respective approaches is the difference between metonymy and metaphor. Monet's paintings are a pictorial example of metonymy, the feminine trope of signification.[21] In metonymy, the signifier suggests the signified through proximity. It describes not the

16. In this chapter, I am not limiting the term "nuisance" to its technical legal meaning. Rather, for lack of another suitable term, I use the term expansively, as shorthand for claims that one person is harmed by the polluting acts of another, regardless of whether such claims are based on tort, property, or other principles. My terminology reflects Calabresi and Melamed's project of developing a unified economic analysis of environmental harms.

17. Guido Calabresi & A. Douglas Melamed, *Property Rules, Liability Rules, and Inalienability: One View of the Cathedral,* 85 HARV. L. REV. 1089 (1972).

18. One numerically inclined pair of authors recently reported that Westlaw listed over 388 law review articles citing the original Calabresi and Melamed article through 1995. *See* James E. Krier & Stewart J. Schwab, *Property Rules and Liability Rules: The Cathedral in Another Light,* 70 N.Y.U. L. REV. 440, 440 n.4 (1995). Another search of Westlaw's journal and law review database revealed that 595 pieces cited the Calabresi and Melamed article. *See* Search of Westlaw, JLR library (Sept. 6, 1998). There are no doubt hundreds of citations not included in the computerized sources. *See* Krier & Schwab, *supra,* at 440 n.4. The *Yale Law Journal* even published a symposium issue, *see Symposium, Property Rules, Liability Rules, and Inalienability: A Twenty-Five Year Retrospective,* 106 YALE L.J. 2081 (1997), based on panel discussions on the impact of the Calabresi and Melamed article at the Association of American Law Schools 1997 Annual Meeting.

19. Calabresi & Melamed, *supra* note 17, at 1089 n.2.

20. *See id.*

21. *See* JANE GALLOP, READING LACAN 121–31 (1985).

thing itself, but parts of the thing or that which surrounds it. Calabresi and Melamed, in contradistinction, adopt the masculine trope of metaphor. In metaphor, the signifier attempts to capture the signified and to reduce signification to meaning by declaring the essential similarity or identity of the signifier and the signified. In metaphor, the signifier stands for the signified; in metonymy, the signifier stands by the signified.[22]

In Chapter 1, I suggested that property serves a purpose in the creation of legal subjectivity, which parallels the role of sexuality in the creation of psychoanalytical subjectivity. In *The Vestal and the Fasces,*[23] I showed how we use anatomic imagery to describe the psychoanalytically phallic concept of property. In this chapter, I further explore the persistent use of masculine and feminine phallic metaphors for property.[24] The masculine metaphor relies on implicit metaphors of the male organ and envisions property as the sensuous grasp of a tangible thing to be displayed and wielded before others. The loss of property is analogized to castration. Property, which is necessarily a mediated trilateral (or even quadrilateral) relationship, is reduced to an immediate bilateral one. Consequently, the masculine metaphor vacillates between identifying property solely with the element of possession—the relationship of the owning subject to the owned object[25]—and identifying it solely with the element of exchange (the relationship between two legal subjects to which the object is irrelevant).[26] In exchange, the object of exchange becomes monetized and irrelevant in that each party is indifferent between retaining its object of exchange and obtaining whatever is offered in exchange. Therefore, Calabresi and Melamed see property regimes (possession) and liability regimes (exchange) as alternatives.[27] This approach reflects the two inconsistent strategies that the masculine position can take in a vain attempt to deny castration. Like Narcissus in order to maintain masculine subjectivity, these strategies are ways to repress the feminine and engage in the homoerotic fantasy of perfect immediate relation.

22. Lacan defined metaphor as the substitution of "one word for another," and metonymy as a substitution "word-to-word." Jacques Lacan, *The Agency of the Letter in the Unconscious or Reason Since Freud* [hereinafter, Lacan, *Agency of the Letter*], in JACQUES LACAN, ÉCRITS: A SELECTION 146, 156–57 (Alan Sheridan trans., 1977) (1966) [hereinafter LACAN, ÉCRITS].

23. SCHROEDER, THE VESTAL AND THE FASCES, *supra* note 4.

24. *See id.* at xvi, 4, 111–12; Jeanne L. Schroeder, *Juno Moneta: On the Erotics of the Market Place,* 54 WASHINGTON & LEE L. REV. 995, 1022 (1997) [hereinafter Schroeder, *Juno Moneta*].

25. *See, e.g.,* JEREMY WALDRON, THE RIGHT TO PRIVATE PROPERTY 34 (1988). The allocation of resources—the identification of the rightful owner—is the definition of possession, which is only one of the three elements of property, albeit the most primitive one. *See* SCHROEDER, THE VESTAL AND THE FASCES, *supra* note 4, at 37–39; *see also* Jeanne L. Schroeder, *Chix Nix Bundle-O-Stix: A Feminist Critique of the Disaggregation of Property,* 95 MICH. L. REV. 239, 264–66 (1994) [hereinafter, Schroeder, *Chix*].

26. *See* Schroeder, *Juno Moneta, supra* note 24, at 1024.

27. *See* Calabresi & Melamed, *supra* note 17, at 1106–10.

In contrast, the feminine phallic metaphor relies on the imagery of the female body. The owning subject identifies with the owned object in such a way as to become indistinguishable from it. Property is that which one enters and enjoys and which one protects from invasion by others. Property is reduced to the single element of enjoyment. Loss of property is imagined as violation, as loss of self.[28]

The law-and-economics debate on environmental "nuisances," based on Calabresi and Melamed's trichotomy, is one of the most extreme examples of the masculine phallic metaphor for property in contemporary legal scholarship. It represses the psychoanalytically feminine aspects of property. It implicitly adopts the masculine phallic metaphor for property as either unmediated possession—the unfettered and exclusive physical custody of tangible objects by an owner—or unmediated alienation through exchange (economic bargaining in which specific objects are irrelevant). Because their trichotomy represses enjoyment—the feminine third—Calabresi and Melamed cannot accurately describe environmental disputes. Environmental nuisances involve neither the taking of a single object nor the exchange of entitlements. Rather, they involve rival claims of enjoyment of different objects by different owners, such that one party claims to be violated by the other.[29]

This debate also represses the necessary *jus tertii* of property law. The unrecognized third—that is, the necessity of mediation—is also an aspect of the "feminine." The debate at one moment imagines that property can be reduced to possession and that possession is a simple, immediate relation of subject to object that exists outside of law. The mediating regime of law does not define the relationship of the owner with other persons in society; it merely enforces the prelegal concept of possession. Property is seen initially as a binary relationship between subject and object rather than a tri-

28. As discussed in Chapter 1, an obvious example of this is Margaret Jane Radin's theory of property for personhood. *See* SCHROEDER, THE VESTAL AND THE FASCES, *supra* note 4, at 4; Schroeder, *Juno Moneta, supra* note 24, at 1016, 1023.

One critique of the Calabresi trichotomy also unwittingly privileges enjoyment over the other elements. Specifically, Madeline Morris collapses Hohfeld's concepts of rights and privileges into a single right of "in-kind enjoyment of the object," thereby not only misunderstanding Hohfeld's taxonomy, which suppresses objects entirely, but also subsuming the right of possession entirely under the right of enjoyment. Madeline Morris, *The Structure of Entitlements,* 78 CORNELL L. REV. 822, 830–33 (1993).

29. The literature only occasionally and sporadically recognizes this point. For example, Polinsky states that environmental nuisances involve "incompatible land use," A. Mitchell Polinsky, *Resolving Nuisance Disputes: The Simple Economics of Injunctive and Damage Remedies,* 32 STAN. L. REV. 1075, 1075 (1980). Polinsky is probably the most insightful scholar working within the Calabresi-Melamed framework, and I refer approvingly to his analysis throughout the notes to this chapter. Unfortunately, he does not internalize that the logical implication of his insight is a rejection of the Calabresi-Melamed taxonomy.

lateral interrelationship of legal subjects with respect to a mediating object of desire. When the debate is forced to recognize the existence of another subject, the relationship once again becomes binary, as the mediating object disappears and is replaced by the intersubjective fungibility of money and economic indifference. Most importantly, the analysis of this immediate two-party relationship of exchange ignores and fails to account for the existence of third parties who are potential rival claimants for the forgotten object of desire. This difficulty explains why law-and-economics has so fervently embraced game theory. Although theoretically possible, multiparty games are not only extremely difficult, but rarely lead to one clear solution.[30] Consequently, the games played by the followers of Calabresi and Melamed involve only two parties, thus reducing all human relationships to binary relations. The recognition of the third (the feminine) is always postponed.[31]

This chapter is not intended to be a comprehensive account of the literature begat by Calabresi and Melamed. Rather, it critiques the assumptions and implicit imagery underlying this literature. First, I introduce the Calabresi-Melamed trichotomy. I argue that it reduces property to a single element, vacillating between possession and exchange. The trichotomy thereby fails to achieve its stated goal of serving as a taxonomy of environmental nuisances involving disputes over enjoyment. Second, I show how the Calabresi-Melamed analysis cannot be applied in a world with more than two

30. *See* John Cassiday, *The Decline of Economics,* The New Yorker, Dec. 2, 1996, at 50. Carol Rose implicitly noted this problem of the standard economic approach. For example, she critiqued the analysis by Ian Ayres and Eric Talley that I critiqued in Schroeder, *Three's a Crowd, supra* note 1, for "removing the large numbers of participants in those cases, and instead treating nuisances as two-party matters." Carol M. Rose, *The Shadow of The Cathedral,* 106 Yale L.J. 2175, 2183 (1997).

31. The other way of reducing multiparty relations to two-party games is to pit an individual player against an aggregate of other parties. An example of this can be found in the first chapter of Eric Rasmusen, Games and Information (1989), one of the standard introductory game theory textbooks. Rasmusen set forth an introductory game based on a hypothetical meeting of OPEC. *See id.* at 21–27. Although he described this as a game among five players who are playing simultaneously—Saudi Arabia, Libya, Venezuela, Kuwait, and Nigeria—in fact the game played in the text is between two parties: Saudi Arabia and "Others." *Id.* at 25, 26.

The prevalence of the masculine metaphor and the repression of the feminine metaphor in the legal literature on environmental nuisances is even more remarkable, considering the historic dominance of the feminine metaphor in discussions of man's exploitation of nature. (For a feminist critique of this tradition, see, for example, Carolyn Merchant, The Death of Nature: Women, Ecology and the Scientific Revolution [1980].) The term "pollution" means "defilement" in the religious and sexual senses and was not extended to environmental harms until the nineteenth century. XII Oxford English Dictionary 43 (2d ed. 1989).

parties. The coherence of the trichotomy depends on maintaining a distinction between property and liability regimes. In a world of three parties (or dynamite), this distinction cannot be maintained.[32]

THREE'S A CROWD: THE CALABRESI AND MELAMED TRICHOTOMY

A sea of ink has been spilled purporting to derive concrete policy recommendations from the Calabresi-Melamed taxonomy. Their trichotomy quickly became one of the foremost schools of property analysis in contemporary American jurisprudence. Their article richly deserves its reputation. It is bold, elegant, concise, and thought-provoking. It is also wrong. It reflects an unworkable, naive conception of property—the masculine phallic metaphor—and concentrates on the wrong elements of property: possession as physical custody and alienation through exchange.

This chapter is a critique, not a criticism, of Calabresi and Melamed. The mere recourse to phallic metaphors cannot be objectionable. My own writings are full of such imagery. All language necessarily consists of metaphor and metonymy.[33] Problems arise, however, when we unconsciously accept our metaphors and let them control the analysis. In this chapter, I try to make the metaphors explicit so that we can be critically aware of how we use them and how they use us.

Calabresi and Melamed tried to unify, and thereby clarify, the seemingly disparate areas of environmental property and tort law.[34] They suggest that all environmental claims involve either assertions of entitlement or allegations of interference with an entitlement.[35] From an economic perspective, the first task of both property and tort law is to decide which of two rivals should be awarded a disputed entitlement.[36] Once the entitlement is allocated, the law must then decide what remedies to use to protect this allocation. Remedies can either maintain or restore the status quo ante with respect to the entitlement or compensate the original entitlement claimant

32. In Schroeder, *Three's a Crowd, supra* note 1, I discuss certain recent refinements of the Calabresi and Melamed thesis proposed by Ian Ayres and Eric Talley and show that these refinements replicate, rather than solve, these inherent flaws. *See* Ian Ayres & Eric Talley, *Solomonic Bargaining: Dividing a Legal Entitlement to Facilitate Coasean Trade,* 104 YALE L.J. 1027 (1995).

33. *See generally* Lacan, *Agency of the Letter, supra* note 22, at 146–59.

34. *See* Calabresi & Melamed, *supra* note 17, at 1089.

35. *See id.* at 1089–92.

36. *See id.* at 1090. Polinsky implicitly recognized that Calabresi and Melamed were incorrect in analyzing this task as an allocation of a "thing." He more accurately described the choice in the environmental nuisance situation as a decision "as to who is entitled to prevail" in a specific dispute. Polinsky, *supra* note 29, at 1076.

for the loss of the entitlement. Sometimes the law entirely removes the entitlement from the market.

Calabresi and Melamed categorize all remedies into three sets: property rules, liability rules, and inalienability rules.[37] This terminology is not merely useless; it is pernicious. It not only fails to reflect any existing legal regime, but also posits a legal regime that is both empirically and theoretically impossible in a world of more than two people.

The trichotomy is flawed for a number of interrelated reasons: (1) it confuses the definition of rights with the enforcement of rights; (2) it suppresses enjoyment, the element of property that classic environmental disputes invoke, and concentrates on possession and alienation; and (3) it inaccurately characterizes property as a binary relationship, preempting description of any actual or possible property regime in which three parties (or dynamite) exist. Indeed, the distinction between property and liability remedies, upon which the taxonomy depends, breaks down in the real world of multiple parties and destruction of property.

Other authors have partially raised a number of these critiques.[38] Nevertheless, these authors treat their insights as quibbles. They basically accept the Calabresi and Melamed paradigm and work within its strictures. This stance is particularly surprising because Calabresi and Melamed purport to

37. Calabresi and Melamed understand that as an empirical matter these categories may not have clearly defined borders: "It should be clear that most entitlements to most goods are mixed." *Id.* at 1093. As I have discussed extensively elsewhere, and will return to later, this uncertainty is probably true of all qualitative distinctions and is not in and of itself a reason to reject the trichotomy. *See, e.g.,* Jeanne L. Schroeder, *Never Jam To-day: On the Impossibility of Takings Jurisprudence,* 84 GEO. L.J. 1531, 1554–58 (1996) [hereinafter, Schroeder, *Never Jam To-day*].

38. For example, Jules Coleman and Jody Kraus chide Calabresi and Melamed for their conflation of the definition of rights and the enforcement of rights *(See* Jules L. Coleman & Jody Kraus, *Rethinking the Theory of Legal Rights,* 95 YALE L. J. 1335, 1342–47 [1986]), and for their confusion of damages for prior harms with a purchase price for involuntary sales. *See id.* at 1356–64. Louis Kaplow and Steven Shavell suggest, as I do, that environmental nuisances cause harms fundamentally distinct from those caused by possessory property disputes. *See* Louis Kaplow & Steven Shavell, *Property Rules Versus Liability Rules: An Economic Analysis,* 109 HARV. L. REV. 713, 715–18 (1996). James Krier and Stewart Schwab note the empirical inaccuracy of the models based on the trichotomy. *See* Krier & Schwab, *supra* note 18, at 477–83. Ian Ayres and Eric Talley challenge Calabresi and Melamed's identification of property with equity. *See* Ayres & Talley, *supra* note 32, at 1031. Dale Nance implicitly recognized a number of my criticisms, including my observations that the trichotomy does not deal adequately with the possibility of the destruction of the object of entitlement, that the property/liability dichotomy cannot be applied prospectively, and that the awarding of limited damages in tort cases does not mean tortfeasors have a "call" on the entitlements of tort victims. *See* Dale A. Nance, *Guidance Rules and Enforcement Rules: A Better View of the Cathedral,* 83 VA. L. REV. 837, 842–58 (1997).

base their paradigm largely on Ronald Coase's *The Problem of Social Cost.*[39] As discussed in the previous chapter, not only does Coase recognize that environmental disputes involve what I call the feminine element of enjoyment; in fact, Coase's primary point was to chide his fellow economists for assuming what I call the masculine phallic metaphor.

I offer a unified critique, showing that these seemingly disparate criticisms all spring from the same fatal flaw, which renders the original thesis worthless: the trichotomy privileges the masculine metaphor for property and represses the feminine. Unable to recognize thirdness, it vacillates between treating property as an immediate binary relation of subject to object (possession confused with physical custody) and treating it as an immediate binary relation of subject to subject (alienation and exchange confused with the physical transfer of custody). The trichotomy ignores the feminine as "the trick of singularity"[40]—the identification of subject with object in enjoyment. Furthermore, it ignores the feminine as trilateral relation—the necessity of mediation in all legal relations. The trichotomy presumes that entitlements exist outside of and prior to law and that the law merely allocates and enforces property. It sees property and liability rules as alternate enforcement regimes. In fact, however, law constitutes entitlements. All property regimes define, rather than merely allocate, entitlements. Rather than being alternates, property rules and liability rules necessarily coexist. These errors all reflect the single perspective of the psychoanalytically masculine sexuated position.

The Trichotomy

Under a Calabresi-Melamed "property" regime, an entitlement can be transferred only with the consent of the holder. Society respects the entitlement holder's idiosyncratic or "subjective" valuation of his entitlement and does not impose its collective valuation. In Calabresi and Melamed's words, "property rules involve a collective decision as to who is to be given an initial entitlement but not as to the value of the entitlement."[41]

Property remedies are, therefore, those that prevent a second party from taking an entitlement holder's property without his consent or those that restore the status quo ante by returning the taken object to the original claimant.[42] While Calabresi and Melamed do not expressly specify what

39. R. H. Coase, *The Problem of Social Cost,* 3 J. L. & Econ. 1 (1960).
40. William Shakespeare, *Twelfth Night* act 2, scene 5 (internal quotation marks omitted).
41. Calabresi & Melamed, *supra* note 17, at 1092.
42. *See id.* at 1118.

actual judicial remedies would fall within these categories, they briefly mention injunctions.[43] They also suggest that meaningful criminal sanctions would be property-like.[44] In context, however, Calabresi and Melamed seem to think primarily in terms of the traditional equitable remedies of injunction, specific performance, and replevin.[45] These are remedies by which possession can be restored.

Unfortunately, the element of property involved in environmental harms is the feminine one of enjoyment. Once enjoyment is violated, it is not clear that the status quo can be restored, because the object itself (and the owning subject) may have been irretrievably changed by the experience. She, as well as her object, are "polluted," in the original sexual and religious sense of violated, desecrated, defiled, or made impure.[46]

Even in the case of a true possessory dispute, the reduction of property rights to injunction, specific performance, and replevin is a fantasy. In a world in which there are more than two possible claimants to the objects of desire and in which objects can be destroyed, the law is often unsuccessful

43. *See id.* at 1116.

44. I say "meaningful" because, as Kaplow and Shavell correctly pointed out, some ostensibly criminal sanctions are so light that they are more accurately characterized as liability rules. *See* Kaplow & Shavell, *supra* note 38, at 753. For example, traffic laws discourage, rather than entirely eliminate, certain behavior. *See id.* In my home town of New York City, the substantial fines charged for illegal parking are treated by delivery companies as a necessary cost of doing business.

45. For example, in one of the best analyses to come out of the Calabresi-Melamed debate, Polinsky largely avoided property-liability terminology in favor of speaking about the relative advantages of injunctive and damage remedies. *See* Polinsky, *supra* note 29, at 1075–78.

46. Interestingly, at least one critic of Calabresi and Melamed implicitly recognized this feminine sexual aspect of pollution. Richard Epstein gives as an example of the absurdity of the notorious Calabresi and Melamed's "hypothetical four," by applying it to the law of rape:

> The enormous risk of this rule should be seen instantly if we propound its analogy for violations to the person. Just to say that "a woman can stop a man from raping her, but if she does she must compensate him" shows how far this position is from an ordinary understanding of rights, and it is with great relief that Calabresi and Melamed do not carry their innovation to this extreme. Rather, they note elsewhere that concern with "bodily integrity" precludes the application of an ordinary liability (take and pay) in these contexts. Obviously [hypothetical four] would be still more grotesque.

Richard A. Epstein, *A Clear View of The Cathedral: The Dominance of Property Rules,* 106 YALE L. J. 2091, 2103–04 (1997) (footnote omitted). Epstein damns Calabresi and Melamed with the faint praise that the only reason that their analysis is not totally "grotesque" is that they do not have the courage of their convictions to apply it to hard cases. *Id.* Of course, Richard Posner, the most ardent believer in law-and-economics, does not flinch from grotesquerie (and does not recognize that the grotesquerie is itself an argument against his analysis). Posner came close to analyzing rape in the market terms Epstein condemn. *See* RICHARD A. POSNER, SEX AND REASON 383–95 (1992).

in preventing a taking; if a taking has occurred, it is often practically and theoretically impossible to restore amends.

Under a Calabresi-Melamed "liability" regime, society imposes its intersubjective valuation on entitlement holders.[47] This means that involuntary transfers will be upheld over the protests of the original entitlement holder, as long as the transferee gives the value of the thing taken to the transferor.[48] Damages are set by reference to market value[49] (intersubjective valuation), regardless of the victim's subjective valuation of her loss.

This supposedly descriptive account in fact works a sea change in the law. As Coleman and Kraus complain, Calabresi and Melamed transform compensation for loss into an option price payable by the tortfeasor for purchase of an entitlement from an involuntary seller.[50] The tortfeasor is, in effect, deemed to have a call option on the tort-victim's "entitlement" to bodily integrity. The Calabresi-Melamed description tries to achieve an immediate binary relation by suppressing the objective aspect of the property relation in favor of the intersubjective. The object of property loses all independent significance because it is completely monetized. In this economy, the parties are completely indifferent between retaining the object of desire and obtaining the purchase price: the object ceases to be desired. In the final part of this chapter, I argue that this shift reflects the second masculine strategy for denying castration. When one is forced to admit that the object of desire is gone, the masculine subject claims that he only temporarily relinquished the object of desire in exchange for a future substitute object.

47. *See* Calabresi & Melamed, *supra* note 17, at 1092. They refer to society's valuation as being "objective[ ]," *Id.* By doing so they were not invoking the definition of "objective" as to external, scientific "truth," The English word "objective" is a chameleon of constantly changing shades of meaning. *See generally* Jeanne L. Schroeder, *Subject: Object,* 47 U. MIAMI L. REV. 1 (1992). Calabresi and Melamed are using the common alternate definition of that which is decided by intersubjective consensus, or what I have called "Community Objectivity." *Id.* at 17–24. This is "objective" in the sense that it is not unique to any one individual subject. *See id.* at 17. Consequently, Calabresi and Melamed referred to objective value as the "collective determination of the value," Calabresi & Melamed, *supra* note 17, at 1106. Although I often adopt this common and useful definition, I avoid it in this chapter as confusing for my present purposes. Unless I expressly state otherwise, I am limiting the word "objective" to the philosophic and psychoanalytic sense of that which relates to object relations. In my terminology, the Calabresi-Melamed trichotomy is "objective" when it attempts to reduce property to the immediate relationship of subject and object—possession as physical custody—even though this attempt also requires the enforcement of the owning subject's "subjective" valuation of the object. The analysis of property rights in terms of exchange and collective valuation of society is more accurately termed "intersubjective."

48. *See id.* at 1092, 1106.

49. *See* Kaplow & Shavell, *supra* note 38, at 731.

50. *See* Coleman & Kraus, *supra* note 38, at 1357.

Even if damages are *economically* equivalent to a call option, it does not follow that they are equivalent for legal, philosophical, or moral purposes. This analysis misperceives not only the nature of the property right being infringed in an environmental harm, but also the nature of the infringing action.

As I discuss, liability remedies may be all that any law can guarantee. This result, however, can never completely be satisfactory. To pretend that monetary compensation is payment for the taken object is to pretend that one consented to castration. According to Coleman and Kraus, a super wealth maximizer like Richard Posner would consider all transfers to be "voluntary" under a proper liability regime; it is just that sometimes the consent is purchased retroactively through the payment of damages.[51] Such an attempt to satisfy retroactively the consensual aspect of exchange is doomed.[52] Even if we can restore the economic value of the lost object of desire, it does not follow that we can relieve the psychic injury of the lost control over one's life. When something is taken without the consent of the holder, there are two harms: first, the loss of the entitlement that Calabresi and Melamed identify; and second, the injury to the claimant's personal autonomy.

To put it another way, if what is violated is not only the masculine element of possession, but also the feminine element of enjoyment, monetary compensation will not restore the lost experience. Damages are metaphor—they substitute one term for another. Even the most rabid Benthamite recognizes the empirical difference between having the right and ability to enjoy a thing, on the one hand, and having no such right but money in the bank, on the other, regardless of their economic equivalence. Accepting arguendo that one could be indifferent between enjoying one's object and possessing money, provided that the price were high enough, it does not necessarily follow that one also would be indifferent between having the exclusive right and power to make this decision and having the choice thrust upon one in exchange for money. This loss of autonomy is violation—the feminine analog to castration.[53]

Moreover, as my hypotheticals will make clear, Calabresi and Melamed are incorrect in identifying a liability rule as a "remedy regime." Their con-

51. Coleman and Kraus recognized that Posner does not state this view expressly, but it is implicit in and required by "the internal logic of his argument." *Id.* at 1358–65.

52. *See id.* at 1359–65. Coleman and Kraus specifically critique Posner for interpreting damages as a form of retroactive consent. *See id.* As they accurately state, this insistence on consent shows a solicitude towards autonomy that is peculiar for a wealth-maximizer like Posner. A true wealth-maximizer need not concern himself with consent so long as wealth is maximized. *See id.* at 1361.

53. Of course, the pure utilitarian would argue that violation is just another form of disutility. Consequently, if damages are designed to make the victim indifferent, they should be set not merely at the victim's subjective valuation of the entitlement itself, but at that amount plus some additional amount to compensate her for her loss of integrity.

cept of a remedy regime presupposes that the entitlement preexists the remedy. On the contrary, the entitlement is nothing but the remedy. The monetization of a right is *by definition* the division of the right between or among claimants. Consequently, a "liability" regime is necessarily a rule of entitlement definition, not merely one of entitlement enforcement.

As its name suggests, under an "inalienability" regime, an entitlement may not be transferred in any (or at least most) market circumstances.[54] For example, in this country, most of my body parts are market-inalienable.[55] Not only will the courts refuse to enforce a contract to sell a kidney, but the state might also use its police power to enjoin such a contract or to impose criminal or civil penalties on the contracting parties.

Most commentators ignore, or give cursory treatment to, this final category and treat the Calabresi-Melamed trichotomy as though it were a dichotomy. This miscategorization occurs because classic law-and-economics theorists usually deem all entitlements monetizable:[56] at the appropriate price, one is indifferent between owning the entitlement or receiving the price. If entitlements are monetizable, then they should also be alienable. Typically, inalienability is defended in terms of paternalism or justice,[57] about which law-and-economic analysis arguably has little to say.

Perhaps more importantly, it seems to many that there is something intuitively wrong with including this last category within a taxonomy of enforcement remedies. As a result, there is a tendency to exclude inalienability rules from the analysis on the grounds that they are fundamentally different from property and liability rules. Calabresi and Melamed somewhat sheepishly step back from their trichotomy because this third category seems to fit poorly with the other two: "Unlike [property and liability] rules, rules of inalienability not only 'protect' the entitlement; they may also be viewed as limiting or regulating the grant of the entitlement itself."[58]

In contradistinction, I defend Calabresi and Melamed's initial instinct that the third category belongs with the other two, but I criticize their belated attempt to distinguish it. The presumption underlying the Calabresi-Melamed taxonomy—that one can analyze environmental nuisances in terms of the possession and exchange of entitlements—logically requires the

54. *See* Calabresi & Melamed, *supra* note 17, at 1111.

55. Blood is a rare exception to this rule, but even the alienation of blood tends to be highly regulated. Some body parts may be alienable in other nonmarket contexts.

56. For example, as I discuss in Chapter 4, Posner champions the goal of wealth maximization.

57. Calabresi and Melamed analyze inalienability in these terms. *See id.* at 1111–13. Of course, there is a utilitarian way of defending inalienability. The sale of body parts might so offend a portion of the population that the aggregate utility lost by society generally would exceed any utility gained by the parties to a contract for such a sale.

58. *Id.* at 1093.

inalienability category. If the ability to be free from pollution or to pollute is a thing that one can possess and alienate through exchange, then this necessarily implies that these exchanges have terms and that society could impose restrictions on these terms.

Furthermore, the very reason that it seems intuitively inappropriate to analyze inalienability as a *remedy* applies equally to property and liability rules. In formulating these rules, Calabresi and Melamed implicitly assume that entitlements preexist law. Entitlements, for them, are unitary, indivisible concepts that the law merely allocates and enforces.[59] Before I apply a standard Hohfeldian analysis to the six possible hypotheticals that the Calabresi-Melamed taxonomy can generate, I would like to set forth a few thoughts on the Coase theorem, on which Calabresi and Melamed think their system is based.

A Word on Coase

Calabresi and Melamed adopt the standard law-and-economics proposition that law should seek to maximize wealth or utility.[60] Under wealth (or utility) maximization, efficiency demands that if the original entitlement holder values her entitlement less than another party, then the original holder must transfer her entitlement to that other party. Ordinarily, based on the assumption that individuals are the best judges of their own values and utilities and that values and utilities can be monetized, legal economists prefer to leave these entitlement transfers to the voluntary world of contract.[61]

Calabresi and Melamed repeat the standard misreading of the Coase Theorem: absent "transaction costs," parties will instantly contract so that all good things immediately end up in the hands of the higher valuing user, regardless of the original location of the entitlement.[62] Indeed, they have always already done so because in the so-called Coasean universe of the perfect market there is no time. Or, to reduce the Coase Theorem to its simplest

59. *See id.* at 1106–10.

60. *Id.* at 1093–1101. I do not mean to imply that Calabresi and Melamed deny that law might also consider other values. Indeed, they were very careful to admit the possibility of distributional and what they called "other justice reasons," although that they were at a loss to imagine an example of the latter which could not be subsumed into the categories of efficiency or distribution. *See id.* at 1102–105.

61. *See id.* 1093–96. *See also* RICHARD A. POSNER, ECONOMIC ANALYSIS OF LAW 86 (5th ed. 1998).

62. *See* Calabresi & Melamed, *supra* note 17, at 1094–95; *see also* Schroeder, *Juno Moneta,* supra note 24, at 995. For a highly amusing critique of the Calabresi-Melamed debate on similar grounds, see Krier & Schwab, *supra* note 18, at 482–83. Krier and Schwab conclude that although this debate is arid, jejune, and often meaningless, engaging in such debate is what all law professors (including themselves) do. *See id.*

formulation, in a world in which all mistakes are instantly corrected, mistakes don't matter. As discussed in the previous chapter, we do not, nor could we ever, live in a Coasean universe—as Coase was the first to point out. Given the existence of various types of transaction costs, Calabresi and Melamed ask: can we manipulate remedial regimes in order to mitigate market failure and encourage good things to flow to higher valuing users?[63]

Although Calabresi and Melamed purport to base their trichotomy largely on the Coase Theorem, Coase himself almost entirely avoids their errors. Coase does not reduce property to possession and alienation. Indeed, Coase expressly emphasizes what I identify as the feminine aspect of environmental disputes, although he does not use my Lacanian terminology. Coase understands that environmental nuisances do not involve disputes over possession or exchange of a single thing. Rather, they involve disputes over necessarily incompatible enjoyments of different things. Consequently, he ends *The Problem of Social Cost* by stating:

> A final reason for the failure to develop a theory adequate to handle the problem of harmful effects stems from a faulty concept of a factor of production. This is usually thought of as a physical entity which the businessman acquires and uses (an acre of land, a ton of fertilizer) instead of as a right to perform certain (physical) actions. We may speak of a person owning land and using it as a factor of production but what the land-owner in fact possesses is the right to carry out a circumscribed list of actions. The rights of a land-owner are not unlimited.[64]

To translate Coase into my terminology: the economic theory of environmental nuisances is inadequate precisely because it reduces property to the single element of possession, imagined as an immediate binary sensuous relationship with a tangible thing. Economic theory often confuses the right of possession with the thing itself. We need to remember not only that property consists of elements other than possession, but also that it is inherently relational. Environmental nuisances, specifically, involve rival claims to competing enjoyments of different objects. Economists (and lawyers) are responsible for determining the relative boundaries of each rival's rights.

Coase demonstrated this idea with the example of an individual who has a chimney of a certain height attached to his fireplace.[65] A neighbor builds a wall on the top of his adjacent house that partially blocks the chimney, so that smoke from the first person's fireplace billows into her flat rather than escaping up the chimney. The chimney owner argues that the neighbor harmed her by building the wall. The court found that one cannot assume

63. *See* Calabresi & Melamed, *supra* note 17, at 1119–21.
64. Coase, *supra* note 39, at 43–44.
65. *See Bryant v. Lefever,* 4 C.P.D. 172, 173 (1879); *see also* Coase, *supra* note 39, at 11–13.

that either party caused harm to the other as a matter of law. Many but-for causes of the "harm" to the first party existed. "But for" the neighbor's enjoyment of his own premises by building a wall, the smoke would not have entered the chimney owner's apartment. It is equally true, however, that there would have been no smoke "but for" the chimney owner's enjoyment of her fireplace by building a fire.

> The smoke nuisance was caused both by the man who built the wall and by the man who lit the fires. Given the fires, there would have been no smoke nuisance without the wall; given the wall, there would have been no smoke nuisance without the fires. Eliminate the wall or the fires and the smoke nuisance would disappear.[66]

In Coase's terminology, the problem lies in the parties' relative claims being "reciprocal," in the sense that "[to] avoid the harm to *B* would inflict harm on *A*."[67] On the one hand, the neighbor's enjoyment of his property (building a wall) makes it impossible for the chimney owner fully to enjoy her property (using the fireplace). On the other hand, recognition of the chimney owner's right to enjoy her fireplace impedes the ability of the neighbor to enjoy his property (i.e., the neighbor would have to refrain from building walls and tear down any wall already built.) What Coase analyzes in terms of necessarily inconsistent claims to enjoyment of two different objects (reciprocity), Calabresi and Melamed misinterpret as disputes regarding symmetrical claims to *possession* of a *single* object.[68]

Coase intuitively replicates Wesley Newcomb Hohfeld's observation that legal rights do not exist in a vacuum but can only be understood as relations between and among specific legal actors.[69] Coase took a step beyond Hohfeld, however, and approached the Hegelian-Lacanian conclusion.[70] If rights are not prelegal, then they must be granted by law. Law is a matter of creation, not discovery; the legal universe is not static, but dynamic. Law is open-ended, and the rights it creates will never be perfectly symmetrical because different legal rules may serve inconsistent competing values.

66. *Id.* at 13.

67. *Id.* at 2 (italics added).

68. As Carol Rose stated, Calabresi and Melamed analyzed entitlements in terms of "bilateral symmetry." Rose, *supra* note 30, at 2177. Rose presented this analysis as one of their two widely cited analytical contributions, *Id.* In fact, I think it is one of the most fundamental failings of the analysis.

69. Ronald H. Coase, The Firm, the Market, and the Law 119–23 (1988) with Wesley Newcomb Hohfeld, Fundamental Legal Conceptions as Applied in Legal Reasoning 74–75 (W. Cook ed. 1919).

70. *See* Coase, *supra* note 39, at 19–28.

SIX HYPOTHETICALS

As a prelude to my critique of the trichotomy, I provide a detailed description of the six paradigmatic hypothetical situations the trichotomy generates. The trichotomy presupposes that there is a preexisting thing—an entitlement—that is to be allocated to one of two rivals.[71] If the non-owner infringes on the entitlement, this infringement is deemed a transfer of the entitlement to the infringing party.[72] In their original article, Calabresi and Melamed stated that their system generates four hypotheticals, although one is rare in the private realm.[73] In fact, if their taxonomy is viable, it generates six hypotheticals, because there are two possible allocations of entitlements and three possible regimes—property, liability, and inalienability.

In my initial analysis of the Calabresi and Melamed hypotheticals, I apply the well known system of jural correlatives developed by Hohfeld.[74] Although I am highly critical of Hohfeld's particular analysis of property[75] and his assumptions of complementarity, his system of jural correlatives is a powerful tool of analysis. Hohfeld developed his taxonomy to identify and define traditional categories of legal relations.[76] No doubt we could invent other taxonomies, and we probably could break down his eight primary categories into subcategories of rights. Hohfeld's system nevertheless has the advantage of being generally familiar. It has met the test of time because it displays that rare quality called elegance—the right balance of simplicity and sophistication. It is easily understood and can be usefully applied to a wide variety of legal topics.[77]

I use Hohfeld's system to show several things. First, Calabresi and Melamed were naive in thinking they could distinguish between remedies and legal rights. Rather, enforcement regimes are part and parcel of the enti-

71. *See* Calabresi & Melamed, *supra* note 17, at 1115–16.

72. *See id.* at 1116.

73. *See id.* at 1116–17; Krier & Schwab, *supra* note 18, at 442–45.

74. *See* HOHFELD, *supra* note 69, at 23, 50–51.

75. I set forth my critique of Hohfeld's property jurisprudence in Schroeder, *Chix, supra* note 25, at 290–99, and SCHROEDER, THE VESTAL AND THE FASCES, *supra* note 4, at 1–7, 168–79.

76. *See* HOHFELD, *supra* note 69, at 27–28, 35–36.

77. Although Hohfeld's project looks unique to modern eyes, Joseph Singer has shown that this judgment is an anachronism. Proposing taxonomies of legal categories was a standard academic exercise in the late nineteenth and in the early twentieth century. Scholars almost immediately recognized Hohfeld's system as so superior to those of his rivals that their systems were virtually forgotten. *See* Joseph William Singer, *The Legal Rights Debate in Analytical Jurisprudence from Bentham to Hohfeld,* 1982 WIS. L. REV. 975, 979. Consequently, Hohfeld, a precursor to the legal realists, is not, as is often thought, the first modern commercial jurisprude. Rather, he serves as the link between the nineteenth and twentieth century because he closed the earlier era. *See id.* at 1049–59.

tlement itself. Consequently, Calabresi and Melamed were correct in lumping "inalienation," which is *expressly* a matter of limiting and defining rights, with property and liability rules, which are *implicitly* matters of limiting and defining rights. Second, Calabresi and Melamed misinterpreted the elements of property involved in environmental nuisances by concentrating on possession and alienation instead of the relevant element of enjoyment. Finally, although Calabresi and Melamed attempted to create a correlative legal system, their understanding of correlative legal conceptions is inaccurate. For example, it may follow from the assertion that A has a right to clean water that B has a duty not to dirty A's water, but it does not follow that if B were to violate his duty by polluting A's water, then B has taken A's right. Even if, after the fact, a court were to find that A's only remedy against B were damages, it does not necessarily follow that B's violation constitutes a taking.

Six simple examples demonstrate how the Calabresi-Melamed model applies in the context of environmental disputes. Suppose that A and B own adjoining plots of land. A's land has a spring that supplies her with drinking water.[78] B owns a widget factory on his adjoining plot. The production of widgets pollutes the water in A's spring. I present each regime separately, allocating "the entitlement" first to A and second to B. For simplicity, each case assumes a pure liability, property, or inalienability regime. In the real world, however, a variety of mixed regimes is more likely to exist.[79]

If A had the initial entitlement and a property rule applied, then A would have the ability to stop B from polluting by obtaining injunctive relief from a court. Perhaps she could also persuade the state to impose criminal penalties against B. In Hohfeldian terms, A would have a right to clean water, and B would have a duty not to pollute. B could not hold off A through the payment of objectively (i.e., intersubjectively) calculated damages. Calabresi and Melamed describe this scenario as a regime in which society respects an entitlement holder's subjective valuation of her entitlement and does not impose its own valuation.[80] The effect of such a regime is that all transfers of

78. The example in the Calabresi and Melamed article is the right to clean air versus the right to pollute. *See* Calabresi & Melamed, *supra* note 17, at 1115–24. I replace air with water to make it slightly more intuitive with regard to the masculine phallic metaphor. It is easier to think of taking water because it is more tangible than air. For simplicity, throughout this chapter I refer to the party who pollutes as a "producer," and the party who is subjected to pollution caused by another as a "consumer." In the real world, however, consumers also pollute, such as when one burns one's leaves or drives one's car, and producers are affected by pollution caused by others.

79. Calabresi and Melamed clearly understood this point. For example, my rights with respect to an entitlement might be protected by a property rule with respect to one person but only be protected by a liability rule vis-à-vis others, such as the state, which can take my property under its power of eminent domain so long as it pays just compensation.

80. *See id.* at 1092–93.

entitlements will be voluntary on the part of the homeowner-transferor. Under a property rule, B has no right to simply "take" the desired entitlement unless he contracted for it with A. In Hohfeldian terms, A has the power to sell her entitlement and the privilege to retain it. B has no right to force A to sell her entitlement.

At first blush, this hypothetical seems successful. Further reflection reveals that this hypothetical is inappropriate because environmental nuisances involve inconsistent rights of enjoyment, not the taking of a single entitlement. Additionally, disputes arise, even in the case of true takings of possessory interests, in a world containing potential third-party claimants.

Specifically, if B violates the law and "takes" A's entitlement to clean water, it is not clear that any remedy could restore the status quo ante. The traditional remedy of replevin (getting back the object) is unavailable because in fact nothing has been "taken." A no longer has clean water, but not because B now has the water. Consequently, the law can only order B to pay damages for the past pollution and enjoin B to clean up the water and prevent future pollution. In the environmental arena, it may be impossible or impracticable as an empirical matter to restore A to her status quo ante through these remedies. This analysis provides the first hint that something is seriously wrong with the Calabresi-Melamed trichotomy.

In the second hypothetical, B has an entitlement to pollute enforced by a property regime. If B pollutes, A can neither stop him nor receive damages. In Hohfeldian terms, B has a privilege and power to pollute, and A has no right to stop him.

Once again, at first blush, this hypothetical seems like a successful description of a common fact situation. For example, when I wrote the first draft of this chapter, I was visiting a campus plagued by fraternities. The local anti-noise rule did not come into effect until 11:00 P.M. Colleagues informed me that the fraternities and the police would ignore noise complaints until that time, but would respond afterwards.[81] Calabresi and Melamed would say that the fraternities had an entitlement to make noise enforced by a property

81. Calabresi and Melamed used the example of the competing entitlements to make noise and to have silence. *See id.* at 1102–04. This example might indicate that they recognized that these nuisances involve not disputes over possession of a single entitlement, but competing rights to enjoy different objects—my right to my ears and the fraternities' right to their stereo systems. Nevertheless, even in this obvious case, Calabresi and Melamed quickly conflate the two objects of property, and thereby change the right from enjoyment to possession. For example, they do not describe the claim of the noisemaker as the right to use her stereo, which incidentally would impinge on my right to use my ears. Rather they see it as "the entitlement to make noise in other people's ears," as though we were fighting over the possession of ears. *Id.* at 1103. From this seemingly innocuous initial slip, they go all the way down the slippery slope, as though there was one single "thing" that is being contested.

Kaplow and Shavell recognized that nuisance disputes are different than takings dis-

regime until 11:00, and I had an entitlement to quiet enforced by a property regime after 11:00.

After a little thought, however, one realizes that, in contrast to hypothetical one, it is more than a little odd to call this an enforcement or remedy regime when the entitlement belongs to the producer. When the consumer is the entitlement holder, as in hypothetical one, the producer can violate the consumer's rights through "self-help"—by producing widgets. The consumer must, therefore, turn to the law's enforcement regime if she wishes to actualize her rights—by obtaining an injunction or other equitable remedy that prevents B from polluting or restores A to the status quo. When the allocations are reversed, however, the producer's right to pollute does not require judicial enforcement to be actualized. He exercises his right through self-help (e.g., B engages in the business of widget manufacture). A cannot violate B's rights through either self-help[82] or legal proceedings. If A were to haul B into court, B's rights would not be vindicated by granting a remedy enjoining A to take or not take any action. Rather, the judge would merely dismiss A's complaint for failure to state a cause of action claim. Indeed, the judge might impose sanctions for abuse of process on the plaintiff and her lawyer.

This asymmetry between hypotheticals one and two provides the second hint that something is wrong with Calabresi and Melamed's attempt to view the environmental dispute as the allocation of a single entitlement which may be involuntarily reallocated if the purchase price (damages) is paid. The Hohfeldian analysis reveals asymmetry between A and B. Consequently, when one allocates entitlements in a property regime, one simultaneously defines the entitlement.

Moreover, the lack of symmetry demonstrates that, in the context of environmental nuisances, A and B cannot possess, and therefore cannot transfer, a single "thing." Because the entitlement that the consumer could have is very different from that which the producer could have, there can never be a simple transfer of A's entitlement to B. The debate generated by the Calabresi-Melamed trichotomy, however, assumes that entitlements can always be conveyed.

---

putes. Nevertheless, they displayed a similar conceptual confusion with respect to the noise-silence hypothetical. *See* Kaplow & Shavell, *supra* note 38, at 766 n.168.

82. Now that the age of Druids is past, A cannot by the unilateral act of drinking water miraculously stop B from polluting and make the water clean. One might be tempted to argue that A can resort to the self-help of sabotage—she can break into B's plant at night and take a hammer to the widget-making machines. Unfortunately, this action changes the hypothetical. A is no longer just interfering with (taking) B's entitlement to pollute. A also is violating a number of B's other legal rights; for example, she is violating B's possessory right to exclude A from his factory.

Jettisoning my arcane academic jargon, we are talking about differences in brute power. The producer does not need the state's assistance to pollute. He does very well, thank you, in a Hobbesian war-of-all-against-all world. The consumer, however, needs societal cooperation—either the good will of the producer or the enforcement power of the state—to enjoy clean water. When B enjoys, he violates A, but for A to enjoy, she must ask B to remain chaste.

If A had the initial entitlement and a liability rule applied, A would have the right to clean water, but if B polluted, A's sole remedy would be money damages. Calabresi and Melamed have described this regime as one in which society imposes its own valuation upon entitlement holders. This is a regime under which B may force A to transfer her entitlement involuntarily, provided he pays damages. In Hohfeldian terms, B has the power to cause an involuntary sale, and as long as he pays the objective purchase price, A has no right to stop the involuntary sale and suffers the liability that B will force a sale.[83]

This Hohfeldian analysis provides our third hint that something is wrong with the Calabresi-Melamed trichotomy. There is now no single entitlement that can be allocated to either party. The Calabresi-Melamed analysis, however, assumes there is a single, allocable entitlement because it implicitly

83. The famous case of *Boomer v. Atlantic Cement Co.*, 257 N.E.2d. 870 (N.Y. 1970), has a holding that is similar in effect to hypothetical three, although based on different reasoning. In this case, the lower court found that a cement plant was a public nuisance that had caused actual harm to neighboring homeowners. *See id.* at 872–73. Because the cost to the manufacturer of closing down the plant was disproportionately high compared to the harm suffered by the homeowners, the lower court refused to grant an injunction, but merely ordered damages for past harms. *See id.* The Court of Appeals disagreed and held that under New York's common law of nuisance, the homeowners were entitled to injunctive relief despite the cost to the defendant. *See id.* at 872. The court claimed to be analyzing the case in terms of hypothetical one (entitlement in the consumers' hands, protected by property rules). Nevertheless, it found that the defendant could postpone imposition of the injunction—keep polluting—so long as it continued to pay the homeowners permanent damages to compensate them for the continuing harm of future pollution. *See id.* at 875.

One might argue that this result is not merely consistent with hypothetical three, but only can be understood in terms of hypothetical three. By the standard conditions of equitable relief, the court never should have issued the injunction (the remedy under property rules). It is blackletter law that equitable relief should not be granted unless the plaintiff would suffer irreparable harm for which no adequate legal remedy, damages, is available. Specifically, the appellate court found that an injunction should be granted because the lower court had found that the cement plant was a nuisance and had caused substantial damage to the plaintiffs. *See id.* at 872. The fact that the appellate court found that the defendant could delay the imposition of the injunction so long as it paid permanent continuing damages to the plaintiffs, however, implies that the court thought that the plaintiffs' harms could be adequately addressed by damages. Consequently, the plaintiffs should not have been granted an injunction, and a property rule should never have applied.

views a property entitlement as a prelegal thing that is necessarily in the sole custody of one of two rivals. A liability regime is not an exclusive allocation of a single entitlement to one party, as Calabresi and Melamed assumed.[84] Rather, a liability regime is an allocation of a number of legal rights between two parties.[85]

Later in this chapter, I consider how hypothetical three would operate in a "true" takings context. Calabresi and Melamed devised their taxonomy to analyze environmental nuisances, which I argue do not involve true takings. Other writers, however, have generalized the Calabresi-Melamed taxonomy to the seemingly more appropriate situation in which one party truly wishes to acquire something that another party owns.[86] The application of a hypothetical three legal regime to the taking of things would require, however, a radical change, not merely in substantive law, but in procedural law as well.

As a self-styled radical feminist, I am certainly not prepared to argue that a proposed change in the law should be opposed merely because it is a sharp break from the past. Nevertheless, one must be critically aware of the logical implications of one's proposals. Calabresi, Melamed, and their followers present themselves as describing the existing structure of American property law for the conservative purpose of increasing efficiency and wealth. In fact, their so-called description rejects two of the most deep-seated American legal principles: judicial respect for the status quo ante (i.e., courts should only redress injuries) and private property rights. These proposals may be good or bad, but their radicalness needs to be acknowledged.

If the initial entitlement belonged to B and a liability rule applied, then B would have the right to pollute but A would have the right and ability to stop him by paying damages. This payment of damages is conceptualized as forcing B involuntarily to sell his entitlement to A in exchange for a purchase price equal to society's intersubjective valuation. Although theoretically conceivable, this regime seems bizarre within our legal system, at least when A is a private citizen. Calabresi and Melamed were refreshingly honest in admitting that empirical examples of this "fourth case" may be rare or nonexistent in the private market, as opposed to governmental actions, and in understanding that finding such examples, or at least formulating plausible hypothetical four regimes, is essential to the validity of their taxonomy.[87]

84. Ayres & Talley make a similar point (*see* Ayres and Talley, *supra* note 32, at 1041), but unfortunately do not recognize its implications. Calabresi and Melamed recognize, of course, that regimes can be mixed and allocations can be divided. *See* Calabresi & Melamed, *supra* note 17, at 1093. Nevertheless, they assumed that in the simple polar hypotheticals one can theoretically have exclusive allocations in a liability regime. This assumption is incorrect.

85. *See* Ayres & Talley, *supra* note 32, at 1041.

86. *See, e.g.*, Kaplow & Shavell, *supra* note 38, at 757–71.

87. *See* Calabresi & Melamed, *supra* note 17, at 1117. They insist on its plausibility, even though this possibility is "easily ignored." *Id. See also* Krier & Schwab, *supra* note 18, at 443–45.

Once again, it is hard to envision hypothetical four as merely an enforcement regime. Rather, like all legal regimes, it defines rights rather than merely allocating them. In hypothetical three, A was the passive party, while B was active. B did not need recourse to the court system in order to take A's entitlement: he just started producing widgets, thereby incidentally causing pollution. In hypothetical four, by contrast, A (the taker) must go to court to force B to take the involuntary purchase price.

Hohfeld's terminology clarifies why hypothetical four is not precisely parallel to hypothetical three. In hypothetical four, B has a privilege to pollute, and A has no right to stop him unless she pays damages. One can easily restate this scenario as an entitlement in favor of A. A has the right or privilege upon the payment of damages to stop B from polluting, and B has the duty to stop, or no right to refuse to stop, if A pays damages. Finally, we could say either that A has the power to stop B from polluting (upon payment of damages), or that B is disabled from preventing A from stopping him (so long as A pays damages) and A is immune from any attempt to do so.

This hypothetical might be more realistic in the public realm; it arguably describes so-called "regulatory takings."[88] These takings occur when a court finds that a government regulation limiting certain uses of property interferes with the rights of the owner to commercially exploit—enjoy—her property to such an extent that the court deems the regulation a taking.[89] Consequently, either the regulation is invalidated (the result under a Calabresi-Melamed property regime) or, if the other conditions of eminent domain are met, the government can maintain the regulation by paying the owner "just compensation."[90]

The coherence of the Calabresi-Melamed trichotomy depends on this hypothetical being at least theoretically possible in the private sector. If the right to pollute is an entitlement that can be possessed and transferred, and if all entitlements can be enforced either by a property regime or by a liability regime, then it must be possible to imagine a liability regime that protects the right to pollute.

Once again it is hard to imagine how such a liability regime could arise within traditional legal principles and procedures. A liability regime arises in the public sector because of the government's unique power to "infringe" on a producer's "right" to pollute through use of its police power and its

88. Calabresi and Melamed give the state's power of eminent domain as an example of hypothetical four (*see* Calabresi & Melamed, *supra* note 17, at 1106—08), and describe a potential hypothetical four regime as a "partial eminent domain coupled with a benefits tax." *Id.* at 1116. Coleman and Kraus refer to a hypothetical four private right of action as a "private takings." Coleman & Kraus, *supra* note 48, at 1357.

89. *See, e.g., Lucas v. South Carolina Coastal Council,* 505 U.S. 1003 (1992).

90. U.S. Const. amend. V.

unique eminent domain power, which allows the government to force involuntary transfers of entitlement. These rights and powers do not exist in the private realm.

When A has the initial entitlement to clean water, she need not act to enjoy it—she can passively let the water flow. When B has the initial entitlement to pollute, however, he cannot passively enjoy his entitlement. Thus A is not hurt by the mere fact that B has the right to pollute. Rather, A is only hurt if B *exercises* his right to pollute. Also, in contrast to hypothetical three but similar to hypothetical two, A cannot, as a practical matter, use "self-help" to infringe. But here, unlike in hypothetical two, which operates under a property regime, A must be able to invoke the police power of the state to take B's original entitlement.

In hypothetical four, A has the power to cause a court to issue an injunction prohibiting B from polluting upon A's tender of the purchase price to B. Recognizing the right of a litigant to initiate a legal action to change the status quo would constitute a departure from American legal principles, which generally leave the status quo in place and only recognize private actions to redress changes to the status quo. Although Calabresi and Melamed recognize that hypothetical four would be unusual in the empirical world, they fail to recognize how radical its occurrence would be because they conceive of damages as the payment of the purchase price for involuntary transfers.[91]

Calabresi and Melamed's followers have been keen to find an example of hypothetical four to demonstrate the accuracy and usefulness of the taxonomy. Consequently, they have seized on the case of *Spur Industries, Inc. v. Del E. Webb Development Co.*[92] Unfortunately, as Krier and Schwab have so eloquently shown, this case does not demonstrate the two-party hypothetical proposed by the taxonomy.[93] These analysts have repressed the fact that this case involves three parties. I discuss this case at length below, when I argue the impracticality, if not outright impossibility, of the legal regimes suggested by the Calabresi-Melamed taxonomy.

If A has the original entitlement and an inalienability rule applies, then A

91. *See* Calabresi & Melamed, *supra* note 17, at 1120.

92. 494 P.2d 700 (Ariz. 1972). As Epstein trenchantly argues, *Spur Industries* does not exemplify hypothetical four, or indeed any other rule—it is, in fact, a sui generis case. *See* Epstein, *supra* note 46, at 2104–05. This case may indeed be "rogue" in the sense that, although it may have resulted in rough justice given the facts of the case, it does violence to both legal substance and legal procedure.

93. Actually, Krier and Schwab introduced this case as an example of hypothetical four. *See* Krier & Schwab, *supra* note 18, at 444–45. Later in their discussion, however, they distinguish it from the archetypical hypothetical four. *See id.* at 469–70.

may not give up her entitlement to clean water, and B may not pollute, regardless of whether A agrees that B may pollute or B agrees to pay damages or otherwise compensate A for the pollution. Applying Hohfeld, A has the right to clean water, and B has the duty not to pollute, which is specifically enforceable. But Hohfeld's correlatives break down when we look at other aspects of the relationship. A has a disability because she has no power to transfer her property. Hohfeld would say that this circumstance means someone else, such as B, must have a corollary immunity. I suppose we could say that if A entered into an illegal contract to sell her entitlement to B, and B defaulted, B would be immune from A's attempt to enforce the contract because it would be void as against public policy. This formulation seems so forced as to be inaccurate.

As I have said, even Calabresi and Melamed recognized that inalienability rules do not seem to jibe with the property and liability rules. But I have already argued that the inalienability rule fits. Property and liability rules are not, as Calabresi and Melamed suggest, merely regimes that enforce preexisting rights, but also are means for defining them. An inalienability rule is similar to a liability rule in that society decides that it will impose its own intersubjective valuation of the entitlement in A's hands over A's own subjective valuation. That is, in a liability regime, society forces a transfer on A even if A highly values the entitlement. In an inalienability regime, by contrast, society prevents a transfer by A even if A ascribes a low value to the entitlement. Consequently, one's intuitive discomfort with the Calabresi-Melamed analysis of inalienability puts us on warning that the difficulty may lie more generally with the assumptions underlying the trichotomy.

Let us briefly consider what an inalienability rule might mean in practice. Suppose that A does not have the right to alienate her right to clean water. Presumably, this rule means that any contract that A attempts to make with B to sell her right would be void as against public policy. An attempt to make such a contract might even subject A, B, or both to civil or criminal sanctions. What if B goes ahead and produces widgets and pollutes A's water with or without A's consent? To say that A's entitlement is inalienable must mean that she theoretically retains the right to the entitlement; even though in fact she is not in a position to exercise that entitlement because she no longer has clean water to drink. The state's only recourse at this point is to punish B, and perhaps A, and to attempt to return A to the status quo ante. A court could order B to stop production and restore the cleanliness of A's water (a property regime). Or, as is likely in the case of environmental nuisances, it may be impossible to restore the status quo ante, and the court will order B to pay damages to A (a liability regime). Inalienability fits with property and liability rules not because it is an alternate enforcement regime, but because inalienability ultimately devolves into property, and property ultimately devolves into liability. That is, they are not three mutually exclusive ways of dividing entitlements, but rather three mutually dependent aspects of defining property rights.

The sense of unease in the Calabresi-Melamed trichotomy graduates to discomfort when one considers the bizarre consequences that would result if we were to allocate the entitlement to B, the polluting factory owner, in an inalienation regime. Neither Calabresi and Melamed nor the resulting debate has considered this embarrassing hypothetical.[94] However, if Calabresi and Melamed were right that their property-liability dichotomy necessitates at least the theoretical possibility of hypothetical four, then the validity of their property-liability-inalienability trichotomy requires the theoretical possibility of hypothetical six. If the right to pollute is to be conceptualized as a thing that can be either taken or transferred to a consumer—as something theoretically alienable—then it follows that society could impose restraints on its alienation. The inability to formulate a realistic hypothetical six is presumably why Calabresi and Melamed half-heartedly suggested that an inalienability regime is substantially different from property and liability regimes, implying that their trichotomy is not really a trichotomy but a dichotomy plus an anomaly.[95]

In hypothetical six, B has an inalienable entitlement to pollute. What could this possibly mean as a practical matter? I suggested in my discussions of hypotheticals two and four that the right of a producer to pollute is more accurately a Hohfeldian power to do so or a privilege against A's attempts to stop him. Saying that this power or privilege is inalienable suggests not only that any contract not to pollute that B enters into would be void as against public policy, and therefore unenforceable by A against B; it also means that if B tries to obey a voluntary contract not to pollute, the government would use its police power to save B from himself. But how can society keep one from alienating one's privilege, right, or power to take certain action, let alone one's immunity from being forced to stop?

Does this mean that the state would force B to pollute? To require such action is likely to raise constitutional questions of involuntary servitude and regulatory takings. Such an absurd result inevitably flows from the conflation of property rights and the object of the property rights, from the conceptualization of entitlements as preexisting things that are merely assigned to one person or another, and from the conflation of interference with property rights and takings. In the environmental nuisance arena, we are speaking not of possession or alienation, but of enjoyment.

94. *See* Calabresi & Melamed, *supra* note 17, at 1115–16.
95. *See id.* at 1093, 1111.

PROPERTY

The Conflation of Property with Object

When Calabresi and Melamed reduce property to the single element of possession, epitomized by physical custody of a tangible thing, they treat property as though it were itself the thing. An entitlement, like any legal right, is a set of relationships between or among legal subjects. When the entitlement is a property right, these relationships concern the possession, alienation, *and enjoyment* of objects. Calabresi and Melamed, however, treat property entitlements not as the right to enjoy objects, but as the right to possess and alienate them.

This construction is similar to, albeit slightly more subtle than, the common error of confusing property and object.[96] Calabresi and Melamed go further and ignore the objects underlying property entitlements (in their hypotheticals, the consumer's water and the producer's factory). Instead, the property entitlement has become the thing.

Parties transfer their entire property interests with respect to specific things millions of times each day in ordinary sales transactions. Sometimes two parties claim inconsistent property rights with respect to the same thing. For example, in a classic priority dispute, A and B may claim to own the same good, purportedly transferred by a double-dealing third party. It does not necessarily follow from this that every interference by one party with a property right of another is equivalent to the transfer of a thing.

When it comes to environmental harms, we are not talking about possessory rights at all. Rather, we are talking about enjoyment rights. More importantly, because of the relational nature of legal rights, it is not always accurate to speak of one person owning a property interest or other entitlement to the exclusion of another person. For example, hypotheticals three and four illustrate that under a liability regime it is not true, as Calabresi and Melamed asserted,[97] that we either allocate the entitlement to clean water to A or the entitlement to pollute to B. Rather, in both hypotheticals, both parties have entitlements (to clean air and to pollute, respectively), but such entitlements are subject to conditions.

96. Thomas Grey calls this the "lay conception" of property. Thomas Grey, *The Disintegration of Property,* XXII NOMOS, PROPERTY 69, 69–70 (J. Roland Pennock & John W. Chapman eds., 1980). I criticize Grey's prediction that property is disintegrating as a meaningful legal concept in SCHROEDER, THE VESTAL AND THE FASCES, *supra* note 4, at 156–85 and Schroeder, *Chix,* supra note 25, at 271–305. Grey is right that property is not the thing, but he (and Hohfeld) are wrong in concluding from this point that things are irrelevant to property. I make an abbreviated version of my argument later in this chapter.

97. *See* Calabresi & Melamed, *supra* note 17, at 1118.

To describe the mutual rights and obligations of individuals involved in a *two*-party relationship in terms of property is risky. It adds little to, and in this case actually detracts from, a legal analysis of two-party relationships that do not involve the conveyance of an object. These rights remain the same regardless of whether we label them contract or property. I agree with Hohfeld that, in our legal system, the term "property" has significance only in the three-party context. Hohfeld defined property as being "multital"—enforceable against "the world," in the sense of a relatively large class of persons.[98]

It becomes meaningful to reify two-party relationships into property only when one of the two parties purports to assign her rights to a third party. For example, assume that B sells a good to A on credit, so that A owes B the purchase price. In accounting and ordinary business parlance, it would be an account receivable.[99] At this stage, these are just terms for A's half of the contract. Now imagine that B assigns his rights against A to C. It now becomes analytically helpful to think of A's account as a specific object that B conveyed to C, enabling the parties to identify exactly what C obtained. Importantly, it helps distinguish the terms of the assignment contract—the relationship between B and C—from that which is assigned pursuant to that contract: the relationship between A and B. Accordingly, Article 9 of the Uniform Commercial Code treats an assigned account as an object that is every bit as capable as a good of serving as collateral.[100]

Returning to the Calabresi-Melamed context of the two-party environmental nuisance, it is misleading to speak of the object of the consumer's property right as A's entitlement—the right to drink clean water. To do so leads to the misperception that if A allows B to pollute subject to payment of compensation, then A is transferring something to B. This misperception assumes, without analysis, that the contract between A and B is a conveyance, and conflates the contract to convey and the thing conveyed. This conflation is the evil that the drafters of the UCC tried to prevent in the law of sales by abandoning the common-law analysis of title

98. Hohfeld incorrectly argued that property was not unique and lumped it into his more general category of "multital rights." HOHFELD, *supra* note 69, at 85. Hohfeld opposes multital rights to "paucital" rights, such as contract, which are enforceable against a specifically identifiable person(s). *See id.* at 72. I believe that property must be intersubjectively recognizable for it to perform its philosophical function of recognition. It must be observed and honored by (enforceable against) others. *See* Jeanne L. Schroeder, *Some Realism About Legal Surrealism,* 37 WM. & MARY L. REV. 455, 255–59 (1996).

99. In commercial law, we call A's obligation an account. *See* U.C.C. §9–102(a)(2) (2000).

100. "Except as otherwise provided . . . this article applies (a) to a transaction, regardless of its form, that creates a security interest in personal property . . . [and also] a sale of accounts . . . ." U.C.C. §9–109(a) (2000).

while preserving the concept of title—ownership—which is, of course, fundamental.[101]

In contrast, Calabresi and Melamed characterized A and B's pollution contract as a conveyance of A's entitlement to B.[102] But this characterization suggests that, upon payment of the purchase price, B would acquire what A possessed. What A "possessed," according to Calabresi and Melamed, was an entitlement to drink clean water at her residence.[103] B, however, does not obtain a right to drink A's water, and the A/B contract would not be enforceable against a class of third parties, as it would be if a conveyance occurred. If A had conveyed her possessory right to clean water at her residence to B, then she would no longer have that right against the world. A would no longer have any right to complain if C, D, or E dumped toxic waste into her water supply. Indeed, if the right had been conveyed to B, B would possess the claim against these other polluters. This is not the case.

101. In Jeanne L. Schroeder, *Death and Transfiguration: The Myth That the U.C.C. Killed "Property,"* 69 TEMP. L. REV. 1281 (1996) [hereinafter, Schroeder, *Death and Transfiguration*], I disprove the old canard that the U.C.C. disaggregated or abandoned the concept of title per se. *See id.* at 1282–83, 1289–91. What it did do was reject a certain common law analysis that determined certain legal disputes based on the location of title.

Karl Llewellyn, the guiding architect of the U.C.C., argued that the common law of sales had become hopelessly confused because common-law title analysis conflated the contract and conveyance aspects of sales. *See* KARL N. LLEWELLYN, CASES AND MATERIALS ON THE LAW OF SALES 64–67 (1930) [hereinafter, *Llewellyn, Sales*]; KARL N. LLEWELLYN, JURISPRUDENCE (1962) (collection of articles); K. N. Llewellyn, *Across Sales on Horseback,* 52 HARV. L. REV. 725 (1939); K. N. Llewellyn, *The First Struggle to Unhorse Sales* 52 HARV. L. REV. 873 (1939); Karl N. Llewellyn, *Some Realism About Realism—Responding to Dean Pound,* 44 HARV. L. REV. 1222 (1931); K. N. Llewellyn, *Through Title to Contract and a Bit Beyond,* 15 N. Y. U. L. Q. REV. 159 (1938) [hereinafter Llewellyn, *Through Title to Contract*]; Karl N. Llewellyn, *Why a Commercial Code?,* 22 TENN. L. REV. 779 (1953). He thought that carefully distinguishing the two would clarify and rationalize the law. *See* Schroeder, *Death and Transfiguration, supra* at 1294–1304. In Llewellyn's words, "Title-thinking [is] Sales law viewed as property law." Llewellyn, *Through Title to Contract, supra* at 191. "The property concept is repeatedly used by courts as a device to settle various issues which in themselves are contract and not "property" issues: i.e., they are matters which the parties have power to arrange at will by express contractual clauses, if they want to, and think about it." LLEWELLYN, SALES, *supra* at 64. In contradistinction, Llewellyn's analytical approach is rooted "in the proposition that the modern law of Sale is a law of contract for future delivery; that the present sale [i.e., the conveyancing of the property right in the good sold] plays little part today in litigation; and that most problems commonly dealt with under the heading of "title" are obscured rather than clarified by that dealing." *Id.* at xiv. The contract for sale, which is two-party in nature, should be entitled to the usual degree of freedom we grant to contracting parties. *See* Schroeder, *Death and Transfiguration, supra* at 1297–1301. Only the conveyance of the good sold under the contract is a property transaction enforceable against third parties and therefore should be subject to certain objective (societally imposed) rules. *See id.*

102. *See* Calabresi & Melamed, *supra* note 17, at 1116.

103. *See id.*

It is equally absurd to think of the entitlement as an object of property and of a pollution contract as a conveyance when B is deemed to be the entitlement holder. In hypotheticals two, four, and six, B possesses the right to make widgets and, incidentally, to pollute A's water. As we have seen, Calabresi and Melamed assert that if A pays B not to pollute, then B transfers the entitlement to A. In fact, A does not acquire B's right to pollute, and B does not lose his right or privilege to pollute A's water.

The problem is that the Calabresi-Melamed analysis assumes that A's and B's property rights relate to the same object. In fact, A's rights relate to one object—her water—and B's rights relate to another object: his widget factory. The right of possession is not involved at all, and the parties are not exercising rights of alienation. Possessory disputes involve mutually inconsistent claims of the right of exclusion with respect to a single object. Environmental disputes involve mutually inconsistent claims of the right to enjoy different objects.

Identifying the Relevant Element of Property

Calabresi and Melamed have been misled by their phallic metaphors. These metaphors reduce the complex set of relations we call property to one element, possession, and implicitly imagine possession as the immediate physical custody of a tangible thing (sensuous grasp). Feminine enjoyment is repressed. Property as sensuous grasp is exclusive: only one party can hold the object of desire in his hand at one time. One violates the right of sensuous grasp by taking or wresting the object from the grasp of another. Consequently, property as sensuous grasp identifies property with the grasped object itself, rather than with the interrelationship of legal subjects with respect to the object. Indeed, possession as sensuous grasp is not a legal right at all, but merely a contingent fact.

All property rights necessarily relate to objects. But Calabresi and Melamed merge property rights with respect to objects with the underlying objects themselves. This analysis is obviously wrong—a variation on what Thomas Grey called the naive lay conception of property,[104] and what I call the positive masculine phallic metaphor for property.

Objects are not, as Hohfeld supposed, irrelevant to property. Property rights can, and often do, include the exclusive right to physical possession of tangible things. For example, individuals ordinarily have the exclusive right to physical possession of their household goods. Even in this case, however, one's property rights cannot be reduced to physical custody. The ordinary

104. *See* Grey, *supra* note 96, at 69–70.

owner has additional rights in her goods (as the term "consumer" implies). Additionally, the right of possession cannot be reduced to an immediate binary relationship between subject and object, epitomized by the sensuous grasp. We are rarely actually in physical contact with the goods we possess nor do we possess many of the goods with which we are in physical contact.[105]

Calabresi and Melamed repress the mediated intersubjective aspect of property and erroneously reduce possession to an immediate relationship between owning subject and owned object. Consequently, they declare that in a property regime society does not impose its intersubjective valuation of the property relationship. The existence of third parties, however, requires the mediation of society and the imposition of its values. Although possession necessarily involves a relationship between subject and object, possession cannot be reduced to that relationship. Empirically no subject ever has perfect possession, in terms of a complete and total right and power to exclude all other subjects, under any and all circumstances, from the object of possession.

Law cannot merely assign the right of possession to one party and then enforce that right, as Calabresi and Melamed presumed. Law must also define possession by detailing those whom the possessor can exclude and under what circumstances she can exclude them. In a world in which third parties or dynamite exists, any limitation of a possessory right is equivalent to imposing an intersubjective valuation on the possessor. Property remedies inevitably merge into liability remedies, and liability regimes presuppose a property regime.

If one thinks of possession as the right of the possessor to exclude another subject from asserting some property interest in the same object, then possession is not necessarily exclusive as a theoretical matter. In the Calabresi-Melamed hypotheticals, it does not necessarily follow from the assignment of an entitlement to a party that the entitlement should be analyzed in terms of the single property right of possession, let alone that any possessory right should be exclusive to the party. Nor does it follow that interference with that entitlement constitutes a transfer of that entitlement to the violator. Not all changes in legal rights consist of or can be usefully analogized to a conveyance.

Alienability is the ability of the subject to sever her relation to the object. Although it is a cliche of American law that we abhor restraints on alienation, most manifestations of alienability are not absolute.[106] Even a fee simple

105. *See* Schroeder, *Legal Surrealism, supra* note 98, at 486–88.

106. *See* Margaret Jane Radin, *Market-Inalienability,* 100 HARV. L. REV. 1849, 1917–21 (1987). I discuss the Hegelian analysis of alienation in SCHROEDER, THE VESTAL AND THE FASCES, *supra* note 4, at 46–52.

owner of real estate is limited by fraudulent transfer principles from alienating her estate in a way that would work a fraud on her creditors.[107] Additionally, when I have relatively broad rights of alienation, I may choose to alienate only a portion of my property rights. For example, when I lease an object to another, I transfer my possessory right to physical custody and sensuous use of the object, but only temporarily, and then conditionally on the receipt of my rent.

The Calabresi-Melamed hypotheticals ostensibly invoke the right of alienation—the ability of a subject to sever her relationships concerning the object. Calabresi and Melamed vacillate between privileging possession in their property regime and privileging alienation through exchange in their liability regime.

In the property regime and liability regime hypotheticals (hypotheticals one and two, and three and four, respectively), the owner supposedly retained the right to alienate her entitlement by contracting. In fact, however, no transfer of property occurred. Even if A contracted away her right to drink clean water, she still retained her water. B obtained no property right in A's water that he can further convey to the world. B obtained neither the right to drink the water himself (enjoyment) nor the right to exclude rivals (including other polluters) from drinking or polluting the water (possession). In addition, A retained the right to prevent all persons other than B from polluting her water and the right exclude from her water all persons *including B*. Rather than severing her relationship with the object or any portion of the object, she simply has changed the nature of her relationship to B with respect to her water. In the liability regime, B supposedly had the power to sever A's relationship with her object—to "take" her entitlement—provided B paid damages. This arrangement, however, should be seen neither as a limitation of A's right of alienation nor as a right of alienation granted to B. Rather, it is a limitation of A's enjoyment rights with respect to her water and an increase in B's enjoyment rights with respect to his factory.

Hypotheticals five and six purport to place limitations on the owner's right and power to alienate her entitlement. In the more realistic hypothetical five, A could not give up her right to clean water. If the conflict between A and B cannot be analyzed in terms of allocating a single object, neither can this paternalistic limitation on A be analyzed in terms of her right to alienate her object. A, as a homeowner, has the usual rights to sell her home and, subject to appropriate licensing or other legal restrictions, to bottle and sell

107. *See, e.g.*, 11 U.S.C. 548 (1994) (fraudulent transfer provision of Bankruptcy Code); Unif. Fraudulent Conveyance Act 4, 7A U.L.A. 652–53 (1985); Unif. Fraudulent Transfer Act 7, *id.* at 509. For an argument that fraudulent conveyance law belies the very distinction between in rem and in personam rights, see Julie Kemperer & Sirota Karchin, *Note, Fraudulent Conveyance Law as a Property Right*, 9 CARDOZO L. REV. 843 (1987).

her water. Consequently, if it is inaccurate to analyze the environmental nuisance hypotheticals in terms of disputes of possession, it is equally inaccurate to analyze them in terms of rights of alienation.

It is the third element of property, the "feminine" element of enjoyment, that is at stake. Enjoyment is the right of a subject to use, consume, collect, or otherwise exploit the object of the property right. In Hegelian terms, enjoyment is the actualization of the subject's mastery over the object.[108] Possessory rights designate those subjects whom the owner can exclude from the object of desire. Alienability rights indicate how the owner rids herself of the object once desired. Enjoyment rights indicate what the owner may do with and to her object of desire.[109]

Once again, it is common to assume that an owner has the unfettered right to do whatever he wants with "his" property—that "a man's home is his castle."[110] However, rights of enjoyment, like those of possession and alienation, often are limited. For example, although I might say that I own my body, in most jurisdictions it is illegal for me to enjoy it in sexual relations with persons other than my husband (particularly if the enjoyment is commercial in nature), or to abuse it by ingesting certain drugs, or to consume it entirely by committing suicide. More importantly for the purposes of this chapter, moralistic or paternalistic restrictions are not the only limitations on enjoyment. Enjoyment is self-limited by the demands of its fundamentally relational nature.

As discussed, the logic of property is recognition—it always involves other persons. Therefore, all legal rights, including property rights, must be intersubjective in nature. Enjoyment, however, seems inherently subjective and

108. *See* G. W. F. Hegel, Elements of the Philosophy of Right 88–90 (Allen W. Wood ed. & H. B. Nisbet trans., 1991) (1820); Schroeder, The Vestal and the Fasces, *supra* note 4, at 43–45.

109. Specifically:

> Just as possession should not be equated with physical custody, enjoyment cannot be limited to sensuous consumption. The nature of the right of enjoyment varies with the type of object involved. A tomato can be eaten, but one can also admire its beautiful color or fragrance or even use it as a weapon by throwing it at some politician. Although during the term of a lease, the lessee has the right to sensuous exploitation of the leased object, the lessor also retains a right of enjoyment in the form of economic exploitation (i.e., the right to rent). Enjoyment is often conflated with possession in the sense of physical custody, because one frequently, or even usually, needs to be in immediate physical contact with, or at least close proximity to, a tangible object in order to enjoy it. But even in the case of tangible goods, the rights of possession and enjoyment are distinguishable. As reflected in the cliche that you can't have your cake and eat it too, it is often the case that enjoyment destroys the object of desire and, therefore, also destroys the other two property elements. Consumption is the ultimate form of enjoyment.

Id. at 43–44.

110. *E.g., Public Util. Comm'n v. Pollak*, 343 U.S. 451, 467 (1952) (Douglas, J., dissenting).

solipsistic in nature.[111] Consequently, I have criticized Margaret Radin's privileging of enjoyment as implicitly individualistic, even virginal.[112]

Yet even enjoyment is necessarily "relational." As total enjoyment cannot be shared, it necessarily envelopes the right of exclusion.[113] Two people cannot eat the same piece of cake. But we already have characterized the right of exclusion as part and parcel of the right of possession. As I have expressed previously, "To say that enjoyment presupposes exclusion is only another way to say that possession is the most primitive element of property."[114]

> Enjoyment is intersubjective not just because the mutual enjoyment of the same object by two different subjects can be inconsistent, but because one's enjoyment of one's own object can hinder or even preclude the ability of another to enjoy his own object. To give an easy example, even rabid libertarians would probably agree that society can legitimately limit the rights of car owners to enjoy their cars by driving them on the side walk because that would interfere with the rights of pedestrians to enjoy their bodily integrity. . . . Exactly what these limitations are (i.e., what degree of interference we will tolerate as a legal matter) must be determined by practical reasoning (i.e., positive law).[115]

In the case of environmental nuisances, B's enjoyment of his object is inconsistent with A's enjoyment with her object. A's objects of desire in our hypothetical are her residence and its well. One of the ways she can enjoy them is by drinking the water. B's object of desire is his widget factory and business. One of the ways he can enjoy this object is by producing widgets. However, the production of widgets pollutes A's water. A's complete enjoyment of her water, therefore, is inconsistent with B's complete enjoyment of his factory. Coase insisted that rival claims in environmental disputes are reciprocal in nature because of the impossibility of simultaneous complete mutual enjoyment.

The question in environmental nuisance is not, therefore, which party possesses an entitlement that may or may not be alienated to the other party. Rather, the question is: what are the borders separating the relative rights of the two parties to enjoy their separate objects.

111. *See* SCHROEDER, THE VESTAL AND THE FASCES, *supra* note 4, at 42–43.

112. See generally Jeanne L. Schroeder, *Virgin Territory: Margaret Radin's Imagery of Property as the Inviolate Feminine Body,* 79 MINN. L. REV. 55 (1994).

113. *Cf.* ALAN BRUDNER, THE UNITY OF THE COMMON LAW: STUDIES IN HEGELIAN JURISPRUDENCE 32–33 (1995).

114. SCHROEDER, THE VESTAL AND THE FASCES, *supra* note 4, at 44. Although one cannot enjoy or alienate an "object" unless one first possesses it, one can theoretically have the right to possess without either of the other two rights, such as in a bailment.

115. *Id.* at 44–45 (footnotes omitted).

PROCEDURAL AND SUBSTANTIVE CRITIQUES

One might be tempted to argue that, even if my argument is technically correct, it is irrelevant given the purposes for which Calabresi and Melamed developed the trichotomy. Might not the trichotomy have pragmatic uses despite its theoretical flaws? Whether we analyze the problem in terms of a single entitlement allocated between two parties or in terms of the determination of the boundaries of two different entitlements held by the two parties, doesn't the Coase theorem suggest that the party who valued the disputed right more will negotiate to pay the other party to allow him to have the right? This should result whether the dispute concerns the right to possess a single object or the rights to enjoy two separate objects. For example, if A valued her enjoyment of her water more than B valued his enjoyment of his widget factory, then the parties would bargain so that B would refrain from enjoyment so that A could indulge in enjoyment, and vice versa. This argument would, in effect, accuse me of conflating a semantic dispute with a substantive one.

The problem is that the Calabresi and Melamed analysis fails in its stated goal of presenting a taxonomy of existing and possible legal remedy regimes. In particular, analyzing a producer's ability to pollute as the allocation of an entitlement is unworkable both in theory and in practice. I have already argued that hypothetical six, in which the producer's "entitlement" to pollute is inalienable, is absurd, and therefore is never discussed in the literature, even though it is logically required by the taxonomy. More importantly, the implementation of either a property or a liability regime protecting such an entitlement (hypotheticals two and four, respectively) would require not merely the recognition of new rights, but also the adoption of radical new legal procedures. Although theorists sometimes recognize this with respect to hypothetical four, it applies equally to hypothetical two. Whether or not Calabresi and Melamed's analysis is amusing as a matter of semantic theory, it does not represent a serious alternative for American law. As Krier and Schwab suggest, although couched in the rhetoric of policy recommendations, the debate inspired by Calabresi and Melamed is purely an aesthetic exercise with no real-world implications.[116]

Even if one agrees with my critique of Calabresi and Melamed's analysis of the allocation of the entitlement to the producer, one might still suggest that it is irrelevant to the bulk of the analysis flowing from their theory. Most analysts expressly or implicitly focus on the two most realistic hypotheticals—

116. *See* Krier & Schwab, *supra* note 18, at 482.

numbers one and three. Assuming the status quo—the consumer has a right to clean water—would efficiency be better served if we protected her right through property or through liability rules?[117] Whether or not Calabresi and Melamed are right in describing this problem as the transfer of a thing, their suggestion does not affect this more fundamental question. Moreover, whatever qualms one may have in applying the taxonomy in its original context of environmental nuisances, surely it is applicable in other contexts in which the parties are, in fact, contesting the ownership of a single thing.

In the following sections, I show that a Calabresi-Melamed analysis is misleading even for these more limited purposes. This analysis requires that the parties negotiate in the shadow of an enforcement regime, which requires that they know what enforcement regime will apply. Negotiation under this condition is not possible because in the real world of third parties and dynamite, property and liability regimes are indistinguishable.

The Empirical Validity of the Trichotomy

The regime that Calabresi and Melamed denominate "property" bears little resemblance to the American property regime. Is this distinction merely a semantic quibble? Perhaps Calabresi and Melamed's choice of the word "property" was unfortunate because the term has other well-understood meanings. This imprecision alone, however, does not mean that the concept designated by this unfortunate term is defective. If I am worried that the term "property" has misleading connotations, perhaps I should merely suggest alternate terminology, such as "injunctive" regime, which seems to fit better with the term "liability" regime. Or why not change the names of both of these categories to the more traditional "equitable" and "legal" remedies?

My objection is not simply that Calabresi and Melamed do not accurately describe the property regime, but that it does not describe *any* remedial regime that does or could exist under any legal system in which objects can be destroyed or in which there are more than two parties. Consequently, the trichotomy is fundamentally unworkable. To see why, let us consider Calabresi and Melamed's definition of a property regime in slightly more detail.

One should intuit that the one problem with Calabresi and Melamed's property regime is its incompleteness. A property regime, they state, is one in which society enforces an entitlement holder's subjective valuation of her property.[118] Consequently, in a property regime, the transfer of an entitlement can only be made with the holder's consent—through purchase. This

117. For example, Polinsky reduced the Calabresi and Melamed analysis to the simpler issue of when we should impose legal remedies and when we should impose equitable ones. *See* Polinsky, *supra* note 29, at 1075–80.

118. *See* Calabresi & Melamed, *supra* note 17, at 1092.

describes the goal of the regime, but fails to describe the remedies adopted to further this goal. In order to understand what a property regime is, one may wish to look at Calabresi and Melamed's description of what it is not: a liability regime. The Calabresi and Melamed analysis subtly changes the traditional nature of damages.

In a liability regime, society imposes its valuation on an entitlement holder. This seems to mean that in a liability regime the only remedy available for a taking is money damages. By negative pregnant, this paucity of remedies implies that the remedy available in a property regime is something other than money damages or "legal" remedies—an "equitable" remedy.

Courts customarily impose damages upon a wrongdoer to compensate the victim for the loss caused by the wrongful act. Calabresi and Melamed suggest that, in economic terms, this remedy is equivalent to setting an objective purchase price for an entitlement, so a rival claimant can force an involuntary transfer on the original entitlement holder.[119] Most acolytes of Calabresi and Melamed treat damages this way.

This interpretation, however, ignores the fact that economic equivalence is not necessarily the same as legal, practical, or ethical equivalence. Quantity is not quality. The Calabresi-Melamed analysis revalorizes takings.[120] Under traditional legal principles, a taking is wrongful. The fact that the payment of damages retroactively heals this wrong does not in and of itself change this judgment. In a liability regime, however, a compensated taking is implicitly rightful. Indeed, if the taker is the higher valuing user, a utilitarian would say that the taking is an affirmatively good thing, which should be encouraged.

Note the legal implications of this valuation. Calabresi and Melamed suggest that the law should adopt a liability regime if it would result in more efficient transfers than a property regime.[121] Efficiency demands that a higher valuing claimant be able to tender the societally imposed "purchase" price to the original entitlement holder in order to take the property. Any attempt by the original entitlement holder to prevent the taking would be dismissed for failure to state a claim, or perhaps converted into a valuation proceeding. This arrangement may or may not be a good idea, but it is a radical change from our current legal system, which tends to protect the status quo

119. Radin makes a similar critique of the American tort regime. She agrees with the law-and-economics approach that requiring a tortfeasor to pay damages, supposedly equivalent to the loss, to the tort victim is tantamount to establishing a market for bodily integrity. Implicitly adopting what I call the feminine phallic metaphor, Radin argues that personal injury is a violation of selfhood that cannot be cured through exchange (i.e., damages). All society can do is acknowledge the victim's loss in a way that respects her dignity. *See* MARGARET JANE RADIN, CONTESTED COMMODITIES 185–205 (1996).

120. *See* Coleman & Kraus, *supra* note 48, at 1352–65.

121. *See* Calabresi & Melamed, *supra* note 17, at 1093–98.

and jealously guards the right of first possession because of its solicitude for private property as an institution.

A Calabresi-Melamed liability rule is at least theoretically possible in the area of environmental nuisances. The producer can "take" the coveted entitlement by going about his usual business of producing widgets. He does not have to enter the consumer's premises or otherwise breach the peace. This is, of course, hypothetical three. Polluters do not have to use law's enforcement mechanism to actualize their "right" to pollute: they have the practical ability to exercise self-help. The availability of this self-help option suggests that it is not just odd, but erroneous, to analyze this as an enforcement regime.

This radical departure from the traditional solicitude towards private property is subtly signaled by Calabresi and Melamed's novel terminology, which changes the meaning of traditional categories. First, they label this regime a "liability," rather than a "damages," regime, thereby avoiding the implication that this is compensation paid for a wrongful act. More importantly, they distinguish this regime from a "property" regime. This is correct. Compensation of involuntary takings is a weakening, if not an outright rejection, of the concept of possession—the right to exclude others. It is impossible to have the other two elements of property without this most primitive element. Hence, Calabresi and Melamed use the weak economic term "entitlement," rather than the resonant legal and philosophic term "property," to describe legal rights.

This terminology is consistent with the utilitarian philosophy underlying law-and-economics. Unlike the libertarian strand of liberalism, utilitarianism does not consider private property to be a natural right.[122] In contrast to the contractarian strand, utilitarianism does not consider property to be a fundamental right established by the positive law of the social contract in order to prevent the war of all against all.[123] It disagrees with Hegelianism, which views property as a necessary step in the creation of subjectivity and the actualization of human freedom.[124] To a utilitarian, these justifications of property are mere sentimental prejudices—the "other justice concerns" to which Calabresi and Melamed pay lip service.[125] The desire for freedom is a preference, a mere matter of taste, which one can reduce to either "utility" or

122. See Kenneth R. Minogue, *The Concept of Property and Its Contemporary Significance,* in PROPERTY NOMOS XXII, supra note 96, at 3, 17; Michel Rosenfeld, *Contract and Justice: The Relation Between Classical Contract Law and Social Contract Theory,* 70 IOWA L. REV. 769, 853–58 (1985).

123. *See* Minogue, *supra* note 122, at 18; Rosenfeld, *supra* note 122, at 790–92.

124. *See* SCHROEDER, THE VESTAL AND THE FASCES, *supra* note 4, at 15. For a description of the Hegelian view, see id. at xv–xvi, 3–4, 15, 19–20, 34, 37–52, 271–73, 294–95, 319–21; Schroeder, *Never Jam To-day, supra* note 37, at 1533–44, 1566–69.

125. *See* Calabresi & Melamed, *supra* note 17, at 1102–05.

market value. Property is merely a tool, like any other, to be used or abandoned to achieve the goal of utility or wealth maximization.

According to Calabresi and Melamed, society should adopt a so-called property regime only insofar as it encourages more efficient transfers of entitlements.[126] Although their "property" regime ostensibly privileges possession, possession is only tentatively justified so long as it encourages efficient alienation. Consequently, the element of possession becomes subordinated to that of alienation through exchange. The element of enjoyment is once again repressed and not discussed. The primary reason why one party would value an object of desire more than another party is because of the anticipated enjoyment that the higher valuing party would have in the object—whether the commercial enjoyment of producing widgets or the sensuous enjoyment of drinking clean water. This unacknowledged feminine ghost of enjoyment haunts environmental nuisances. What is repressed in the symbolic (law) always returns in the real.

This hostility toward property results from the implicit adoption of the masculine phallic metaphor of property as possession, and of possession as sole and unfettered custody of a tangible thing—property as sensuous grasp. As we have seen, the masculine phallic metaphor pops up most explicitly in the Calabresi-Melamed model's assumption that the entitlement is a thing that is assigned to one party or the other. If one holds this view of property, property must be disparaged in any situation in which these absolutist views are unworkable or absurd. Consequently, Hohfeld thinks that traditional property analysis is illogical and proposes the abandonment of property as a separate legal category.[127] He lumps rights traditionally falling within the rubric of "property" into a new, broader category, which he calls "multital rights." Calabresi and Melamed go further and declare that a liability rule is nonproperty.

Regardless of the ethical implications of the Calabresi-Melamed liability

126. Calabresi and Melamed's policy conclusion reflects common misreadings of Coase. For example, Barbara White stated, "Coase asserts that courts, when ruling on entitlement disputes, must assign the property right not on the basis of traditional notions of property rights, but on the basis of maximizing total product." Barbara White, *Coase and the Courts: Economics for the Common Man,* 72 IOWA L. REV. 577, 586 (1987). Unfortunately, White mischaracterized the Coasean language she quoted to support her interpretation. As discussed in Chapter 2, Coase says that different allocations of rights can be expected to have different effects on economic efficiency. Coase never suggests, however, that courts should decide cases based on economic efficiency alone. He expressly states that economic and legal decisions "should be carried out in broader terms than [mere consideration of efficiency] and that the total effect of these arrangements in all spheres of life should be taken into account." Coase, *supra* note 39, at 43. Society should also examine aesthetics and morality. Consequently, Coase's analysis has plenty of room for respect for "traditional notions of property rights." *Id.*

127. Grey made a similar conceptual error. *See* SCHROEDER, THE VESTAL AND THE FASCES, *supra* note 4, at 163–79; Schroeder, *Chix, supra* note 25, at 242–44, 271–75, 299–300.

analysis or its relevance to the analysis of environmental nuisances, the taxonomy becomes fanciful when applied to true possessory disputes. For example, suppose that the object of desire is a diamond engagement ring that A, the owner, always wears. In order to take the ring from an unwilling A through self-help, B would have to assault her physically. This behavior would interfere not only with A's property rights, but also with A's autonomy and bodily integrity. Consequently, Calabresi and Melamed must have been proposing that B be able to enforce his right to impose an involuntary sale on A through the courts, through an "enforcement regime." Perhaps B could tender the "purchase price," or pay it into the court and then obtain an injunction ordering A to turn over the ring. A regime that gives a plaintiff the right to use the courts to change the status quo is alien to our capitalist legal system, which jealously defends property rights.

Of course, no one is seriously suggesting that we institute a Calabresi-Melamed liability regime in the case of consumer goods. Let us therefore consider its implications in a situation debated in the literature: the efficient allocation of commercially productive property.[128]

Suppose that X owns a business that Y could operate more profitably. Standard economic analysis suggests that because Y is the higher valuing user, society would benefit from the transfer of control of the corporation from X to Y. Under current law and practice, Y cannot take the business away from X without X's consent. This protection exists in part because a property regime protects X's entitlement. X has an enforceable right of possession in the business. As a result, the only way Y can acquire the business is by bargaining with X.[129]

Under a liability regime, however, Y would have the power to force onto X an involuntary transfer by paying X society's valuation of the object. If the object is control of a corporation, however, there is no practical way for Y to "take" X's object through self-help. Consequently, we must devise a procedure whereby Y could invoke the enforcement power of the state.

Perhaps society would permit Y to bring a legal action against X seeking an injunction ordering X to transfer title to his equity in the corporation to Y upon Y's paying X the "purchase price." This transfer is involuntary with regard to X, and thus the purchase price would not respect X's subjective val-

128. For example, Ayres and Talley started their article with an analysis of a piece of real estate. The real estate begins in the hands of an owner who uses it for one purpose, but it is desired by another party, who believes that he could develop the property in a more profitable manner. *See* Ayres & Talley, *supra* note 32, at 1030–31.

129. If the business is a public company, then X would not be an individual, but a collective of shareholders. Y could "bargain" with these shareholders by negotiating a business combination with the managers of the business, who would then, in most cases, be required to submit the proposal to a vote of the shareholders. Alternately, Y could circumvent management and make a tender offer directly to the shareholders.

uation. Consequently, the action must include some form of valuation proceeding. Every corporate and bankruptcy lawyer, however, knows that judicial valuation proceedings are time-consuming and that the financial world has scant confidence in their accuracy.

As Zohar Goshen suggests, society arguably adopts a modified liability regime, including a valuation proceeding, in the limited area of "squeeze-out" mergers.[130] Under certain limited circumstances, disgruntled minority stockholders can bring an action in which interested officers and directors have the burden of proof for showing both the procedural and substantive fairness of the squeeze-out and the compensation paid to the minority in exchange for their stock.[131] Goshen suggests that this action is equivalent to allowing the majority to take the minority's interest in the corporation under a liability rule: the minority receives a societally imposed price for its entitlement.[132]

Does anyone in the Calabresi-Melamed debating society really believes that any state legislature would, in the foreseeable future, consider extending the liability rule of squeeze-outs to all corporate acquisitions, thereby creating a whole new class of complex and expensive lawsuits? Upon reflection, it is apparent that the squeeze-out rule Goshen describes is not the exception that proves the rule at all. It is not a rejection of the fundamental proposition that a property regime generally applies to stockholding; it is, instead, an attempt to deal with certain unique problems that arise in collective ownership.[133] The squeeze-out rule is a relatively recent alternative to earlier corporate law, which applied a rigid property regime to shareholders individually. Until the early twentieth century, a merger required unanimous shareholder approval on the grounds that majority rule would violate dissenters' property and contract rights in their stock.[134] Even under current law, squeeze-outs can only occur after the acquirer first purchases, in voluntary transactions with the original owners, the requisite percentage of shares

130. See Zohar Goshen, *Breaking the Tyranny of the Majority in Corporate Conflict of Interests Voting: Liability Rule or Property Rule?* (1998) (unpublished manuscript, on file with author).

131. *See id.* at 4–5.

132. *See id.* at 19–20.

133. As is true in another instance in which a court will occasionally order an involuntary sale—a partition action.

134. Obviously, this limitation gave veto power to individual stockholders and rendered the negotiation of mergers of widely held public corporations extremely difficult, if not impossible. Recognizing that property rights need not be absolute, we now acknowledge that the extent of a stockholder's property rights may be limited by statute or by the corporate charter. Consequently, recognizing that corporations are a collective means of transacting business and holding property, modern corporate law provides that many decisions be made collectively—i.e., by majority or supermajority rule.

to force a merger, allowing these original owners to receive a subjective valuation for their shares.[135]

Calabresi and Melamed actually suggest a regime similar to my takeover example in their notorious hypothetical four: B, the producer, has an entitlement to pollute protected by a liability regime. It is difficult to find examples of hypothetical four in the private realm. A, the consumer, cannot "take" B's entitlement to pollute by tendering the purchase price and seeking self-help because she cannot shut down widget production without trespassing.[136] This limitation contrasts with the state's power of eminent domain. Therefore, for this regime to work, A would need a procedure to change the property status quo: we would have to invent a "private" takings regime. Participants in the Calabresi and Melamed debate have assumed that they finally found an example of such a private takings regime in *Spur Industries, Inc. v. Del E. Webb Development Co.*[137] This, however, is a wishful reading of this case.

In *Spur Industries,* a plaintiff real estate developer brought an action to enjoin the neighboring defendants from continuing their cattle fattening business.[138] The court ruled that the defendants shut down their operation, but required the plaintiff to compensate the defendants for their resulting losses.[139] This situation, however, is not the two-party conflict presented in hypothetical four. The Calabresians repress the fact that this was a three-party dispute in which one bad actor had harmed two comparatively innocent ones. In reality, the court fashioned a custom-fit remedy to ensure that the two innocent parties would be made whole at the expense of the wrongdoer.

In *Spur Industries,* an unscrupulous developer built a retirement community next to the cattle fattening operation, but apparently failed to disclose this to the purchasers of the homes. Needless to say, the resident retirees were horrified by the nauseous filth of their neighbor's business and com-

135. Goshen also suggests that Delaware further modifies this "liability" rule with respect to squeeze-outs by layering on top of it a modified "property" regime in favor of the minority as a class. Parties forcing a squeeze-out can shift the burden of fairness by obtaining the approval of a majority of the minority. *See id.* at 21. Because this approval is voluntarily given by voting after full disclosure, the price received by the minority as a class reflects the class's subjective valuation. *See id.* This regime is still arguably a liability regime for class members as *individuals* because dissenting minority members do not receive their idiosyncratic valuation.

136. By entering B's property, A would not only be taking B's right to possess his entitlement; she would also be infringing other rights.

137. 494 P.2d 700 (Ariz. 1972). Most commentators assume that this case is an example of hypothetical four. *See, e.g.,* Ayres & Talley, *supra* note 32, at 1040 n.46; Coleman & Kraus, *supra* note 48, at 1338; Krier & Schwab, *supra* note 18, at 444–45. Epstein is one of the few analysts who recognizes that this case is, instead, sui generis.

138. *See Spur Industries,* 494 P.2d at 705.

139. 494 P.2d. at 706–07.

plained to the developer.[140] The developer, trying to protect his investment, sued the cattle operation.[141] The judge was in a difficult position because the cattle operation had done nothing wrong.[142] Cattle fattening is an insalubrious business, which is why the cattlemen originally located their business far from any residential communities. It was the developer who chose to move in next to the cattlemen. The land was cheap precisely because it was next to a cattle fattening operation.[143] Even if the retirees were negligent, they were clearly more innocent than the developer, who had misrepresented the quality of the homes.

The usual result for a lawsuit like the developer's would be that the status quo ante for the innocent cattle fatteners would be preserved but the old folk would be permitted to sue the developer for damages equal to the difference between the value of the houses as warranted and the value of houses next to a cattle feeding operation.[144] This result was unsatisfactory as a human, if not legal, matter. Elderly people had sunk their life savings into the dream of spending the lay end of their years in quiet contemplation of the Arizona desert. During retirement, people are typically more interested in consumption (enjoyment) than saving. The judge recognized, law-and-economics to the contrary, that giving retirees smelly homes plus money damages would not make them whole, although it might ultimately please their laughing heirs. The court noted that if the residents had been parties to the action, they would have been entitled to an injunction against the cattle operation as a public nuisance.[145]

In contrast to the residents, the cattle feeders' interest was commercial in nature. Economic theory more nearly fits their situation. They should be indifferent between continuing their operations at the same location, on the one hand, and receiving damages equal to lost profits and expenses incurred in relocating, on the other.[146] The question was how to reach this result. The court solved this problem not by inventing new substantive rights (à la hypothetical four), but by in effect crafting a novel procedure.[147]

140. The court noted, "There is no doubt that some of the citizens of [the retirement community] were unable to enjoy the outdoor living which Del Webb had advertised" and that they had made "strong and consistent complaints." 494 P.2d at 705. The odor and flies from the operation were "annoying if not unhealthy." *Id.* Nothing in the reported opinion indicates whether any of the residents had attempted to bring legal action against the developer.

141. Not only were the operation's odor and vermin objectionable, they were causing "sales resistance from prospective purchasers." *Id.*

142. *See* 494 P.2d. at 708.

143. *See* 494 P.2d. at 707.

144. *See* 494 P.2d. at 706.

145. *See id.*

146. *See* COASE, *supra* note 69, at 158; Coase, *supra* note 39, at 15, 34.

147. *See Spur Industries*, 494 P.2d at 706–07.

The court's language indicates that the he was not allocating a single entitlement between the developer and the cattle operation. This case is not an example of a liability regime described in hypothetical four. On the contrary, the court stated that *if* this were a classic two-party dispute between the developer and the cattle operation, he would not have granted an injunction because this was a classic "coming to the nuisance case."[148] In Calabresi and Melamed's terminology, between the cattle operation and the developer, the former had the entitlement to fatten cattle, protected by a property rule. The court suggested, however, that if this were a classic two-party dispute between the residents and the cattlemen, he would have granted an injunction in favor of the residents and against the cattlemen—but would *not* have ordered the *residents* to pay damages to the cattlemen. Vis-à-vis the residents, the cattle operation was a classic "public nuisance."[149] In Calabresi and Melamed's terminology, between the cattlemen and the residents, the residents had an entitlement to clean air enforced by a property regime. The court, however, recognized that, although there were only two named parties to the litigation, the dispute was in fact tripartite.[150]

Under conventional procedure, the court should have dismissed the developer's suit against the cattlemen, as the cattle operation did not violate any rights of the developer. The residents would then have had the option of bringing a suit for violation of their rights either against the developer for damages or against the cattlemen for equitable relief. If the residents chose the latter route and obtained an injunction, the cattlemen could then have brought an action against the developer for damages.[151] The court, instead, invented a procedure to, in effect, consolidate these three potential actions. The court implicitly allowed the developer to act as a proxy for the residents in order bring a claim to enforce the residents' rights against the cattlemen. The cattlemen then, in effect, sued the developer in his individual capacity as a third-party defendant. The court concluded:

> [The developer] is entitled to the relief prayed for (a permanent injunction), not because [he] is blameless, but because of the damage to the people who have been encouraged to purchase homes in [the retirement community]. It

148. *Id.*

149. 494 P.2d. at 706.

150. *See id.*

151. *See* 494 P.2d. at 708. The court was insistent that it was not recognizing any entitlement with respect to the developer itself, but merely using the developer as a proxy to assert the rights of the residents: "It should be noted that this relief to [the cattlemen] is limited to a case wherein a developer has, with foreseeability, brought into a previously agricultural or industrial area the population which makes necessary the granting of the injunction against a lawful business and for which the business has no adequate relief." Id.

does not equitably or legally follow, however, that [the developer], being entitled to the injunction, is then free of any liability to [the cattle operation] if [the developer] has in fact been the cause of the damage [the cattle operation] has sustained.[152]

When described as a three-party case, this case is a procedural anomaly. It is not, however, either *substantively* novel or an illustration of a Calabresi-Melamed two-party liability regime. *Spur Industries* represents a rare case in which a court crafted an equitable resolution of an inconsistent enjoyment dispute by applying familiar three-party possessory dispute principles within a two-party dispute—a rare judicial recognition of the elusive *jus tertii.* This (perhaps sui generis) case implicitly analogized nuisances (interferences with enjoyment) to the most empirically common type of possessory conflict: the three-party conflict known as a priority dispute. The Calabresi-Melamed taxonomy, however, utterly fails to account for three-party disputes.

The Theoretical and Empirical Impossibility of Calabresi and Melamed's Distinction Between Property and Liability

The analytical utility of the liability-property dichotomy (temporarily putting aside the pesky inalienability embarrassment) depends on the parties knowing which regime applies to any specific entitlement. Calabresi and Melamed assume that parties bargain within the shadow of a known remedy regime. Claimants must therefore be reasonably sure which regime is likely to apply in any given case. The problem, however, is that regardless of the property regime, the parties can never have this assurance in a world in which either (1) the object of the property right can be destroyed, or (2) third-party claimants are possible. Because this describes our world, injunctive and monetary remedies are both necessary and complementary remedies of a property regime.[153]

This conclusion is a variation on the familiar proposition that we only really care about the difference between property and contract when scarcity exists. If multiple substitutes for the object of desire are available on the market, and if the defendant is rich enough to pay damages, then the plaintiff may be economically indifferent between getting the original object back and receiving damages sufficient for her to go to the market and buy a substitute object. Unfortunately, scarcity means that there is an inadequate

152. *Id.*

153. Polinsky correctly argues that although there is a distinction between injunctive and monetary relief, this distinction breaks down because entitlements are rarely, if ever, absolute. *See* Polinsky, *supra* note 29, at 1086–87. I am making a slightly different point.

number of objects to satisfy all property claimants; property remedies are often unavailable or inadequate precisely when it is needed.

The legal economist might argue that, although a party to a property dispute might destroy the coveted object of desire in the messy empirical world, destruction cannot occur in their hypothetically perfect market, in which all actors are economically rational. The parties fight over possession of a valuable entitlement. It would be irrational for either party to destroy the entitlement they both desire. To do so would be the irrational act of the jealous lover who shouts: "If I can't have you, then nobody will!"

My use of this misogynistic analogy is intentional. These analysts repress the feminine. They want to see property as possession of the phallic object of desire (analogous to the male organ and the female body). Perhaps the *rational* lover would not destroy what he desires—but since when is love rational? You always (or too frequently) hurt the one you love. Calabresi and Melamed's analysis represses the fact that the classic environmental nuisance does not involve the masculine right to possess and alienate the (feminine) object of desire.

Enjoyment often destroys the object of desire. The ultimate form of enjoyment is consumption. If the object of desire is a limited resource—the old-growth forests of the Pacific Northwest, for example—enjoyment in the sense of commercial exploitation eventually will destroy the resource.[154]

More importantly, in classic environmental nuisances, enjoyment by one party of his object of desire may permanently and irreparably destroy the other party's ability to enjoy her quite separate object of desire. Indeed, the enjoyment of the first may destroy the second object altogether. If environmentalists are correct, then the lumber company's commercial enjoyment of the old-growth forests through logging will destroy not only the forest as object of desire, but also the spotted owl.[155]

For example, let us assume that the water our hapless consumer drinks comes from an underground river that passes under the neighboring widget

154. Of course, modern logging practices in this country frequently include reforestation. If one thinks of the forest purely as an economic resource, logging no more destroys the "forest" than harvesting this season's wheat crop destroys the farm. If, however, one views a forest as an ecosystem, then an old-growth forest may be very different from a reforested one, meaning that logging destroys the desired resource. Much of the irreconcilable conflict in this area springs precisely from the fact that loggers and environmentalists do not value the forest in the same way.

155. Ayres and Talley noted that the competing rights with respect to the spotted owl and old-growth forests are "qualitatively incompatible." Ayres & Talley, *supra* note 32, at 1091. Their discussion, however, reveals that they do not fully realize that this problem of qualitatively incompatible uses and the possibility of destruction of the object of desire are typical of environmental nuisances. Nor do they recognize the implications of this problem for the validity and utility of the Calabresi-Melamed trichotomy.

factory. These "widgets" are plutonium batteries that power space vehicles. Their production irradiates the aquifers under the factory. This radiation lasts longer than the expected life of the consumer and of her children; in fact, it is so difficult to clean out of the aquifers that it lasts for the economic equivalent of "forever."

Therefore, once B violates A's rights, it is impossible to put A back in the same empirical position she was in before the violation. The only remedy that a court *can* give A is damages. Consequently, as in a liability regime, we have (in Calabresi-Melamed terminology) a "forced sale." One can give the consumer the right to an injunction forbidding B from opening his plant, but defendants can, and often do, ignore injunctions. When they do, the plaintiffs must go back to court and get some other form of relief.

Consequently, the only way to make a property regime truly distinguishable from a liability regime in many environmental nuisance situations is not to impose equitable remedies. Rather, courts must impose sanctions for violation of the property right that are so draconian that no rational actor would ever risk them.[156] This is why Ayres and Talley suggest that a true property remedy (in the Calabresi-Melamed sense of the term) must consist of either exorbitant damages or significant criminal sanctions.[157] The government can impose damages or penalties large enough to prevent, rather than remedy, environmental harms. Environmental harms and theft of property rights are often crimes. We also permit punitive damages in some cases in which we believe the defendant acted egregiously. Theoretically, we could criminalize or impose punitive damages for all property violations. But to impose punitive damages on a party who loses a priority dispute, let alone to throw her in jail, would be a radical departure from current law.

Even if the property-liability dichotomy is unworkable for analyzing when an object might be destroyed, one might be tempted to argue that it remains workable in property disputes that truly are possessory in nature. No rational claimant would destroy the single object of desire being fought over. Although this may be theoretically true in a universe of two economically rational parties, in the real world of more than two potential claimants, the dichotomy breaks down for another reason—the impossibility of giving Calabresi-Melamedian property remedies to more than one person. The existence of a third party in a possessory dispute is equivalent to dynamite

156. For example, although Kaplow and Shavell assume that a property regime consists primarily of equitable remedies and criminal sanctions, their description is broad enough to cover draconian damages as well. *See* Kaplow & Shavell, *supra* note 38, at 723.

157. *See* Ayres & Talley, *supra* note 32, at 1036 & n.35. These, of course, are the options available in our legal system. In other systems—such as those established by organized crime—other options are not only available but used, such as threatening to kidnap the taker's kids or to send the taker to "sleep with the fishes."

in the enjoyment dispute. If property is a hysterically erotic relation, then in property, as in love, three's a crowd.

Consider the basic priority dispute that forms the first lesson in the typical introductory commercial law class.[158] On day one, A has the exclusive right of possession. On day two, B somehow obtains power over the object without A's consent to B becoming the permanent possessor of the object.[159]

When B fails to live up to his contractual obligations with respect to the object (for example, B fails to pay the purchase price for the object sold pursuant to a "cash sale" or return entrusted goods), he violates A's property rights. One of the classic rights available to A is replevin—the right to force B to return the good to A, restoring the status quo. This looks like a classic Calabresi-Melamed property regime.

But things are not so simple. Another classic remedy for violation of property rights is available—trover (the tort of conversion). The court treats B's interference with A's property right as a sale and orders B to pay a determined purchase price: the object is "put" to B. Calabresi and Melamed would argue, persuasively at this juncture, that so long as the election of remedies belongs to the original owner, this result is consistent with their definition of a property regime. Although trover involves an intersubjective valuation, A will never elect trover over replevin unless she anticipates that the intersubjective valuation will be greater or equal to her subjective valuation.

Unfortunately, the universe of property is never two-party in nature. There are always potential claimants for possession of the object. All but the totally self-sufficient hermit has creditors who have inchoate claims to one's assets in the event that one does not pay one's debts. A defender of Calabresi and Melamed might argue that the mere theoretical existence of these potential claimants with their inchoate claims does not necessarily impinge on their system. If A has taken whatever steps are necessary to protect her property rights in the object, then A should retain her alternate replevin and trover claims and prevail over the creditors. The fact that certain creditors will prevail over certain "owners" does not change this analysis so long as the object is still in B's hands when the dispute arises. The problem with this is contingency. The validity of the dichotomy requires that the parties know

158. For example, the first chapter of the Farnsworth, Honnold, Harris, and Mooney commercial law casebook, which I use, is devoted to variations on this problem under Articles 2, 3, and 7 of the U.C.C. *See* E. ALLAN FARNSWORTH ET AL., COMMERCIAL LAW: CASES AND MATERIALS (5th ed. 1993).

159. This transfer of possession could happen in a number of ways. Because of the absolutist rules American law applies to theft, for simplicity we will posit that B did not "steal" the object, but obtained the power in some other way. For example, B may have purchased the object from A on credit extended against fraudulent misrepresentations to A as to his ability or intent to pay for the object. Another classic example of B obtaining power over an object is when A entrusts a good to B as a bailee.

what remedy would apply before bargaining begins. This validity is lost if the remedy depends on later facts.

Let us now be more realistic. People who cheat other people frequently, if not usually, do so for financial gain. Consequently, if B takes A's object without paying for it, more likely than not, he will try to monetize his gain by "selling" the object to a third party. Moreover, the fact that B violated A's property rights often suggests that B has a tendency to cheat people generally. If B has not paid his debt to A, chances are he will not or cannot afford to pay his debts to others.

In the classic priority hypothetical, therefore, B purports to transfer A's object to C,[160] who may be a very sympathetic character. C may be not merely unaware of B's wrongdoing, but his actions even may be also "as pure as grace / As infinite as man may undergo."[161] C may have paid cash for the object. He may be a tort victim who seeks to attach the good in order to pay a judgment obtained against B. Either way, the problem is the same: we now have three claimants for the same object.

It is easy to dispose of B, the crook. But we must decide which of A's and C's innocent but mutually inconsistent claims of possession should prevail. The point is that only one of the two parties can get the object back and exclude the other rival—Calabresi and Melamed's definition of property. Calabresi and Melamed might counter that their description of property is accurate in the sense that, in a dispute between A and C, the court will decide that only one of the parties has a property right and will cut off the property claims of the other. Consequently, property and specific performance seem to go together.

The problem is that this analysis considers only one leg of the triangle at any given time, repressing the feminine third. The dispute that Calabresi and Melamed examine is not that between A and C, a third-party claimant. It is the original two-party dispute between A and B. There is no question that A has a property claim enforceable against *B,* even if a court finds that A's claim is cut off against *C.* Indeed, A's loss of her claim against C confirms B's act as wrongful. Yet there is no way for A to regain the object. A cannot go against C under the relevant priority rules; B no longer has the object and, as the wrongdoer, cannot replevy the good from C.

A's enforceable property claim against B can only take the form of money damages. Although a court will calculate these money damages according to property law principles, they will result in the imposition of society's inter-

160. I say "purports" because a sale is the conveyance for value of title from one party to another. The dishonest B often does not have good title. He may have only the fact of actual custody and a voidable title—as in the fraudulent misrepresentation case—or no title, but a limited conditional right of possession in the form of custody, as in the entrustment case.

161. William Shakespeare, *Hamlet, Prince of Denmark,* act 1, scene 4.

subjective valuation upon the unfortunate A. A will retain her option of remedies: replevin and trover. Trover (conversion) is precisely the type of forced sale that Calabresi and Melamed called a liability regime. A will be able to deem the taking a sale of the object to B as of the date of the taking and will be entitled to the market price on that date.

It is the replevin remedy that necessarily changes in the "lost object" scenario. A has the right to have the object back—the meaning of possession. However, there is no object in B's hands to return. Consequently, the most that she can get is restitution damages. The goal of restitution is to place the plaintiff in the identical economic position she would have been in if the taking had never taken place. She is entitled to the value of the lost object as of the date of the judgment.

In other words, if the lost object goes down in value between the date of the taking and the date of the judgment, then the plaintiff should prefer the conversion action and its turnover remedy—sale as of the date of the taking. If, on the other hand, it goes up in value, she should prefer the remedy of restitution damages—sale as of the date of judgment. In either case, society imposes its intersubjective valuation on the plaintiff—the plaintiff only gets to choose the date of valuation.

It is impossible in a society with more than one potential claimant to impose the liability/property dichotomy that Calabresi and Melamed propose. Because we can never assure a property owner ahead of time that she will be able to recover an object taken from her, claimants must consider the remedy for a taking to be money damages. A property regime is not an alternative to a liability regime. It requires a liability regime to function.

CONCLUSION: THE MASCULINE PHALLIC METAPHOR

The difficulty with Calabresi and Melamed's dichotomy springs from their adoption of the masculine phallic metaphor. They analyze environmental nuisances in terms of disputes over the possession of entitlements, essentially making them priority disputes. Because priority disputes always have the possibility of third-party claimants, no priority regime could be a Calabresi-Melamed property regime.

The classic environmental nuisance is not, however, a priority dispute at all. The parties are not contesting possession of a single thing. They are contesting necessarily inconsistent enjoyments of different things. As we have seen, these enjoyment disputes do not presuppose a theoretically unlimited class of third-party claimants. It is, therefore, theoretically and often pragmatically possible to impose a regime whereby one set of enjoyers always has an injunctive right against the limited universe of conflicting enjoyers. For example, homeowner A could always get an injunction to stop widget-maker B from polluting her water, regardless of whether B has made a contract with C to pollute his water.[162]

Therefore, it is impossible to have a variation of the pure Calabresi-Melamed "property" (injunctive remedy) regime applicable to classic environmental torts. Unfortunately, because the Calabresi-Melamed taxonomy confuses environmental disputes with priority disputes, it does not and cannot describe American environmental law. This shortcoming is why several of the six possible hypotheticals generated by Calabresi-Melamed are alien and absurd.

Property is phallic. It entails the creation of subjectivity through the possession, enjoyment, and exchange of an object of desire. Property, being legal, is symbolic. As with subjectivity, however, our desire to achieve the wholeness of the real leads us to identify the symbolic with natural analogs. We are drawn to identify property with the physical. When we stand in the masculine position, we concentrate on the masculine elements of possession and alienation. We confuse possessing and alienating with holding, exchanging, and taking tangible things that remind us of the penis and the female body. Furthermore, when we stand in the masculine position, we tend to repress the feminine element of enjoyment. As we have seen, despite the fact that environmental nuisances involve disputes over the feminine element of enjoyment, analysts have persisted in analyzing them in terms of the obviously inapplicable masculine elements of possession and alienation. But whatever is repressed in the symbolic returns in the real. Thus a feminine phallic metaphor for property is also implicit, but hidden, in property discourse.

Perhaps the reason inalienability rules are all but ignored is because they dimly reflect the repressed feminine aspect of property and environmental nuisances. Inalienability rules deny the adequacy and potency of the masculine regime of possession and of exchange. These rules imply a unique relationship between the "entitlement claimant" and her "entitlement," which suggests the feminine position of identifying with one's objects of desire. Unlike the masculine regimes, which pretend that castration can be cured, inalienability regimes recognize that some losses—like loss of virginity—are permanent and irremediable. Inalienability—the removal of certain objects from the market regardless of the owner's wishes—is, however, the mascu-

162. Of course, if we grant an entitlement to be free from pollution to a large class of consumers, it may be impracticable for a potential polluter to contract with all of them. Negotiating with large classes raises the possibility of both holdouts and free-riders—two of the classic market failures, which Calabresi and Melamed suggested a liability regime might mitigate. *See* Calabresi & Melamed, *supra* note 17, at 1107–08.

line response to the imagined fragility of feminine integrity—"the forced chastity of the veil."[163]

The Calabresi-Melamed analysis necessarily fails as a taxonomy of enforcement regimes because the remedies they propose do not relate to the harm committed. The trichotomy is not only an inadequate description of the legal relationship known as property, but neither can it serve as a limited analytical tool in a universe of more than two legal actors. As a result, what at first blush seems like a politically conservative debate about the increase of economic efficiency is in fact a call for the radical restructuring of American legal principles.

In other words, Calabresi and Melamed do not present a view of that cathedral we call property. Rather, in order to present something that can be viewed, they clandestinely attempt to destroy the actual, sublime cathedral and replace it with something simple and banal. Monet used metonymy to frame human experience, depicting only that which is proximate to it. Calabresi and Melamed erect a metaphor to stand in for experience, claiming to have captured its essential qualities through similarity. Monet tried to suggest how human subjects experience the cathedral's facade; Calabresi and Melamed build a facade and call it a cathedral.

163. SCHROEDER, THE VESTAL AND THE FASCES, *supra* note 4, at 232–35.

Chapter 4

The Midas Touch

The Lethal Effect of Wealth Maximization[1]

PROLOGUE: THE GOLDEN TOUCH

Ovid told two myths about King Midas, which on first reading seem quite diverse.[2] Lacanian psychoanalysis explains their hidden connection.

The first is *Midas Aureus*—literally *Golden Midas,* but more commonly known as the *Midas Touch.* This tale is so familiar that it has led to a common English expression. As is so often the case, however, the cliché represses the myth's original, and true, meaning. When we say that someone has "the Midas touch," we express admiration for or envy of the man who profits again and again through an uncanny combination of acumen and good luck. Yet according to Ovid, no man was as foolish and unfortunate as poor Midas.

Midas, king of Phrygia, came upon an obese satyr incapacitated by drink. He brought the satyr home to the palace, where he "recuperated" by spending several more days in drunken revels, amusing the king with fantastic anecdotes about a continent across the Atlantic Ocean "where splendid cities abound . . . [with] a remarkable legal system."[3] It turned out that the satyr was none other than Silenus—Dionysus's Falstaff. In gratitude for the king's

1. An earlier version of this chapter was published as Jeanne L. Schroeder, *The Midas Touch: The Lethal Effect of Wealth Maximization,* 1999 Wis. L. Rev. 687 (1999).

2. Ovid, The Metamorphoses (More trans.) www.perseus.tufts.edu/cgi-bin/text?lookup = ov.+met+11.85+vers+english;more.

3. Robert Graves, The Greek Myths 282 (1955). Although I rely primarily on Ovid's account, my retelling of the Midas myths is derived from a number of sources. Robert Graves cites Aeliean, *Varia Historia* iii, 18 for Silenus's tales of a Western continent that seems more like America than Atlantis. *Id.* at 283 n. 3.

hospitality toward his old friend, Dionysus, god of wine and ecstasy, granted Midas one wish.[4]

His avarice having been whetted by Silenus's tales, Midas asked that everything he touched be turned to gold. Dionysus pleaded with Midas to reconsider his hasty request, but Midas was adamant. Dionysus sadly granted the foolish king his wish and laughed at his folly. Within minutes Midas became the richest man in all history.

What he desired in haste, Midas learned to regret at leisure. When he started to drink to his wisdom and blessings, he was initially delighted when the goblet turned to gold. Delight quickly changed to horror when the wine itself became liquified gold the moment it passed his lips.

Dionysus, being half human, was the kindest of all gods. When the starving Midas prayed for relief, Dionysus granted it. Following the god's instructions, Midas bathed in the river Pactolus, which washed away the curse.[5]

Midas was the legal economist of ancient Greece. He sought to change worldly possessions he enjoyed into gold he could spend. By doing so, however, he found that he destroyed the ability to enjoy. Similarly, the wealth maximizer would have society maximize not goodness, or morality, or happiness, but wealth—the goods of the world expressed in money. He requires that we translate our subjective use value into objective exchange value.

Like Midas, the legal economist neglects to think through the logic of his own position. What is the wealth that we are supposed to maximize? As is the case with the ideal of the perfect market, there is surprisingly little literature that even discusses how to define wealth, or the necessarily related definitions of money and time. Midas did not pause to consider that the golden touch would destroy his ability not only to enjoy but to live. Similarly, the law-and-economics movement fails to see that its goal of wealth maximization, when coupled with its ideal of the perfect market and classic price theory, would also destroy not only all use value or utility, but freedom and subjectivity. In the perfect market all use value would be reduced to exchange value—all things are reduced to useless gold—at which point market participants become perfectly indifferent to all goods in the marketplace and all exchange must cease. If wealth maximization is the end of the market, the market will end when its end is reached.

Once again, both the logic of this dialectic and the reason why the pro-

4. Shakespeare tells us that Henry V could only assume his role as king by renouncing not only his youthful excesses but also his companion in debauchery. William Shakespeare, *Henry IV, Part II,* act 5, scene 5. Dionysus, in contrast, was destined to become not a mortal monarch, but the divine personification of inebriation itself. He therefore continued, even after his apotheosis, to cherish the silly old man who introduced him to the pleasures of the cup.

5. Which explains why gold is found in the river's sands to this day. OVID, *supra* note 2, at lines 224–27, GRAVES, *supra* note 3, at 282.

ponents of wealth maximization repress it are explained by Lacanian theory. Midas, the wealth maximizer, is driven by the desire to achieve the ideal of perfect immediacy, the instantaneous fulfillment of desire—the real. As discussed, law and actual markets, like language and sexuality, are symbolic. It is only friction, separation, and desire that creates human subjectivity. To achieve the real—to gain the golden touch and maximize wealth—is to destroy the market, lose subjectivity, and achieve oblivion.

Psychoanalysis also reveals that the paradox of wealth maximization reflects the fundamental paradox of human subjectivity—the sexual impasse. The wealth maximizer takes on the "masculine" position while repressing the equally necessarily "feminine" one because the two sexual positions are fundamentally incompatible. In Lacan's terms, there is no sexual relationship.[6] Consequently, we seek to take on one position and eliminate the other. The Lacanian paradox, however, is that despite their incompatibility, the two sexes simultaneously require each other: each is created by its failure to relate to the other. It is precisely this contradiction and tension between the sexes that causes desire. Desire is the engine of movement in the symbolic order that is necessary for the operation of actual markets and law and the actualization of human freedom. It is lucky that all attempts to resolve the sexual impasse and eliminate either sexual position are impossible, because success would be lethal. Thus the imaginary regime of wealth maximization is characterized not by desire, like actual markets, but by the death drive.

This chapter proceeds as follows. First, I examine the scanty law-and-economics literature on the definition of wealth in order to explore its implicit, if repressed, internal logic. This necessitates an examination of the subsidiary concepts of money and time. I show that wealth maximization is the Midas touch. I then show why law-and-economics continues to make Midas's foolish decision not despite, but just because of its self-destructive implications. Wealth maximization analysis is yet another example of how the law-and-economics movement privileges the masculine regime of possession and exchange and represses the feminine act of enjoyment. However, actual markets function only because they are haunted by the hidden presence of the ghostly repressed feminine. I compare the legal economic concept of wealth maximization with Georges Bataille's analysis of capitalism as the continuous postponement of the "sovereign" moment of enjoyment.

6. JACQUES LACAN, THE SEMINAR OF JACQUES LACAN. BOOK XX: ENCORE, ON FEMININE SEXUALITY, THE LIMITS OF LOVE AND KNOWLEDGE, 1972–1973 9 (Jacques-Alain Miller ed. & Bruce Fink trans., 1998) [hereinafter, LACAN, SEMINAR XX]. Ellie Ragland-Sullivan, *The Sexual Masquerade: A Lacanian Theory of Sexual Difference,* in LACAN AND THE SUBJECT OF LANGUAGE 49, 67 (E. Ragland-Sullivan & M. Bracher eds., 1991); *see* ELIZABETH GROSZ, JACQUES LACAN: A FEMINIST INTRODUCTION 137 (1990).

Or, more accurately, wealth maximization reflects the relationship toward enjoyment that characterizes drive, not desire. Drive is the idiotic satisfaction achieved through repetitive purposeless activity divorced from any attempt to achieve a goal.

Finally, I relate Ovid's second myth of Midas as a fitting coda to this chapter. This second story warns that we cannot avoid the errors of wealth maximization theory through a romantic rejection of market values in favor of the cultivation of immediate enjoyment. Romanticism, as the simple negation of wealth maximization, is its mirror image, reflecting it back in inverted form. As an attempt to privilege the feminine and repress the masculine, romanticism is just as deluded, and lethal, as wealth maximization.

DEFINING WEALTH

The proposition, most closely associated with Judge Richard Posner, that law should maximize wealth,[7] has consumed an enormous number of law review pages. Much of the critical literature concentrates either on the accuracy of the descriptive claim or on the desirability of the normative one. Some question Posner's claim that wealth maximization differs in any fundamental way from utilitarianism, let alone cures its flaws.[8] Even some of the literature that accepts Posner's general economic approach disagrees with Posner's adoption of the Kaldor-Hicks definition of efficiency, as opposed to Pareto supe-

7. Wealth maximization has both positive and normative aspects. The former posits "that the common law is best understood on the 'as if' assumption that judges try to maximize the wealth of society." RICHARD A. POSNER, OVERCOMING LAW 172–73 (1995) [hereinafter, POSNER, OVERCOMING LAW]. The latter posits that "judges should interpret . . . antitrust statutes to make them conform to the dictates of wealth maximization." *Id.* at 173. *See also* Lewis A. Kornhauser, *Wealth Maximization,* THE DICTIONARY OF LAW AND ECONOMICS 679 (1998). Even Posner now admits that "not all questions that come up in law, however, can be effortlessly recast as economic questions." POSNER, OVERCOMING LAW, *supra* at 22. "In recent years, Posner has weakened his claim from one that asserted that common law courts should be exclusively concerned with wealth maximization to one that asserts that wealth maximization is one of the values that common law courts ought to pursue." Kornhauser, *supra* at 682.

8. *See, e.g.,* "Wealth maximization . . . is neither more defensible than utilitarianism nor is it an alternative efficiency criterion. Indeed it is not an efficiency criterion at all." Jules L. Coleman, *Efficiency, Utility, and Wealth Maximization,* 8 HOFSTRA L. REV. 509, 521 (1980) [hereinafter, Coleman, *Efficiency*]. "The only area in which wealth maximization escapes the condemnation accorded utilitarianism is in measurement. It is much easier to measure wealth than utility, although the need to hypothesize markets reveals that even wealth measurement is not without difficulty." Lewis A. Kornhauser, *A Guide to the Perplexed Claims of Efficiency in the Law,* 8 HOFSTRA L. REV. 591, 603 (1980). For an excellent critique of Posner's claim to distinguish wealth maximization from utilitarianism, *see* Robin Grant, *Judge Richard Posner's Wealth Maximization Principle: Another Form of Utilitarianism?,* 10 CARDOZO L. REV. 815 (1989).

riority.[9] I agree with many of these critiques, and believe that expanding and elaborating them would be a worthy scholarly task. Nevertheless, I shall resist the temptation to travel down these roads here.

My aim is other and very specific. Although I base my analysis on the critical theoretical tradition frequently associated with left-wing or even Marxist economics, I am a believer in free markets and am not criticizing capitalism per se. Indeed, in this book I argue that market transactions play a fundamental role in the development of subjectivity and the actualization of human freedom, and that contract is a primitive form of "love." Nor do I deny that economics, or any other branch of knowledge, might have a useful role to play in jurisprudence or legal analysis. Consequently, in the last section of this chapter, I return to an argument I introduced in Chapter 1, that a simplistic romantic rejection of economic values and market relations is merely the mirror image of utilitarianism or wealth maximization and replicates their errors.

I am, however, criticizing much of the analysis associated with the self-described law-and-economics movement in the American academy generally, and particularly that subsection of the movement that adopts some variation of the wealth maximization criterion. In this chapter, I examine only the central concept underlying this scholarly debate on wealth maximization. Surprisingly, this is precisely the idea that is *least* discussed in the literature: the definitions of "wealth" itself and of its components, money and time.

If the literature on the ideal of the perfect market is scant, it is voluminous when compared to that on the definition of wealth. Virtually all that is written on the subject comprises a few passing paragraphs in a small number of articles written by Posner and his critics in the early 1980s. Since that time, legal scholars have squared off as being either for or against the economic analysis of law promoted by Posner, apparently assuming that the underlying conception of wealth is as simple as it is coherent. A quick computer search will locate scores of articles that merely quote Posner and then move on without further analysis of the definition itself. This concept is paradoxical, if not impossible, but there are powerful psychoanalytical reasons why we are drawn to the chimera of wealth, yet fear to examine it.

To maximize wealth is to achieve market perfection, and therefore to merge into the deadly order of the real. We will never do so, however, because the concept of wealth includes two mutually inconsistent positions toward money and time, which replicate the two sexuated positions. In other words, the paradox of wealth maximization reflects the sexual impasse that characterizes all human relations. The two sexual positions, like the two con-

9. Once again, since nothing in this book turns on the difference between the different standards of efficiency, I will not discuss them here.

cepts of money, paradoxically require and create each other, even as they can never exist simultaneously. It is this failure of sexual relations that maintains the symbolic order of language, law, and actual markets that prevents us from becoming submerged in the deadly immediacy of the real of the perfect market and wealth maximization.

Definitions

Posner, the foremost proponent of wealth maximization as an economic and legal goal, argues that his theory avoids the perceived problems of classic utilitarianism.[10] He calls his criterion a form of "constrained utilitarianism"[11]—a sort of conceptual plastic surgery that lopped off the grotesque features of utilitarianism while preserving the attractive ones. Some critics argue that the line Posner attempts to draw between wealth maximization and utilitarianism is a distinction without meaningful difference in that wealth maximization shares all of the problems of utilitarianism identified by Posner. I am sympathetic to this argument, but it is beyond the scope of this chapter. Here I take Posner's claim seriously because the secret to the deadly failure of wealth maximization lies precisely in the distinction that Posner draws between it and utilitarianism—namely, wealth maximization's repression of enjoyment.

Other critics have argued that, insofar as Posner is successful in distinguishing the two criteria, his surgery so mutilated the patient as to leave post-op wealth maximization more grotesque than pre-op utilitarianism.[12] For example, Ronald Dworkin recognizes that, despite its problems, the basic premise of utilitarianism—one should work to increase happiness in the world—has great intuitive appeal.[13] If wealth maximization can be distinguished from utilitarianism, it is only because it lacks this one saving grace.[14] There is nothing intuitively appealing about the proposition that one should

10. Richard A. Posner, *Utilitarianism, Economics, and Legal Theory,* 9 J. LEG. STUD. 103, 103–105 (1980) [hereinafter, Posner, *Utilitarianism*].

11. Richard A. Posner, *The Ethical and Political Base of the Efficiency Norm in Common Law Adjudication,* 8 HOFSTRA L. REV. 487, 497 (1980) [hereinafter, Posner, *The Efficiency Norm*].

12. *See, e.g.,* "Wealth maximization is not a happy compromise between utilitarianism and Pareto superiority, a compromise which somehow retains the best and eliminates the worst features of these other two principles. If anything, just the opposite is true: wealth maximization exhibits the vices of both and the virtues of neither." Anthony T. Kronman, *Wealth Maximization as a Normative Principle,* 9 J. LEG. STUD. 227, 228 (1980).

13. *See, e.g.,* Ronald M. Dworkin, *Is Wealth a Value?,* 9 J. LEG. STUD. 191, 200–201 (1980) [hereinafter, Dworkin, *Is Wealth a Value?*]. *See also,* "Unlike happiness or well-being, wealth is not something of intrinsic value." Coleman, *Efficiency, supra* note 8, at 527.

14. "Once social wealth is divorced from utility, at least, it loses all plausibility as a component of value. It loses even the spurious appeal given to utilitarianism." Dworkin, *Is Wealth a Value?, supra* note 13, at 200.

increase the amount of wealth in the world. It contradicts the intuition that wealth should only be desired instrumentally, as a means of achieving other ends.[15] In the words of Richard Schmalback, "The problem [with wealth maximization], it seems, is that hardly anyone since King Midas has really believed that wealth is an ultimate goal."[16] Once again, I am sympathetic to this critique, but my analysis is not based primarily on the charge that wealth maximization confuses means with ends. Rather, I argue that the seeds of wealth maximization's doom lie in its chosen ends.

As Posner defines wealth maximization by contrasting it to utilitarianism, we will analyze the latter to understand the former.

Posner identifies utilitarianism as a philosophy—or at least a policy—that seeks to maximize the aggregate amount of happiness, or "utility," in the world, understood as the surplus of pleasure over pain.[17] I contingently accept this definition for the limited purposes of this chapter.[18]

15. As Georg Simmel has stated, "Money is the purest form of the tool . . . it is an institution through which the individual concentrates his activity and possessions in order to attain goals that he could not attain directly." GEORG SIMMEL, THE PHILOSOPHY OF MONEY 210 (David Frisby ed. & Tom Bottomore and David Frisby trans., 2d ed. 1990).

In Dworkin's words, "Money or its equivalent is useful so far as it enables someone to lead a more valuable, successful, happier, or moral life. Anyone who counts it for more than that is a fetishist of little green paper." Dworkin, *Is Wealth a Value?, supra* note 13, at 201. "If the pursuit of wealth is a good, it must be because pursuing wealth promotes other things of value." Coleman, *Efficiency, supra* note 8, at 527. Similarly, "simple 'desire for wealth' is not a meaningful starting point, because while one may be able to give meaning to a desire for happiness, say, apart from other characteristics, one cannot give meaning to 'wealth' and hence to a desire for wealth in such an abstract state." Guido Calabresi, *About Law and Economics,* 8 HOFSTRA L. REV. 553, 555 (1980). He adds, "That even with a starting point it is hard to see how an increase in wealth constitutes an improvement in society unless it furthers some other goal, like utility or equality." *Id.* at 556. And for Edwin Baker, "Before one can normatively employ the wealth-maximization criterion, one must show that wealth, as contrasted to utility for example, is a property measure of value; or, at least, one must show that wealth is something that society, whatever its other concerns, should seek to increase." C. Edwin Baker, *Starting Points in Economic Analysis of Law,* 8 HOFSTRA L. REV. 939, 939–40 (1980).

One supporter of Posner defends wealth maximization on the grounds that wealth is not merely a value that can serve as an appropriate end, but that it is the only criteria of value. D. Bruce Johnsen, *Wealth Is* Value, 15 J. LEG. STUD. 263 (1986).

16. Richard Schmalback, *The Justice of Economics: An Analysis of Wealth Maximization as a Normative Goal* (book review of RICHARD A. POSNER, THE ECONOMICS OF JUSTICE), 83 COLUM. L. REV. 488, 492 (1983).

17. "Utilitarianism, as ordinarily understood and as I shall use the term in this paper, holds that the moral worth of an action (or of a practice, institution, law, etc.) is to be judged by its effect in promoting happiness—'the surplus of pleasure over pain' aggregated across all of the inhabitants . . . of 'society' " (citations deleted). Posner, *Utilitarianism, supra* note 8, at 104. "Happiness, utility, is maximized when people (or creatures) are able to satisfy their preferences, whatever those preferences may be, to the greatest possible extent." *Id.* at 111–12.

18. In this chapter, I refer to utilitarianism purely as a foil for wealth maximization. Posner's is arguably an impoverished account of this philosophy. Much economic literature implicitly

Posner's formulation of wealth maximization is designed to avoid certain widely recognized problems of utilitarianism. Two classic criticisms of utilitarianism are the difficulty or impossibility of measuring utilities and the possibility of monstrous results.[19] The first problem relates to the suspicion (or assertion) that there is no way to know whether the pleasure or pain of any individual is commensurable with that of any other.[20] Consequently, we cannot formulate a single universal standard of measurement necessary to compare the aggregate utility created by alternate policies. In other words, it is not clear that we can translate subjective utilities into a single objective standard. In the absence of such commensurability, utilitarianism is an impossibility. The second problem relates to the proposition that if the only standard to be applied is *aggregate* utility, then utilitarianism would support any number of monstrous institutions, such as slavery or torture, *if* it could be shown that the aggregate pleasure experienced by the masters or sadists would exceed the pain suffered by the slaves and other victims.[21] Indeed, no proposal is off the table in utilitarianism. Utilitarianism even stands ready to abolish itself if that would increase utility in the world.

The Posnerian "solution" to these problems is to sever the direct connection between the objective criterion to be maximized by society in the aggregate and the subjective enjoyment of society's members as individuals.[22] Rather than maximizing pleasure, wealth maximization, as its name implies, seeks to maximize the aggregate "wealth" of society. According to Posner: "Wealth is the value in dollars or dollar equivalents [an important qualification, as we are about to see] of everything in society. It is measured by what people are willing to pay for something or, if they already own it, what they demand in money to give it up."[23] Although Posner seeks to distinguish his

---

assumes that utilitarianism posits that individuals are atomistic utility maximizers. In fact, utilitarianism is radically anti-individualistic. The utilitarian stands ready and willing to sacrifice his own individual utility for the sake of the aggregate utility of others.

19. Richard A. Posner, *The Value of Wealth: A Comment on Dworkin and Kronman*, 9 J. Leg. Stud. 243, 251 (1980) [hereinafter, Posner, *Value*]. A third problem raised by Posner regards boundaries (must we include all feeling beings, including sheep and rats, in the utility calculus?). This is beyond the scope of this chapter.

20. "Partly because there is no common currency in which to compare happiness, sharing, and protection of rights, it is unclear how to make the necessary trade-offs among these things in the design of a social system. Wealth maximization makes the trade-offs automatically." *Id.* at 247. *See also* Posner, *Utilitarianism, supra* note 10, at 115.

21. This is the problem of "moral monstrousness." *Id.* at 115–17.

22. Posner admits that wealth maximization might have an indirect relationship to enjoyment. *See, e.g.*, "Of course, in [making certain arguments] I am 'hitching' wealth maximization to utility maximization, but I am willing to do this because happiness is one of the ultimate goods to which wealth maximization is conducive." Posner, *Value, supra* note 19, at 244.

23. Posner, *Utilitarianism, supra* note 10, at 119–20.

theory from utilitarianism by emphasizing wealth over utility, the use of money "as a proxy for utility"[24] dates back to Jeremy Bentham, the founder of modern utilitarianism. As Ian Shapiro explains, however, "whereas Bentham saw preserving abundance as one necessary condition for maximizing utility," Posner's wealth maximization criterion makes "any connection with happiness purely contingent."[25]

Posner presents wealth maximization's estrangement from enjoyment as a mark of its ethical superiority over utilitarianism: "What is missing from utilitarianism is any very direct concern with the productive side of human activity; all the focus is on the consuming, the appetitive. . . . Wealth maximization reverses the order, and this is a mark in its favor."[26] Supposedly, one of the problems with utilitarianism is that if we assigned entitlements on the basis of pleasure, "people would cultivate the faculty of enjoyment rather than hard work."[27] Posner finds it "odd to give consumption moral precedence over production, to sacrifice the frugal for the pleasure-loving."[28] Posner does not, however, adopt a neo-Marxian labor theory that locates the source of value in production. Rather, Posnerian value is created entirely through exchange.

> To summarize, the wealth-maximization principle encourages and rewards the traditional "Calvinist" or "Protestant" virtues and capacities associated with economic progress. It may be doubted whether the happiness principle also implies the same constellation of virtues and capacities, especially given the degree of self-denial implicit in adherence to them. Utilitarianism would have to give capacity for enjoyment, self-indulgence, and other hedonistic and epicurean values at least equal emphasis with diligence and honesty, which the utilitarian values only because they end to increase wealth and hence *might* increase happiness.[29]

One should not assume from this definition, however, that Posner limits "wealth" to economic goods traded in the market. Rather, it includes any good thing, tangible or intangible, that a member of society would be will-

24. Ian Shapiro, *Richard Posner's Praxis,* 49 OHIO S. L. J. 999, 1002 (1987).

25. *Id.*

26. Richard A. Posner, *Wealth Maximization Revisited* 2 J. L. ETH. & PUB. POL. 85, 97 (1985) [hereinafter, Posner, *Wealth Maximization Revisited*]. *See also:* "Utilitarianism can be purged of its absurdities by the substitution of wealth for happiness as the social maximand. This substitution excludes the claims of the unproductive and thus gets rid of the thief, the "utility monster," and other unappealing claimants to whom the strict utilitarian must, however reluctantly, give ear." Posner, *Value, supra* note 19, at 248.

27. Posner, *Wealth Maximization Revisited, supra* note 26, at 93.

28. *Id.* at 97.

29. RICHARD A. POSNER, ECONOMICS OF JUSTICE 68–69 (1981) [hereinafter, POSNER, ECONOMICS OF JUSTICE].

ing to pay to have, or would have to be paid to be willing to give up.[30] Consequently, it is not necessary for there to be an explicit market for the good thing.[31] As Posner states: "Even today, much of economic life is organized on barter principles; the 'marriage market,' child rearing, and a friendly game of bridge are some examples. These services have value which could be monetized by reference to substitute services sold in explicit markets or in other ways."[32]

In the absence of actual markets, Posner argues, the monetary value of other good things can be determined by reference to hypothetical markets, although these should be used sparingly for practical reasons:[33] "Since . . . the determination of value (that is, of willingness to pay) made by a court is less accurate than that made by a market, the hypothetical market approach should be reserved for cases, such as the typical accident case, where market-transaction costs preclude use of an actual market to allocate resources efficiently."[34]

The inclusion of all good things that any person might want—as opposed to those things exchanged in explicit markets—in the maximand would risk reducing wealth maximization to utilitarianism but for one important restraint.

> The difference between wealth and utility is that wanting something very much, but not being able to pay more for it than its owner or competing demanders, does not establish a claim to a good in a system of wealth maximization, although it might do so in a system of utility maximization. Wealth maximization thus excludes claims based on pure desire—claims not backed up by willingness (implying ability) to pay.[35]

In other words, for a preference to be counted in a wealth-maximization regime, it is not enough that an object would make a member of society more happy or that the member be able to monetize his desire or even that he be theoretically willing to pay for it. The member must also actually *be able*

30. "A person's wealth includes not only those goods, rights, or services that he could sell on an established market, but also those objects of value, such as friendship or free time, that could conceivably be monetized." ERIC RAKOWSKI, EQUAL JUSTICE 202 (1991).

31. "Posner defines value as willingness to pay. To be exact, value is defined as willingness to forgo other valued goods. The distinction is far from trivial since much of what an individual forgoes in competing to establish exclusive use of valued goods is not always transferred to others as payment; rather, it may be dissipated." Johnsen, *supra* note 15, at 267.

32. Posner, *Utilitarianism, supra* note 10, at 120.

33. *See id.*

34. *Id.*

35. Posner, *Value, supra* note 19, at 243 (footnote omitted).

to pay for it.[36] Wealth maximization, thereby, severs the direct relationship between society's members and the enjoyment of the objects of their desires and replaces it with possession of the means of exchange and the ability to engage in exchange.[37] Although Posner's concept of being able to "pay for something" seems simple and intuitive at first blush, upon further examination it is revealed to be complex and paradoxical.

Wealth maximization is not a rights-based philosophy. Unlike Lockean libertarianism and Kantianism, it does not make a priori arguments in favor of property, liberty, or duty to the moral law. Nevertheless, in his early work, Posner argues that wealth maximization, by coincidence, supports the type of voluntary transactions and relatively free markets intuitively favored by libertarians, albeit for pragmatic rather than foundationalist reasons.

Wealth maximization seeks to allocate good things to the highest valuing user. This goal is therefore dependent on the individual subjectivity of each member of society. In this respect, wealth maximization is similar to utilitarianism. But, as we have seen, this is problematical if we accept Posner's assumption that we can never directly know the private subjective valuation of another person, let alone compare it to our own or to the rest of society.[38] Consequently, one reason why Posner champions wealth maximization over utilitarianism is because the former supplies a universal standard of measurement to use in determining whether resources have been efficiently allocated. But having a standard does not alone solve the problem of measurement. One must also have a methodology for applying the standard to the thing to be measured. The paradox of wealth maximization is that while Posner purports to find an "objective" standard of measurement, the thing to be measured is still the "subjective" valuation of market participants.

According to Posner, voluntary market transactions in a perfect market—in which each market participant translates her own subjective valuation into the objective standard of exchange value—serve an important evidentiary

36. Dworkin writes:

> Posner is very strict about how economic analysis must understand the verb "to value." Someone values something more than someone else (and the system of economic analysis depends on this) only if he is willing (and able) to pay more for it. If (for reasons other than market imperfections) the natural owner is unable to pay what the owner of the right would take, then he does *not* value it more."

Dworkin, *Is Wealth a Value?*, *supra* note 13, at 209.

37. Simmel, writing at the beginning of the twentieth century, anticipated this concept of money when he stated that "money has no inherent relation to the specific purpose the attainment of which it aids. Money is totally indifferent to the objects because it is separated from them by the fact of exchange. What money mediates is not the possession of an object but the exchange of objects." SIMMEL, *supra* note 15, at 211.

38. Indeed, the theory of the unconscious questions whether we can ever be sure of our own subjective valuations.

function.[39] The fact that two fully informed participants in an efficient market enter into a sales contract is not merely evidence that the purchaser values the object transferred more than the seller;[40] it is the definition of what market preferences are. Unfortunately, no actual markets are perfect. Even if two parties to an exchange correctly measure their own valuations, two-party transactions inevitably create externalities. The aggregate wealth of society as a whole might therefore be diminished, rather than increased, by the transfer. But Posner nevertheless proposes that voluntary transfers are the best evidence we have of wealth-maximizing activity, and, coincidentally, favoring contractual transfers also has the advantage of serving the intuitively attractive goals of autonomy and negative freedom.[41] Posner's analysis, in fact, goes beyond assigning a mere evidentiary function to exchange. Not merely actual subjective use value, but enjoyment itself, is excluded from his system. Exchange value becomes the *only* criterion of value recognized by wealth maximization.[42] Use value is implicitly excluded.

39. "It is true that Posner and others recommend market transactions except in cases in which transaction costs . . . are high. But it is crucial that they recommend market transactions for their *evidentiary value.*" Dworkin, *Is Wealth a Value?, supra* note 13, at 197.

40. The alternative device of adopting legal rules that "mimic" market transactions is consistent with wealth maximization principles but is not to be favored for practical reasons. Posner writes: "A coerced exchange, with the legal system later trying to guess whether the exchange increased or reduced efficiency, is a less efficient method of allocating resources than a market transaction—where market transactions are feasible. But often they are not, and then the choice is between a necessarily crude system of legally regulated forced exchanges and the even greater inefficiencies of forbidding all forced exchanges, which means all exchanges, as all have some third-party effects." POSNER, ECONOMICS OF JUSTICE, *supra* note 29, at 15.

41. In his early work, in which he tried to justify wealth-maximization on moral grounds, Posner argued that his theory was consistent with traditional Kantian consent theory. Posner, *The Efficiency Norm, supra* note 11. But Posner's concept of "consent is hypothetical rather than express. After all, common law rules are announced by judges rather than enacted by unanimous acclamation of those acted by them." Kornhauser, *supra* note 7, at 681. But even early Posner maintained that "voluntariness is, however, too restrictive a condition to impose on the wealth-maximization criterion." Posner, *Utilitarianism, supra* note 10, at 130.

Moreover, Posner's argument that wealth maximization might lead to the same substantive results as the Kantian categorical imperative is antithetical to Kantian ethical philosophy by definition. Kantian ethics insist on a total divorce between the good (substantive results) and the right. *See* Immanuel Kant, *Religion Within the Boundaries of Mere Reason, in* IMMANUEL KANT, RELIGION WITHIN THE BOUNDARIES OF MERE REASON AND OTHER WRITINGS 45, 52–54 (Allen Wood & George di Giovanni trans. & eds., 1998); Jeanne L. Schroeder & David Gray Carlson, *Kenneth Starr: Diabolically Evil? (Book Review Essay)*, 88 CAL. L. REV. 653 (2000); Jeanne L. Schroeder, *The Stumbling Block: Freedom, Rationality and Legal Scholarship*, 44 WM. & MARY L. REV. 263 (2002).

42. This, of course, raises one of the most common criticisms of the wealth maximization criterion. The proposition that voluntary transfers are favored by wealth maximization only instrumentally, as a means towards the end of efficient transfers, coupled with the fact that the degree to which voluntary transfers serve their evidentiary function depends on the relative efficiency of the empirical market raises questions as to the practicality and intuitive attractiveness

Before I continue, I need to make an aside regarding the context of the debate I am analyzing. In the early 1980s, Posner replied to criticism from moral philosophers by arguing that wealth maximization would, in fact, be expected to yield results that were consistent with the moral intuitions of his critics.[43] Wealth maximization would generally support contractual transactions over forced reallocations of resources, protect traditional property rights and criminalize theft, support personal freedom and prohibit slavery, and protect a woman's sexual autonomy and criminalize rape. It is in this context Posner and his critics discussed their definition of wealth.[44]

One such moment in Posner's writing is his attempt to appease libertarian intuition by arguing that a wealth maximization regime would support freedom on the grounds that, in the state of nature, slaves could be expected to purchase their freedom.[45] Libertarians, following Locke, start with the

---

of wealth maximization as a criterion when significant transaction costs or other forms of market failure exist. *If* transfers in a perfect market are deemed to be equivalent to Kaldor-Hicks efficiency transfers, *then* wealth maximization would suggest that the law should not support just any voluntary transfers in an imperfect market, but only those that approximate those that *would* hypothetically occur in a perfect market. Those who favor voluntarism per se seek legal devices that may either reduce potential transaction costs or cause the participants to act in ways that mimic the actions they would take in a perfect market. The true wealth maximizer, however, would also support a legal regime that enforced involuntary transfers, if they could be shown to be efficient. This argument has been eloquently made elsewhere *(see, e.g.,* Ronald Dworkin, *Is Wealth a Value?, supra* note 13, at 196–98; *and* Ronald Dworkin, *Why Efficiency? A Response to Professors Calabresi and Posner,* 8 HOFSTRA L. REV. 563, 575 [1980] [hereinafter, Dworkin, *Why Efficiency*]), and will not be explored further here. In any event, Posner has finally granted the force of the rights-based critique, and therefore no longer purports to defend wealth maximization on the grounds that it leads to the same results as libertarianism.

43. *See* Posner, *The Efficiency Norm, supra* note 11; Posner, *Utilitarianism, supra* note 10; Posner, *Wealth Maximization Revisited, supra* note 26; *and* Posner, *Value, supra* note 19. These discussions were later rewritten and published as a chapter in POSNER, ECONOMICS OF JUSTICE, *supra* note 29.

44. More recently, in two lectures delivered at Harvard Law School, Posner has partially renounced his earlier position. He now concedes that legal and public policy decisions cannot be justified by moral theory. Richard A. Posner, *The Problematics of Moral and Legal Theory,* 111 HARV. L. REV. 1638, 1669–70 (1998). These lectures form the basis of RICHARD A. POSNER, THE PROBLEMATICS OF MORAL AND LEGAL THEORY (1999). Posner has not, however, rejected an economic analysis of law. Rather, he continues to support economic analysis on the grounds that it is a form of pragmatic reasoning—a tool for achieving society's goals, whatever they might be. *See, e.g.,* "What the economist can say, which is a lot, but not everything, is that if a society values prosperity (or freedom or equality), these are various policies that will conduce to that goal." *Id. See also* POSNER, OVERCOMING LAW, *supra* note 7, at 15–17 in which he identifies economic reasoning as a form of pragmatism.

Insofar as he still supports wealth maximization, however, he still requires a definition of wealth. As far as I am able to determine from his recent work, Posner has not attempted to reformulate his definition of wealth.

45. A literal-minded approach to a libertarian conception of dessert would lead to a form of economic montanism, whereby no present allocation of resources would be justified unless

intuition that each individual has the natural right to own herself and the products of her labor.[46] In other words, nature demands that society prohibit slavery and protect property rights. Posner, who bases his theory not on a notion of natural rights but on wealth maximization, must try to justify this regime through instrumental reasoning by reference to a hypothetical market.[47] Moreover, because Posner is not a utilitarian, it will not be enough to argue that each man values his own freedom more than any other man could value his servitude. To argue that wealth maximization would support freedom, he must also show how each individual would be able to outbid every potential rival for his freedom.

Posner initially posits that each individual's labor is, as a general rule,[48] worth more (i.e., generates a larger income stream) in the hands of the individual laborer than if allocated to a "master" owning the laborer as a "slave." This is because it is empirically observable (and consistent with our under-

---

one could trace it back through an unbroken string of legitimate transfers to an legitimate first acquirer. Indeed, some radical libertarians seem to adopt something close to this extreme view. *See, e.g.*, ROBERT NOZICK, ANARCHY, STATE AND UTOPIA (1974). As this is clearly impossible as a practical matter, wealth maximizers seeks to develop some other basic principles of allocation and transfer.

Posner in effect argues that the Coase Theorem obviates the libertarian's preoccupation with initial legitimate acquisition. In Posner's formulation, "if transaction costs are low, the law's assignment of rights and liabilities is unlikely to affect the allocation of resources significantly." POSNER, OVERCOMING LAW, *supra* note 7, at 406–07.

As discussed in Chapter 2, Posner quotes Coase out of context to use him as support for a position that is diametrically opposed to Coase's point.

Nevertheless, based on his misreading of the Coase Theorem, Posner believes that he can legitimately skip the libertarian's founding assumptions as to property rights and allocate resources in the hypothetically most efficient manner, since this is the way resources would eventually be allocated in any event. In this way, Posner tries to argue that wealth maximization is consistent with Lockean or Kantian consent theory, even though it assigns property without actual consent: "If there is no reliable mechanism for eliciting express consent, it follows, not that we must abandon the principle of consent, but rather that we should look for implied consent, as by trying to answer the hypothetical question whether, if transaction costs were zero, the affected parties would have agreed to the institution." Posner, *The Efficiency Norm, supra* note 11, at 494.

46. JOHN LOCKE, TWO TREATISES ON GOVERNMENT (Peter Lachelt ed., 2d ed. 1967) (3d ed. 1698).

47. "The rights derived from economic theory are not, to be sure, bestowed by God or otherwise transcendental; they are "mere" instruments of wealth maximization." Posner, *Utilitarianism, supra* note 10, at 127.

48. "If assigned randomly to strangers these rights [that is, the right of a worker to his productive capacity, and the right of a woman to her sexual access] would generally (not invariably) be repurchased by the worker and woman respectively." *Id.* at 125. Because Posner is trying to establish generally applicable principles or default rules, he only needs to posit how people can be expected to act on the average, not how any individual actually acts.

standing of human nature) that people are willing to work harder when they own the fruit of their labors and more likely to slack off when others own the fruit. Consequently, in a hypothetical auction market, the average individual can be expected to outbid any other potential claimant to purchase himself.[49]

At first blush, one might be tempted to object that this result will not come about, given the criterion that valuation will only be recognized if the bidder *is able* to pay the purchase price. One might assume that by definition a slave will always be impoverished because anything the slave claims as property ultimately belongs to his master. This would seem to suggest that masters always have the ability to outbid slaves and preserve the status quo.

This conclusion does not, however, consider that wealth maximization analysis refers not merely to actual markets but also to hypothetical markets. To understand Posner's argument one must, therefore, consider the radical conditions of Posner's hypothetical.

First, because the issue of freedom versus slavery relates to the establishment of basic rights, the hypothetical auction is held before the establishment of the state—i.e., in the state of nature, prior to the allocation of resources. In other words, before the auction, neither the potential slave nor the potential master owns any property or money whatsoever: neither the potential master nor the potential slave owns the "slave's" productive capacity. All potential property in the state of nature—including each person's productive capacity—is contingently held by a hypothetically perfect auctioneer who will auction off all entitlements. Consequently, the "slave" will not be attempting to purchase his freedom from his "master." Rather, the potential master will be bidding for the right to be a master, and the potential slave will be bidding for his freedom. It is potentially misleading to refer to the participants in the auction as "slave" and "master," because these terms presuppose that the "master" will win the bid and become the owner of the "slave's" productive capacity. Indeed, in the state of nature each man is simultaneously bidding for the productive capacity of every other man, so that any man might become a slave, a master, or a freeman owned by and owning no one else. Nevertheless, I follow Posner and Dworkin in calling one participant the "slave" and one the "master" because I cannot think of a better alternative.

Second, since this is a hypothetically "perfect" market, all market participants must have perfect knowledge of all relevant information. This includes

49. As I have stated, Posner no longer tries to justify wealth maximization on the grounds that it can be expected to yield results that are attractive to our moral intuitions. It is therefore unclear whether he still holds to his assumption as to the relative value of a person's labor if free or if enslaved.

knowledge not only of the relative subjective valuations of all of the market participants but also the objective future income stream that each market participant would be able to earn from owning the disputed object.

Third, because neither the potential slave nor the potential master owns any property before the auction, each must borrow the purchase price he is willing to pay for the slave's productive capacity.[50] This being a perfect market, there can be no barriers to financing efficient transactions. Consequently, the theoretically perfect auctioneer is ready, willing, and able to make a "purchase money" loan[51] to the higher bidder in an amount equal to his valuation, secured by a security interest in the future income stream to be earned by the bidder through exploitation of the object being auctioned.[52] In other words, the ability of each participant to bid will not be

50. If one really took Posner's perfect market assumptions seriously, there would be no need for such purchase money financing. One of the conditions of the perfect market is that there is no time. The winning bidder would receive the income attributable to the slave's labor instantaneously upon the assignment of the entitlement of his labor to the bidder. The bidder would therefore be able to pay the purchase price in cash. As neither Posner nor his critics realize this implication of perfect market theory, I will not discuss it in the text. Nevertheless, as we shall see, the true purpose of including an auctioneer in the hypothetical is not to provide financing, but to insure that use value (enjoyment) does not enter into the calculation of bids.

51. A purchase money loan is a loan advanced for the purpose of allowing the borrower to acquire rights in an object. *See, e.g.,* Uniform Commercial Code Section §9–103 (2000). As in the hypothetical, purchase money loans are typically secured by a "purchase money security interest" in the property acquired.

52. Neither Posner nor Dworkin discuss the express terms of the auction, but they both implicitly assume that the parties have to borrow the purchase price of the entitlement auctioned. For example, Posner cites the lack of an efficient credit market for human capital as a high transaction cost that justifies our allocation of individuals' productive capacity and access to feminine sexuality by law rather than leaving this matter to the market: "No doubt the inherent difficulties of borrowing against human capital would defeat some efforts by the natural owner to buy back the right of his labor or body even from someone who did not really value it more highly than he did—but that is simply a further reason for initially vesting the right in the natural owner." Posner, *Utilitarianism, supra* note 10, at 125. In other passages, Posner refers to the fact that the slave's ransom of her freedom will be financed by purchase money lending. *See, e.g.:*

> Suppose the value of her output to [her master] is $1 million, but if she were free she could produce [economic activity] worth $1.2 million in the same amount of time. Then presumably she could produce [economic activity] worth $1 million in less time and have time left over for [leisure activity]. If so, she could and would buy her freedom. Having done so, she will be worse off than if she had been free from the outset (she owes $1 million, plus interest, to whoever financed the purchase of her freedom). But that is not the point. The point is that wealth maximization leads to a determinate solution in the [slave-master] case once it is assumed that she could produce more if she were free than if she were a slave. Since she would retain her freedom if given it from the first and would purchase it if she began as [her master's] slave, the initial assignment does not determine the final assignment.

Posner, *Value, supra* note 19, at 110–11.

based on his wealth prior to the auction (because neither man has any wealth before the auction), but on the predicted future wealth that he would generate if he were to win the auction.

If it can be expected that as a general rule the potential "slave" would earn more from his labor if he were the owner than the potential master would earn from the slave's labor, the auctioneer would be willing to make a larger loan to the slave than to the master, enabling the slave to win the auction. Consequently, wealth maximization would suggest that freedom (in the sense that each individual owns the fruits of his own labor) would be the default rule in an efficient society.

Even this brief introduction raises many issues which this analysis needs to address, including the question of what it could mean to bid in the state of nature, before one has any assets to bid, and why the freedman wouldn't be as likely to shirk in order to cheat his creditor as he would to cheat his master. I will return to this hypothetical and its implications when I discuss in more detail Posner's repression of enjoyment.[53] From this hypothetical, however, it is possible to tease out the definition of wealth that underlies Posner's work.

To analyze the definition of wealth implicit in the slavery parable, one must also uncover the implicit definitions of money and time that underlay

---

Anthony Kronman has deduced a description of the Posnerian auction that is similar to mine:

> Let us assume the auctioneer is prepared to extend credit to each of the bidders by assigning them rights before the rights have been paid for (in the same way seller of goods might extend credit to his buyer). Of course, the amount of credit the auctioneer extends to a particular bidder bidding on a particular entitlement will depend upon the auctioneer's estimate of the magnitude of the income which the asset in question is likely to generate if its ownership is given to that bidder rather than another. Thus, for example, *on the assumption that* X's labor power will generate more revenue if he is its owner rather than someone else (because of well-known difficulties involved in the extraction of slave labor), X will receive a larger loan from the auctioneer and will, therefore, be able to outbid his competitors and obtain the entitlement himself.

Kronman, *supra* note 12, at 240–41.

53. The libertarian objection to this proposition should be obvious. The wealth maximizer supports liberty and property only contingently, as a means of achieving efficiency. If, for example, one could empirically falsify Posner's hypothesis that in the vast majority of cases each individual's labor would be worth more in the hands of the individual than in someone else's hands, then wealth maximization would no longer support liberty and property. In other words, under wealth maximization, liberty and property are not "rights" but temporary accommodations. As Shapiro correctly states, "There is in fact no particular reason to respect property rights at all from the standpoint of this radically consequentialist ethic: if state ownership of the means of production could be shown to maximize overall wealth it should be preferred on [Posner's] theory." Shapiro, *supra* note 24, at 1006.

it. The necessity of examining money is obvious: if wealth is to be measured only in terms of money or money's worth, it serves to know what money is. Wealth is not the same thing as money, however.[54]

As Posner points out, "Money . . . is just a measure of one's entitlement to houses, cars, rewarding work, leisure, privacy and countless other 'things' that constitute a person's wealth."[55] Even though Posner speaks of wealth in terms of "value in dollars or dollar equivalents,"[56] Posner is obviously not proposing that wealth can be reduced to currency. Otherwise, as has been suggested by Jules Coleman, wealth maximization would support scarcity or other economic policies that would increase the price of goods.[57] Instead, Posner insists that "value is not the same thing as price."[58]

Money is a measure, or more accurately, a repository, of the value of other things. Money so understood has no characteristics of its own. It is a purely transparent mediator of exchange. Money is pure negativity. Value is defined not in terms of what it is, but in terms of what it is not: the alternative for which it can be traded. Money so conceptualized is a "master signifier." It stands for the general concept of a neutral measure of the comparative valuation of the goods in society, a measure that might be contingently stated in terms of a currency, such as dollars.[59] Consequently, Posner states that "when [he] used money as a component of wealth . . . it was just as a shorthand for the things money can buy."[60]

In other words, money is another term for value, understood as that which one would give or accept in exchange for an object. As sociologist Georg Simmel argued in his *Philosophy of Money,*

> Money has been defined as "abstract value." . . . [M]oney is the substance that embodies abstract economic value. . . . If the economic value of objects is con-

54. Posner, *Wealth Maximization Revisited, supra* note 26, at 85–86.

55. *Id.* at 86.

56. Posner, *Utilitarianism, supra* note 10, at 119.

57. "Because the principle of wealth maximization necessarily involves the existence of prices, a proponent of wealth maximization would have to condemn as wealth reducing any recommendation to eliminate scarcity. Prices, after all, are necessary only in so far as scarce goods must be allocated. The elimination of scarcity eliminates the need for prices. The elimination of scarcity eliminates prices and, therefore, wealth." Coleman, *Efficiency, supra* note 8, at 524.

Despite his flippancy, Coleman intuits the point I make later in this chapter that if one takes the logic of wealth maximization to its logical extreme, then if wealth were ever maximized, wealth would immediately evaporate. *See also* David Gray Carlson, *Secured Lending as a Zero-Sum Gain,* 19 CARDOZO L. REV. 1635, 1703 (1998).

58. POSNER, THE ECONOMICS OF JUSTICE, *supra* note 29, at 60.

59. "Dollars or dollar equivalents provide a convenient way of expressing the measurement. They serve as a common denominator of value." Johnsen, *supra* note 15, at 270.

60. *Id.* at 87.

> stituted by their mutual relationship of exchangeability, then money is the autonomous expression of this relationship. . . .
>
> The money price of a commodity indicates the degree of exchangeability between this commodity and the aggregate of all other commodities.[61]

Simmel continues: "Money is simply 'that which is valuable,' and economic value means 'to be exchangeable for something else.' "[62]

Money as a neutral measure is equivalent to the familiar economic concept of "exchange value." Thus Posner speaks of wealth in terms of "what people are willing to pay for something or, if they already own it, what they demand in money to give it up."[63] Economic goods not traded in actual markets "have value which could be monetized by reference to substitute services sold in explicit markets or in other ways."[64]

This concept of money as exchange value is the corollary to the familiar economic doctrine that all costs can be analyzed in terms of opportunity costs. If costs represent the existence of forgone alternatives, then value represents the existence of acceptable alternatives.[65] In other words, value is the absence and cost is the presence of a better alternative.

Elsewhere, however, Posner does not limit wealth to the pure negativity of exchange value, but tries to give money an affirmative character. That is, he argues that wealth must include what economists call "use value" in addition to exchange value. Posner specifically confirms this by stipulating that wealth encompasses the concept of consumer surplus.[66] Consumer surplus is the amount by which a person subjectively values her property (use value) over the market price (exchange value). The fact that an individual does not sell a good at the prevailing market price indicates that she must subjectively value the good at least as much, if not more, than the objective, exchange value. And if goods are retained because of consumer surplus, the goods are being retained precisely to *consume* them or *enjoy* them. Wealth, then, must be about enjoyment, not exchange.

61. SIMMEL, *supra* note 15, at 120, 121. As Mark Hager has noted, "The neoclassical market model stresses that wealth is created in the sphere of circulation, not production." Mark M. Hager, *The Emperor's Clothes Are Not Efficient: Posner's Jurisprudence of Class,* 41 AM. U. L. REV. 7, 31 (1991). Unfortunately, Hager draws from this correct characterization the non sequitur that Posnerian wealth maximization would support an increased *number* of exchanges. *Id.*

62. SIMMEL, *supra* note 15, at 121.

63. *Id.* at 119.

64. *Id.* at 120.

65. GEORGE J. STIGLER, THE THEORY OF PRICE 112 (4th ed. 1987). Simmel states: "Value is determined not by the relation to the demanding subject, but by the fact that this relation depends on the cost of a sacrifice which, for the other party, appears as a value to be enjoyed while the object itself appears as a sacrifice." SIMMEL, *supra* note 15, at 80.

66. RICHARD A. POSNER, ECONOMIC ANALYSIS OF LAW 16 (5th ed. 1998); Posner, *Wealth Maximization Revisited, supra* note 26, at 88–89.

How does Posner reconcile these two different concepts of money as exchange value and as use value? He doesn't. Posner merely gives lip service to enjoyment (use value) indirectly through his references to consumer surplus. In fact, wealth maximization is incapable of acknowledging use value directly. A subjective valuation by any member of society is given recognition if and only if she translates it into the objective valuation of the market (exchange value). I will argue, when I return to Posner's analysis of slavery to add his analysis of rape, that no market participant is ever permitted to enjoy her goods. She must exploit them commercially, possessing goods only temporarily, in anticipation of future exchange in order to produce a future income stream.[67] Consequently, Posner condemns incentives to hedonism as the vice of utilitarianism that wealth maximization must stamp out.[68]

The reconciliation of the negativity of exchange value and the positivity of use value could only occur in the perfect market. In the perfect market, all objects are priced so that the use value and exchange value of every subject with respect to every object in the market are equalized. Of course, if this happens, each object is equivalent to all others. Each subject becomes perfectly indifferent between owning any specific object in the market and owning its exchange value. The particularity essential to enjoyment ceases, and use value evaporates. Moreover, since all market participants are indifferent, all exchange ceases. If exchange ceases, then there is no exchange value. Paradoxically, at the moment when wealth is maximized, wealth (value measured in either negative or positive money) immediately evaporates.

This result is already implicit in the very definition of money as the transparent medium of exchange. To express the value of objects in money is to translate use value into exchange value. But, as the medium of exchange, money has no positive value. It is radically negative. Value requires exchange if it is to appear. Yet objects, valued in money, lose their individualistic characteristics and become equivalent. In other words, objects valued in money become equivalent to money: totally negative, without any positive content. Having no individuating positive characteristics, monetized objects cannot be enjoyed: they are merely repositories of value that can be temporarily possessed in anticipation of future exchange. Expressing the value of objects in money means precisely that one would be indifferent between having the object and having money—with money being defined as that which has no content.

A perfect monetization of objects would therefore have the lethal effect

67. Posner asserts that one's buying capacity almost always springs from productive activity (either the buyer's or her ancestors'). POSNER, ECONOMICS OF JUSTICE, *supra* note 29, at 66, Posner, *Utilitarianism, supra* note 10, at 128–29, 135.

68. POSNER, ECONOMICS OF JUSTICE, *supra* note 29, at 68–69.

of the Midas touch. At the moment of wealth maximization, all actual market exchanges would cease, and all wealth would evaporate.

As I argued in Chapter 1, actual market exchanges require that objects *not* be perfectly monetized in the way that Posner proposes. The only reason why one engages in market exchange is because one is *not* indifferent between having the object to be transferred and the object to be acquired. As discussed in Chapter 1, exchange reflects the identity of identity and difference.[69] On the one hand, exchange only occurs if the two parties recognize an essential equivalence between the two objects to be exchanged. This equivalence is expressed and shared by the two parties in a single "objective" valuation of the two goods in terms of money. On the other hand, exchange only occurs if the parties also recognize a fundamental difference between the two objects to be exchanged, so that each party prefers the object to be acquired over the object to be transferred. This differentiation is implicit in each party's "subjective" valuation of the two goods.

Consequently, although the market can directly recognize money only in terms of the public, objective realm of exchange value, it must implicitly preserve the possibility of a separate category of use value. Use value exists as the boundary of exchange value. Although exchange value cannot capture use value, exchange only occurs insofar as each party believes that he can thereby realize a surplus of use value over exchange value. Indeed, this is the very reason why exchange is supposed to lead to an increase in wealth.

As we have seen, contract is the most primitive form of love. The lover sees in his beloved more than she is. When love is requited, it has the alchemical effect of enabling the beloved to give more than she has. The lover and beloved exchange places, so that the lover knows himself as the recipient of love. Both parties are enriched in that they become more than they once were.

Similarly, contractual exchange only occurs if each party sees that the other potentially has more than she has. As stated by Simmel, "It is the object of exchange to increase the sum of value; each party offers to the other more than he possessed before."[70] That is, the first party sees that the object owned by the second party would have greater use value in the hands of the first party. Conversely, the second party can only fulfill the first party's desire if she similarly sees that the first party owns an object that would have greater use value in the hands of the second party. In exchange, each party gives to

69. G. W. F. HEGEL, HEGEL'S SCIENCE OF LOGIC 424 (A. V. Miller trans., 1969) [hereinafter, HEGEL, THE GREATER LOGIC].

70. SIMMEL, *supra* note 15, at 82. Although Simmel was writing before the full development of classic price theory, his neo-Kantian theory of value looks forward to later developments. Simmel's analysis of the increase in value through exchange reflects my analysis of contract as love.

the other something that doesn't exist when the object is held in her own hands, creating the alchemical effect of increasing the total amount of value. As in love, the successful consummation of a contract results in each party attaining more than she had at the beginning of the transaction. There would be no exchange unless the parties disagreed as to the relative use values of the objects to be exchanged, even while they come to a temporary and contingent meeting of minds as to their equivalent exchange values.

Consequently, if objective exchange value were ever to become equivalent to the subjective use value of all parties, all exchange—and all value—would come to an end. Paradoxically, for the market to function, it requires that use value exist, but also that the market never completely captures use value. Surplus use value can never be observed directly, but only retroactively posited by the fact that an exchange has occurred.

This necessarily follows from Posner's definition of wealth as the good things of the world measured in money. As we have seen, Posner defines money as a pure means of exchange. As such, it has no qualities of its own or, to put this another way, its only quality is quantity.[71] Enjoyment of an object, however, is precisely the recognition of the unique qualities of the object. From a Hegelian standpoint, "quality refers to the specific, affirmative aspect of a thing which distinguishes it from other things that exist—*i.e.*, it is the aspect of a thing which is not shared; it is that which enables us to tell two 'things' apart."[72] Quantity, by contrast, is indifferent to qualitative difference.[73] As I have stated elsewhere,

> The concept of more or less is the same regardless of whether we are talking about more of this, or less of that. . . . Quantity is, therefore, indifferent to quality.
>
> In simple English, quality is differentiation, quantity is commensuration. Quality is difference, quantity is identity. . . . Qualities are the differences of

71. In Simmel's words, "Since money is nothing but the indifferent means for concrete and infinitely varied purposes, its quantity is its only important determination as far as we are concerned. With reference to money, we do not ask what and how, but how much. This quality or lack of quality of money first emerges in all of its psychological purity, however, only after it has been acquired. Only when money is transformed into positive values does it become evident that the quantity exclusively determines the importance of money, namely its power as a means." *Id.* at 259.

72. Jeanne L. Schroeder, *Never Jam To-day: On the Impossibility of Takings Jurisprudence,* 84 GEORGETOWN L. J. 1531, 1556 (1996) [hereinafter, Schroeder, *Never Jam To-day*]. Quality is what Hegel called "determinate being." HEGEL, THE GREATER LOGIC, *supra* note 69, at 111. It is "being in-itself." *Id.* at 131. I barely touch the tip of the iceberg of Hegel's theory of quality and quantity here. *See* Schroeder, *Never Jam To-day, supra* at 1554–66.

73. If quality is "being in-itself," quantity is "being-for-self." *Id.* at 1558. HEGEL, THE GREATER LOGIC, *supra* note 69, at 177–78.

> self from other. Quantity, in contradistinction, is what self and other have in common. Qualitative difference is a matter of is or is not. Quantitative difference is a matter of more or less. Quality asks "is it X or Y?" Quantity asks "how much Z do X and Y have?"[74]

To translate one's use value of an object into exchange value would be to erase the qualitative distinctions between objects necessary for enjoyment and replace them with mere contentless quantity. This is reflected in Posner's attempt to account for consumer surplus (enjoyment) as the amount one would accept in exchange for the objects one possesses; thus, in Posner's system, no one ever enjoys her objects, but only holds them temporarily in anticipation of future sale.[75] Indeed, insofar as the enjoyment of an object frequently results in the consumption of the object, and therefore reduction of the aggregate amount of wealth in the world, the very concept of present enjoyment is antithetical to wealth maximization. In that wealth maximization opposes consumption, it embraces the Midas touch.

The relationship between exchange value and use value parallels the relationship between the symbolic and the real, and that between the masculine and the feminine. Consequently, exchange value is "masculine money" and use value is "feminine" money. In each pair, the latter serves as the limit of the former; the latter is defined as that which the former is not. The former, therefore, simultaneously requires the existence of the latter as its defining other, while it can never capture the other. The relationship within the dyad is therefore an essential failure of relationship—an impasse. The subject of the market, like the subject of law and sexuality, is split between the masculine and the feminine, the symbolic and the real. The dream that this split can be overcome is imaginary.

In fact, if the split could ever be overcome, if wealth were maximized and the perfect market achieved, all markets would cease. Consequently, although Posnerian wealth maximization tries to deny, destroy, or defer enjoyment, it can only *repress* it in the technical psychoanalytic sense. The market cannot recognize enjoyment directly, but secretly preserves it so that it operates *sub rosa.*

The relationship of wealth to time may not be as obvious at first blush, but

74. Schroeder, *Never Jam To-day, supra* note 72, at 1556–67.

75. Posner defines property "as a right to exclude everyone else from the use of some scarce resource." POSNER, ECONOMICS OF JUSTICE, *supra* note 29, at 70. As discussed in the previous chapter, this is my definition of "possession." Tellingly, this definition fails to recognize the owner's additional right of enjoyment. More interestingly, however, is its failure to account for the right of alienation, given that the Posnerian owner only possesses his property temporarily and contingently until he receives an offer for exchange at the appropriate price.

it is just as necessary. First, wealth itself is defined as having a particular relationship with dilatory time.

> "Income" is a flow concept, "wealth" is the corresponding stock concept. The important thing to bear in mind is that income (and therefore wealth, which is the discounted present value of anticipated future income) refers to real rather than monetary phenomena—to housing or transportation services or leisure, not to wages or dividends.[76]

In other words, unlike income, wealth does not exist in and over time. Rather, it is outside of time in the sense that it collapses future time into present value. Actual markets, however, always exist within time.

Second, the negative concept of money as exchange value is also an attempt to freeze the time that necessarily exists in actual markets—to collapse the future into the present. One accumulates money today in the hope of acquiring the object of desire tomorrow.

> A person who accumulates more money than he spends during his lifetime is, in effect, deferring some of his spending until after his death, when it will be done by surrogates, his heirs. If, after taking . . . [a]gency costs of ne'er-do-well-children into account, he nevertheless leaves them money, they become, in effect, his agents to spend it after his death.[77]

Because market transactions require time, and because the goal of markets is to maximize wealth, time is viewed as a transaction cost in the Coasean sense. It stands between the market and its goal. Money as exchange value exists as a means of dealing with this transaction cost. As I discussed in Chapter 2, by definition there are no transaction costs in the perfect market. Consequently, there is no time in the perfect market. If there is no time in the perfect market, there is no money. If wealth is the aggregate goods of the world valued in money, there is no wealth in the perfect market. Paradoxically, therefore, if the perfect market were ever achieved and wealth maximized, all wealth would vanish.

There is a long tradition of condemning the money economy as destructive of human nature and freedom.

> Money, according to this conception, also destroys, necessarily replacing personal bonds with calculative instrumental ties, corrupting cultural meanings with materialist concerns. Indeed, from Karl Marx to Jürgen Habermas, from

76. Posner, *Wealth Maximization Revisited, supra* note 26, at 87 n. 5.

77. *Id.* at 98. *See also:* "Nor is the justice of this reward system undermined when some people live off inherited wealth and make no personal contribution to augmenting the wealth of society. The expenditure of inherited wealth represents simply the deferral of part of the accumulator's consumption beyond his lifetime." Posner, *Utilitarianism, supra* note 10, at 135.

> Georg Simmel to Robert Bellah, observers of commercialization in Western countries have thought they saw devastating consequences of money's irresistible spread: the inexorable homogenization and flattening of social ties. Conservatives have deplored capitalism's dehumanization, but both have seen the swelling cash nexus as the source of evil.[78]

As discussed in Chapter 1, probably the most prominent proponent of what I am calling "romanticism"—the fear that market transactions will result in an alienating universal commodification, not only of objects but of subjects—is Margaret Jane Radin.[79] I agree that the logic of the Posnerian conception of money as exchange value ("masculine" money) would be the deadly golden touch that destroys the differentiation necessary for use value (feminine money). Nevertheless, I break from these critics and support market relations. The mistake these critics of markets make is the same one made by those proponents of wealth maximization who seek to defend markets: they assume that the money economy is, or could be, successful in destroying differentiation and breaking the connection with enjoyment. I argue that Gresham is wrong in this case: masculine money will never drive out feminine money. Wealth maximization's very attempt to repress enjoyment and to define money as exchange value proves the necessity of feminine use value. In other words, the myth of the golden touch is just that—only a myth.

THE DENIAL OF ENJOYMENT

Wealth is utility—subjective use value—mistranslated into money's worth (objective exchange value). The criterion of wealth maximization is not what one wants or would enjoy, but what someone else would pay for it. To apply wealth maximization therefore requires that we recognize an individual's valuation of the object of desire only insofar as he can express it in terms of money he has (for objects he does not yet own) or would take (for objects he does own). This follows from the definition of value as the existence of acceptable alternatives—that which one would exchange to acquire what one doesn't have, or that which one would accept to give up what one does have. Wealth maximization therefore requires that we repress enjoyment (use value) in favor of possession and exchange (exchange value). In other words, nothing may be "used" because everything is held in reserve for future exchange. This is consistent with the fact that the enjoyment of an object frequently leads to its consumption, and therefore a decrease in the amount of wealth in the world.

78. Viviana A. Zelizer, The Social Meaning of Money 1 (1994).
79. Margaret Jane Radin, Contested Commodities 93 (1996).

Simmel, who adopts a concept of money similar to Posner's concept of wealth, insists that this conception necessarily leads to a break from present enjoyment:

> Money, as the *absolute* means, provides unlimited possibilities for enjoyment, while at the same time, as the absolute *means* it leaves enjoyment as yet completely untouched during the stage of its unused ownership. In this respect the significance of money coincides with that of power; money, like power, is a mere potentiality which stores up a merely subjectively anticipatable future in the form of an objectively existing present.[80]

Because money is a means of congealing time, wealth maximization is always a postponement of enjoyment.

Posner presents the severance of wealth maximization from enjoyment as an untrammeled good. While aesthetic utilitarianism incentivizes the culti-

80. SIMMEL, *supra* note 15. Simmel had mixed feelings about what he thought were the necessary implications of money as exchange value, which forever separates us from direct enjoyment. On the one hand, the modern monetized capitalist economy is leading to an increase in human freedom, as the interchangeability of the market releases people from the rigidity of status and allows the development of individuality. *See, e.g.*, his conclusion that the development of money payment "has been regarded, to some extent, as a *magna carta* of personal freedom in the domain of civil law." *Id.* at 285–86.

> Money's importance in gaining individual freedom serves to illustrate a very far-reaching definition of the concept of freedom. At first glance, freedom seems to possess a merely negative character. It only has meaning in contrast to a form of bondage; it is always freedom from something and corresponds to the concept by expressing the absence of obstacles. However, the concept of freedom is not confined to this negative meaning. Freedom would be without meaning and value if the casting off of commitments were not, at the same time, supplemented by a gain in possessions or power: freedom from something implies, at the same time, freedom to do something.

Id. at 400. On the other hand, he worries that (masculine) money inevitability leads to the interchangeability of people, as well as objects, making relationships impersonal and leading to universal alienation: "Yet however much money encourages such freedom, it cannot be denied that, from the standpoint of a free, independent and self-sufficient existence, the exchange of property and achievements for money depersonalizes life after a tight network of transactions originally enclosed and intertwined people." *Id.* at 407. See also:

> Money thoroughly destroys that self-respect that characterizes the distinguished person and becomes embedded in certain objects and their appreciation; it forces an extraneous standard upon things, a standard that is quite alien to distinction. By arranging things in a series in which only quantitative differences are valid, it deprives them, and on the one hand, of their difference and distance of one from another and on the other of the right to reject any relationship or any qualification by comparison with others—these are precisely the two factors whose combination determines the peculiar ideal of distinction.

Id. at 394.

Simmel comes to this depressing conclusion precisely because he believes that masculine money is successful in its goal of driving out feminine money.

vation of the capacity for enjoyment, ascetic wealth maximization incentivizes the cultivation of the capacity for thrift and hard work.

Although Posner renounces enjoyment, he in fact only succeeds in repressing it. But psychoanalysis tells us that repression is not destruction, but preservation. What is not spoken or acknowledged always returns to function elsewhere. Indeed, repression actually increases the efficacy of that which is repressed. When one tries to repress something, one always implicitly admits both its existence and its power. Although wealth maximization officially denigrates enjoyment, the hidden possibility of enjoyment is the engine that drives the market.

Indeed, when Posner celebrates squelching enjoyment through wealth maximization, he forgets what he implies elsewhere: one seeks wealth in order to effectuate one's preferences and obtain the object of desire. In other words, according to Posner's atomistic individualistic calculus, the reason why economic actors want the object of desire is so that they can enjoy it.

Psychoanalysis reveals wealth maximization's internal deadly paradox. It is an attempt to take on the "masculine" position of subjectivity, which privileges possession and exchange. The masculine position is created through the repression of the "feminine" position, which includes enjoyment. If wealth maximization (the masculine position) were ever successful in achieving its goal and destroying enjoyment (the feminine position), it would destroy itself as well. Luckily, the masculine position is always a failure, the repressed feminine always returns, and markets continue to function. Actual markets are impervious to the logical implosions of economic theory.

Slavery

Posner's repression of enjoyment and his antipathy to the "feminine" can be seen in his discussion of slavery. As already introduced, Posner suggests that wealth maximization would prohibit slavery on efficiency grounds. If the right to one's productive capacity were allocated to a master in a perfect market with no transaction costs and perfect financing, the slave, as the higher valuing user of his own productive capacity, would outbid the master and buy his freedom. Consequently, we should allocate productive capacity to the "natural" owner *ab initio.*

In wealth maximization, not only must preferences be translated into money, but the purchaser must also have the ability to pay his offer price; thus Posner's argument relies on certain express and implicit assumptions. First, the slave's productive capacity is worth more in the slave's hands than in the master's: one works harder if one retains the fruits of one's labor (and the ability to enjoy) than if one works for others. Second, one can borrow the purchase price of one's labor from some hypothetical banker, securing the debt with one's future earnings.

The structure of the hypothetical auction is designed to eliminate certain problems that might arise in actual markets. First, in an actual market one cannot assume that the master will set his asking price for his slave at the present value of the expected fruits of the slave's productive capacity in the master's hands. The master might also value the social status of the continued existence of slavery. This surplus enjoyment by the master might be greater or less than the value the slave would put on his autonomy (over and above the value of his productive capacity). In our hypothetical market, however, the relative hedonic pleasure of the master and slave will not be given any weight. This is because no resources have yet been allocated in the state of nature: neither party owns any money or other property. All purchases must be financed through purchase money loans made by the hypothetical auctioneer. The auctioneer will only lend money up to the amount of the collateral that the buyer can supply. Neither the slave nor the master will be able to borrow against their anticipated hedonic pleasure, precisely because it is subjective and cannot be turned into objective exchange value that could be used to pay down the loan.[81] The only collateral that either party can put up is the relative future income streams that the slave and master can earn from exploitation of the slave's labor.

81. Simmel made a similar argument that value understood in terms of money does not directly reflect the capacity for enjoyment:

> The intensity of demand by itself does not necessarily increase the economic value of objects; since value is expressed only through exchange, demand can affect the value only to the extent that it modifies exchange. Even though I crave an object this does not determine its equivalent in exchange. Either I do not yet possess the object, in which case my desire for the object, unless I express it, will not exert any influence upon the demand of the present owner and he will ask a price in accordance with his own or the average interest in the object, or I do possess the object, and in that case my price may be so high that the object cannot be exchanged at all (i.e. it is no longer an economic value), or else I shall have to reduce the price to correspond with the degree of interest shown by a prospective buyer.

Id. at 92. Posner would, of course, disagree with the second half or Simmel's analysis because Posner, in his definition of wealth, includes consumer surplus. Nevertheless, Simmel's analysis has bite.

First, in this context Simmel implicitly defines economic value in terms of market value or price. This is reflected in our legal system, which awards damages for violations of property rights in terms of objective standards, not in terms of the victim's idiosyncratic, subjective valuation. Second, Simmel is correct that the notion that subjective valuation can only be given economic recognition when it is revealed in price means that the concept of price requires that the owner enter into a contract to exchange the object. This intuitively reflects my analysis that in Posner's system, consumer surplus (i.e., excess feminine enjoyment) can only be retroactively hypothesized as having existed in the past after the owner contracts to sell it.

Indeed, the true function the auctioneer plays in the hypothetical is as a means of eliminating the parties' enjoyment from the calculation. Within the criterion of wealth maximization, we could eliminate the auctioneer and assign the slave's labor initially to either the slave or the master only if they were both perfectly rational and only cared about increasing their wealth (as opposed to utility). The "rational" wealth-maximizing master would understand that slavery creates the negative incentive that causes the slave to "shirk." The master would therefore rationally seek to incentivize the slave to work harder by sharing at least some of the profit from his labor with the slave—that is, by giving the slave at least partial freedom and making the slave his partner. This would bring the same result as that of the hypothetical auction. Posner recognizes, however, that individuals are more likely to maximize utility, rather than wealth.[82] The "rational" utility maximizing master might decide that the pleasure he would get from dominating the slave would exceed any additional pleasure he might get if a more autonomous slave earned him more money. If so, the master would not agree to transfer the slave's autonomy.[83] Consequently, the presence of an auctioneer who requires payment in money serves to prevent the parties from actualizing the excess of use value over exchange value. From a Lacanian analysis, the auctioneer serves as the guardian of the symbolic order—the Name-of-the-Father—which prohibits enjoyment.

To recapitulate, each party must borrow the purchase price for the slave's productive capacity from someone else and pay it back with appropriate interest. The transaction between the master and the slave results in a purchase price somewhere between the master's asking price and the slave's offer price—but wealth maximization is indifferent as to how the difference is allocated. However, as Dworkin has argued, the slave will only obtain any enjoyment if the purchase price is something below his maximum offer price; otherwise he merely exchanges one master for another. If the auctioneer has a purchase money security interest in *all* the worker's income

82. "Not only can wealth not be equated to happiness, but, to state the same point in the language of economics, people are not just wealth maximizers. Wealth is an important element in most people's preferences, and wealth maximization thus resembles utilitarianism in assigning substantial weight to preferences, but it is not the sum total of those preferences." POSNER, ECONOMICS OF JUSTICE, *supra* note 29, at 64.

83. Rakowski so criticizes Posner's assertion that the master would sell the slave if he could receive a purchase price higher than the expected future income stream of the slave's labor in his hands: "Posner manages to lend some creditability to his example by stipulating that Sir George views Agatha as a productive asset. But once this arbitrary stipulation is removed, Agatha's hopes of gaining release rapidly fade. If Sir George regards her not only as a pulp mill but also as a sexual plaything, or if he simply takes delight in the feeling of domination that slaveholding fosters, then he might demand more to part with Agatha than she could ever earn on her own." RAKOWSKI, *supra* note 30, at 206–207.

from his labor, then the auctioneer is just as much the owner of the worker's productive capacity as a master, and the worker would have the exact same incentive to shirk. Consequently, the worker must be able to earn and keep at least *some* income over and above the amount he must earn to pay back the auctioneer in order to incentivize him to work hard enough to increase society's wealth.

Rather than drawing from the historic American experience of plantation slavery, Dworkin poses the twee hypothetical of a slave, Agatha, owned by a master, Sir George. Agatha has an extraordinary talent for writing murder mysteries but a preference to engage in the nonremunerative hobby of gardening.[84] Both Dworkin and Posner ignore the possibility that by gardening Agatha might increase her consumer surplus in her home, thereby increasing the wealth of society. This omission unconsciously suggests that there can be no consumer surplus in the Posnerian ideal market.

Agatha, Dworkin suggests, would not buy her freedom under wealth maximization because, if she did so, she would have to continue to engage in the hateful activity of writing mysteries in order to pay back her loan to the hypothetical auctioneer. In other words, she would merely be exchanging masters.[85] Posner counters that if we assume that a free Agatha would be so much more productive than an enslaved Agatha that she could write enough mysteries to pay off her debt and then have extra time left over for gardening, then she would buy her freedom.[86]

84. Dworkin, *Is Wealth a Value?, supra* note 13, at 209–11.

85. *Id.* at 210. As described by Rakowski: "As Dworkin notes, Agatha would have to forfeit her financial security for a slight increase in the control she exercises over her life, and many people would doubtless consider this an unattractive trade. Third, to the extent that Agatha's productivity would be affected by the actuality or the prospect of liberation, it is hard to imagine the paper freedom she would have if sir George originally owned her labor and sold it to her at its net present value making any difference at all. She would, as Dworkin points out, remain the slave, formalities apart, of either Sir George or some moneylender." RAKOWSKI, *supra* note 30, at 206.

86. POSNER, ECONOMICS OF JUSTICE, *supra* note 29, at 110. This hypothetical raises another problem beyond the scope of this book: the "state of nature" assumption used by the early Posner to allocate resources. This, as Posner admits, is the extreme version of the "wealth" effect of varying allocations of resources.

That is, the amount of money Agatha will be able to earn depends not only on the market for the goods and services she produces. The market for goods and services depends on the supply and demand curves for these goods and services generated by all other persons in the market, as well as the supply and demand curves of all other alternative goods and services in the economy. These, in turn, depend on the allocation of resources. In the state of nature, however, resources are not yet allocated, so we do not know what the supply and demand curves will be for any goods and services. In other words, we have defined value in terms of alternatives, but in the state of nature we do not yet know what alternatives will exist once an industrialized society is developed.

To say this more concretely, Agatha writes murder mysteries. Although popular in late twen-

The question is whether the incremental difference between the slave's expected return and the master's expected return is great enough to make this transaction occur. Consequently, as Posner realizes, his early argument that wealth maximization would support the elimination of slavery requires not merely that we assume that the productive value of the slave's labor is higher in the slave's hands than in the master's, but also that we assume that the former exceeds the latter by an amount sufficient to pay interest on the purchase money loan incurred by the slave to acquire his freedom, and providing enough excess capacity for the slave to spend for his own purposes. Perhaps it is the inability to generate any meaningful empirical support for these fanciful assumptions that has led Posner eventually to abandon the moralistic argument for wealth maximization in favor of a self-proclaimed pragmatic one.

Rape

Wealth maximization excludes all enjoyment, and is therefore the Midas touch. This point can be seen more starkly in Posner's argument that wealth maximization explains the legal prohibition of rape. His analysis is supposed parallel to that of slavery. Posner might complain that I place too much emphasis on his analysis of rape, which is arguably at the margin of his theory. As Jacques Derrida has argued, however, it is often the marginal case that illustrates the essence of a theory[87] (just as marginal costs set the price of goods in a competitive market).

Posner hypothesizes that access to feminine sexuality would be auctioned off in the state of nature. He argues that, just as most individuals would outbid potential rivals to their productive capacity, most women would outbid potential rivals for their sexuality. Posner argues that even if we were initially to allocate women's sexuality to rapists,[88] we could expect that in the vast majority of cases, each woman would redeem her own sexuality.[89] This

tieth century developed economies, murder mysteries are a relatively recent literary genre. What could it even mean to say that there is a market for mystery novels in the state of nature before the allocation of goods and the formation of the state? By definition, before rights are allocated, there could be no concept of murder since there is no right to life that could be violated. Moreover, if Agatha lives in a perfect market in which information is perfect, how could there be any mysteries?

87. JACQUES DERRIDA, *Tympan,* MARGINS OF PHILOSOPHY ix, xxiii (Alan Bass trans., 1982).

88. As I mentioned in my introduction to the slavery hypothetical, it is hard to come up with appropriate language to discuss these hypotheticals, since our terminology reflects the status quo. If we were, in fact, to allocate a woman's sexuality to a man, he would not be a "rapist" if he were to exploit his valid property right over the unlawful protests of the woman.

89. "If assigned randomly to strangers, these rights would generally (not invariably) be repurchased by the worker and the woman; the costs of the rectifying transaction can be avoided

would be an efficient reallocation of sexuality. According to the Coase Theorem, however, this efficient reallocation can only be guaranteed in a perfect market with no transaction costs. Given the existence of transaction costs, we should allocate resources in a way that is efficient *ab initio.*[90] Consequently, wealth maximization suggests that we should allocate each woman's bodily integrity to that woman.[91]

However, Posner forgets that this is the utilitarian, not the wealth maximizing, answer. It is not enough that the woman value her sexual autonomy—she must be able to pay for it. In contradistinction to Posner's analysis of the case of slavery, it is hard to argue that the woman would be able to borrow the purchase price, since the value of her bodily integrity to her is not related to productive capacity per se. In other words, a woman's preference for sexual integrity is hedonic and subjective. She seeks to enjoy herself, for herself.[92]

In contrast, Posner can only think of women and feminine sexuality as commodities exchanged by men, and never as the property of a woman for herself. This necessarily follows, as a psychoanalytic matter, from the Posnerian definition of the market, which represses the feminine element of enjoyment. According to both a Lacanian and economic analysis, when viewed from the woman's standpoint, chastity is as much an enjoyment or use of a woman's body as is sexual congress. To equate the enjoyment of sexuality with sexual congress is to take the masculine position towards feminine sexuality.

Let us examine the hypothetical auction of feminine sexuality. First, the

---

if the right is assigned at the outset to the user who values it so highly that he might not resell it to the 'natural' owner." POSNER, ECONOMICS OF JUSTICE, *supra* note 29, at 71.

90. "If transaction costs are positive (though presumably low, for otherwise it would be inefficient to create an absolute right), the wealth-maximization principle requires the initial vesting of rights in those who are likely to value them most, so as to minimize transaction costs. This is the economic reason for giving a worker the right to sell his labor and a woman the right to determine her sexual partners." *Id.* at 71.

91. "This is the economic reason for giving a worker the right to sell his labor and a woman the right to determine her sexual partners. If assigned randomly to strangers these rights would generally (not invariably) be repurchased by the worker and woman respectively." Posner, *Utilitarianism, supra* note 10, at 124.

92. Surprisingly, Posner *does* recognize the necessity of excluding utility in the rapist's calculation. As Richard Markovits notes, "Posner acknowledges that a prospective rapist might obtain extra pleasure from the dominance he would be exercising by imposing himself on his victim. . . . However, Posner claims that this extra pleasure should not count in any evaluation of rape because under his approach, value must be measured by the price that would be established through a voluntary market transaction or contract (unless conventional transaction costs would preclude such an arrangement)." Richard S. Markovits, *Legal Analysis and the Economic Analysis of Allocative Efficiency: A Response to Professor Posner's Reply*, 11 HOFSTRA L. REV. 667, 674–75 (1983).

rapist himself can not bid for the woman because his interest is also purely hedonistic—he wishes to enjoy her. But certainly the madam and procurer who make their living selling women's sexuality would be "willing" (i.e., able) to bid. Consequently, in the hypothetical market for the initial allocation of feminine sexuality in the state of nature, there can be expected to be an effective bidding war for women's sexuality by pimps.

Second, although it may be true that the woman may have a greater capacity to enjoy her sexual integrity than any potential procurer or customer, under wealth maximization we give no weight to enjoyment. We do not recognize her claim to her own sexuality unless she turns her desire to bid into an ability to bid. She has no power to bid for her sexuality unless she intends to use her sexuality as a means of producing an income stream that could be used to secure the auctioneer's purchase money loan.

In order to do so, she might become a freelance prostitute. She could outbid the procurer if she would turn more tricks as a free agent then as the employee of a procurer, because she would be willing to work "harder" and resist "shirking." Ironically, in order to buy his slavery, the male slave must argue that he would be less likely to lie down on the job if he were free then if he were enslaved, while the prostitute must argue just the opposite. As Iago taunted his wife: "Nay it is true, or else I am a Turk. / You rise to play, and go to bed to work."[93]

Perhaps, alternatively, she might offer to move to a traditional society that places a premium on feminine virginity and use her chastity as a bargaining chip to negotiate a favorable marriage (or concubinage) that will result in a greater income stream then her exploitation by a procurer. She could outbid the procurer (or more accurately, her future husband would be able to outbid the procurer) if her chaste body had greater economic value when exclusively exploited by her husband (perhaps in the production of sons) than if promiscuously exploited in prostitution.

This hypothetical auction leads to an infinite regress.[94] On the one

93. William Shakespeare, *Othello, Moor of Venice,* act 2, scene 1.

94. Coleman has made a similar point briefly elsewhere: "Wealth maximization requires a fixed set of relative prices. The prices of goods depend, among other things, on the relative demand for them. The demand for goods depends in turn on the distribution of wealth. And the distribution of wealth is of course a function of what individuals are entitled to. Therefore, the system of wealth maximization must presuppose a set of initial entitlements in order to get started; and these initial entitlements cannot, by hypothesis, be accounted for on wealth-maximizing grounds. The system of wealth maximization therefore cannot provide a basis for an initial assignment of entitlements." Coleman, *Efficiency, supra* note 8, at 524–25.

This is known in the literature as the problem of "wealth effects." Dworkin briefly raises and disposes of this issue. Dworkin, *Is Wealth a Value?, supra* note 13, at 192. Posner chides Dworkin for not having the courage of his convictions in proposing his hypothetical slave auction in the state of nature:

hand, if the husband purchases the virgin bride purely for his own sexual pleasure (or love), he cannot outbid the procurer. In the hypothetical auction, the husband does not start out with any money that he could use to buy an object purely for consumption. Consequently, he must buy her for money-making activities. But what could it possibly mean to do something to make money before resources are allocated, when there is no one who yet owns money to buy any goods and services? How could the husband offer to breed his wife in order to produce children who could engage in productive labor when, at this point, we do not yet know who will end up as the owner of the children's labor? On the other hand, how could the procurer offer to sell the woman's sexuality, when no one has any value to give in exchange for her services? The potential johns do not yet own any money in the state of nature. Indeed, potential customers cannot even offer to pay for the woman's sexuality in kind, by working for the procurer, because we do not yet know who will own the customer's productive capacity. No customer knows whether he will be a

---

> A problem of indeterminacy may arise, however, if rights are being assigned when a society first comes in to existence. In the [slave-master] example it was easy to obtain a determinate rights assignment, because only one good in society was unowned—[slaves'] labor. With every other good having a market or shadow price, one could compute, in principle at least, the effects on aggregate wealth of assigning [the slave's] labor to herself or to [the master]. But suppose no goods are yet owned: land, labor, sexual access—everything is up for grabs. How can each good be assigned to its most valuable use when no values—no market or shadow prices—exist? This is the problem of wealth effects with a vengeance. All rights have yet to be assigned; assignment of rights on so massive a scale is bound to affect prices; and prices in turn will affect the question of whom the rights should be assigned to.

Posner, Economics of Justice, *supra* note 29, at 110. Posner proffers the rather unconvincing argument (given the radical nature of hypothetical market assumptions) that "the problem is exaggerated in two respects. First we need not be troubled in any case where the particular issue of policy that we are concerned with is marginal to the society as a whole. . . . Second, the assignment of rights at the outset of social development is unlikely to determine the allocation of resources many generations later." *Id.* According to Posner, no empirical study has found, and no one has proposed, a realistic hypothetical finding extreme wealth effects of this type. Posner, *Value, supra* note 19, at 246. Posner's answer ignores the fact that his own hypothetical is not intended as a realistic description of any empirical market, but is based on the highly abstract conditions of the state of nature, in which all values are up for grabs. Consequently, several of Posner's critics maintain that wealth effects make it impossible to use wealth maximization as a means of determining initial allocations of rights. *See, e.g.,* Coleman, *Efficiency, supra* note 8; Calabresi, *supra* note 15. "The preceding analysis indicates that the efficiency norm is incapable of uniquely assigning fundamental rights. Pure wealth effects make it possible to find that any existing allocation of rights will be efficient." Mario J. Rizzo, *The Mirage of Efficiency,* 8 Hofstra L. Rev. 641, 651 (1980); Kornhauser, *supra* note 7, at 679–80.

free man who can offer his services to the procurer, or the slave of another.[95]

Even assuming that we could get beyond the circularity of what it means to bid for an entitlement in the state of nature, any Posnerian alternative would still require the woman to realize the financial value of her sexuality by selling it, presumably to men.[96] If, instead, the woman wished not to have sex with men, or wished not to live in a world where her social and financial status depended on her marriage, or even if she accepted such a marital arrangement but rejected the concept that financial considerations should be the only or the paramount consideration for choosing a husband, she would not be able to raise money to secure a loan from the auctioneer. Posner's is a world of compulsory whoredom with no room for the nun, the romantic, the feminist, the lesbian, or even, for that matter, the traditional American housewife. Because of wealth maximization's repression of feminine enjoyment, it cannot accommodate women's sexuality as belonging to women.

There are no feminine subjects recognized in the regime of wealth maximization, only feminine objects. Wealth maximization can only analyze feminine sexuality as a commodity traded among masculine subjects. Posner's definition of wealth is masculine in the technical, psychoanalytic sense, and the masculine always defines itself by expulsion or abjection of the feminine.

This should not surprise us. Not only has Claude Lévi-Strauss shown that most primitive cultures are based on literal exchanges of brides among

95. In the words of Rakowski, "This difficulty [i.e., the problem of wealth effects] cannot be removed by Posner's suggestion that people should be thought of as able to borrow against their future incomes in bidding for rights at the moment when they are initially assigned. For the amount that people will later be capable of earning is in turn a function of how entitlements, including labor rights, are first distributed. To appeal to future income to determine initial shares, when future income depends on initial shares, is to turn an embarrassingly tight circle." Rakowski, *supra* note 30, at 208. Posner tries to counter this type of argument by making the unsupported empirical claim that any hypothetical differences in allocations of resources resulting from wealth effects would dissipate over time.

> Suppose at the beginning one man owned all the wealth in a society. To exploit that wealth, he would have to share it with other people—he would have to pay them to work for him. His remaining wealth would be divided among his children or other heirs at his death. Thus, over time, the goods and services produced and consumed in the society would be determined not by his preferences but by those of his employees and heirs. Probably after several generations most prices in this society, both market and shadow prices, would be similar to those in societies in which the initial distribution of wealth was more equal. If so, it means the initial distribution of wealth will eventually cease to have an important effect on the society's aggregate wealth.

Posner, Economics of Justice, *supra* note 29, at 111–12.

96. Theoretically, she might be able to sell her body in lesbian prostitution as well.

men of different kinship groups—indeed, the exchange of women is the beginning of culture. As I have discussed at length elsewhere,[97] Lacanian theory argues more generally that the masculine subject and the symbolic order are created through the imagined exchange of a feminine object of desire.

LACAN *AVEC* POSNER

The Sexuated Positions

In this section, I briefly summarize those aspects of my theory of the erotic nature of law and markets that are necessary to explicate the sexual implications of Posner's theories. Just as Lacanian theory posits that the masculine position is created by repressing the feminine, my theory predicts that a market theory such as wealth maximization, which emphasizes the masculine property elements of possession and exchange, cannot directly acknowledge the feminine element of enjoyment. Repression is not destruction, however. The masculine must always fail in his goal of destroying the feminine because the masculine can only define himself in contrast to the feminine. Similarly, in order for actual markets to function, the ideal of wealth maximization must fail, and enjoyment must secretly remain the guiding principle of the market.

To reiterate points made in previous chapters, as one matures, learns to speak, and takes on a sexual identity—that is, as one becomes a subject—one's subjectivity is split between three orders called the symbolic, the imaginary, and the real. The subject experiences this split not as a pregiven "fact of life," but as the tragic result of a hypothesized primal act of violence. It is not just that the subject in the symbolic order of the Other happens to feel split; rather he feels that he has been split by the Other.

Sexuality is the position the subject takes in response to castration. The masculine position is denial. The feminine position is acceptance. The masculine subject claims, falsely, to possess the phallus and to exchange it with other masculine subjects. The feminine knows that the phallus is forever lost, and she can only nostalgically pine for it. Rather than seeking to attain the phallus the feminine identifies with the lost phallus, and longs to ecstatically enjoy it.

The lost object of desire—the phallus—is exiled to the real. The feminine, insofar as she accepts castration, identifies with this real aspect of selfhood. Because the real is that which by definition cannot be captured in words or images, it is literally everything that is unspeakable and unimaginable. The

97. JEANNE L. SCHROEDER, THE VESTAL AND THE FASCES: HEGEL, LACAN, PROPERTY AND THE FEMININE (1998) [hereinafter, SCHROEDER, THE VESTAL AND THE FASCES].

feminine as the phallus is therefore impossibility or radical negativity. This corresponds to the feminine desire of Thanatos—the identification with the phallus is the desire to achieve the negativity of the real.

Paradoxically, the feminine portion of the personality is able to cross over occasionally from the symbolic realm of speech to the real. The term for the temporary achievement of the real—"feminine *jouissance*"—has a connotation of ecstacy. As we have seen, however, feminine *jouissance* is not enjoyable in the conventional sense of the term. Enjoyment is ecstasy, the achievement of desire, but since our desire is *Thanatos,* when we enjoy we stare into the abyss. Enjoyment is gut-wrenching horror as well as sublime joy.

The two sexes are two positions one can take with respect to castration—denial and acceptance. The masculine, which feels that he has lost a precious part of himself, falsely claims to possess and exchange the object of desire. The feminine, which feels that she has lost her selfhood, accepts the role of identification with and enjoyment of the object of desire. The masculine must lie to himself and pretend nothing has been lost. He must deny the existence of the real and act as though the symbolic were complete. The formula for masculinity is therefore "all subjects are submitted to the symbolic order."

How does the masculine reconcile this with his feeling of castration? By identifying castration with the feminine, and then repressing the feminine. If the feminine is the aspect of personality that is identified with castration, then one can avoid dealing with castration by not acknowledging the feminine. The feminine is therefore that aspect of personality that cannot be directly acknowledged in the symbolic realm. In Lacan's notorious formulation, Woman does not exist. She is that which is literally unspeakable in the symbolic order and unseeable in the imaginary. She is the lost phallus, lack per se, the radical negativity and impossibility of the real.

Consequently, although the masculine creates himself by distinguishing himself from the feminine, he can never directly acknowledge the feminine because the feminine is precisely the part of personality that he denies. Similarly, although the feminine is created by the masculine, the feminine cannot directly acknowledge the masculine, since the feminine position is the realization that the masculine position is a lie. If the masculine formula claims that "all subjects are subjected to the symbolic order," the feminine is the opposite claim, "*pas-toute,*" which can be translated either as "not-all subjects are subjected to the symbolic order" or "the subject is not wholly so subjected."[98] The two sexes require each other but can never exist simultane-

98. LACAN, SEMINAR XX, *supra* note 6, at 70, 80. Lacan's term "pas-toute" has also been translated as "not-all." JACQUES LACAN AND THE ÉCOLE FREUDIENNE, FEMININE SEXUALITY 145 (Juliet Mitchell & Jacqueline Rose eds. & Jacqueline Rose trans., 1985) [hereinafter, LACAN, FEMININE SEXUALITY].

ously. In Lacan's terms, there are no sexual relations. Or, perhaps more accurately, sexuality *is* constituted by the fundamental nonrelation between the two sexes.

The Real

Before we apply my interpretation of Lacanian theory to wealth maximization, I wish to reiterate and develop one additional aspect of the concept of the "real" relevant to a discussion of enjoyment and use value in wealth maximization. I have described the real as the order that serves as the impossible border of the other two orders—as that which literally cannot be captured in words or pictures. We experience the real as that which was "lost" or left behind when we entered the symbolic—as the "hard kernel" of reality that resists sublation.

Any such experience is a delusion. The real was created at the same time as the other two orders, when we learned language. In other words, the symbolic (law, language, sexuality) and the imaginary (imagery, meaning) are limited, bounded orders. The real is created solely to act as their border. It is that part of our experience that cannot be reduced to words or pictures. The real is the radical negativity and loss of consciousness that is the other of the symbolic and the imaginary. However, we retroactively hypothesize that the real must have an affirmative content by clues that we interpret as the "stains" or "traces" of its retreat in the symbolic and the imaginary.[99] Whenever we encounter the uncanny—the sense that our language and imagery is incompetent—rather than realizing that this is the inevitable failure of language and imagery, we interpret this as evidence that there is something beyond language and imagery. In the words of the advertising slogan for *The X-Files,* we feel "the truth is out there."

This is reflected in the traditional male preoccupation with female virginity. Virginity in and of itself is a purely negative quality—it is the lack of sexual relations. It achieves a positive significance only retroactively, from the judgment that it is something that is "lost" by women. Sexually active women are deemed to be split—deflowered. Defloration, like the achievement of language and submission to the symbolic, is a gain—the achievement of the ability to engage in intersubjective (sexual) relations (however imperfect they must necessarily be). Nevertheless, we retroactively describe defloration as the loss of a presymbolic integrity and wholeness. In the words of Shakespeare, "Loss of virginity is rational increase, and there was never vir-

99. Slavoj Žižek, Tarrying with the Negative: Kant, Hegel, and the Critique of Ideology 36–37 (1994) [hereinafter Žižek, Tarrying with the Negative]

gin got till virginity was first lost. . . . Virginity, by being once lost, may be ten times found; by being ever kept, it is ever lost."[100] Thus, in traditional societies, virginity can never be affirmatively proven because it is always at risk of being lost: the virgin could never claim to be chaste because tomorrow's indiscretion would be conclusive proof of yesterday's bawdy predilection. This, no doubt, is why unmarried women were frequently sequestered. Past virginity could literally only be posited retroactively, by the public display of the bloody stain of its loss on the marriage bed sheets.

In other words, there was never a time when we were one with the world. It is only our feeling of being split in the symbolic that enables us to imagine what wholeness must be like. It is only our feeling of loneliness that enables us to imagine what love might be and experience desire. The real is therefore not that which is not-yet-lost, but that which is not-yet-gained. Its traces in the symbolic are not what is left in its retreat, but the building blocks of its creation.

The Sexual Impasse of Wealth Maximization

Wealth maximization privileges the masculine position and represses the feminine position. Repression is not destruction, however, but preservation. In Lacan's famous slogan, what is repressed in the symbolic returns in the real.[101] Interestingly, Lacan himself adopts a monetary metaphor to express this idea: "Repression and the return of the repressed are just two sides of the same coin."[102]

Consequently, as I explore at length in the last chapter, the masculine creates himself through the repression of the feminine, and the feminine only comes into being through her own repression by the masculine. And so, I argue that the Posnerian system depends on the repressed feminine to function. The masculine element of exchange only occurs because of the hidden possibility of future feminine enjoyment; the masculine vision of money as exchange value implicitly requires its feminine shadow of money as use value; the masculine vision of time as a transaction cost to be eliminated requires a competing feminine vision of time as an object of desire to be cherished and prolonged.

100. William Shakespeare, *All's Well That Ends Well*, act 1, scene 1.

101. "What happens, then, when what is not symbolized reappears in the real? . . . Thus what is repressed nevertheless expresses itself, repression and the return of the repressed being one and the same thing." JACQUES LACAN, THE SEMINAR OF JACQUES LACAN. BOOK III: THE PSYCHOSES, 1955–1956 86 (Jacques-Alain Miller ed. & Russell Grigg trans., 1993) [hereinafter, LACAN, SEMINAR III].

102. *Id.* at 12.

Similarly, the feminine moment of wealth maximization cannot be resolved with the masculine moment. Actual markets—exchange—are in the order of the symbolic. They can recognize exchange but not use value. In contrast, use value—feminine enjoyment—is in the real. The symbolic order of exchange therefore cannot directly express use value. Nevertheless, just as the symbolic requires the real to act as its border, exchange requires enjoyment, even if it cannot capture it. Just as the real is only posited retroactively by the traces that appear as the stain of its retreat left in the symbolic, the existence of a prior, lost enjoyment can only be indirectly posited after an exchange has been made. In other words, we can only posit retroactively that the seller's subjective use value in the good sold must have once exceeded the objective exchange value and that his surplus enjoyment must no longer exist. As in the Lacanian theory of desire, the effect precedes the cause.

Sexuality is an impasse. But it is precisely this impasse—this moment of contradiction—that is the dynamic source of life in the symbolic order. The masculine is the moment of subjectivity that is unfree, in that it is totally constrained by the symbolic order of law, language, and markets. The feminine, being at least partially exiled from the symbolic into the real, is the moment of freedom in subjectivity. It is wealth maximization's failure to acknowledge the paradoxical necessity of the feminine that threatens to make it deadly.

We are now in a position to develop more fully a psychoanalysis of wealth and money. When Posner speaks of money, he is using it as shorthand for the trade-offs one makes in order to obtain, or retain, one's objects of desire. It is the acceptance of alternatives. Money is therefore only a temporary receptacle of exchange value. Money as exchange value is "masculine" money.

As we have seen, law-and-economics scholarship views time as a transaction cost. Time is an impediment that interferes with the instantaneous satisfaction of desires that is characteristic of the perfect market. In the case of wealth maximization, the desire to be satisfied is the movement of goods to the highest valuing user. As we have seen, if value is conceptualized in terms of alternatives, it can only be identified at the moment of exchange.[103] Immediate exchange of alternatives—barter—is impracticable in a developed economy such as ours. For example, we sell our productive capacity now in order to purchase alternatives later. Money serves as the mediator between the object sold today and the unknown future alternative.

Money conceived as the transparent medium of exchange is a means for solving the problems posed by time. Money coagulates exchange value over

103. Simmel intuits that this is the inevitable result of defining money in terms of exchange value: "Just as money is real money only at the moment when it buys something, i.e. when it exercises the function of money, so the commodity becomes a commodity only when it is sold; until that time, it is only a possible object for sale, an ideal anticipation." SIMMEL, *supra* note 15, at 138.

time, it makes two transactions occurring at different times (the sale of my labor for money and my use of money to purchase goods) equivalent to a single transaction occurring at one time (the exchange of my labor for goods). Intriguingly, this conceptualization of money was made explicit on the very first coin minted by the American government in 1787. The copper cent piece pictured a sun above an hourglass and the word "fugio," Latin for "I fly."[104] The personified unit of money identifies itself with time in the well-known adage *tempus fugit* (time flies).

Posner's view of money as the means of exchange—as the acceptance of future but unknown alternatives—is consistent with Slavoj Žižek's analysis of money as an illustration of signification and subjectivity. Ironically, although Posner reaches his conclusions as a means of supporting capitalist markets and the American free enterprise system, Lacanian theory owes a debt to Karl Marx.

The symbolic order of language, law, and sexuality is characterized by what Lacan calls "signification." Signification is the relationship of a word, or signifier, to a concept, or signified. This relationship should not be confused with a simplistic, unchanging, one-to-one relation between a name and an external object.[105] Such a simple identification and perfect correlation is what Lacan called "meaning," which characterizes the order of the imaginary.[106]

The imaginary realm is that of simple mirror images, negation, correspondence, and picture thinking, which we associate with animalistic thinking. For example, when a bird attacks a red object, it is not because he associates the color red with other birds that might be rivals for a mate.[107] Rather, red *means* "Attack!" In the imaginary, we act as though we were capable of the type of direct, immediate relationship that is in fact lost in the real. Meaning concentrates on the signified and assumes a direct correspondence between signifier and signified. Lacan's understanding of meaning is "imaginary" in several senses of the term—it involves picture thinking, it is delusional, and it is also the creation of imagination.

Signification, in contrast, exists entirely within the symbolic realm. There can be no direct relationship between speaking subjects within the symbolic

104. Jack Weatherford, The History of Money 119 (1997). The coin also bore the punning motto: "Mind your business." *Id.*

105. For example, in his otherwise excellent book on the brain science of language, Terence Deacon summarily dismisses Saussure (Lacan's precursor) for such a naive "mapping" view of language. Terence W. Deacon, The Symbolic Species: The Co-Evolution of Language and the Brain 69–70 (1977). From his description, however, it is clear that Deacon could not have read Lacan or any of his followers, but must be relying on simplified third-party accounts because Lacan's actual theory of language shows many similarities to Deacon's notion of symbolization.

106. Lacan, Seminar III, *supra* note 101, at 54.

107. *Id.* 9–10.

order and external objects in the real, because the real is defined as that which is beyond the border of the symbolic. Indeed, "the barrier separating the Symbolic from the Real is impossible to trespass, since the Symbolic *is* this very barrier."[108] Therefore, signifiers cannot refer directly to the object world. In signification, each signified is itself a signifier that refers to another signifier, which in turn refers to another signifier in an unending chain like "rings of a necklace that is a ring in another necklace made of rings."[109] Thus, in markets, exchange value never refers directly to the use value of the thing itself, but always to the exchange value of another object, which is in turn understood only in terms of the exchange value of yet another object ad infinitum in the unending signifying chain of available alternatives.

For Hegel and Lacan, a concept can only be understood in terms of what it is not: by its own negation. Each signifier relates to its signified not merely in terms of the similarity of the two, but also in terms of their essential differences.[110] Language is unified by a "master signifier" that can serve as the negative of all other signifiers.[111] The master signifier is the signifier with no signified.[112] Because the master signifier stands for nothing, it can serve as the starting point for the chain of signification.[113] Having no affirmative content of its own, only the negative, split subject can serve as the master signifier.[114]

108. Slavoj Žižek, For They Know Not What They Do: Enjoyment as a Political Factor 201 (1991) [hereinafter, Žižek, For They Know Not What They Do].

109. William J. Richardson, *Lacan and the Subject of Psychoanalysis,* Interpreting Lacan, 6 Psychiatry and the Humanities 51, 54 (Joseph Smith & William Kerrigan eds., 1983) (quoting Jacques Lacan, Écrits: A Selection (Alan Sheridan trans., 1977) [hereafter, Lacan, Écrits]). See also: "The meaning of this chain does not 'consist' in any one of these elements but rather 'insists' in the whole, where the 'whole' may be taken to be the entire interlude as described, whose meaning, or rather whose 'effect' of meaning, is discerned retroactively." *Id.* at 55.

110. "Within a signifier's dyad, a signifier thus always appears against the background of its possible absence which is materialized—which assumes positive existence—in the presence of its opposite." Žižek, For They Know Not What They Do, *supra* note 108, at 22.

In other words, signification is yet another example of the identity of identity and difference.

111. "The only possible way out of this impasse [that is, the dispersal of signification] is that we simply *reverse* the series of equivalences and ascribe to *one* signifier the function of representing the subject (the palace of inscription) for all of the others (which thereby become "all"—that is, are totalized): in this way, the proper *Master-Signifier* is produced." *Id.* at 23.

112. "This signifier is, on the contrary, a 'reflective' one: in it, the very failure, the very impossibility of the signifier's representation is reflected into this representation itself. In other words, this paradoxical signifier represents (gives body to) the very impossibility of the subject's signifying representation—to resort to the worn-out Lacanian formula, it functions as the 'signifier of the lack of the signifier,' as the place of the reflective inversion of the lacking signifier into the signifier of the lack." *Id.* at 24–25.

113. *Id.* at 23.

114. *Id.* at 22, 76.

In other words, it is the speaking subject that gives signification to language. The symbolic order is therefore always in the process of being made. Unlike the imaginary relationship of meaning, the symbolic interrelationship of signification is in a state of flux, slippage, and growth. Each subject gives signification to language by acting as the master subject and distinguishing herself from the language she uses to define herself. On the one hand, the subject is only a subject insofar as he is able to speak and engage in other symbolic interrelations, such as bearing legal rights, trading in the market, and having sex. Yet simultaneously, each subject also experiences herself as external to and separate from the language, law, market relations, and sexuality that define her. In other words, we all feel that there is a part of us that cannot be captured in words or reduced to our role in society. We feel we have an essential essence that endures over time, over and above our ephemeral and accidental position in the symbolic order. This is another way of saying that the subject is split between the orders of the symbolic (language), the imaginary, and the real, and between the masculine and the feminine. The part of the subject that is totally defined in speech is the masculine. The part of the subject that cannot be so captured is the feminine.

Žižek compares Lacan's reasoning to Marx's account of how society moves from barter (in which each object is valued directly, in terms of the specific other object for which it is exchanged) to a monetary economy (in which exchange value is generalized by reference to money, understood as the means of exchange).

> First, the commodity which serves as "general equivalent" is the one which is most often exchanged, which has the greatest use value (furs, corn, and so on); then, the relationship is inverted and the role of "general equivalent" is taken over by a commodity with no use value (or at least with negligible use-value)—*money* (the "money form). Following the same logic, the "general form" of the signifying equivalence ("a signifier represents the subject for *all of the other* signifiers").[115]

In other words, money as the medium of exchange is the one thing that cannot be enjoyed.[116] Just as the speaking subject, as a master signifier with no independent significance, serves to give signification to other signifiers, money is the master commodity. Money can serve as the universal unit of

115. *Id.* at 23–24. (citations omitted).

116. Money is the "commodity with no use value (or at least with negligible use value)." *Id.* at 26. I analogize Lacan's analysis of the subject as master signifier with Marx's analysis of money as the master commodity. Interestingly, Fink points out that Marx's analysis of the alienation of the worker through the commodification of his labor prefigures Lacan's theory of the split subject:

value for other commodities because it has no independent value of its own. Money can only be created through exchange for another commodity, temporarily possessed, and then exchanged for another object.[117] Simmel, trying to develop an alternative to Marx's labor theory of value, nevertheless comes to a similar conclusion: "The condition of money is obviously the same as what is called its lack of qualities and lack of individuality. Since it stands

---

> Castration can thus be associated with other processes in other domains: in the economic register, capitalism requires the extraction or subtraction from the worker of a certain quantum of value, "surplus value." That value (which is not so much a plus or surplus as a minus from the worker's point of view) is taken away from the worker—the worker is subjected to an experience of loss—and transferred to the Other qua "free" market. Surplus value, equated in the last chapter with surplus jouissance (Lacan's *plus-de-joiur*), circulates in an "alien" world of "abstract market forces." Capitalism creates a loss in its field, which allows an enormous market mechanism to develop. Similarly, our advent as speaking beings creates a loss, and that loss is at the center of civilization and culture.

BRUCE FINK, THE LACANIAN SUBJECT: BETWEEN LANGUAGE AND JOUISSANCE 100 (1995).

117. "In addition [dollars or dollar equivalents] are valued by market participants not in and of themselves but in the sense that they represent exclusive command over scarce goods." Johnsen, *supra* note 15, at 270.

Jason Scott Johnston comes to a similar conclusion that money as exchange value is a means of eliminating the differentiation among commodities, but from a very different vantage point. He tries to explain why many scholars resist valuing intimate relations in money.

> Money is money precisely because the cost of ascertaining what money will do is low. Under a barter system, by contrast, each side to a transaction must determine both the physical and market characteristics of the good or service. . . . But as the complexity of the economy and the number of goods and services, multiply, it will become more and more difficult for traders to execute in-kind transactions. . . . Without money, asymmetric information about the physical and market qualities of goods will act as a tax on transactions, thus preventing many value-enhancing deals.

Jason Scott Johnston, *Million-Dollar Mountains: Prices, Sanctions, and the Legal Regulation of Collective Social and Environmental Goods,* 146 PA. L. REV. 1327, 1337–38 (1998). In other words, Johnston considers distinction to be inimical to markets because exchange necessarily requires that we treat the objects to be exchanged as equivalent. In contrast, we view intimate relations as unique—the idiosyncracies of a potential mate are of the utmost importance. Consequently, money, which eliminates or hides differences, has little role to play in these relations. *Id.* at 1338.

Of course, Johnston's analysis of exchange overlooks my point that exchange actualizes the identity of identity and difference—that the parties must simultaneously treat the objects to be exchanged as equivalent and distinguishable. Perhaps a better analysis is that the phenomena that Johnston is trying to describe relates to money conceptualized as a way of congealing time. In a barter economy—what Karl Llewellen calls a "farmer's transaction." (Karl Llewellyn, *Across Sales on Horseback,* 52 HARV. L. REV. 725, 727 (1939))—there is no time dimension in the sense that the relinquishment of the object to be transferred and the receipt of the object to be acquired happen roughly simultaneously. Time, however, is an important factor in a modern mercantile (or postmodern information) economy. *See* Jeanne L. Schroeder, *Death and Transfiguration: The Myth That the U.C.C. Killed "Property,"* 69 TEMPLE L. REV. 1281, 1307–11 (1996).

between individual objects and in an equal relation to each of them, it has to be completely neutral."[118] Simmel continues, "Money is not only the absolutely interchangeable object, each quantity of which can be replaced without distinction by any other; it is , so to speak, interchangeability personified."[119] In Hegelian terms, quantity is indifferent to quality in the sense that the concept of "more or less" does not require one to know more or less "of what."

This conception of money epitomizes the Posnerian concept of wealth maximization, in which subjects repress enjoyment in favor of the productive activity of possession and exchange. In Simmel's analysis, the interchangeability of money threatens to make all objects interchangeable, robbing them of their unique characteristics.[120] Money so imagined is masculine in the Lacanian sense.

By treating money as though it were perfectly transparent, the wealth maximizer seeks to transform the trilateral mediated relationships of the market, whereby two subjects exchange objects, into bilateral, immediate relationships whereby two subjects interrelate. In Simmel's formulation, "Money represents pure interaction in its purest form; it makes comprehensible the most abstract concept; it is an individual thing whose essential significance is to reach beyond individualities."[121] This is another example of masculine desire as Eros. But note, the result is that the objects exchanged lose all positive particularity—being monetized, they are, like money, purely negative. At the moment of exchange, goods cannot be enjoyed, even as exchange never occurs but for the possibility of future enjoyment.

Simmel's fears (and Posner's hopes) are unfounded in that the interchangeability of objects in monetization does not destroy the differentiation of objects. As discussed in Chapter 1, the fact that two subjects engage in exchange is conclusive evidence that they recognize a fundamental difference between the objects exchanged.[122]

The relationship of exchange and use value necessarily flows from the logical connection between quality and quantity, which Hegel calls "measure."[123] Masculine money as exchange value is quantitative in nature. Feminine money—enjoyment or use value—in contrast, is qualitative. Quantity

118. SIMMEL, *supra* note 15, at 123.

119. *Id.* at 124.

120. *Id.* at 123.

121. *Id.* at 129.

122. As Žižek says, "Claude Lévi-Strauss pointed out how the very fact of exchange attests a structural flaw, an imbalance that pertains to the symbolic." SLAVOJ ŽIŽEK, ENJOY YOUR SYMPTOM!: JACQUES LACAN IN HOLLYWOOD AND OUT 18 (1992) [hereinafter, ŽIŽEK, ENJOY YOUR SYMPTOM!]. Actual markets, being symbolic, are always characterized by imperfection and differentiation—hence exchange.

123. *See* Schroeder, *Never Jam To-day, supra* note 72.

as commensuration is the suppression of quality as differentiation, in the same sense that the masculine position is the denial of the feminine. This should not be read as implying that quantity (or masculinity, or exchange value) can exist without quality (or femininity, or use value). Rather, it means the opposite: quantity can only be understood with respect to quality, and only perceived by its grace. Quantity is the sublation of the contradictions of quality, and therefore it requires quality as the condition of its existence.[124] If quality is difference and quantity is identity, then, according to the doctrine of the identity of identity and difference, quality and quantity share a moment of identity despite their difference.[125] To put this another way, to make a quantitative judgment is to assert that there is a moment of essential similarity between two things *despite* their difference. A quantitative statement is therefore always an implicit acknowledgement of qualitative difference. We require a concept of masculine money understood as an objective metric of exchange value—as a tool that enables us to commensurate and connect different commodities—precisely because the things to be exchanged are distinguishable by quality as well as by time and space. If all commodities were in fact interchangeable, we would not engage in exchange, and therefore would not need money as a universal metric of value. Money exists as a means to fill a gap, and therefore can only exist insofar as there is a gap that needs to be filled. To use another metaphor, money is a translator, and the fact of translation is not an assertion that two languages are the same, but testimony to the fact that they are not. To paraphrase Derrida, translation is necessary not despite, but just because of, its impossibility.[126]

This analysis of the relationship of quantity to quality seeks to break the logjam seen in contemporary discussions of commensurability and difference, which so often degenerate into the trading of "is too"–"is not" assertions typical of a playground argument.[127] Both proponents and opponents

124. *Id.* at 1556.

125. *Id.* at 1557.

126. Jacques Derrida, *Des Tours de Babel, in* DIFFERANCE IN TRANSLATION 165, 171 (Joseph F. Graham ed. & trans., 1985).

127. *See generally, Symposium: Law and Incommensurability,* 146 PENN. L. REV. 1169 (1998). In a refreshing, but only partially successful, attempt to break out of the sterile iteration that forms so much of this dreary argument, Frederick Schauer has suggested that "commensurability and comparability often have, or can be constructed to have, the character of attitudes, dispositions, presumptions, or conceptual frameworks, and, as such, they are best thought of as being chosen rather than as simply existing and, furthermore, as being chosen for instrumental and not intrinsic reasons." Frederick Schauer, *Instrumental Commensurability,* 146 PENN. L. REV. 1215, 1217 (1998). To paraphrase Schauer's point, although most writers assume that one mush choose between commensurability and incommensurability for all purposes, in fact, two things might be commensurable in some contexts yet incommensurable for others. The Hegelian

of commensurability assume that an acknowledgement of the proposition that the fact that people frequently make tragic choices means that people can and do measure things with respect to a common metric, despite their assertions to the contrary. Further, both assume that such commensuration would necessarily lead to universal commodification of both subjects and objects. Consequently, wealth maximizer Eric Posner uses the assertion of commensurability as support for an economic or cost-benefit analysis of all areas of law and morality,[128] while romantic Radin couches much of her condemnation of commodification in terms of a denial of commensurability.[129] By contrast, I argue that we frequently and necessarily commensurate, in the sense of comparing two qualitatively different objects, but I insist that this neither leads to the destruction of qualitative differences nor suggests that an economic approach privileging the moment of quantitative commensuration and repressing the moment of qualitative differentiation is appropriate for the analysis of human relations. Hegel reveals that quantity and quality—like repression and the return of the repressed—are always two sides of the same coin.

This suggests the ghost of the repressed feminine vision of money as use value—the congealment of enjoyment—can always be glimpsed flitting behind the masculine vision of money as exchange value (the congealment of time). Being real, enjoyment must be hypothesized to exist as the boundary of exchange. Posner does occasionally recognize the existence of this feminine twin to money as exchange value, but is unsuccessful in integrating the two precisely because the sexual impasse makes them logically inconsistent. Being two sides of the same coin, only one can be "heads" at any given time.

As we have seen, Posner flirts with the feminine when he states that wealth cannot be reduced to the Gross Domestic Product or any other gauge that tries to measure the good things of the economy in terms of their market price (exchange value), but must also include consumer surplus—the excess by which any individual's subjective use valuation of her possessions exceeds the market's objective exchange value. This admission reflects a shift in the definition of money from the medium of exchange to the congealment of enjoyment. This concession reflects the repressed, unconscious understanding that capitalist markets cannot, as Posner suggests, suppress the capacity for enjoyment, but implicitly requires that its members cultivate an exquisite capacity for future enjoyment.

---

analysis agrees with this claim, but goes a step further in suggesting that the very concepts of commensurability and incommensurability necessarily require each other.

128. Eric A. Posner, *The Strategic Basis of Principled Behavior: A Critique of the Incommensurability Thesis,* 146 PENN. L. REV. 1185 (1998).

129. *See, e.g.,* RADIN, *supra* note 79, at 1–15.

Nevertheless, despite these occasional fleeting glimpses of enjoyment (feminine money as use value) in Posner's writings, his system of wealth maximization, which necessarily conceptualizes money as exchange value, cannot recognize or fully account for use value. As we have seen, in a wealth maximization world, we only recognize a party's preferences insofar as that party is able to actualize them in market relations. In other words, it is not enough that she desire the object, she must have enough money to buy it.

Posner's critics have suggested that Posner's system depends on an asymmetric recognition of exchange value. He recognizes and protects the present enjoyment of the rich, while forbidding the future enjoyment of the poor.[130] This critique is based on Posner's definition of the value of the good things in the world as the amount of money one would spend to acquire an object that one does not yet possess plus the amount of money one would require in order to give up what one already possesses. This analysis asserts that although Posner recognizes only the exchange value of the have-nots, he does recognize both the exchange and use value of the haves.

A more subtle analysis, however, shows that even in the case of the rich, Posner never fully recognizes the feminine element of enjoyment or truly values objects in terms of use value. Rather he only expressly recognizes the two masculine elements of exchange and possession and the masculine form of money as exchange value.

The Posnerian analysis of slavery and rape shows how his models are incapable of recognizing enjoyment (use value), but can only conceptualize money in terms of exchange value. To repeat, in the state of nature, resources, including money, have not yet been allocated. The rival parties must therefore obtain purchase money financing to pay the purchase price in the auction. This requires that each party commercially exploit the object purchased. It is irrelevant that the object has greater use value than exchange value in one of the party's hands, because this use value is totally subjective and cannot be used to raise money to pay back the purchase money loan. This means that the purchase price in the Posnerian auction is always capped by the exchange value of the object.

In other words, although on the one hand Posner insists on including use value in the form of enjoyment in his definition of the aggregate wealth, or money, that exists in the economy, on the other hand he does not include it in the amount of value that may be exchanged to create additional value. Use value *seems* passive in that it cannot be spent unless it is first converted into exchange value. At first blush, this might not seem like a contradiction. If a person's use value in an object exceeds its exchange value, she would

130. Rakowski, *supra* note 30, at 211.

have no reason to want to exchange it. But this means that use value cannot be conceptualized in terms of masculine money understood as the means of exchange. As we have seen, however, Posner states that money is a "measure of one's entitlement" to good things—that is, what one can spend in order to make one's preferences "count." Consequently, even though wealth is supposed to include consumer surplus (enjoyment), and even though wealth is supposed to be the good things of the world measured in money, his definition of money is limited to exchange value.

This result is duplicated in one of Posner's criticisms of utilitarianism. Utilitarianism seeks to maximize the aggregate utility—enjoyment, use value—of all members of society. But, by Posner's own definition, utilities are incommensurable. Enjoyment is purely individualistic, solipsistic—subjective. A quality cannot be aggregated unless it is made general, interrelational, commensurable—objective. Wealth maximization is precisely an attempt to replace the subjective standard of enjoyment with the objective standard of wealth. On its own terms, wealth maximization cannot directly recognize utility.

This is obvious in the case of Posner's analysis of money in the hands of the "have-not." Because the have-not does not possess the object of his desire, he wishes to engage in exchange in order to acquire it. Under a wealth maximization regime, however, we only recognize the have-not's desire insofar as he has the means of actualizing his desire—if he possesses the exchange value of the object of desire.

But Posner's analysis is equally masculine with respect to the "have." I call this party the "have" because in Posner's analysis this party never enjoys his object of desire, he merely "has" it: he excludes others from the object of desire. Moreover, he hypothetically possesses the object of desire only temporarily and contingently, until another party offers him money sufficient to persuade him to part with it. In other words, even in the hands of the rich possessor, valuation never refers to the solipsistic, subjective use value of any one party, but is always defined in terms of a future intersubjective, objective exchange value of multiple parties. This follows from a definition of value as the acceptance of alternatives—one values things not in terms of what they are (enjoyment, use value), but in terms of what they are not (exchange value).

Current enjoyment is antithetical to wealth maximization. As reflected in the old saw "you can't have your cake and eat it too," the enjoyment of an object of desire eventually leads to its consumption. Once it has been consumed, the object can no longer be possessed or exchanged. Consequently, enjoyment of the object reduces the aggregate amount of wealth in society. As we have seen in our discussion of the Posnerian auction of feminine sexuality, under wealth maximization, no party can ever obtain an object for his own hedonic purposes. He always acquires the object of desire for future productive activity. Enjoyment, therefore, must always be postponed.

This symbolic order can directly recognize only the masculine position of the speaking subject, necessarily repressing the feminine subject and exiling her to the real. Nevertheless, the symbolic order only exists because it is bounded by the real; the masculine only exists because of the continued shadow existence of the feminine, who serves as his defining other. Similarly, wealth maximization can only recognize masculine money as exchange value, and cannot directly recognize feminine money (enjoyment as use value). Nevertheless, actual markets, being symbolic, require the continued existence of feminine money, in that exchange occurs only because market participants long to enjoy the objects of their desire. As a result, although at first blush it is tempting to interpret the silence of feminine negativity as passivity, in fact, the feminine is the engine that drives the entire symbolic order.[131]

Feminine money is *Juno Moneta*—she who reminds and warns. No matter how much we try to repress feminine money, she always returns as a nagging reminder of her existence and a warning of the lethal effects of ignoring her.

Lacan notoriously asserted that woman is a symptom of man.[132] Similarly, use value is the "symptom" of exchange value. This is not to say that feminine enjoyment is merely an unfortunate, unintended, and inessential result or consequence of masculine exchange, which could be cured. Rather, in Lacanian theory a symptom is the

> particular signifying formation which confers on the subject its very ontological consistency, enabling it to structure its basic, constitutive relationship to *enjoyment (jouissance)*, . . . if the symptom is dissolved, the subject itself loses the ground under his feet, disintegrates. In this sense, "woman is a symptom of man" means that *man himself exists only through woman qua his symptom:* all his ontological consistency hangs on, is suspended from his symptom, is "externalized" in his symptom.[133]

Use value is therefore the symptom of exchange value. Exchange value requires the use value it expels as the very grounds of its possibility.

Lacanian linguistics suggests another reason why wealth maximization is

131. In Žižek's words, "Woman is therefore no longer conceived of as fundamentally 'passive' in contrast to male activity: the act as such, in its fundamental dimension, is 'feminine.' " Žižek, Enjoy Your Symptom!, *supra* note 122, at 156.

132. Lacan, Feminine Sexuality, *supra* note 98, at 168; Žižek, Enjoy Your Symptom!, *supra* note 122, at 155.

133. *Id.*

unable to capture use value directly, although it does on occasion try to refer to it indirectly. Just as there are two sexuated positions the speaking subject can take in the symbolic order, speech also has two modes of signification—the masculine trope of metaphor and the feminine trope of metonymy.[134]

In signification, each signifier refers to a signified, which is, in fact, another signifier in an unending chain of shifting signification.[135] Lacan modifies Saussure's system and expresses this as "S/*s*."[136] The bar between the signifier on top and the signified on the bottom represents the fact that there can be no direct, immediate, or "natural" connection between the two (as there would be in the imaginary relationship of meaning), and therefore signification always contains an arbitrary, subjective, and contingent aspect.[137] In Hegelese, that which is above and below the bar are *qualitatively* different—incommensurate. Similarly, there can be no direct relationship between the exchange value of an object and the object itself because exchange value is defined solely in terms of alternatives. Meaning constantly slips as signifiers shift above and below the bar, and signifieds shift below.

Metaphor is the impossible crossing of the bar of signification.[138] In metaphor, the subject creates a *point de capiton,* or upholstery button, by which he temporarily "quilts" the two layers of signification together.[139] The subject

134. JANE GALLOP, READING LACAN 114–32 (1985).

135. "One cannot go further along this line of thought than to demonstrate that no signification can be sustained other than by reference to another signification." LACAN, ÉCRITS, *supra* note 109, at 150. "We are forced, then, to accept the notion of an incessant sliding of the signified under the signifier." *Id.* at 154.

136. *Id.* at 149. "Lacan reverses Saussure's formula, signified/signifier, giving primacy to the material element (the signifier) in the genesis of the concept (the signified). His own formula for the sign is thus 'S/*s*,' 'which is read as: the signifier over the signified, 'over' corresponding to the bar separating the two stages.' The signifier is granted priority because, in Lacan's understanding, the signified is in fact simply another signifier occupying a different position, a position 'below the bar' within signification." GROSZ, *supra* note 6, at 94.

137. "Saussure also meant for the bar to indicate the arbitrary nature of the relation between the signifier and signified. . . . But Lacan stresses the importance of this 'bar,' conceiving it as indeed a 'barrier' to any one-to-one relationship between signifier and signified, insisting that any given signifier refers not to any corresponding signified but rather to another signifier in a sequence or 'chain' of signifiers." Richardson, *supra* note 109, at 54.

138. "The formula for metaphor contains an addition sign: +. Lacan writes of this 'the + sign . . . here manifesting the crossing of the bar.' . . . The 'bar' is always represented in Lacan's notations as a horizontal line; it is therefore 'crossed' by the vertical line in the + sign." GALLOP, *supra* note 134, at 119 (citations omitted). *See generally,* LACAN, ÉCRITS, *supra* note 109, at 156–58.

139. ŽIŽEK, FOR THEY KNOW NOT WHAT THEY DO, *supra* note 108, at 16–20. In this passage, Žižek speaks specifically about the broader concept of the quilting point as the central idea that one adopts to unify and explain the symbolic order as a whole, such as the fear of God, or racism, or anti-Semitism. *See also,* "Metaphor occurs at the precise point at which sense emerges from non-sense." LACAN, ÉCRITS, *supra* note 109, at 158.

insists that S (the signifier) *is* like *s* (the signified)—that there is an essential identity between the two, that signification can be frozen into meaning. This temporary quilting of signification into meaning, which requires a willful forgetting of contingency and difference, is necessary for speech.[140]

Metaphor is appropriate to exchange value because they are both dependent on quantitative distinctions. Quantity is identity, commensuration, and the suppression of difference. Both exchange and metaphor are the insistence that two "things" are essentially identical, despite their surface differences. Money as exchange value, like metaphor, is a temporary and contingent "quilting" or binding of two different things in a moment of equivalence. But the very fact that one needs the invisible needle of masculine money to sew two objects together as commodities in order for them to be exchanged as equivalents suggests, by negative implication, that for all other purposes the two objects are fundamentally different. If there were no essential differences between the two objects, there would be no reason to exchange them.

Metaphor is masculine because it denies castration. Castration rules out all immediate relationships. And yet, in order to speak we claim to have an immediate relationship between our thoughts and our words, between the signifier and the signified, which characterizes meaning. When the masculine subject denies castration, he claims to have the phallus, understood as whatever it is that is missing. To speak is to claim to have "it," meaning, to speak is to commensurate the incommensurable. Metaphor is the spending of masculine money—the acceptance that two alternatives are equivalent. It is the claim to be able to capture meaning and relate to it directly. Of course, it is impossible to freeze signification and to have the immediate relations with others implied by the ideal of perfect communication. Nevertheless, through the masculine trope of metaphor, we act as though we could achieve the goal of some degree of mediated relationship and imperfect communication. Through money, exchange occurs not despite, but just because of, the fundamental qualitative differentiation between commodities.

In contrast to metaphor, metonymy does not cross the line of signification. Metonymy is the shifting of signifiers above the line of signification.[141] In metonymy, one does not claim to be able to match a specific signifier with a signified. Rather, through metonymy one indirectly suggests the signified through reference to that which surrounds or is associated with the signi-

140. Consequently, the subject as master signifier is itself the quilting point that ties together the symbolic order. ŽIŽEK, FOR THEY KNOW NOT WHAT THEY DO, *supra* note 108, at 78.

141. LACAN, ÉCRITS, *supra* note 109, at 157.

fied.[142] In metonymy, the signified always remains hidden and negative. It is only inferred from the traces of its absence.[143]

Metonymy is appropriate to enjoyment because both depend on qualitative distinctions. As previously discussed, the differentiation necessary for enjoyment is what Hegel called the "quality" of "determinate being": "But a quality can only be defined in terms of what it is not—it is defined by its own negation in the sense of 'this is not that.' "[144] Quality, and therefore enjoyment, can never be described directly.

Metonymy is feminine in that it is an acceptance of castration. It is a reminder and a warning, like *Juno Moneta.* When we use metonymy, we remember that signification is not meaning and that one can never have direct access or immediate relationships. We do not arrogantly claim to have "it"; we only modestly refer to what it is not. Metonymy is the minting of feminine money—it is the realization that enjoyment requires the insistence on uniqueness and the rejection of alternatives. In metaphor, the signifier stands for the signified, whereas in metonymy the signifier stands by the signified.

Accordingly, we can use the masculine trope of metaphor and claim to describe masculine money (exchange value) directly in words. Conversely, feminine money (use value) only be alluded to indirectly through the feminine trope of metonymy. This explains why wealth maximization can capture masculine money, but feminine money always slips through its fingers. Feminine money is the fundamental fact of differentiation between commodities that persists despite their temporary commensuration in exchange value (masculine money)—feminine money is the reason for the exchange made possible through masculine money.

Masculine money—money as the "means" of exchange—is revealed to be the way the market deals with time (i.e., the problem that exchange is not immediate). Money is, in this sense, congealed time. Money is both time and the negation of time. As time is a transaction cost, the need for money is itself

142. Perhaps the best known form of metonymy is synecdoche—the use of the part for the whole. Lacan quotes from a grammar book that refers to thirty ships as thirty sails. *Id.* at 156. The part (the sail) implies the whole (the ship). Lacan probably chose this example because it is somewhat more complex and ambiguous than a simple synecdoche. A sailing ship frequently has more than one sail. Consequently, a literal-minded reference to thirty sails does not necessarily imply thirty ships—it could be one ship with thirty sails: "The part taken for the whole . . . and if the thing is to be taken seriously, we are left with very little idea of the importance of this fleet, which 'thirty sails' is precisely supposed to give us: for each ship to have just one sail is in fact the least likely possibility." *Id.*

143. *See* Michel Rosenfeld, *The Identity of the Constitutional Subject,* in LAW AND THE POSTMODERN MIND at 157–65 (Peter Goodrich and David Gray Carlson eds., 1998).

144. *Id. See also* HEGEL, THE GREATER LOGIC, *supra* note 69, at 129.

a transaction cost. If, however, there is also a necessarily repressed feminine conception of money, this suggests that wealth maximization must also have a repressed feminine understanding of time as well. The sexual impasse suggests that masculine and feminine time, like masculine and feminine subjectivity, and masculine and feminine money, must require each other yet be mutually inconsistent.

To recap, the ideal of the perfect market underlying the wealth maximization analysis views time as a transaction cost. As discussed in Chapter 2, in a truly perfect market, time would be eliminated or, to say the same thing, there would either be no time so that all desires would be instantaneously fulfilled, or there would be an infinite amount of time so that all desires would eventually be fulfilled. This fear and loathing of time explains Posner's repression of enjoyment.

If one concentrates on the masculine elements of possession and exchange, time can only be conceptualized as a cost. Value is created when we equate an object with an alternative. Time is a cost because it is the gap between the identification of a better alternative and the exchange that enables one to acquire the better alternative.[145] Money is a means of filling in the gap—a way of making two alternatives equivalent despite their separation by time.

One engages in exchange in order to obtain possession of one's object of desire. Time is a delay in the consummation of exchange that prevents the instantaneous satisfaction of one's desire. Exchange wants to destroy time. But exchange can only take place during time. The purpose of money is to make two commodities equivalent, but exchange only takes place insofar as commodities are different. Difference only exists at the level of enjoyment, since exchange is the moment of equality. Exchange always looks forward to future enjoyment. Exchange, therefore, requires enjoyment, differentiation, and time. Exchange wants to exist in the present, as an unmediated moment of unity of the two things exchanged. However, as Kant recognizes,[146] time and space are basic conditions of possibility for experience. The conscious act of exchange therefore requires time. Exchange requires mediation in that the differentiated commodities exchanged only become equivalent through the mediation of the means of exchange—money.

By contrast, enjoyment requires time in that experience takes place over time. Nevertheless, there can be no time in enjoyment. To enjoy is to become

145. *See also* David Gray Carlson, *On the Margins of Microeconomics,* in DECONSTRUCTION AND THE POSSIBILITY OF JUSTICE 265, 277–79 (Drucilla Cornell, Michel Rosenfeld & David Gray Carlson eds., 1992).

146. IMMANUEL KANT, THE CRITIQUE OF PURE REASON 21–33 (J. M. D. Meiklejohn trans., 1978).

one with the experience—to have an immediate relationship, to merge with the real. The moment one realizes that one is having an experience, one's relationship with the experience is already mediated. One is thrown back into time, as one either anticipates or remembers enjoyment—and enjoyment is lost.

Not surprisingly, the paradoxical relationship of the masculine and feminine elements of property and time reflects the Lacanian paradox of sexuation. The sexes are defined as an impossible nonrelationship. Exchange is masculine and enjoyment is feminine. Exchange hates time, even as it is necessary for the existence of exchange. Enjoyment loves time but always obliterates it. Consequently, the masculine and feminine can never coexist.

Lacan's concept of the sexuated positions is based in part on Hegel's critique (following Kant) of the Cartesian cogito.[147] According to Hegel and Lacan, there are two inconsistent ways of reading Descartes's statement of subjectivity, "I think, therefore I am." These two readings are based on the proposition that one can be in the position of existing *or* thinking, but one cannot be in both positions at the same time.

The Lacanian rereading of the Cartesian cogito reflects the Heisenberg Uncertainty Principle: subatomic particles can either have exact position (being) or exact momentum (having) but it is impossible for them to have both simultaneously.[148]

The masculine is the aspect of personality that claims to be that which exists (that has positive content), but in so claiming, the masculine puts himself in the position of conscious thinking (i.e., speaking), rather than being. In other words, by trying to contemplate his own existence, the masculine subject is always in the position of losing immediate relationship with existence. When he reinterprets his existence by thinking about it, he is the thing-thinking who finds himself saying: I think "therefore I am."[149] The masculine subject is the master signifier that gives signification to the symbolic order through speech.

Conversely, the feminine is the aspect of personality that seeks to be the active position of thinking, speaking, and acting. By concentrating solely on her action, however, she becomes lost in her activity (achieves ecstasy). She achieves immediate relationship with her activity and momentarily ceases to interpret it. She becomes pure existence: "I think (therefore I am)."[150] The

147. Žižek, Tarrying With the Negative, *supra* note 99, at 56–69.

148. Fink, *supra* note 116, at 133–34. The Heisenberg Uncertainty Principle is often misunderstood as a matter of empirical impossibility—that any attempt to measure position inevitably results in a change in momentum and vice versa. The principle, in fact, is much more radical, arguing that it was theoretically, not merely empirically, impossible for an object to have exact position and momentum simultaneously. Norwood R. Hanson, Patterns of Discovery 136–49 (1965).

149. Žižek, Tarrying With the Negative, *supra* note 99, at 59–61.

150. *Id.* at 61–62.

feminine subject serves as the master signifier whose radical negativity gives affirmative signification to other signifiers through contrast.

In both sexuated positions, one loses what one seeks.[151] The masculine who claims to be the free acting subject wielding the phallus is totally constrained by, and subject to, the symbolic order (the mediated relationships of speech and law).[152] The feminine accepts the objectified position of the lost phallus. But by doing so, she at least partially escapes the constraints of the symbolic order and has access to the real order of immediacy: she achieves the possibility of free subjectivity.[153]

The masculine (who seeks the immediacy—pure existence—that he can never achieve) wishes to do away with time so that he can engage in market exchange and possess the object of desire. But he can never do so. He is always located within time. The moment he thinks, he is either anticipating future enjoyment or remembering past enjoyment. He is the thing-thinking, and time is a basic unit of thought. The masculine is the position of the economist positing the ideal of the perfect market. The feminine, in contrast, wishes to have time to engage in the ecstatic enjoyment of *jouissance.* But upon the achievement of *jouissance,* she loses access to time. At the moment of ecstasy, we are in the position of pure existence, not conscious thought—

151. "I think where I am not, therefore, I am where I do not think." Lacan, Écrits, *supra* note 109, at 166. *See also* Fink, *supra* note 116, at 44–48. In Žižek's words:

> The "masculine" *cogito* chooses being, the "I am," yet what it gets is being which is merely thought, not real being (*cogito "ergo sum,"* I think "therefore I am," as Lacan writes it), *i.e.,* it gets the fantasy-being, the being of a "person,: the being in "reality" whose frame is structured by fantasy.
>
> —the "feminine" *cogito* chooses thought, the pure "I think," yet what it gets is thought bereft of any further predicates, though which coincides with pure being, or, more precisely, the hyperbolic point which is neither thought not being.

Žižek, Tarrying With the Negative, *supra* note 99, at 61–62.

152. Consequently, the matheme for the masculine position is "$\forall x \Phi x$." This can be translated as "for the class of X, all X's are submitted to the phallic function." Lacan, Seminar XX, *supra* note 6, at 78–81.

153. Consequently, the matheme of the feminine is $\overline{\forall x}\ \Phi x$."For the class of X, not all X's are submitted to the phallic function." *Id.* at 78–81. See also:

> When I write [the matheme of the feminine], a never-before-seen function in which the negation is placed on the quantifier, which should be read "not whole," it means that when any speaking being whatsoever situates itself under the banner "women," it is on the basis of the following—that it grounds itself as being not-whole in situating itself in the phallic function.

Id. at 72.

> The fact remains that if she is excluded by the nature of things, it is precisely in the following respect: being not-whole, she has a supplementary jouissance compared to what the phallic function designates by way of jouissance.

Id. at 73.

we are experiencing not interpreting. There can be no time where there is no thought. Law-and-economics tends to repress this feminine side of the dialectic for the good reason that is impossible to reconcile with the masculine one.

Consequently, Simmel bases his definition of money as exchange value (what I have termed masculine money) and his rejection of use value (what I have termed feminine money) in part on the proposition that there can be no consciousness, and therefore no intersubjective relationship, in the purely subjective experience of enjoyment:

> Human enjoyment of an object is a completely undivided act. At such moments we have an experience that does not include an awareness of an object confronting us or an awareness of the self as distinct from its present condition. Phenomena of the basest and the highest kind meet here.[154]

Being heavily influenced by Kant, Simmel accepts the proposition that space and time are the conditions of thought.[155] In order for a subject to desire, therefore, he must never achieve enjoyment in the present: "The possibility of enjoyment must be separated, as an image of the future, from our present condition in order for us to desire things that now stand at a distance from us."[156]

My analysis of the uneasy relationship between wealth maximization and enjoyment has strong affinities to Georges Bataille's theory of the relationship between capitalism and what he calls "sovereignty."[157] American economics is supposed to be driven by the rational Apollonian ideal of investment and increased production. In contrast, Bataille's theory of the "accursed share" is that economies are in fact driven by a Dionysian frenzy of nonproductive consumption and destruction. Bataille anticipates my thesis that the repressed desire of the market is its own destruction: the perfect market is the end of the actual market. The Dionysian frenzy extolled by Bataille is feminine *jouissance*—enjoyment.

Bataille's concept of sovereignty is not limited to the simplistic idea of an actual empirical individual serving as king. His terminology reflects the role played by kings in monarchies. Bataille does not adopt the more common,

154. SIMMEL, *supra* note 15, at 65.

155. *Id.* at 104.

156. *Id.* at 71.

157. Bataille first introduced his concept of sovereignty in the early 1950s in L'EXPÉRIENCE INTÉRIEUR (published in English as GEORGES BATAILLE, INNER EXPERIENCE [Leslie Anne Boldt trans., 1988]). *See* Jacques Derrida, *From Restricted to General Economy: A Hegelianism Without Reserve,* in JACQUES DERRIDA, WRITING AND DIFFERENCE 251 (Alan Bass trans., 1978). Bataille's final theory of sovereignty was published posthumously in France in 1976 (and published in English translation in 1993) as the third part of THE ACCURSED SHARE. GEORGES BATAILLE, THE ACCURSED SHARE (Robert Hurley trans., 1993) [hereinafter, BATAILLE, THE ACCURSED SHARE].

jurisprudential definition of the concept of the sovereign as he who is not subject to the rules imposed by another.[158] Instead Bataille proposes an economic conception of sovereignty.

Sovereignty is that which "is opposed to the servile and the subordinate."[159] It is the free subjectivity that is the essence of human nature.[160] Sovereignty is radical freedom as total negativity. It is *jouissance* as the fulfillment of all desires. Sovereignty, therefore, is the end of the market and capitalism—both its goal and its doom. Bataille believed that the secret of capitalism's incredible productivity is precisely that it has no place in the present for a sovereign. Instead sovereignty, like the feminine, is always postponed. It is yesterday and tomorrow, but never today.

To Bataille, the sovereign is "he who consumes," as opposed to "he who produces."[161] Most members of society are involved in useful or productive activity. Confusingly for the purposes of this book, Bataille calls this productive activity "utility." Obviously, Bataille is not invoking the American economic definition of utility (happiness); rather his terminology is closer to the colloquial or lay definition of usefulness.[162]

Productive activity, according to Bataille, is useful in the sense that it serves some goal; it is the means to an end. To serve another's ends is, by definition, servile. To serve as a means is always to postpone one's desire, "to employ the *present* time for the sake of the *future*."[163] Consequently, there is always an inevitably servile aspect of productive activity.

According to Bataille, "Life *beyond utility* [productive activity] is the domain of the sovereign."[164] Sovereignty (enjoyment) is the total negation of utility (wealth maximization).[165] To be the sovereign is to be one's own end. It is to live in the present and not to anticipate the future or dwell in the past. It is the ethical decision that further postponement of desire is procrastination. Sovereignty is experienced as "miraculous"[166]—ecstatic.

158. *See, e.g.*, H. L. A. Hart, The Concept of Law 50–71 (1961).

159. Bataille, The Accursed Share, *supra* note 157, at II, 197.

160. *See id.* at II, 237–57.

161. *Id.* at II, 198.

162. Indeed, Bataille's use of the term "utility" is almost precisely the opposite from American utilitarianism. Posner identifies utility with the capacity for enjoyment, in contrast to wealth, which is the capacity for production and exchange. Bataille identifies utility with production and exchange, in contrast to the capacity for enjoyment, which he calls sovereignty. In other words, Bataille's "utility" is roughly equivalent to Posner's wealth maximizing activity, and Bataille's "sovereignty" to Posner's utility.

163. *Id.* at II, 198.

164. *Id.* at II, 198.

165. *Id.* at II, 343.

166. *Id.* at II, 207.

The sovereign moment is the temporary achievement of the real in feminine *jouissance*. To be totally in the present is to lose consciousness. "Consciousness of the moment is not truly such, is not sovereign, except in *unknowing*. Only by canceling, or at least neutralizing, every operation of knowledge within ourselves are we in the moment, without fleeing it."[167] All individuals occasionally experience this, as when they are suddenly overcome by tears or laughter.[168] "The miraculous moment when anticipation dissolves into *nothing*, detaching us from the ground on which we are groveling, in the concatenation of useful activity."[169] The sovereign moment as the realization of desire is the breakdown of the subject-object distinction, which destroys both subject and object. The subject consumes the object, losing the object that defines the subject. In other words, Bataille agrees with Kant that time and space are necessary for thought. Insofar as the sovereign exists only in the present, he is outside time. Insofar as the sovereign destroys the separation of objects, he is beyond space. Consequently, sovereignty is unconsciousness. The sovereign moment is real: impossible,[170] divine,[171] deadly.[172] To actually achieve sovereignty as a permanent state is therefore obliteration.

Every individual occasionally achieves the sovereign moment. But most individuals are not positioned in the role of the sovereign per se. Traditional monarchical (or, in Bataille's Marxist terminology, "feudal") societies positioned certain individuals, or classes, in the role of "the sovereign." This does not mean, of course, that these individuals were continually experiencing *jouissance*. Rather, as an institution, they were placed beyond the necessity of leading a useful life. They were the ones who had the right to consume what the rest of society produced. As the end, rather than the means, they were theoretically free from the restraints of society, who had the right and ability to

167. *Id.* at II, 203.

168. *Id.* There is a fundamental relationship between laughter and oblivion. Laughter is, in effect, the confrontation of the real—the realm of the phallus.

> One must simply remember that the element in comedy that satisfies us, the element that makes us laugh, that makes us appreciate it in its full human dimension, not excluding the unconscious, is not so much the triumph of life as its flight, the fact that life slips away, runs off, escapes all those barriers that oppose it, including precisely those that are the most essential, those that are constituted by the agency of the signifier.
>
> The phallus is nothing more than a signifier, the signifier of this flight.

Jacques Lacan, The Seminar of Jacques Lacan. Book VII: The Ethics of Psychoanalysis, 1959–1960 (Jacques-Alain Miller ed. & Dennis Porter trans., 1992) 314 (1988).

169. Bataille, The Accursed Share, *supra* note 157, at II, 203.

170. *Id.* at II, 215.

171. *Id.* at II, 215.

172. *Id.* at II, 213.

act arbitrarily. Being free from restraint, the sovereign was in the position of subjectivity. Being merely useful, the means to the sovereign's ends, most of society was in the position of objectivity. They were the sovereign's "subjects" in the sense that they were *subject to* the will of the one sovereign subject.[173]

Once again, this creates a paradox. Sovereignty is freedom in the sense of radical negativity. It is the achievement of the end of absolute subjectivity, which necessarily ends subjectivity. The instant sovereignty—*jouissance*—is achieved, the sovereign is obliterated. Sovereignty is the freedom that destroys freedom.

Bataille's analysis reveals that the genius of capitalism is the denial of sovereignty. Bataille thinks this means that capitalism's goal is not the consumption of productivity but the accumulation of productivity. In Posnerian terminology, capitalization seeks not to cultivate the capacity for enjoyment, but to maximize wealth. Accumulated productivity is capital, which is then reinvested to increase productivity, which is then accumulated, and so on. This does not mean, of course, that no individual in capitalism ever experiences the sovereign moment, or that all production is reinvested as capital. On the contrary, capitalism allows for increased consumption of luxuries and an increase in freedom and subjectivity in representative governments. Bataille's point is that no person, class, or institution in a truly capitalist society is positioned as the sovereign: as he who consumes and enjoys, who is beyond utility understood as the need to maximize wealth.

In capitalism, the rich and powerful are not the leisure class of feudalism. The dominant class of capitalism—the bourgeoisie—sees itself as the preeminent productive class. Wealthy Americans take pride in being called workaholics. Their role is not to consume, but to invest, to increase productivity and profitability and to reinvest these profits. This is not to deny that capitalists often consume. Bataille's point is that, in contradistinction to feudalism, such subjective moments are not essential, but only accidental, to capitalism.

One might be tempted to argue that Bataille's analysis ignores (or, given that he was writing in the 1950s, fails to anticipate) the oft-cited sovereignty of the consumer in modern society. Doesn't our economy revolve around satisfying consumer desires? This critique does not understand Bataille's point, which is not a denial of the fact of consumption, but an analysis of the theoretical political-economic role of consumption. To the capitalist, the fulfillment of consumer desire is not the end, but one means to his desire. The

173. Bataille apologizes for this "awkward" but "unavoidable play on words" (*Id.* at II, 240) which inevitability arises out of the necessarily contradictory meanings of subject and object. The subjects project their subjectivity onto the sovereign, and therefore experience it vicariously through him in the spectacle of public displays of court life.

desire of the capitalist is the production, accumulation, and reinvestment of profits. One way a business can make profits is by creating consumer goods and services, but this is only one segment of our economy.

Nevertheless, Bataille's theory of the "accursed share" posits that the sovereign moment is necessary to all successful societies. That is, all healthy organisms, including societies, produce more energy than they need for their own survival.[174] They must therefore find a way of dealing with this excess. The simplest way is to use this energy for reproduction, but the ability to reproduce is bounded by any number of physical limitations. Consequently, societies must develop a means of nonproductive consumption or destruction—the sovereign moment.[175]

For capitalism to continue to function, it can never make a place for sovereignty in the present. In this sense, sovereignty and capitalism are inconsistent. This explains why the ideal of absolute monarchies was quickly replaced by that of representative democratic government upon the development of capitalism in early modern European history. Thus at first blush, capitalism seems to be an anomaly—a society that avoids the curse of the accursed share.

Bataille, however, errs when he infers from the idea that capitalism must deny enjoyment and cannot accommodate sovereignty in the present that "today, sovereignty is no longer alive except in the perspectives of communism"[176] and that sovereignty does not function in capitalism. In contradistinction, sovereignty is absolutely necessary for capitalism. Under Bataille's own analysis, capitalism represses sovereign enjoyment—but repression and

174. As much as I admire Bataille's analysis of capitalism, I find his attempts to universalize his concept of the accursed share not only to all human societies but also to the physical world to be dubious at best, if not outright fanciful.

175. In the first volume of THE ACCURSED SHARE, Bataille explores the variant institutions that many historical societies have developed to deal with the problem of this excess. Ancient Aztec society, for example, developed a religion founded on human sacrifice as a means of destroying this excess. Potlatch and war are other examples of institutions whose economic function is destruction.

In his last volume, on sovereignty, Bataille analyzes mid-twentieth-century capitalism and Stalinist communism as sharing a unique solution to this "problem"—postponement. Both turned the accursed share into "capital," which was used to increase production, thereby increasing the accursed share, which was turned into capital, etc. According to Bataille, the primary difference between capitalism and Stalinism is that the former represses any express role for the sovereign, while the latter accepted it but transfigured it in a new and terrifying way. Stalinism identified the sovereign with the abstract concept of "the people," and then declared that "the people" exercise its sovereignty by "freely" renouncing their own freedom. As a result, Stalinism was able to change sovereignty from a moment of subjective freedom into pure objective power and restraint.

176. *Id.* at II, 261.

the return of the repressed are two sides of the same coin. Consequently, capitalism does not destroy sovereign enjoyment; it merely postpones it so that enjoyment can serve as its goal, the object of its desire.

Sovereign enjoyment is what capitalism claims to expel in order to define itself. This is why wealth maximization represses the capacity to enjoy and forever postpones the moment of consumption. Actual markets are erotic, and desire is created by the perpetually unsuccessful attempt to achieve the impossible goal of *jouissance.* By ostensibly postponing and repressing present enjoyment, capitalism actually produces the possibility of a future enjoyment that can serve as its goal. The sovereign consequently serves as the feminine, the real. That is, capitalism's sovereign is not a king, but a queen whose presence is denied and deferred.

Specifically, the sovereign is Persephone, the goddess of the hope of spring who is also necessarily the queen of death. Her very name means "The Bringer of Destruction."[177] Sovereignty is not presently alive in capitalism precisely because it performs the "real" function of its own future death. Capitalism does not, therefore, destroy but represses the sovereign. It is this repression of the sovereign that creates both the sovereign and the possibility of capitalism. The endless means of the accumulation of capital must implicitly have an end. This end, we have seen, is the ideal of the perfect market. The perfect market is the sovereign.

This ideal of the perfect market is efficiency, in the sense of the fulfillment of all desire through the maximization of wealth. The perfect market is therefore universal consumption. In the perfect market, consumers instantly finance, produce, and consume production.[178] Production and consumption become the same thing. Given that sovereignty is the ability to consume and achieve one's desire, in the perfect market, all participants will achieve sovereignty. Efficiency is therefore the achievement of universal sovereignty.

To be sovereign, however, is to be beyond usefulness, to cease to be a means, to be an end. Once one achieves sovereignty, one ceases to produce. The market economy by necessity stops. Similarly, as Coase insists, markets are a means to achieve the ends of efficiency. Once wealth is maximized through the transfer of all objects to the highest valuing user, all exchange will stop. Only then can market participants finally stop procrastinating and enjoy their objects of desire. The achievement of the perfect market would fulfill the end of the actual market and result in the end of the actual market. For capitalism to continue, therefore, it must continue to postpone the fulfillment of its desire. Sovereignty—the perfect market—is simultaneously

177. GRAVES, *supra* note 3, at 93. *See* SCHROEDER, THE VESTAL AND THE FASCES, *supra* note 97, at 332–34, for a Lacanian reading of the myth of the Rape of Persephone.

178. David Gray Carlson, *On the Efficiency of Secured Lending,* 80 VA. L. REV. 2177, 2183 (1994).

necessary to and inconsistent with desire, freedom, and creation. Because the feminine moment of sovereignty is both necessary and impossible, it can only function through prohibition and postponement.

Now that we have analyzed the relationship of desire and enjoyment—the erotic, sexual nature of actual markets—we are in a position to analyze more fully the relationship of Posner's fantasy to enjoyment. I wish to suggest a reason why we may be drawn to models such as wealth maximization despite their unrealistic assumptions and potentially lethal implications: these models themselves create *jouissance* or enjoyment, albeit in a different form from that of actual markets.

Up to now, when I have spoken about enjoyment, I have been speaking in terms of the relationship we have to enjoyment in desire—desire being the longing for wholeness. As discussed in Chapter 1, we seek this wholeness through intersubjective recognition, but intersubjective recognition must be mediated by relationships of possession, exchange, and enjoyment of a hypothesized object of desire. As we have seen, although the hypothetical phallic object of desire is always already lost, we substitute other objects to serve as the object cause of desire (the *objet petit a*). In desire, *jouissance,* enjoyment in the sense of achieving the object of desire, is the goal—albeit one that is never completely achieved. This is the impulse that impels actual markets.

The Posnerian wealth maximization fantasy, by contrast, is impelled not by desire, but by what Lacan called libido, the myth of the lamella, or most frequently the "drive."[179] Distancing himself from Freud, Lacan did not equate drive either with the animal mating instinct or with human sexuality, which is characterized by desire. Rather, drive is a uniquely human, nonsexual impulse—it may be thought of as that which is left over from the primordial "real" animal instinct *after* its sexual aspect has been symbolized as desire.[180]

Both animal instinct and desire have goals. In the former, this goal is always easily fulfilled by the physical act of mating (or eating, or whatever). In the latter, the goal (the object of desire, *jouissance,* immediate sexual rela-

179. RENATA SALECL, (PER)VERSIONS OF LOVE AND HATE 48 (1999). Lacan's most thorough discussion of the drive are contained in his eleventh seminar, translated into English as JACQUES LACAN, THE FOUR FUNDAMENTAL CONCEPTS OF PSYCHO-ANALYSIS (Jacques-Alain Miller ed. & Alan Sheridan trans., 1977) [hereinafter, LACAN, THE FOUR FUNDAMENTAL CONCEPTS], and in the essay *Positions of the Unconscious* [hereinafter, Lacan, *Positions*], which was published in the French (but not the English) edition of *Écrits,* and has been recently published in READING SEMINAR XI: LACAN'S FOUR FUNDAMENTAL CONCEPTS OF PSYCHOANALYSIS 259 (Richard Feldstein, Bruce Fink, Maire Jaanus eds., 1995) [hereinafter, READING SEMINAR XI].

180. SALECL, *supra* note 179, at 48. In Lacan's words, "My lamella [Lacan's mythic personification of the drive] represents here the part of a living being that is lost when that being is produced through the straits of sex." Lacan, *The Positions of the Unconscious, supra* note 179, at 274.

tionship, wholeness, escape into death, etc.) is never fully achieved, but always pursued. By contrast, drive has no goal; it only has *aim*.[181] The subject of drive is driven to do what he does not because he wants to, but because he can't help himself.[182]

By this, Lacan means that drive has impulse or thrust but no purpose. Drive does not impel us to achieve a goal (possible in the case of instinct, and impossible in the case of desire), but pressures us to continue doing what we are doing. Drive has no purpose but its own activity.

Drive is an attempt to get beyond the impossibility of desire by forswearing desire entirely. The relationship of drive to enjoyment is the obverse of that of desire and enjoyment.[183] Enjoyment is the elusive goal of desire that impels us on and allows for (admittedly imperfect) intersubjective relations and love. It is always the partial failure of desire that is the engine of desire. In drive, however, the subject achieves a certain idiotic enjoyment merely by endlessly engaging in an activity without purpose.[184] Rather than trying to achieve the object of desire, drive doesn't even try, but merely circles around it. Because drive has no goal that can be thwarted, subjects driven by the drive of wealth maximization achieve a certain type of satisfaction (or, perhaps more accurately, can never be unsatisfied).[185] The drive results in an obscene enjoyment through compulsive repetitive activity to its utter

181. Marie-Helene Brousse, *The Drive (II), in* READING SEMINAR XI, *supra* note 179, 109, 112; Antonio Quinet, *The Gaze as an Object, in* READING SEMINAR XI, *supra* note 179, 139, 140–41.

182. One desires something because one cannot have it. One does something out of drive merely because it feels good. The logic of desire is: " 'It is prohibited to do this, but I will nonetheless do it.' Drive, in contrast, does not care about prohibition: it is not concerned about overcoming the law [i.e., the symbolic order]. Drive's logic is: 'I do not want this, but I am nonetheless doing it.' " SALECL, *supra* note 179, at 50.

183. "Desire and drive are clearly opposed with respect to the way they relate to *jouissance*. . . . Desire stands for the economy in which whatever object we get hold of is 'never *it*,' the 'Real thing,' that which the subject is forever trying to attain but which eludes him again and again, while drive stands for the opposite economy within which the stain of *jouissance* always accompanies our acts." SLAVOJ ŽIŽEK, THE TICKLISH SUBJECT: THE ABSENT CENTRE OF POLITICAL ONTOLOGY 291 (1999) [hereafter, ŽIŽEK, THE TICKLISH SUBJECT].

184. In Žižek's words, "An idiotic-happy circuit of the apparatus which produces *jouissance*, is this not the very definition of *drive?*" *Id.* at 295. *See also* Brousse, *supra* note 181, at 112; *see also*, Quinet, *supra* note 181, 140–41.

185. "Drive paradoxically always finds satisfaction, while desire has to remain unsatisfied, endlessly going from one object to another, positing new limits and prohibitions. Drive is thus a constant pressure, a circulation around the object *a*, which produces *jouissance*—a painful satisfaction. The object *a*, the object around which drive circulates, thus needs to be understood as a special kind of satisfaction: 'The object that corresponds to drive is *satisfaction as object*.' In this search for satisfaction, drive resembles perversion." SALECL, *supra* note 179, at 50 (quoting Jacques-Alain, Miller, *On Perversion*, in READING SEMINARS I AND II: LACAN'S RETURN TO FREUD 313 (Richard Feldstein, Bruce Fink & Maire Jaanus eds., 1996) [hereinafter, READING SEMINARS I AND II]. *See also* LACAN, THE FOUR FUNDAMENTALS, *supra* note 179, at 166–67.

destructive limit, no matter what the consequences. Paradoxically, the very denial of *jouissance* causes its own *jouissance*—the repressed and the return of the repressed are two sides of the same coin.[186]

It is *this* sterile, asexual, solipsistic satisfaction that is the enjoyment of wealth maximization. Consequently, I was oversimplifying when I implied earlier in this chapter that there is *no* enjoyment in Posner's system. Rather, enjoyment takes a different form from the enjoyment found in desire and actual markets. Actual markets, being characterized by desire, aim toward the achievement of enjoyment—I engage in trade in order eventually to acquire those objects I think I will eventually enjoy. Because no *objet petit a* ever really substitutes for the lost phallic object of desire, I continually engage in market transactions in the vain hope that the next object I acquire will lead to the level of *jouissance* I desire.

In Posner's imaginary system, market participants do *not* engage in market transactions in order to attain objects to be enjoyed, because no objects are ever enjoyed in his system. Rather, they engage in market transactions for the purpose of engaging in market transactions—i.e., they exchange one object in order to achieve its exchange value to acquire another object which, in turn, is exchanged in order to achieve its exchange value, ad infinitum. As Posner's terminology makes clear, what is maximized is *wealth*—the ability to enter into future exchanges in order to produce more wealth. Posner's imaginary market has no goal other than self-perpetuation. Wealth maximization has an aim, but not a goal. By the logic of drive, wealth maximization achieves a perverse enjoyment from expressly rejecting enjoyment as a goal.

Most significantly for my thesis, Lacan, departing from Freud, insists that all drives are, in fact, *death* drives.[187] Drives do not have any creative or reproductive goal. They ceaselessly circle around the subject's painful pleasure at

186. Žižek describes the logic of drive as follows: "For Lacan, the trouble with *jouissance* is not only that it is unattainable, always-already lost, that it forever eludes our grasp, but, even more, that *one can never get rid of it,* that its stain drags on forever—that is the point of Lacan's concept of surplus-enjoyment; the very renunciation of *jouissance* brings about a remainder/surplus of *jouissance* . . . drive . . . finds satisfaction in (i.e. besmirches with the stain of satisfaction) the very movement destined to 'repress' satisfaction." SLAVOJ ŽIŽEK, THE TICKLISH SUBJECT: THE ABSENT CENTRE OF POLITICAL ONTOLOGY 290 (1999) [hereinafter, ŽIŽEK, THE TICKLISH SUBJECT]. Later he says that "desire desperately strives to achieve *jouissance,* its ultimate object which forever eludes it; while drive, on the contrary, involves the opposite impossibility—not the impossibility of attaining *jouissance,* but the impossibility of getting *rid of it.*" *Id.* at 293.

187. Lacan, *Positions of Unconscious, supra* note 179, at 275. In Lacan's rewriting of Freud, the death drive has nothing to do with the "desire" to die. In fact, Žižek intimates that the death drive is the immortal part of our soul—its universality. ŽIŽEK, TICKLISH SUBJECT, *supra* note 186, at 292–94. The death drive is the same as the pleasure principal. The death drive as compulsion is the very inability to die, or to realize Thanatos, the desire for death as release.

The death drive is the "satisfaction in aberration, and even in aberrant acts directed against yourself, that is, finding satisfaction in aggression for the sake of aggression." Jacques-Alain

always being satisfied because he has no goal. Consequently, the subject of the death drive is curiously immortal—in the sense that the living dead are immortal. The subject of the drive is always dead because he is unable to live.[188] Being obsessively and mindlessly driven, the subject of a drive loses her freedom and becomes a passive object.

Actual markets, like law, language, and sexuality, are symbolic. The symbolic implies castration, which results in the sexual impasse. Masculinity and femininity are two different failed attempts at achieving wholeness. The masculine is created by the repression of the feminine. Consequently, the masculine requires the feminine, even as it is structurally impossible for the masculine to recognize the feminine directly.

This is the same paradox we saw in wealth, time, and money. The symbolic order of capitalist markets and wealth maximization is created by privileging the masculine and repressing the feminine. The market must ostensibly emphasize productive activities, exchange value, and the elimination of time as a transaction cost. But for any actual market to function, all parties must look forward to enjoyment. Money must be understood as congealed future use value. Because enjoyment and use value are always in the future, time must be preserved. The masculine, public, intersubjective order of economics therefore requires that there be a hidden and only partially acknowledged feminine, private world of ecstatic and solipsistic enjoyment.

The feminine is the defining other of the masculine order. Not only is the feminine the moment of unbounded freedom necessary for any market to exist, but the impossibility of fulfilling desire is what makes desire function. The masculine position that seeks to repress the feminine is therefore both cruel and hypocritical.

It would be equally futile, however, to try to reverse the sexual status quo and privilege the feminine while repressing the masculine. The feminine, as the freedom of the real, is only created through her repression. To destroy the masculine would destroy the conditions of femininity. As I develop at length in my conclusion, the repression of the feminine is the masculine generative act that enables the feminine to give birth to the masculine. The paradox of the feminine part of personality is that she is only free and creative

---

Miller, *A Discussion of Lacan's "Kant with Sade," in* READING SEMINARS I AND II, *supra* note 185, at 212, 220 (Richard Feldstein et al. eds., 1996).

188. "The 'death drive' designates the dimension of what horror fiction calls the 'undead,' a strange, immortal, indestructible life that persists beyond death." ŽIŽEK, THE TICKLISH SUBJECT, *supra* note 186, at 294. Caught in this unending circle of perverse satisfaction and pressure, the subject of drive—like the legendary vampire of fiction—learns to escape into true death. Lacan introduces this uncanny aspect of the death drive in his famously bizarre myth of the lamella—the monstrous, immortal living dead, asexual twin born with each human subject. Lacan, *Positions of the Unconscious, supra* note 179, at 273–76.

because she has been violated and rejected by the masculine. Pure enjoyment, without possession and exchange, is pure nothingness. Pure enjoyment would be the satisfaction of all desires, the cure of castration, and the loss of consciousness. The capitalist market could not function if its members demanded present enjoyment.[189]

The impossibility of overcoming the sexual impasse is one reason why Lacan said the subject was split. It also explains the workings of the economy.

As Bataille has shown, this does not mean that individuals in a wealth maximization regime do not in fact enjoy their property as an empirical matter. But this enjoyment is merely accidental to the theoretical ideal of wealth maximization. Indeed, enjoyment only occurs because of transaction costs that inhibit the achievement of the perfect market, in which all use value is reduced to exchange value. Consequently, transaction costs serve the same function in economics as castration does in psychoanalysis—they are the "cut" or gap that separates actual markets, which exist in the symbolic, from the perfect market, which exists in the real. This means that transaction costs—the flaws of actual markets—are paradoxically necessary for the operation of actual markets. Indeed, as wealth (exchange value) evaporates in the perfect market, wealth is itself revealed as an imperfection—the detritus of transaction costs. Enjoyment—which must be denied by wealth maximization—is necessary for wealth maximization.

One of Lacan's most famous depictions of the workings of the three orders of the symbolic, the imaginary, and the real is based on an analysis of Edgar Allan Poe's *The Purloined Letter.*[190] As is well known, the thief is able to hide the stolen missive of the title from the police by changing its appearance and displaying it in the most obvious place in his office.

Lacan was a notoriously difficult writer—indeed he claimed that he was intentionally obscure because he didn't want to speak to idiots.[191] He frequently adopted the method he identified in *The Purloined Letter,* hiding his meaning by disguising it slightly and then placing it in plain sight. Similarly, the secret of a Lacanian analysis of money in postindustrial capitalist society is hidden in plain sight.

One of Lacan's most annoying affectations is his use of quasi-mathematical symbols called "mathemes" to stand for his central concepts.

189. Consequently, if I criticize Posner for privileging exchange over enjoyment, I also chide Radin for doing the opposite. SCHROEDER, THE VESTAL AND THE FASCES, *supra* note 97, at 259. In other words, I agree with Posner's assessment that there is ethical value in an economic system that seeks to increase productive activity by favoring the ant over the grasshopper.

190. Jacques Lacan, *Seminar on "The Purloined Letter"* (Jeffrey Mehlman trans.), THE PURLOINED POE: LACAN, DERRIDA AND PSYCHOANALYTIC READING 28 (John P. Muller & William J. Richardson eds., 1988).

191. STUART SCHNEIDERMAN, JACQUES LACAN: DEATH OF AN INTELLECTUAL HERO 19–20 (1983).

Although they are supposedly designed to provide mathematical rigor, and therefore clarity, to his theories, these mathemes often have the opposite effect, making his presentation unnecessarily difficult. Difficult, that is, until one remembers Lacan's love of hide-and-go-seek.

One of his earliest and most consistently used mathemes is that devised for the split subject. This consists of a capital S standing for the subject and the (master) signifier, bifurcated by a bar representing its constituent split: $S\!\!\!/$.[192]

I know of no commentator who has acknowledged the striking resemblance between the matheme for subjectivity and the American dollar sign. Nevertheless, once it is seen, it is clear that Lacan has hidden in plain sight the message that money and the subject serve parallel roles in the creation of the symbolic order of law, language, sexuality, and markets. They are both master signifiers that can give signification to other signifiers precisely because they have no content in and of themselves. The masculine speaking subject in the symbolic order of language, law, and sexuality is defined only by the silent, repressed feminine subject in the real. The masculine concept of money as exchange value in the symbolic order of the market is similarly defined only by the unacknowledged, forever postponed feminine concept of money as use value. To maximize wealth in the Posnerian sense of suppressing, rather than repressing, enjoyment would destroy exchange. Wealth maximization is the golden touch. Luckily, the golden touch is only a myth. Despite its denials, the masculine is only successful in repressing, not suppressing, the feminine.

EPILOGUE: THE ASS'S EARS

The golden touch was not Midas's only foolish decision. Midas's story does not stop with the happy ending when Dionysus answered his prayer and lifted this curse. Relieved of his burden, Midas renounced wealth maximization and became a romantic—he abdicated his crown, took to the hills, and became a devotee of the rustic god Pan.

One day he was asked to help decide an unusual dispute. Pan, having invented his eponymous pipe, bragged that he was a better musician than

192. FINK, *supra* note 116, at 45. Lacan's alteration in this case is slight. The line bifurcating or barring the S of subjectivity is usually drawn at an angle, rather than the strict perpendicular of the dollar sign. Despite the obvious similarity of the two symbols, I have not been able to find any commentator who has noticed it. Even though Žižek discusses Lacan's matheme for subjectivity a page before he compares the subject as master signifier to money as master commodity and even though his book prints the matheme with a perpendicular bar like a dollar sign, he fails to note the remarkable resemblance between the two. ŽIŽEK, FOR THEY KNOW NOT WHAT THEY DO, *supra* note 108, at 22.

Apollo, god of reason, culture, and the arts, including music. When Apollo objected to Pan's boast, the gods decided that the dispute should be decided by the ancient god Tmolus, the Old Man of the Mountain. Tmolus asked Midas to counsel him. The trial took the form of a music contest pitting Pan and his panpipe against Apollo and his lyre.

Consistent with his newfound romanticism, Midas announced that he preferred the simpleminded, earthy tooting of vulgar Pan over the sophisticated, celestial lyrics of Olympian Apollo. Tmolus ignored Midas's ignorant advice and decided for Apollo. After all, the true gravamen of the dispute was not one of aesthetics, which can be judged by man, but one of blasphemy, which can only be determined by god. Apollo punished Midas for his bad counsel by changing his ears into those of an ass.

For a time Midas succeeded in hiding his deformity by wearing a Phrygian cap[193]—the ancient symbol of liberty—at all times. Of course, this is the typical romantic position that tries to cloak foolish license under claims of freedom. Even Midas's wife was fooled by his eccentric insistence on wearing his hat to bed.[194] He could not keep his shame from his barber, however. Midas assured his barber that he would experience a slow, painful death if he ever revealed the royal embarrassment.

Like all men, the poor barber desired nothing more than to spread this all-too-delicious gossip. The barber felt that he was about to burst and was terrified that he would slip and blurt out the truth. He finally arrived at a solution. He crept out in the middle of the night, dug a hole in the side of the river bank, and unburdened himself by whispering into the hole and filling it in. Relieved of his linguistic constipation, the barber went home and slept soundly for the first time in months.

In the spring, a reed sprung from the river bank. When it swayed in the wind, it made a tiny rustling noise. The nearby grasses, swaying in rhythm, picked up the sound, which spread in turn to the bushes and eventually to the trees, growing louder with every repetition. Finally, whenever the wind blew, the entire country echoed with the "secret": "King Midas has ass's ears!"

What could this strange myth mean? At first blush, a simple explanation seems sufficient. Apollo punished the foolish judge by branding him in the flesh with a visible sign of his bad decision. Thus what is repressed in the symbolic returns in the real. The real includes our understanding of the physical world, our sense of our bodies. Consequently, traumas repressed in the

193. GRAVES, *supra* note 3, at 283.

194. Not everyone can believe this. The ever practical Wife of Bath insisted that it was Midas's queen, not his barber, who must have discovered and inadvertently revealed the secret. GEOFFREY CHAUCER, THE WIFE OF BATH'S TALE, *in* THE CANTERBURY TALES 240, 243 (David Wright trans., 1985).

symbolic can return as psychosomatic symptoms in the body. Myth reveals psychoanalytic truth by giving it a literal form. Midas in his capacity as judge in the symbolic order of law repressed the inconvenient evidence presented to him. As Midas sinned in the symbolic through his ears, his ears took on the real form of his sin. As he stubbornly refused to face his own prejudices, his ears took on the form of the most stubborn of all creatures.

A more satisfactory interpretation of the two stories is suggested by the fact that Ovid gave them almost perfectly homophonic titles: *Midas Aureus* (Golden Midas) and *Midaes Aures* (Midas's ears). In the poet's words, these two seemingly diverse stories are actually two retellings of one and the same story of how Midas "from his foolish mind . . . by an absurd decision harmed his life."[195] This is further revealed by the parallel structures of the two myths. More accurately, the two stories are mirror images. The potentially tragic story of golden Midas has a happy ending when Midas realizes his error and the god lifts the curse. The potentially comic story of Midas's ears has a sad one as the god's curse leads to Midas's public humiliation. This relates to the fact that the story of the golden Midas reflects the masculine position, characterized by the comic desire of Eros, whereas the story of Midas's ears reflects the feminine position, characterized by the tragic desire of Thanatos.

Classical mythology presents the human condition as hovering between the divine—represented by the anthropomorphic Olympian gods—and the bestial, represented by half-animal races such as centaurs and satyrs. In both tales, Midas first meets a goat-man who tempts him with his brutish, simple-minded ways. God then appears and asks Midas to make a decision as to his true nature. In each case, Midas foolishly follows the example of a goat-man and chooses his animal nature over the divine to his own peril.

In the tale of golden Midas, Midas is seduced by Silenus's tales of the wealthy, law-obsessed land beyond the Atlantic that so eerily prefigures capitalist America. God takes the form of Dionysus, the personification of ecstacy—the real. When God offers Midas the opportunity to join with the real and achieve immediacy, Midas foolishly chooses to postpone enjoyment. He follows the satyr and chooses the simplistic rationality of wealth maximization, which privileges possession and exchange and denies the enjoyment necessary to make the other two elements valuable. He takes on the masculine position and represses the feminine, personified by Dionysus.[196]

195. OVID, *supra* note 2, at lines 231–32.

196. Although Dionysus is a male god who is usually presented as the heterosexual lover of Ariadne, his myth insists on that he was ostentatiously effeminate, wearing long hair, makeup, perfume, and feminine robes and leading women in orgiastic rites. In THE VESTAL AND THE FASCES, *supra* note 97, at 335–37, I have suggested that the mysterious, silent, faceless goddess Hestia (the Roman Vesta) was a personification of the Lacanian feminine. Tellingly, upon his ascension to Olympus in his apotheosis, Hestia let Dionysus sit on her throne among the

In the tale of Midas's ears, Midas is seduced by Pan's promise of simple pleasures. God takes the form of Apollo, the personification of reason—the symbolic. The crucial aspect of the musical content is the difference in the two performances. Pan plays a pipe and Apollo a lyre. Pan can produce only one note at a time on the panpipe, enabling him to play only the simplest melody. Apollo can not only produce harmony with his lyre, but he can also sing along. When God speaks to Midas and offers him the opportunity to stop and hear divine words—to submit to the symbolic order—Midas instead chooses immediate enjoyment. He follows goat-footed Pan and chooses the simplistic emotionality of romanticism, which privileges the immediate enjoyment of flute music over the complex, mediated, intersubjective communication of Apollo's lyrics. He takes on the feminine position and rejects the masculine, personified by Apollo.

In both tales, Midas makes the error that characterizes equally utilitarianism and romanticism—the idea that passion and reason are opposites that one can choose between. This simplistic, mirror image world of complements and simple negation is the animalistic order of the imaginary—the order of the goat. Moreover, in both stories Midas is the author of his own fate. Midas expressly asks for the golden touch and nearly starves to death when his feminine enjoyment is postponed forever. But Midas is equally the author of his fate after the musical contest. Apollo in fact does nothing to Midas; Midas makes an ass of himself. All Apollo does is to note that Midas is a fool and predict that Midas's foolishness will soon become apparent to others.

There is, however, a "divine," fuller understanding of these myths. Paradoxically, passion and reason, like the sexuated positions, create and require each other, even though they cannot exist simultaneously. They are the two sides of the single coin of human subjectivity. As the Greeks understood, Apollo and Dionysus are equally God. One can never choose but only dynamically vacillate between them. This is the contradiction that enables us to love and gives us the divine capacity for freedom. Consequently, according to the myth, what initially appears as passion is revealed to require reason, and reason is only accessible through passion.

Olympians, thereby ensuring that the number of the high gods would remain at the magic number of twelve and not be increased to the unlucky one of thirteen. That is, Dionysus is, mysteriously, identical to Hestia. This is why the Vestal Virgins of Rome administered the obscene rites of orgiastic Bacchus (Dionysus) as well as the pure rites of chaste Vesta (Hestia).

Chapter 5

The Eumenides' Return

The Founding of Law Through the Repression of the Feminine

PROLOGUE: THE DEUS EX MACHINA

The Eumenides,[1] Aeschylus's account of legal origins, reveals that postmodernism precedes, rather that succeeds, modernism.

Relating the trial of Orestes for the murder of his mother Clytemnestra, *The Eumenides* illustrates the moment when law and civilization supplants chaos and barbarism—the moment when we become subjects by submitting to the symbolic. Specifically, it tells how Athens comes to decide that accusations of murder will thereafter be addressed through public trial by jury rather than the spiraling blood bath of private vendetta.[2]

Surprisingly, the play contains absolutely no discussion of the relative morality, justice, wisdom, or practical effect of the two rival regimes. The debate is framed entirely and expressly in terms of whether the masculine or feminine principle should prevail. The rule of law is newly written by Father Zeus and is represented by Apollo—a solar god personifying masculine culture. In contradistinction, the prelegal, natural regime of vengeance is the primordial rule of Mother Night and is represented by the Furies (the *Erinyes*)—infernal goddesses personifying the maternal superego or feminine *jouissance* in its ecstatic, destructive mode.

The Furies and Apollo argue over whether the mother or the father is the true parent of the child, and which relationship, motherhood or marriage, is the more significant. In other words, in Lacanian terms, the issue adjudi-

1. Aeschylus, *The Eumenides* [hereinafter Aeschylus, *The Eumenides*], *in* AESCHYLUS, THE ORESTEIA *at* 231 (Robert Fagles trans., 1975) [hereinafter, AESCHYLUS, THE ORESTEIA].

2. Although the Furies speak of the rule of Mother Night as the ancient law, it is not "law" in the sense of public order. The private regime of vengeance and guilt is natural and prelegal.

cated is whether nature (the real) or law (the symbolic) is more fundamental. If the feminine, real, natural principle prevails, then Orestes' matricide was an unforgivable atrocity. If the masculine, symbolic, legal principle prevails, it was justifiable homicide.

The jury splits. Athena, goddess of wisdom, casts the deciding vote, establishing legal process and exonerating Orestes on the grounds that she "honour[s] the male in all things."[3] The rule of law requires that the symbolic be given precedence over the real. Having established the rule of law, Athena tames the Furies. She renames them the "Kindly Ones" (the *Eumenides*) and has them assume the duties of the tutelary goddesses known as the "Solemn Ones" (the *Semnai*). She then hides them away in a grotto under the Acropolis.

The secret of the play, however, is that it is one long deus ex machina[4]: Apollo arrives to save Orestes in the very first scene. In his seminar on *The Ethics of Psychoanalysis,*[5] Jacques Lacan explains the nature and function of this dramatic device. Just as the conflict appears to be at an impasse, a god appears to reconcile the irreconcilable—pulling a happy ending out of a tragic hat. To a modern audience, the deus ex machina seems hopelessly artificial and unconvincing. The unsatisfying nature of the device makes us feel self-satisfied, as we contemplate our intellectual and aesthetic superiority over our cultural forefathers. "How could the Athenians have been so gullible?" we smirk.

But our smugness is unjustified. It is we, not the Athenians, who are easily undone because of our inflated sense of sophistication. They at least intuited that a deus ex machina is never the true end of a drama: "Everyone has known for a long time that [the god] simply serves as a frame and limit to tragedy, that we don't have to take any more account of it than we do of the supports that define the area of the stage."[6]

In other words, when the god "appears like the curtain falling,"[7] he is only veiling the horror that the audience knows must inevitably ensue. This veiling actually increases the horror. Lacan famously argued that the phallus only functions insofar as it is veiled.[8] That is because the phallus is real. The

3. *Id.* at 264, ll. 749–56.

4. The nitpicking historian might cavil that *The Eumenides* does not *literally* involve a deus ex machina because the "machine" by which the actor impersonating the god was lowered to the stage was not used until the generation after Aeschylus. I use the term in the more general sense of divine intervention resolving the conflict posed by a play.

5. JACQUES LACAN, THE SEMINAR OF JACQUES LACAN. BOOK VII: THE ETHICS OF PSYCHOANALYSIS, 1959–1960 (Jacques-Alain Miller ed. & Dennis Porter trans., 1986) [hereinafter, LACAN, SEMINAR VII].

6. *Id.* at 320.

7. *Id.*

8. The phallus "can play its role only when veiled, that is to say, as itself a sign of the latency with which any signifiable is stuck, when it is raised *(aufgehoben)* to the function of

real is literally unspeakable and unimaginable because it has no content—the real is radical negativity and impossibility. It is the abyss. By hiding the phallus's true nature, we create fantasms that make it function as though it had a positive existence.

Similarly, the tragic ending—obliteration of the hero—is real. It therefore functions through veiling. Not being able to see the tragedy, the audience is deprived of the imaginary; not being permitted to speak of the true ending, it is cast out of the symbolic. The audience is forced to confront the abyss and is trapped in the real of annihilation. The audience experiences the terrifying ecstatic immediacy of *jouissance.*

Like the emperor's new clothes in the eponymous fairy tale,[9] the deus ex machina is a fiction that is maintained by the unspoken conspiratorial agreement of the audience. According to Hans Christian Andersen, the adults "knew" that the emperor was naked, but refused to see or speak the truth. It was the pre-oedipal child who naively described what he saw.[10] Although subjectivity, like the emperor's clothes, is a fiction, the universal lie that it exists enables it to function. The emperor walked down the street without shame, and the spectators viewed him without embarrassment only so long as everyone acted *as though* he were clothed. The potency of the imperial phallus is lost the moment we acknowledge that it is unveiled.

Consequently, the implied hidden meaning of *The Eumenides* is that the Furies were never tamed, Orestes not saved. This reflects the Lacanian understanding that only the masculine is completely circumscribed by the law: the feminine always escapes. Indeed, the rule of law is a masculine fantasy erected to veil or hide the truth of feminine freedom.

---

signifier." JACQUES LACAN, ÉCRITS: A SELECTION 288 (Alan Sheridan trans., 1977) [hereinafter, LACAN, ÉCRITS].

9. Hans Christian Andersen, *The Emperor's New Clothes, in* HANS CHRISTIAN ANDERSEN, ANDERSEN'S FAIRY TALES (E. V. Lucas & H. B. Paul trans., 1948) *at* 199. *See* SLAVOJ ŽIŽEK, FOR THEY KNOW NOT WHAT THEY DO: ENJOYMENT AS A POLITICAL FACTOR 11–12 (1991) [hereinafter, ŽIŽEK, FOR THEY KNOW NOT WHAT THEY DO]. *See also* Jeanne L. Schroeder & David Gray Carlson, *The Subject is Nothing,* 5 LAW & CRITIQUE 93, 100–101 (1994).

10. Andersen presents this story as a contrast between the pure innocence of childhood and the hypocritical conformism of adulthood. To a Lacanian, however, the story illustrates how children are not fully integrated into the symbolic. All human institutions— and subjectivity as well—are every bit as fictional as the emperor's clothes. In Lacan's words:

> If I do say "The king is naked," it is not the same way as the child who is supposed to have exposed the universal illusion, but more in the manner of Alphonse Allais, who gathered a crowd around him by announcing in a sonorous voice, "How shocking! Look at that woman! Beneath her dress she's stark naked!" Yet in truth I don't even say that.
>
> If the king is, in fact, naked, it is only insofar as he is so beneath a certain number of clothes—no doubt fictitious but nevertheless essential to his nudity.

LACAN, SEMINAR VII, *supra* note 5, 13–14.

And yet, the paradoxical moral of the play is that it is precisely our refusal to recognize tragedy and injustice, our insistence on an happy ending, that enables law to function. Law must repress not only the extralegal forces of violence,[11] but *its own* necessary moment of subjectivity—the illegal moment of its own founding. As the Furies argued, the jury that established the law was in fact lawless: declaring its own paternal jurisdiction, it revolted against the preexisting maternal one. We must believe, and act, as though the law and the masculine were everything they claim to be—objective, complete, constraining, and in control. But the phallus is not merely the masculine claim to power; it is also the symbol of the repressed feminine. In order for the masculine law to function, we must invoke the deus ex machina and veil the law's feminine origins.

The Eumenides can be read as an allegory of the Lacanian theory of the interrelation between sexuality and law. Lacan showed that sexuality is legal—or "symbolic." I posit that the converse is equally true: law is sexual in nature, characterized by the nonrelationship of the sexual impasse. Every promulgation and application of a law is itself a sexual act.

Although every subject is split between the three psychic orders of the symbolic, the imaginary, and the real, the masculine subject creates himself by totally submitting to the symbolic. He does this by identifying the nonlegal aspects of his personality with the feminine and exiling the feminine, at least partially, to the order of the real.

As discussed in Chapter 4, this is an "impossible" situation. The masculine exists only in opposition to the feminine. He needs her to be constantly present as his defining other, even though he can never acknowledge her openly. In this chapter I will explore in more detail how the feminine that the masculine represses in the symbolic always returns in the real.[12] In Aeschylus's retelling of the myth, the masculine rule of law requires that the feminine violence represented by the Furies leave the scene of judgment, while returning in secret to serve literally as the law's subterranean support. As Aeschylus insists, the Furies do not stand in the place of judgment, but hide in the cave beneath it.

This dialectic is reflected in every legal act. I argue that in order to claim legitimacy, the judge take on a masculine role. He must claim to be "objective," a passive object totally bound by the dictates of the law. He must therefore disclaim the "feminine" aspect of his personality—the free, "subjective" side that is not totally constrained by the past. Nevertheless, every new appli-

11. *See* Jacques Derrida, *Force of Law: The "Mystical Foundation of Authority,"* 11 CARDOZO L. REV. 919 (1990).

12. JACQUES LACAN, THE SEMINAR OF JACQUES LACAN. BOOK III: THE PSYCHOSES, 1955–1956 86 (Jacques-Alain Miller ed. Russell Grigg trans., 1993) [hereinafter, LACAN, SEMINAR III].

cation of law necessarily contains some novel moment not anticipated by the statutory language or by precedent. In order to render his decision, therefore, the judge must inevitably exercise some freedom and discretion—take on the feminine position. If it were otherwise, there would be no need for trials and judges, as the outcome of every legal dispute would be predetermined—an absurd proposition belied by the very fact that the litigants are willing and able to argue their divergent positions. This is why we correctly call a ruling a "judgment" or an "opinion." The feminine position, repressed when the masculine judge invokes the symbolic order of the law, reappears in the very real effect of the ruling on the litigants. In this sense, even the most benevolent application of the law contains within it a moment of violence.

It is a common misunderstanding to assume that Lacan thought that all subjects are totally trapped within the symbolic order. This is sometimes expressed in the hopelessly depressing (and trite) cliché that, since subjectivity is socially constructed, freedom is an illusion. This is a grave misreading of Lacan. It is only the masculine aspect of personality that is circumscribed by the phallic order of the symbolic. All subjects have an essential, if repressed, feminine aspect as well. Indeed, subjectivity is nothing but the failure to integrate entirely into the symbolic. The symbolic exists because we insist on its existence. There is no need, however, to insist on that which is self-evident. It is our very uncertainty about how we fit into the symbolic—our very alienation—that causes us to insist on the efficacy of the symbolic. In the fairy tale, the people loudly praised the emperor's new clothes precisely because they couldn't see them.[13] Paradoxically, by claiming the role of free, active subjectivity, the masculine binds himself to passive objectivity; by repressing the feminine and trying to exile her from the symbolic order, the masculine allows the feminine to break free.

In other words, in *The Emperor's New Clothes* the adults did not insist that the emperor was clothed despite but *just because* of his nakedness. Masculine

13. In the fairy tale, each adult insisted he saw the emperor's clothes because he believed that failure to do so was proof that he was not integrated into the symbolic order. According to Andersen, a pair of con men sought to exploit the vanity of the emperor. They claimed to possess a magical fabric that revealed the ethical character of humanity because it could not be seen by fools or those who were unfit for their position. Given this claim, neither the emperor nor his courtiers dared to admit that they could not see the nonexistent cloth. The emperor paid the fraudsters handsomely for a new suit made from the miraculous fabric. He arranged for a parade to test his subjects. Each subject, fearing that he was the only one who did not fit into the symbolic order, loudly praised the beauty of the royal raiment. It was only when the little child shouted out, "But he has no clothes!" that the spell was broken. How could a child be unfit to be a child? The crowd roared with laughter at the obscene spectacle of the naked emperor who had no choice but to continue his long procession back to the palace.

subjects do not insist that they have the phallus despite but *just because* of their castration. Judges do not claim to know the law despite but *just because* of its indeterminacy.

THE *ERINYES*

In this chapter, I first examine the text of the play in detail and explicate its sexual content. In the following sections, I show how this content reflects the relationship of law to sexuality. It is not accidental that Aeschylus defends law in terms of sexual difference. In the penultimate section, I bring these ideas together to propose a theory of the sexual nature of judging. I present *The Eumenides* as an allegory of how a judge must on the one hand ostensibly privilege the masculine, legal side of personality and repress the feminine side, while on the other hand momentarily and surreptitiously giving way to the freedom of the feminine. I conclude with some necessarily unanswerable questions about what my theory might predict about feminism and empirical women.

The Play

The Eumenides begins as Pythia, the Delphic sibyl, invokes the gods. Her prayer prefigures the sexual agon that will form the drama.

After invoking Mother Earth as the most ancient deity,[14] Pythia evokes a fantasy of how the masculine regime of law and culture supplanted the feminine prelegal regime in relating the myth of how the titaness Phoebe, the original goddess of the oracle at Delphi, voluntarily handed her seat over to Phoebus Apollo "as a birthday gift."[15] Apollo, she claims, is the source of order "who tamed the savage country, civilized the wilds."[16] She prays to "Father Zeus"[17] as the source of her prophetic powers.

The repressed feminine slowly returns in the sibyl's prayers. Pythia addresses Athena, a goddess who identifies with the masculine over the feminine.[18] She next praises the nymphs, more conventionally feminine deities.[19] She then turns to the effeminate Dionysus, god of ecstacy, whom she identifies as ruler over the land.[20] Finally, feminine *jouissance*, the opposite of the order supposedly set down by Apollo and Zeus, is alluded to in the

14. Aeschylus, *supra* note 1, at 231, ll. 1–2.
15. *Id.*, ll. 3–20.
16. *Id.*, ll. 13–14.
17. *Id.*, l.20.
18. *Id.* at 232, l.21.
19. *Id.*, ll. 22–23.
20. *Id.*, l.24.

form of the Maenads—Dionysus's frenzied female devotees, who bring obliteration in their divine ecstasy. This contradicts Pythia's previous assertion that Apollo, god of order, had tamed the wilds: "I never forget that day [Dionysus] marshalled his wild women in arms—he was all god, he ripped Pentheus down like a hare in the nets of doom."[21] This is a telling point. As the translator notes, this passage is intended to prefigure "the fate of Orestes if he is handed over to the Furies."[22]

The ancient Greek plays were performed during a religious festival in honor of Dionysus.[23] And yet *The Eumenides* supposedly tells how the Apollonian values of law and order supplanted the Dionysian ones of chaos and ecstasy. Presumably, Aeschylus did not intend to blaspheme the god of drama. If not, it suggests that his hidden moral is that the Apollonian requires the Dionysian.[24] *Jouissance*—personified by the Maenads and the Furies—continues to dance behind the veil.

Earlier in the day, the Athenian audience would have seen the immediately preceding play of the *Oresteia* trilogy. *The Libation Bearers*[25] recounts how Orestes murdered his mother, Clytemnestra, in revenge for her murder of Agamemnon, her husband and his father. That play ends as the Furies, goddesses of blood vengeance, rise up and pursue Orestes offstage. In that play, *jouissance* is only alluded to: no one but Orestes can see his invisible tormentors.[26] Now *jouissance* in its physical, personified form appears when

21. *Id.*, ll. 24–26.

22. Robert Fagles & W. B. Stanford, *Notes, in* AESCHYLUS, ORESTEIA, *supra* note 1, *at* 285, 318 n.24.

23. Robert Fagles & W. B. Stanford, *A Reading of "The Oresteia": The Serpent and the Eagle, in* AESCHYLUS, THE ORESTEIA, *supra* note 1, *at* 13, 18–19.

24. Indeed, Dionysus even took over the oracle of Delphi from Apollo during the three winter months. *Id.*

25. Aeschylus, *The Libation Bearers, in* AESCHYLUS, THE ORESTEIA, *supra* note 1, *at* 173 [hereinafter, Aeschylus, *The Libation Bearers*].

26. In the closing scene, Orestes shouts:

No, no! Women—look—like Gorgons,
shrouded in black, their heads wreathed,
swarming serpents!

. . . .

No dreams, these torments,
not to me, they're clear, real—the hounds
of mother's hate.

. . . .

You can't see them
I can, they drive me on! I must move on—

Aeschylus, *The Libation Bearers, supra* note 25 at 173, ll. 1048–50, 1053–55, 1059–60. Orestes' crime is only the latest in a long legacy of atrocities by the Atreides, including murder, canni-

Pythia opens the temple door to reveal a tableau of Orestes surrounded by the sleeping Furies.

Orestes is, however, already accompanied by two male gods, Apollo and Hermes. Taking on the role of deus ex machina, Apollo announces that he is there to save the hero.[27] Apollo not only claims to expiate Orestes for matricide, he admits responsibility for the deed, as his oracle encouraged Orestes.[28] But even now the masculine claim to power appears as mere pretense. Despite his boast that he saved Orestes, Apollo admits that he cannot lift the curse and that Orestes must travel to Athens and embrace Athena's idol. Orestes exits, temporarily protected by the masculine—guarded by Hermes, identified by Apollo as "brother, blood of our common Father."[29]

The primitive maternal superego now makes her appearance—*literally*. The ghost of Clytemnestra enters to rouse the Furies from their slumbers, and demands vengeance.[30] The Furies' leader immediately begins debating with Apollo over the sexual struggle.

The Fury insists on the blood guilt of the matricide, who has broken the "first law," and bemoans the dominion of the new young gods.[31] Apollo expressly identifies the Furies' *jouissance* not merely as generalized destruction, but as castration.[32] He denies that matricide is the primal crime. Matricide was appropriate in this case as a means of punishing the more serious crime of a wife murdering her husband.[33] The Fury replies that such a violation of the legal (i.e., symbolic) relationship of marriage cannot compare with the elemental sin of destroying one's own flesh and blood (i.e., destroying a real relationship of motherhood).[34] Apollo,

---

balism, and incestuous rape. Orestes justifies his matricide on the grounds that Clytemnestra killed his father Agamemnon. Clytemnestra earlier justified that murder on the grounds that Agamemnon not only sacrificed their daughter Iphigenia to the gods, but had previously murdered her first husband and her infant child by him. Aegisthus, Clytemnestra's lover and Agamemnon's cousin, justified his abetting of the murder on the ground that Agamemnon's father (Aegisthus's uncle) had murdered Aegisthus's two half-brothers and fed their flesh to their father. Aegisthus was himself the product of his father's rape of his mother-sister—who was at the time married to Agamemnon's father under false pretenses.

27. "No I will never fail you, through to the end / your guardian standing by your side or worlds away!" Aeschylus, *The Eumenides, supra* note 1, at 233, l. 67.

28. "I persuaded you to take your mother's life." *Id.* at 234, l. 87.

29. *Id.*, l. 92.

30. *Id.* at 235, l. 97–139.

31. *Id.* at 237, ll. 144–75.

32. "Go where . . . castrations, wasted seed, young men's glories butchered, extremities maimed . . . " *Id.* at 239, ll. 183–87.

33. *Id.*, ll. 199–200.

34. *Id.*, l. 210.

unable to reconcile the real of feminine blood guilt with the symbolic of masculine law, escapes into the imaginary realm.[35] He invokes the masculine fantasy of tamed femininity—the perfect mate who can make man whole through immediate sexual relationships—and contrasts this fantasm with the real of the destructive feminine of Clytemnestra and the Furies.[36] Clytemnestra's crime was more serious than Orestes' precisely because a wife's murder of her husband reveals the imaginary nature of marriage. There is no sexual relationship.

Unable to "cut [the Furies'] power with [his] logic,"[37] Apollo flees to Athens to seek Athena's assistance. In hot pursuit, the Furies give way to an ecstatic dance of *jouissance.* It is impossible perfectly to translate the Furies' song into English because in the original Greek there are no verbs in the refrain. This conveyed the fact that "the Furies 'are not ministers of vengeance but Vengeance itself, so their charm is not a cause of madness but madness embodied in words and actions.' "[38]

Mother who bore me,
O dear Mother Night,
to avenge the blinded dead
and those who see by day,
now hear me. . . .
to atone away the mother-blood at last.

Over the victim's burning head
this chant this frenzy striking frenzy
lightning crazing the mind
this hymn of Fury
chaining the senses, ripping the lyre,
withering lives of men![39]

35. "What defines the imaginary order is the appearance of a complementary relationship between thesis and antithesis, the illusion that they form a harmonious Whole, filling out each other's lack; what the thesis lacks is provided by an antithesis and vice versa (the idea that Man and Woman form a harmonious Whole, for example)." SLAVOJ ŽIŽEK, TARRYING WITH THE NEGATIVE: KANT, HEGEL, AND THE CRITIQUE OF IDEOLOGY 123 (1994) [hereinafter, ŽIŽEK, TARRYING WITH THE NEGATIVE].

36. "Why, you'd disgrace—obliterate the bonds of Zeus and Hera queen of brides! And the queen of love you'd throw to the winds at a word, disgrace love, the source of mankind's nearest, dearest ties. Marriage of man and wife is Fate itself, stronger than oaths, and Justice guards its life." Aeschylus, *The Eumenides, supra* note 1, at 240, ll. 211–16.

37. *Id.* at 241, l. 225.

38. Fagles & Stanford, *supra* note 22, *at* 322, n.330f (quoting, H. J. ROSE, A COMMENTARY ON THE SURVIVING PLAYS OF AESCHYLUS [1958]).

39. Aeschylus, *The Eumenides, supra* note 1, at 245, ll. 321–34.

The Furies are the real that existed before the creation of the symbolic law: "Even at birth, I say, our rights were so ordained."[40] The Furies are the denial of all masculine claims to power.

> And all men's dreams of grandeur
> tempting the heavens,
> all melt down, under earth their pride goes down—[41]
> . . . .
> Then where is the man
> not stirred with awe, not gripped by fear
> to hear us tell the law that
> Fate ordains, the gods concede the Furies
> absolute till the end of time?
> And so it holds, our ancient power still holds.[42]

Zeus's law is the replacement of private vendetta by public legal process. And so, Athena begins the creation of law by assembling a jury of ten men "so that you can learn my everlasting laws."[43] The Furies correctly predict that if Orestes were acquitted, it would be the end of the primitive maternal rule:

> Here, now, is the overthrow
> of every binding law—once his appeal,
> his outrage wins the day,
> his matricide![44]

In other words, this founding jury is different from all other juries in that the issue it is to decide is its own jurisdiction. It pretends to apply the law when in fact it is engaging in a violent revolution, overturning the old regime and writing a new law. The law of this jury is lawless. The masculine objectivity of the law is established by an act of feminine subjectivity which, of course, is why only a goddess, Athena, can empanel the jury.

Athena presides over the trial. The senior Fury acts as prosecutor. Apollo is counsel for the defense. The Fury makes a simple case: killing one's mother creates blood guilt because it is the killing of one's own blood. Orestes cannot justify matricide as vengeance for his father's death because "the blood of the man [Clytemnestra] killed was not her own."[45] The relationship of marriage is only symbolic (legal), not real (natural).

40. *Id.* at 246, l. 348.
41. *Id.* at 247, ll. 370–73.
42. *Id.* at 248, ll. 399–404.
43. *Id.* at 256, ll. 577–78.
44. *Id.* at 253, ll. 506–09.
45. *Id.* at 258, line 611.

Apollo urges Athena to reject the rule of the mother and enact the law of the father. He invokes the paternal nature of Zeus:

The Olympian Father.
This is *his* justice—omnipotent, I warn you.
Bend to the will of Zeus. No oath can match
the power of the Father.[46]

He deplores the impropriety for a "noble man to die . . . by a woman's hand."[47]

Most significantly, Apollo denies any connection between a child and his mother—in order to insist on the symbolic relationships between husband and wife and father and son, he must repress and deny the real relationship between mother and child. Law requires the son to submit to the father. Because law is located in the symbolic order, symbolic, legal relationships (marriage and fatherhood) must have priority over real, natural ones (motherhood).

The woman you call the mother of the child
is not the parent, just a nurse to the seed,
the new-sown seed that grows and swells insider her.
The *man* is the source of life—the one who mounts.
She, like a stranger for a stranger, keeps
the shoot alive unless god hurts the roots.[48]

As proof, Apollo refers Athena to her own birth. Having "sprung full-blown"[49] from the brow of Zeus, she is living proof that "the father can father forth without a mother."[50]

Athena, having heard enough,[51] tells the jury to vote, and declares the establishment of law.

And now
if you would harm my law, you men of Greece,
you who will judge the first trial of bloodshed.
Now and forever more, for Aegeus' people
this will be the court where judges reign.[52]

The jurors split five to five. This is because the masculine jury cannot take the act of the free, feminine, subjective violence necessary to overthrow the

46. *Id.* at 259, ll. 625–29.
47. *Id.*, ll. 632–34.
48. *Id.* at 260, ll. 665–71.
49. *Id.* at 261, line 675.
50. *Id.*, l. 673.
51. *Id.*, ll. 684–86.
52. *Id.* at 261–62, ll. 691–95.

existing order and give birth to the binding, masculine objectivity of law. Athena, the virgin goddess, must herself establish the law in the name of the father.

> My work is here, to render the final judgement.
> Orestes, I will cast my lot for you.
> No mother gave me birth.
> *I honour the male, in all things but marriage.*
> Yes, with all my heart I am my Father's child.
> I cannot set more store by the woman's death—
> she killed her husband, guardian of their house.
> Even if the vote is equal, Orestes wins.[53]

Orestes declares himself free. But this claim of masculine dominance is once again a lie. The Furies protest that the feminine is merely repressed, not destroyed. They threaten to punish mankind for this injustice and to put a curse on "the land to burn it sterile."[54]

> You, you younger gods!—you have ridden down
> the ancient laws, wrenched them from my grasp—
> and I, robbed of my birthright, suffering, great with wrath.[55]

Athena stoops to toadying flattery in her attempt to persuade the Furies to abandon Mother Night and submit to Father Zeus. She succeeds in mollifying them, however, only when she herself admits that the Furies are entitled to the reverence they claim as the most ancient of deities.[56] She promises them the highest honors and sacrifices,[57] and begs them to replace their curses with a benevolent spell.[58]

Having wrested this admission of their continued predominance from the representative of the symbolic order, the Furies accept the offer to become tutelary deities of Athens and agree to be known as the Kindly Ones, the

53. *Id.* at 264, ll. 749–56 (emphasis added).
54. *Id.* at 266, line 797.
55. *Id.*, ll. 792–94.
56. No, I will never tire of telling you your gifts. So that you
the older gods, can never say that I,
a young god and the mortals of my city drove you outcast, outlawed
from the land.

But if you have any reverence for Persuasion
the majesty of Persuasion,
the spell of my voice that would appease your fury—
Oh please stay.

Id. at 270, ll. 888–96.
57. *Id.* at 269, ll. 862–66.
58. *Id.*, ll. 900–13.

Solemn Ones. They resign their role as bringers of vengeance[59] and reject their former feminine *jouissance.* They enter the imaginary order and replicate the affirmative masculine fantasy image of femininity previously invoked by Apollo—the perfect mate that can heal the scar of castration through immediate sexual relations.

> But the lovely girl who finds a mate's embrace,
> the deep joy of wedded life—O grant that gift, that prize,
> you gods of wedlock, grant it, goddesses of Fate!
> Sisters born of the Night our mother,
> spirits steering law, sharing at all our hearths,
> at all times bearing down
> to make our lives more just,
> all realms exalt you highest of the gods.[60]

The play ends as the women of Athens, "girls and mothers, trains of aged women,"[61] assemble and lead the Kindly Ones into a cave beneath the Acropolis—the home of the Solemn Ones. All femininity joins in submitting to the law of the Father and repressing the feminine.

The Actuality

No amount of poetry can establish the defeat of the feminine. The continued vitality of the Furies' feminine power is demonstrated by the fact that over a quarter of the play consists of Athena's attempt to gain the Furies' subsequent acquiescence to the trial and vindication of Orestes. Athena eventually subordinates her divine prerogatives to the Furies' prior claim to reverence. This reflects the paradox that the repression of the feminine by masculine law does not destroy her. It brings her into being and allows her to function as the law's hidden support—its necessary moment of feminine subjectivity, which establishes the boundaries of masculine objectivity.

That this is the true moral of the play is revealed not only by the deus ex machina. We also know that the Furies were not defeated. Euripides tells us in *Iphigenia at Tauris* that the Furies continued to hound Orestes even after his "expiation" at the hands of the masculine gods in Athens, until he submitted to the goddess Artemis.

Indeed, Aeschylus's contemporaries disputed his identification of the Furies with the mysterious but beneficent *Semnai.* The Solemn Ones were

59. "And the lightning stroke / that cuts men down before their prime, I curse." *Id.* at 273, ll. 968–69.

60. *Id.*, ll. 970–78.

61. *Id.* at 276, ll. 1036–37.

always depicted as dignified matrons. The Furies, in contrast, had the terrifying features of gorgons—snakes for hair, bats' wings, bronze claws, blood and disgusting discharges dripping from their eyes, and, in some accounts, dogs' heads. The title "Kindly Ones" was probably intended not as an accurate description of the goddesses, but as a form of flattery designed to propitiate them.[62] This interpretation fits the dialogue of the play, in that Athena can only assuage the Furies' wrath through obsequious references to their wisdom and power.

Aeschylus left clues to the story's hidden meaning—traces of the real—in his text. No doubt he left them unintentionally: as a believer in the rule of law, he would have to repress the horrific substrate that underwrites the truth.

First, as mentioned, the Furies are neither destroyed nor exiled. Athena orders that they shall now be honored before all gods and receive the first sacrifice. Most importantly, the Furies take up residence in a cave beneath the seat of law, indicating that they are the law's hidden origin. They remain, merely changing their name. Their new title is a euphemism adopted precisely because they are so dangerously powerful. The real of feminine *jouissance* cannot be described in the symbolic order of law and language.

Another strong hint that the play's ending is false is the reason Athena gives for favoring the male. She accepts Apollo's account of her birth and agrees that she does not have a mother. But myth says otherwise and suggests Athena might have secretly wanted revenge against the masculine.

According to Hesiod's authoritative account,[63] Athena—the goddess of wisdom—in fact had an appropriate mother: Metis (i.e., Counsel), titaness of occult wisdom and arcane knowledge.[64] Metis was Zeus's first wife.[65] The Fates declared that Metis would bear a child greater than its father.[66] Remembering how he had cruelly overthrown his own father, Cronus, and how Cronus had earlier risen up and castrated *his* father, Uranus, Zeus had good reason to fear a powerful son who might carry on the family tradition of parricide. Accordingly, he swallowed Metis alive. He thought that this would simultaneously allow him to continue to benefit from her wise counsel, as the immortal titaness would remain alive but imprisoned within him, while he avoided his unwelcome destiny.[67] However, the feminine Fates—whom the Furies name as their sisters—cannot be defeated, even by almighty

62. Robert Graves, The Greek Myths 122 (1955).
63. Hesiod, Theogony, Works and Days 29 (M. L. West 1988).
64. Graves, *supra* note 62, at 46.
65. Hesiod, *supra* note 63, at 29.
66. *Id.*
67. *Id.*

"Father" Zeus himself. The repression of the feminine does not destroy her, but makes her more powerful.

Metis was pregnant at the time she was devoured. She gave birth to Athena within Zeus' skull. Only when her daughter was fully grown, and schooled in her mother's wisdom, did the titaness send her forth. As Athena tried to force her way out of Zeus's brain, he fell prostrate with pain. Zeus finally prayed to Hephaestus, the divine blacksmith, to cleave his skull in two. Athena leapt out in full armor, shouting a war cry.[68] It was this grotesque humiliation—this castration—of Zeus that led to the reemergence of feminine wisdom in the world. Athena is the (feminine) real that always escapes the strictures of the (masculine) symbolic. This is why she remains an unviolated virgin warrior and never submits to the symbolic law of marriage or adopts the imaginary role of docile mate.

Indeed, Aeschylus himself surreptitiously indicated that Athena may have actually voted against Orestes and upheld the maternal regime. Athena stated that she sided with the male in all things *other than in marriage.* Orestes' crime was the latest of a string of masculine betrayals of feminine marital rights. It was the masculine, in the guise of Father Zeus the law giver, who betrayed her mother Metis's rights of marriage and deprived her of her freedom and her recognition as queen of heaven and mother of Zeus's heir. It was the masculine, in the guise of Agamemnon, who betrayed Clytemnestra's marriage bed by murdering her first husband and child, sacrificing their daughter Iphigenia, and finally installing Cassandra as his mistress. It was the masculine, in the guise of Orestes, who denied the reverence due to Clytemnestra, who, as wife and mother, is the founder of the household and giver of life.

THE LAW'S NECESSARY REPRESSION OF THE FEMININE

The Eumenides as the Lacanian Account of Law

The Eumenides is a story of the creation of law, and therefore also of the creation of legal subjectivity. Psychoanalytical theory is a story of the creation of the symbolic order and psychic subjectivity. Law and sexuality are symbolic. Not surprisingly, therefore, both the form and substance, the structure and meaning, of *The Eumenides* reflect the interrelationship between law and sexuality.

Another Lacanian term for castration—the operation that creates the symbolic—is "submission to the Law of the Father." Because he insists that sexuality is symbolic, not natural, Lacan must rewrite Freud's family

68. HESIOD, *supra* note 63, at 30; GRAVES, *supra* note 62, at 46.

romance to denaturalize and dephysicalize it.[69] Lacan does not believe that the child in the Oedipal stage literally lusts after his mother. Rather, the child initially identifies with the feminine in the form of his "mother" (i.e., the initial caregiver of either biological sex who serves the role that our society identifies as maternal). Consequently, the Freudian term "incest taboo" is a misnomer.[70] The child does not mature by internalizing a law that forbids physical incest with his mother; rather, he achieves subjectivity by shifting his identification from the feminine, and the real order she represents, to the masculine, and the symbolic order associated with the paternal role. In other words, the Law of the Father is not the injunction "thou shalt not sleep with thy mother!" but rather "thou shalt not identify with the feminine." By obeying this law and turning away from the feminine, the masculine subject forever loses the possibility of immediate relationship with the phallic mother—he is castrated.

As we have seen, the masculine is the position entirely circumscribed by the symbolic order.[71] The masculine claims to be the bearer of subjectivity. Moreover, in creating the symbolic order and his subjectivity, and in the acts of speaking and judging, the subject must repress the feminine moment of personality. In other words, in order for the symbolic order (and, therefore, masculinity) to function, it must deny its subjectivity and claim to be objective. This means that, although the masculine initially claims the position of being the subject, the masculine paradoxically identifies subjectivity as the

69. Famously, Lacan insisted that his theory was a "return to Freud." *See, e.g., The Freudian Thing, or the Meaning of the Return to Freud in Psychoanalysis* (published in LACAN, ÉCRITS, *supra* note 8, at 114). *See generally*, PHILIPPE JULIEN, JACQUES LACAN'S RETURN TO FREUD: THE REAL, THE SYMBOLIC, AND THE IMAGINARY (Devra Beck Simiu trans., 1994). This should not be misinterpreted as an uncritical acceptance of Sigmund Freud's writings. Rather, Lacan's point was that the first encounter with Freud (including his own early work), had been a failure. *Id.* at 7. American Freudianism, in particular, was a cult, treating Freud's theory as dogma. If psychoanalysis is to be the science that its proponents claim it to be, it must be self-critical and progressive. Consequently, psychanalysis needs to return to Freud in order to reexamine its origins before moving on: "More than any other post-Freudian, Lacan questions the taken-for-granted interpretations of Freud's texts." ELIZABETH GROSZ, JACQUES LACAN: A FEMINIST INTRODUCTION 3 (1990). Further: "Lacan's project for a return to Freud thus took the form of an *Aufhebung* [i.e., sublation], in the sense of an un-doing. . . . " JULIEN, *supra,* at 5.

70. "Thus, the incest taboo is not so much a biological 'no,' as it is a strong cultural injunction to boys to identify away from the maternal and the feminine, to substitute the name of a lineage to the desire of a mother." Ellie Ragland-Sullivan, *The Sexual Masquerade: A Lacanian Theory of Sexual Difference,* in LACAN AND THE SUBJECT OF LANGUAGE 49, 50–51 (E. Ragland-Sullivan & M. Bracher eds., 1991)

71. JACQUES LACAN, THE SEMINAR OF JACQUES LACAN. BOOK XX: ENCORE, ON FEMININE SEXUALITY, THE LIMITS OF LOVE AND KNOWLEDGE, 1972–1973 79–98 (Jacques-Alain Miller ed. & Bruce Fink trans., 1998) [hereinafter, LACAN, SEMINAR XX]. ŽIŽEK, FOR THEY KNOW NOT WHAT THEY DO, *supra* note 9, at 122–25.

feminine. In order to appear objective, the masculine judge must reject his subjectivity and exile it from the symbolic into the real. As the feminine is also at least partially exiled into the real, subjectivity becomes the position of the feminine. Indeed, it is precisely this masculine repression of the feminine that creates the feminine as radical freedom, and it is only this moment of feminine subjectivity that enables masculine objectivity to function. As the masculine defines himself in opposition to the feminine, he must create and preserve the feminine as his defining other.

Judging is psychoanalytically masculine. Consequently, in *The Eumenides,* civilized law is created by rejecting the primal loyalty to the mother, as personified by the Furies, and submitting to the law of the father, as personified by Zeus.[72] Accordingly, in *The Eumenides,* not only the legally recognized subject (the defendant, Orestes) but his defense attorney (the god Apollo) and the judges (the ten jurors) are all empirically male. Although Athena is female, she claims to be acting on behalf of Father Zeus in favoring the male. In order to establish the law, the masculine must be vindicated. It is not enough that the feminine be tamed; she must be repressed, hidden away. Their fury extinguished, the Kindly Ones solemnly retreat to the grotto.

However, as we have seen, the deus ex machina is just the falling of the curtain, the veil that hides the true ending of the story. In truth, the masculine is not completely successful. The untamed Furies remain hidden beneath the place of judgment, merely veiled.

This also is the true story of law and subjectivity. In order to act, the ostensibly "masculine" judge must ultimately give way to the feminine side of personality. That which the symbolic needs to hide behind the veil is the phallus. The symbolic order of law (i.e., the masculine) succeeds only in repressing, not taming, the feminine. What is repressed in the symbolic always returns in the real. The feminine is the hidden, veiled support of the law: she is that which permits law to function. In the guise of the Furies, the radical negativity that is the feminine appears as the total annihilation, or the death beyond death, of the real. Clearly, the primitive, prelegal regime of self-help and private vendetta must be repressed for any civilized society to exist.

The phallic order of the symbolic only functions through veiling because the masculine claim to have the phallus—to be powerful and objective—is, in fact, a fiction. The masculine objectivity of law is only created through lawless feminine subjectivity. If the phallus were revealed to us unveiled, we would have to admit its artificiality and fragility and would no longer obey it. Like the Wizard of Oz, the law is great and powerful only so long as we pay no attention to the man behind the curtain.

72. In Hegel's words, judging is primary partition. G. W. F. HEGEL, HEGEL'S PHILOSOPHY OF MIND (William Wallace & A. V. Miller trans., 1971) §398.

Lacan insists that the Father who writes the law is the absent or dead father, who never appears. The law is therefore written not *by* the Father, but *in his name.*[73] This is why Father Zeus is never seen and does not act directly, but only indirectly, through a feminine proxy who invokes his name. It also explains why Apollo lacks the power to exonerate Orestes and why the masculine jury deadlocks on the subject of its own jurisdiction. Only the goddess Athena acting in the name of the Father is able to call the jury, break the deadlock, acquit Orestes and mollify the Furies. This is because Zeus's pretense that he was founding the law was itself an act of violence—a violation of the preexisting regime of Mother Night.

Law and the Masculine; Justice and the Feminine

I have discussed the real in terms of radical negativity, the annihilation of individual subjectivity, the impossible dream of fulfillment, and the horror of the abyss. But it is more that this.

The symbolic and imaginary function as closed systems: they have boundaries. The real functions as the border to the two other systems. Although we hypothesize that the walls that create the symbolic and the imaginary must be walling something out—i.e., the real must have some preexisting positive content of its own—this is a fiction. That which is walled off (the feminine) is radical negativity with *no* positive content. Of course, this is another reason why the real is so terrifying.

But there is, nevertheless, an affirmative aspect of negativity.[74] If the symbolic and imaginary are bounded systems, then the real beyond the boundaries is freedom from their constraints. This is Kant and Hegel's understanding of the freedom that is the one essential element of personality. The real is the radical freedom that is the heart and soul of the subject.

Perhaps more importantly, the feminine is the respect for freedom that can prevent masculine law from degenerating into closed rigidity. Feminine freedom pries open the possibility of (and therefore ethical obligation for) justice. In other words, this understanding of the feminine enables us to retain the heart of the modern liberal values created in the Enlightenment, even in the postmodern state. The feminine is therefore the possibility that the subject can escape the determinism often assumed by postmodernist "social construction" theory as well as neo-Darwinian socio-biologists.

73. Lacan, *Introduction to the Names-of-the-Father Seminar* [hereinafter, Lacan, *Names-of-the-Father Seminar*], *in* Jacques Lacan, Television: A Challenge to the Psychoanalytic Establishment *at* 81 (Joan Copjec ed. & Dennis Hollier et al. trans., 1990) (1974).

74. As Hegel argued in his *Greater Logic,* nothing is always something. As he explains in the opening dialectic, just as pure being necessarily implies pure negativity, pure negativity also implies pure being. G. W. F. Hegel, Hegel's Science of Logic (A. V. Miller trans., 1969).

Although Athena claims to be acting *on behalf* of the masculine, in so doing, she acts *as* the feminine.

Indeed, since the masculine erotic desire reflects the false memory of a perfect relationship with the mother in the past and the vain hope for a perfect wife in the future, the feminine *is* the dream of immediacy. Since the feminine thanatotic desire reflects a false memory of being complete and intact in the past, and the dream of recovering oneself in the future, the feminine is also the dream of perfect integrity. Consequently, for Athena to personify the pure moment of feminine freedom (the real), which is able to accept the law freely, she must be virginal. She can create the symbolic order only because she is not yet subject to the symbolic order.[75]

Before going further, we should consider the usual Lacanian disclaimers that I have been making throughout this book: The sexuated positions are symbolic and should not be confused with anatomy (the real); all human subjects are sometimes standing in one sexual position, sometimes in the other, but most often are uncomfortably straddling the two positions, which are simultaneous, inconsistent, and redundant.

By now you should be enough of a Lacanian to distrust the foregoing disclaimers. After all, one of my central theses is that denial—whether in the form of drawing the curtain over a tragedy either by trotting out the deus ex machina or by claiming objectivity when judging—is a form of repression. And the repressed always returns to wreak its vengeance.

And so, the more a Lacanian denies the real nature of the sexuated positions, the more certain you are that sexuality has reality. Specifically, we live our lives as though the symbolic positions of sexuality were real. Sexuality is a fiction, but we make the fiction of sex into our reality by acting upon it. The real is not reality, but merely our intuition that reality exists. Nevertheless we conflate the real with reality.

This is revealed by Lacan's terminology. No purported claim to gender neutrality by Lacanians can get past the fact that Lacan calls the two supposedly abstract positions by the concrete terms "masculine" and "feminine," or that he maintains that they describe empirical personality traits that we generally associate with men and women, respectively. The Lacanian claim that the term for the signifier of subjectivity—the "phallus"—is abstract and neutral flunks the giggle test. Rather, it is chosen because the masculine claims to have the phallus, and the masculine is identified with the male, who really has the penis.

75. Of course, since the real is created by the symbolic, this also means that Athena's virginity must constantly be created by the law. As protector of the law, she must remain virgin forever not only because her virginity gives her the power to create the law, but because the law's recognition of her as its creator (i.e., as she who is prior to the law) creates and reinforces her virginity.

In other words, Lacanian terminology reflects the concrete actuality of the sexual hierarchy. It is not neutral. It is blatantly, expressly, and essentially misogynistic because our society is misogynist. The symbolic necessarily excludes the real; law necessarily suppresses freedom; objectivity necessarily denies subjectivity; and the masculine necessarily represses the feminine. My thesis as a feminist, however, is that this does not mean that Lacanianism is a misogynist theory, even though the historical individual known as Jacques Lacan may very well have been a virulent misogynist.

I believe that Lacanianism should be read as a theory *of* misogyny in the sense that it explicates the existence and persistence of misogyny. The Lacanian understanding of the sexuated positions undermines from within the traditional gender stereotypes and the status quo.

The two positions are two different and equally unsuccessful ways of dealing with the impossible human condition. They do not together form a whole person, since they are each failed attempts at wholeness. When we try to put them together and achieve a perfect sexual relationship, we are left with unfilled gaps and fulsome overlaps. Of course, this may be for the best. If we were ever to fit together and achieve a perfect relationship, we would merge into the real and lose the individuality that enabled us to have relations in the first place.

This means that the sexual positions are supplementary, not complementary[76]—one is not the simple, mirror-image negation of the other, and

76. "You will notice that I said 'supplementary.' If I had said 'complementary' what a mess we'd be in!" LACAN, SEMINAR XX, *supra* note 71, at 73. Also:

> The woman belongs on the side of the Other in this second sense, for in so far as *jouissance* is defined as phallic so she might be said to be somewhere else. The woman is implicated, of necessity, in phallic sexuality, but at the same time it is 'elsewhere' that she upholds the question of her own *jouissance,* that is, the question of her status as desiring subject. Lacan designates this *jouissance* supplementary so as to avoid any notion of complement, of woman as a complement to man's phallic nature (which is precisely the fantasy). But it is also a recognition of the 'something more,' the 'more than *jouissance* which Lacan locates in the Freudian concept of repetition—what escapes or is left over from the phallic function, and exceeds it. Woman is, therefore, placed *beyond* (beyond the phallus). That 'beyond' refers at once to her most total mystification as absolute Other (and hence nothing other than other), and to a *question,* the question of her own *jouissance,* of her greater or lesser access to the residue of the dialectic to which she is constantly subjected. The problem is that once the notion of 'woman' has been so relentlessly exposed as a fantasy, then any such question becomes an almost impossible one to pose.

Jacqueline Rose, *Introduction II, in* JACQUES LACAN AND THE ÉCOLE FREUDIENNE, FEMININE SEXUALITY (Juliet Mitchell & Jacqueline Rose eds. & Jacqueline Rose trans., 1985) 27, 51 (citations omitted). In the words of Ragland-Sullivan, "The idea of a symmetrical opposition is founded on the mistaken assumption that the male/female opposition also gives rise to a relation." Ragland-Sullivan, *supra* note 70, at 50.

the two do not fit together like yin and yang. Lacanian-Hegelian thought rejects all simple complementary dualities in the symbolic order, which defines sexuality, language, and law. Complementarity belongs instead in the imaginary. We cannot ascribe characteristics such as "passive" and "active" to the sexes precisely because these terms are themselves philosophically and psychoanalytically inept. To seek to act is to become passively acted upon. To seek to be passive requires action.[77] Accordingly, the masculine is the opposite of what it claims to be.

The Law of the Father (the "incest taboo") castrates the masculine subject by forbidding access to the feminine real. Nevertheless, as we have seen, the masculine reaction to castration is denial, and the feminine reaction to castration is acceptance. Those who disobey the Law of the Father and continue to identify with the feminine are exiled from the masculine community. This is because that which is lost in castration is equated with union with the mother. The feminine, therefore, becomes identified with loss—with negativity per se. Women, like the Furies, are the very personification of castration.

If the feminine position sounds depressing, that is because it is. On further examination, however, the Lacanian masculine position can be seen to be equally, or perhaps more, grim. The masculine subject can never achieve his desire. There is no "thing" that can cure castration because the thing that we retroactively hypothesize was lost never existed. The concept of the phallus is the logic of the double negative. We feel that we lack, and feel that there must be a thing to take away the lack—that is the lack of the lack.

Moreover, the very masculine repression and denigration of the feminine makes the masculine myth of exchange impossible. No new mate can make him whole, precisely because he identifies the feminine with lack. No mate can give him the positive content he desires. Every woman is Juno Moneta, a reminder and warning of his own castration. "The masculine gives up what he never had (the feminine in the form of the phallic mother) in exchange for something that doesn't exist (the feminine in the form of a perfect mate) to achieve something with no content (subjectivity)."[78]

The masculine claim not to be castrated is false. The masculine, which

77. "Let us simply consider the terms 'active' and 'passive,' for example, that dominate everything that was cogitated regarding the relationship between form and matter, a relationship that was so fundamental, and to which each of Plato's steps refers, and then Aristotle's, concerning the nature of things. It is visible and palpable that their statement are based only on fantasy by which they tried to make up for what can in no way be said . . . , namely, the sexual relationship." LACAN, SEMINAR XX, *supra* note 71, at 82.

78. JEANNE LORRAINE SCHROEDER, THE VESTAL AND THE FASCES: HEGEL, LACAN, PROPERTY, AND THE FEMININE (1998) [hereinafter SCHROEDER, THE VESTAL AND THE FASCES]. Also: "I give *something in exchange for nothing*—or (and therein consists its fundamental paradox) in so far as the incestuous object is in itself impossible, I give *nothing in exchange for something* (the 'permit-

denies castration, can be seen as cowardly, lying, or delusional. Lacan therefore rewrites Freud's concept of castration anxiety. It is not the fear of being physically maimed, but the fear of having to confront one's own castration or, more importantly, of not being able to keep up appearances and prevent others from learning that he is castrated. Castration anxiety is the emperor's fear that others will realize (or, more importantly, acknowledge) that he has no clothes.

The feminine is braver than the masculine in that she faces and accepts her fate. The feminine is the understanding not only that castration has occurred, but also that it cannot be cured without the loss of the subjectivity that was created by castration. On the one hand, as I have suggested, this "brave" position can be depressing; it is the realization that the battle is always already lost. Consequently, the feminine suffers from *peniseid.* This is not to be understood as Freud's notion that the little girl is so impressed with their brother's anatomical superfluity that she literally wants it for herself. Rather, it is a nostalgic mourning for a forever lost integrity.[79] Indeed, perhaps the reason why Lacan uses Freud's original German as a technical term rather than translating it into French (as penis envy) is precisely because he rejects Freud's hope that women could possibly feel that men are superior. To Lacan, the feminine is the position of sadness because the feminine judges herself by her own impossible, internal, subjective standard of integrity, not because empirical women compare themselves to pathetic men. The masculine is the position of envy in that he evaluates himself by external, objective standards. The masculine is the frustration that I do not have what I claim to have, while the feminine is the disappointment that I am not who I want to be.

There is an alternative, more optimistic reading of Lacan, however. As I discuss below when I consider judging, the masculine can be seen as heroic—a refusal to acknowledge fear. He writes a fiction of wholeness where one does not exist, and continues to fight an unwinnable battle.

Although the feminine is the depressed mourning of castration, mourn-

---

ted' non-incestuous object)." ŽIŽEK, FOR THEY KNOW NOT WHAT THEY DO, *supra* note 9, at 230–31.

79. "Freud tells us that in the end the aspiration of the patient collapses into an ineradicable nostalgia for the fact that there is no way he can be the phallus, and that since he cannot be it, he can only have it in the condition of the *Peniseid* in a woman or of castration in a man." LACAN, SEMINAR VII, *supra* note 5, at 299. Jane Gallop adds: "Lacan uses the word 'nostalgia' rather than the more usual 'deprivation' or 'envy.' JANE GALLOP, READING LACAN 146 (1985). Also: "Nostalgia here is a regret for a lost past that occurs as a result of the present view of that past moment." *Id.* at 147. This is to be contrasted to the castration anxiety felt in the masculine position: "For the boy, the moment of loss is always an imminent future, a threat, an anticipation; for the girl there is no moment of loss, but loss is inferred on the basis of a retrospective view that sees the past as fuller than the present. Something must have been lost." *Id.* at 148.

ing is the necessary first step in recovery. Mourning is the ability to accept death and eventually move on. The masculine who denies the reality of castration, like the bereaved person who is unable to accept the death of a loved one, can never move on, but is stuck in sterile objectivity. The feminine is the position of freedom and the dream of perfect integrity and immediate relationship to which the masculine aspires. The phallus is the symbol of subjectivity. Consequently, while the masculine claims to have subjectivity, the Lacanian subject is a woman.[80] The feminine therefore comprises the potentiality of becoming a free, active, fertile, creative subject. As I have said, the feminine is created only through her abjection by the masculine. This is why the feminine loves the masculine as much as she hates him. Women resent men not because men have what women want, but because the masculine makes the feminine what she is.

However, Hegel argues that one can only retroactively know that something is potential after it is actualized. The question for feminist jurisprudence is whether the hypothesized potentiality of the feminine—the promise of human freedom—can be actualized in law.

The symbolic and the imaginary constrain the masculine subject. To reiterate, the masculine is completely circumscribed by the symbolic order of language and law. The postmodern cliché that "everything is socially constructed" is, besides being self-contradictory, too often misconstrued as determinism and a denial of the modern "liberal" claim that all men are free. This is a grave error because it is only the masculine side of personality that fits the deterministic stereotype of social construction theory. The masculine is the submission to socially constructed chains from which the feminine slips. Or, more accurately, if the masculine is the aspect of personality that is perfectly circumscribed by the symbolic order, then the feminine is the aspect that is at least partially outside of that order.

Postmodernism is not the simple negation of modernism—it does not replace it entirely. Rather, postmodernism is the sublation of both modernism and premodernism; it preserves as well as negates the two earlier understandings of human nature. This is the sense of my earlier quip that postmodernism precedes modernism, and my claim that the Hellenes understood Lacan.

Social construction theory recognizes postmodernism's reclamation of the premodern understanding that man is defined in terms of his status in society and is subject to inexorable fate. It fails, however, to see postmodernism's preservation of the modern understanding that each person is

80. SCHROEDER, THE VESTAL AND THE FASCES, *supra* note 78, at 328–29. *See also* SLAVOJ ŽIŽEK, THE INDIVISIBLE REMAINDER: AN ESSAY ON SCHELLING AND RELATED MATTERS 114 (1996) [hereinafter, ŽIŽEK, THE INDIVISIBLE REMAINDER] ("Woman . . . is *more subject than man*").

simultaneously a free individual with personal rights and responsibilities, who always ultimately chooses his fate. Consequently, a postmodernist might reject as simplistic neo-con (i.e., classical liberal libertarian) denunciations of affirmative action that emphasize the ideal of freedom and the equality of individuals in the abstract, while repressing the fact of the concrete limitations imposed by society on any given person.[81] But a postmodernist should be equally suspicious of simplistic "left-wing" victimology and political correctness, which make the mirror-image error of seeing only the actuality of restraint and ignoring the possibility of freedom.[82]

Modern liberal freedom, as understood by Kant and Hegel, is totally negative. As the absence of restraints, it must be completely arbitrary, with no affirmative content. Purpose and content necessarily imply limitations and restraints. Negative liberal freedom is therefore real. Nevertheless, the Lacanian-Hegelian understanding of personality is precisely that the boundaries formed by the symbolic and the imaginary (i.e., social constructs) produce an essential unbound moment as well.[83] Paradoxically, although the real is necessary for the existence of the symbolic and the imaginary, in order for the symbolic and the imaginary to function, they must repress the real (wall it out). It is my hypothesis that, although the law of the modern state is based on the proposition that all humans are inherently free, in order to

81. Which is why Stanley Fish, despite his "right-wing" intuitions, is nevertheless a fervent supporter of some forms of affirmative action. *See, e.g.,* Stanley Fish, *When Principles Get in the Way,* THE NEW YORK TIMES A. 27 (Dec. 26, 1996).

82. Which is why Žižek, despite his "left-wing" leanings, critiques PC. *See, e.g.,* ŽIŽEK, THE INDIVISIBLE REMAINDER, *supra* note 80, at 190–93. Similarly, I do not reject the longing for equality and dignity that invigorated the so-called PC movement of the early nineteen-nineties. But, to the postmodernist, the acknowledgement of prejudice and injustice is only the first, not the last, step of analysis.

The trap of PC, of course, is its internal inconsistency. If the victim is socially constructed, so, by the same logic, is his tormentor—the rich white protestant male is *equally* trapped by his background. The social constructionist position has no moral purchase. Having deprived man of moral responsibility, the victim has no way of judging his tormentor. Moreover, if society is merely the brute fact of dominance and subordination, why should the dominant listen to the pleas of the subordinates? I have explicated this analysis in terms of a critique of "different voice" feminism in Jeanne L. Schroeder, *Abduction From the Seraglio: Feminist Methodologies and the Logic of Imagination,* 70 TEX. L. REV. 179 (1991) Catharine MacKinnon tries unsuccessfully to get around this paradox by juxtaposing premodernism and modernism and dressing it up in postmodern lingo. She posits that women are the totally constrained subjects of social constructionism (i.e., premodernism), while men are free individuals (i.e., modernism). I critique her position in Jeanne L. Schroeder, *The Taming of the Shrew: The Liberal Attempt to Mainstream Radical Feminism,* 5 YALE J. L. & FEMINISM 123 (1992).

83. Žižek relates the Lacanian-Hegelian understanding of the necessary moment of freedom created by the closed symbolic order with quantum physics, which hypothesizes that the bound, deterministic universe necessarily requires a moment of pure arbitrariness. ŽIŽEK, THE INDIVISIBLE REMAINDER, *supra* note 80, at 189–231.

function the law must act as though it were closed and constrained all human activities. Law must claim to be objective and repress the logically necessary subjective aspect of the act of judging.

It is often thought that Lacan held that the active position of subjectivity is masculine, and that he relegates the feminine to the passive position of objectivity, making Lacanianism just another restatement of traditional Western gender stereotypes. This is another grave misreading.

The masculine claims to *have* subjectivity—that is, to have "it," whatever "it" might be that could make him potent, that makes action possible. In judging, "it" is certainty, knowing what the law "is." Consequently, as soon as the judge pronounces a judgment, she becomes masculine. That is, the masculine in the symbolic claims to be complete—there is nothing walled out into another real. Lack, failure, emptiness, mediation, the possibility of unplanned contingencies, arbitrariness, and unmotivated behavior—anything and everything that would reveal the lie of the masculine claim to be in control—are prohibited by the masculine. Free will and judicial discretion must be denied.

This creates several paradoxes, of which I will only discuss a few here. To say that one knows what the law "is" is to imagine that the law is "objective": it is to declare that one is bound by the law, and that one is not exercising subjectivity. Consequently, by proclaiming his active subjectivity, the masculine finds himself in the position of passive objectivity. The subjectivity that is repressed by the judge is the feminine.

This is why the masculine's claims to subjectivity, freedom, and activity are hollow; the masculine is not merely castrated, but totally constrained by the symbolic order, and is therefore objective, bound, impotent, and passive. He has boxed himself in so tightly that he has no room left to move. But by repressing the feminine, the masculine symbolic order expels the feminine at least partly from that order.[84]

This generates several more paradoxes. First, as *The Eumenides* illustrates, the foundation of law's binding, masculine objectivity is necessarily an act of free, feminine subjectivity. Second, it is precisely the prohibition of the feminine that calls her into being and allows her to function. Her very exile releases the feminine from some of the constraints that bind the masculine. It is the denial of freedom that creates the possibility of freedom.

To repeat, although we experience the real as that which preexists the symbolic, as the hard kernel of reality that cannot be symbolized, in fact the real was created by the same operation that created the symbolic. When the masculine writes the fiction of the closed symbolic order, this fiction necessarily also implies the real that it expels. The masculine's claim that the

84. "A woman can but be excluded by the nature of things, which is the nature of words, and it must be said that if there is something that women themselves complain about enough for the time being, that's it." LACAN, SEMINAR XX, *supra* note 71, at 73.

symbolic order is complete rings hollow precisely because of the incest taboo. But by repressing the feminine (i.e., lack, mediation, freedom), the masculine is admitting her existence—and her power.[85] The more the masculine represses the feminine, the stronger she becomes.[86] One does not prohibit that which does not exist.[87]

Before the incest taboo was imposed, that which is placed in the real was impossible—the real did not preexist the symbolic. We were never one with the mother. We were never totally self-sufficient and never comprised the entire universe. Immediate relationship, perfect wholeness, radical freedom are only retroactive reconstructions of the adult mind. They act as the borders of that which is possible in the symbolic. By prohibiting them, however, we act as though what was impossible is in fact possible, but merely off limits. When writing the fiction of our subjectivities, therefore, we are able to act as though freedom was possible. And it is this very feminine freedom that enables the masculine to write the symbolic order that excludes the feminine. In other words, the sexes are mutually constituted. The masculine is created by feminine freedom, the feminine by masculine abjection. Only the feminine can give birth to the masculine, but the feminine cannot function without the masculine generative act. In the depressing Lacanian formulation, however, even though the two sexes require each other, they can never fit together. The masculine is passive and impotent. He can neither procreate nor satisfy the feminine because he is castrated. The feminine is active and fertile. But she only brings forth because she has been violated and can never forgive the masculine.

Before considering in more detail the masculine moment of judging and declaring the law, and the inevitable repression of the feminine, we need to consider the nature of the freedom that Lacanians locate in the feminine.

The feminine is not only immediacy, but lack. In this sense, the feminine is radical negativity.[88] It is the possibility of being outside the constraints of

85. I am not making the palpably silly statement that empirically female human beings are not oppressed in patriarchal societies. Of course they are, and cruelly so.

86. SCHROEDER, THE VESTAL AND THE FASCES, *supra* note 78, at 322–27?]. Also:

> In other words, man literally ex-sists: his entire being lies "out there," in woman. Woman on the other hand, does *not* exist, she *insists,* which is why she does not come to be only through man. Something in her escapes the relation to Man, the reference to the phallic enjoyment; and, as is well known, Lacan endeavored to capture this excess by the notion of a *"non-all" feminine jouissance.*

ŽIŽEK, TARRYING WITH THE NEGATIVE, *supra* note 35, at 188 (footnote omitted).

87. SCHROEDER, THE VESTAL AND THE FASCES, *supra* note 78, at 321–27.

88. In the words of Slavoj Žižek, "In short, by playing upon the somewhat worn-out Hegelian formula, we can say that the 'enigma of woman' ultimately conceals the fact that there is nothing to conceal." ŽIŽEK, THE METASTASES OF ENJOYMENT: SIX ESSAYS ON WOMAN AND CAUSALITY 143 (1994) (footnotes omitted).

the symbolic and the imaginary. The feminine therefore can have no positive content. All attempts to give content to the feminine are masculine fantasies written in the imaginary.

This radical negativity is the Kantian-Hegelian concept of free will. To reiterate an argument made in the first chapter, Kant and Hegel agree that the bare minimum conception one could have of personhood is self-consciousness as free will.[89]

Pure freedom must, however, be totally negative, contentless, arbitrary. If an action was motivated, it would not be completely free, but at least partially constrained. This minimum aspect of personhood is the foundation stone, the first building block for the construction of more developed notions of the individual. All such more developed manifestations must therefore preserve at their heart a moment of negative freedom.

As discussed in Chapter 1, the concepts of the abstract individual and pure negative freedom are self-contradictory and must be sublated. Logically, the next more developed notion of personhood is subjectivity understood as the ability to bear legal rights and duties—that is, positive freedom. Subjectivity is a symbolic construct. Or, more accurately, the regime of private law and legal subjectivity are mutually constituting in the same way that the regime of sexuality and psychoanalytical subjectivity are. Consequently, for law and subjectivity to function, subjectivity must retain a moment of arbitrary freedom. The law, which claims to be objective, must retain a (repressed) subjective moment. The masculine requires the feminine.

We can now understand the paradox of the Lacanian superego. The traditional Freudian account of the superego is roughly equivalent to the lay understanding of the conscience: it is the part of the psyche that enjoins us to obey the law—"Don't enjoy!" Nevertheless, Lacan insisted that the superego simultaneously enjoins us to disobey the law—"Enjoy!"[90] This apparent contradiction is logically necessary and another example of the sexual impasse.

The first aspect of the superego is paternal. It is the Law of the Father, which establishes a masculine position totally constrained by the symbolic order. The law cannot function, however, if subjects are so completely objectified by the law. As I explained in the previous chapter, action is real, not symbolic. Consequently, the superego must simultaneously create the subjective freedom, the freedom *from* law, that will enable action to occur and the law to function. This can only be done if the subject escapes and trans-

89. G. W. F. HEGEL, ELEMENTS OF THE PHILOSOPHY OF RIGHT 67–68 (Allen W. Wood ed. & H. B. Nisbet trans., 1991) [hereinafter, HEGEL, THE PHILOSOPHY OF RIGHT]. Also: "The will is *free,* so that freedom constitutes its substance and destiny." *Id.* at 35.

90. LACAN, SEMINAR XX, *supra* note 71, at 3.

gresses the law.[91] By doing so, the superego opens a gap, the space in the law necessary for movement and growth. This second aspect of the superego is, of course, maternal—the regime of Mother Night. It is access to the repressed feminine exiled into the real.

To put this another way, as we have seen, the dialectic of abstract right tells us that the abstract person creates law as a means of actualizing his freedom. To be totally constrained by law, however, would be the opposite of freedom. Consequently, by its own internal logic, for law to function, it must always partially fail. Just as the achievement of the perfect market would be the end of all actual markets, the achievement of perfect law would be the end of all law—and the death of the subject.

Paradoxically, although the subject requires a "real" moment of radical freedom, the real is the destruction of subjectivity. That which is lost in the real is not only the freedom of not being constrained by the symbolic. It is also the dream of wholeness and immediate relationship—perfect virginity and unity with the mother. The problem is, of course, that subjectivity requires recognition. If all are joined as one in the real, there is no possibility of recognition. To recognize you, I need to understand you as different than and separate from me.[92] But such separation is the opposite of the unity of the real. If one is completely whole, there is no need, demand, or desire to recognize others, and recognition does not occur.

The radical freedom of the real, therefore, cannot function until it is given content by the symbolic and the imaginary. To say that the feminine requires abjection by the masculine to call it into being, even as the masculine is called into being by a feminine act of freedom, is another way of saying that the real cannot preexist the symbolic. All three orders are created together.

Because the radical freedom of the real is the destruction of the conditions of subjectivity, the feminine is radically destructive. The feminine form of desire—to *be* the phallic mother and recover the real—is Thanatos. This is why the feminine must be prohibited, or repressed, by the masculine. Ecstasy is the destruction of subjectivity. As soon as we imagine or describe our experience, we are already interpreting it. In the moment of ecstasy, we are briefly one with our experience, and therefore without consciousness. Once we become conscious of our experience, we are once again back in the symbolic and the imaginary.

Our mediated experiences in the imaginary and the symbolic orders in anticipation and memory enable us to hypothesize that there must have been one past moment of immediacy, which is now lost. Feminine *jouissance*

91. *See* LACAN, SEMINAR VII, *supra* note 5, at 176–77.

92. ALAN BRUDNER, THE UNITY OF THE COMMON LAW: ESSAYS IN HEGELIAN JURISPRUDENCE 19 (1995); SCHROEDER, THE VESTAL AND THE FASCES, *supra* note 78, at 275, 278–82.

reflects the feminine position of being and enjoying the phallus.[93] As discussed in Chapter 2, *jouissance* is not merely obliteration; it the horror of staring into the abyss. What is truly horrifying about this is that Lacanian-Hegelian thought reveals that the abyss is the radical negativity that is the heart of our own personhood. The truth of subjectivity is revealed to be its own negation.

In *The Eumenides,* feminine *jouissance* takes the metaphorical form of the Furies. The Furies were called into being by Orestes' rejection of the feminine. According to Aeschylus, the Furies are the spirits of maternal vengeance called forth by Orestes' murder of Clytemnestra. They are literally roused from their slumber by Clytemnestra's ghost. Reflecting the fact that one becomes an adult subject by submitting to the injunction to reject the maternal in favor of the paternal (the incest taboo), Orestes *literally* murders his mother in the name of revenge for his father and then is exonerated by the law of Father Zeus. As the play shows, *jouissance* is not the simple destruction of nonbeing. The Furies do not kill Orestes. *Jouissance* is the continuing horror of the awareness of obliteration that has not yet come, but has always already overtaken him.

The feminine is also necessarily present at thc founding of paternal law. Father Zeus, as wielder of the phallus, never appears because the he can only function when veiled. The law can only be written in his name. The attempts of Apollo, the masculine god of culture, to declare the rule of law were impotent. Apollo's defense of Orestes rang hollow precisely because the god had previously failed to declare the rule of law and publicly try Clytemnestra for murder. Instead, Apollo perpetuated the ancient maternal regime of private vengeance by urging Orestes to commit matricide. Because Orestes' masculine jurors could not act until they took the lawless act of overthrowing the existing feminine regime, only the goddess Athena could call the jury and cast the deciding vote in favor of its jurisdiction. Moreover, as an unacknowledged moment of feminine subjectivity remains necessary in order for the masculine judge to reach his opinion objectively, the Furies, tamed as the Eumenides, remain hidden in the grotto beneath the bench.

The Masculine Writing of the Law

Law, like language, is in the symbolic order. It is the "genius" of the common law to recognize that law, like language, is always in a state of flux. The law

93. "There is a jouissance that is hers . . . that belongs to that "she" . . . that doesn't exist and doesn't signify anything. There is a jouissance that is hers about which she herself perhaps knows nothing if not that she experiences it—that much she knows." LACAN, SEMINAR XX, *supra* note 71, at 75. Because the feminine is not totally circumscribed by the phallic function, she has more than one possible relationship to the phallus. *Id.* at 81.

does not refer directly to natural reality, but only to other law. In the common law system, one never knows what the law is until the *next* case is decided. This is equally true in the case of statutory law. Because it is impossible for the legislature to anticipate all possible fact situations, one never knows the precise contours of a statute until it is applied in the *next* case.

The legal subject, however, is split between the three orders of the symbolic, imaginary, and real. In order for the judge—as a legal subject—to apply the law to other legal subjects, therefore, law itself must be split between the three orders.

On the one hand, for the law to function as law, the judge must act as though the law were fixed. To be just, the judge cannot merely express his personal opinion. He must declare what the law is. That is, the judge's decision must be objective—bound by the law—not subjective, or free and arbitrary.[94] The judge must therefore take on the masculine position of denying castration. He must use metaphor, quilting the signifier of the judgment to the signified of the case.[95] He must claim to have "it," whatever it is that enables him to achieve immediate relationship. In this case "it" is the true rule of law that achieves justice, understood as a perfect immediate relationship between generalized law and the specific case in dispute.

Judging is therefore located at least partially in the realm of the imaginary. It is the fantasy that we can reduce signification to meaning. This is imaginary because no actual law can be as complete and objective as the masculine position must claim it is. In order to operate as a closed system, the law would have to anticipate every situation that would, or could, ever occur.[96] As every lawyer knows, however, each application of the law is unique. Each case involves a new, unanticipated fact and a new argument that can be made. This is demonstrated by the very fact that the parties to a litigation disagree and are forced to submit their dispute to a judge.

This may make the masculine act of judging seem delusional at best, and fraudulent at worst. There is an alternate reading, however. The masculine act of judging reflects the fact that law is a human creation, not a divine, preexisting "thing." In order to speak the law, one must necessarily write a fiction. This takes imagination, which is part of the order of the imaginary.

94. I am, of course, giving a simplified schematic account of judging. The most insightful judges and jurisprudes are, of course, critically aware of the necessary subjective moment of judging. *See, e.g.,* Justice Benjamin Cardozo's recognition that "we may try to see things as objectively as we please. Nevertheless, we can never see them with any eyes except our own." BENJAMIN N. CARDOZO, THE NATURE OF THE JUDICIAL PROCESS 13 (1921).

Nevertheless, even Cardozo sought to make law into a science and to minimize the subjective element.

95. *See* Derrida, *supra* note 11.

96. *See generally,* David Gray Carlson, The Traumatic Dimension of Law, 24 CARDOZO L. REV. (forthcoming 2003).

Judging is an act of courage in the sense of daring to do the impossible. We must imagine that the judge has the phallus veiled by his robe.

To say that law is artificial is not a denial that it functions, any more than saying that the fact that the computer I am typing on is a human invention means that it does not work. Indeed, the law functions *only because* it is a human invention. The feminine understanding that perfect justice (immediate relationship between the law and the case) is legally impossible leads to the depressed impotence of a castrated law. Without the imaginary strength of the law, the litigants are left with the chaotic violence of self-help and the unending cycle of blood vengeance. Ironically, however, by insisting on the objectivity and completeness of the law, the masculine not only denies his freedom and subjectivity; he defines freedom and subjectivity as feminine.

I am not making the vulgar assertion associated with the critical legal studies movement that because law is indeterminate it does not exist.[97] It is the way we live our lives. Or rather, if law does not exist, it is only in the sense that, in Lacan's notorious slogans, "Woman does not exist"[98] and the "Big Other does not exist."[99] Lacan does not, of course, deny the empirical existence of female human beings or law. Neither does he deny the efficacy of the feminine. His point is that the feminine cannot be reduced to any pregiven, constrained abstraction. The feminine, as freedom, is always in a state of creation.

Rather, to a Hegelian, nothing exists more than law *precisely* because it is a human creation. To be a postmodern person is to be free and creative. Law is the fruit of our creativity. Paradoxically, the constraints of the law are precisely the actualization of our own freedom. Law is our life, our desire. As my

97. This position is most closely associated with Pierre Schlag. As Carlson explains (quoting from numerous works by Schlag):

> Schlag blames law, conceived here as a historically situated, vaguely defined American linguistic practice, for its want of a "robust referent." Instead of delivering any such referent, as it promises to do, law tenders an endless set of signifiers (which Schlag likes to call "ontological entities"), each of which disappointingly refers only to other signifiers. In the end, law signifies nothing. It literally does not exist. Law engages in the petty pace of an infinite regress—a bad infinity—without ever reaching the ultimate signified. Law in Schlag's opinion, is pseudoscience: nonsense rendered plausible; madness; deficient in its authority and ontology; "faked, bluffed, or simulated" ; mere belief and no knowledge of a Real Thing; a Mobius strip, language game circling around nothing at all. In Austinian terms, it pretends to be constantive (i.e., reporting a pre-existing reality), but is merely performative. It illegitimately reifies (i.e. "thingifies") imaginary concepts.

David Gray Carlson, *Duellism in Modern American Jurisprudence*, 99 COLUM. L. REV. 1908, 1912–14 (1999).

98. LACAN, SEMINAR XX, *supra* note 71, at 72–73.

99. *See* Jeanne L. Schroeder, *The Stumbling Block: Freedom, Rationality and Legal Scholarship*, 41 WM. & MARY L. REV. 263 (2002).

colleague Arthur Jacobson has said, the jurisprudence of duty is an act of love of God, an attempt to achieve perfection by emulating the Almighty.[100] The jurisprudence of right is an act of love of man, an attempt to achieve relationship by making others perfect.[101]

But equally, the statement that law in the abstract exists and functions as both the cause and effect of human desire means that no specific concrete law has any permanent status. No positive law can ever live up to its claim to be law. Justice is always yet to be achieved. This inability to achieve justice—this castration of law from its desire—is necessary for law to function. If law were perfectly objective, it would destroy the subjective freedom that is its basis. The law, like the feminine, is, in Lacan's terminology, *pas-toute*—not all or not whole.[102] This feminine understanding that the law (like the feminine subject) is castrated and incomplete does not mean merely that it is imperfect; it also means that it has the capacity—and therefore the ethical mandate—to become more.

The Eumenides can now be seen not merely as a myth of the foundation of ancient law, but as an allegory of the practice of contemporary law. According to Aeschylus, the unending circle of blood violence could only be stopped by the adoption of a legal regime—in the case of Athens, trial by jury. But the adoption of the new peaceful regime was itself an act of violence, in that it was the overthrow of the preexisting one. Since law did not preexist the first trial, the rule of law could only be created through a lawless act. In *The Eumenides*, the prelegal regime is feminine, maternal, violent, and real. The law—masculine, paternal and symbolic—is written in the name of the Father. The law can only be established by declaring the rule of the masculine and the defeat of the feminine. Nevertheless, because this very declaration of masculine law is itself a feminine lawless act, it cannot be accomplished by Zeus, Apollo, or the male jury, but only by the goddess Athena. Even though Athena claims to favor the masculine in so acting, she implicitly admits the primacy of the feminine by ceding the right to first sacrifice to the Furies. Most importantly, in a startlingly literal depiction of the Lacanian theory of how the masculine position relies on the feminine while not directly acknowledging her, the Furies hide in a cave beneath the seat of judgment to serve as the true deities of law.

The repression of the feminine moment of *jouissance* by the law is a necessary moment in the creation of society and civility, as *The Eumenides* suggests. What is repressed in the symbolic always returns in the real. Consequently, judging is always also partially located in the order of the real.

100. This is the jurisprudence of Kant and Rabbinical Judaism. Arthur J. Jacobson, *Hegel's Legal Plenum*, 10 CARDOZO L. REV. 877, 892–95 (1989).

101. This is the jurisprudence of Hegel. *Id.* at 895–900.

102. LACAN, SEMINAR XX, *supra* note 71, at 72–73.

The feminine is freedom. If unrepressed, she is pure negativity, arbitrariness, chaos, oblivion, *jouissance.* When she is repressed, she can be channeled. To judge is ostensibly to take on the masculine role of being totally constrained by the symbolic order of law, of pure neutral objectivity. Paradoxically, if law is a fiction, judging also requires a moment of feminine subjectivity—the freedom and creativity to write the fiction. That is, by trying to be free, the masculine binds itself, but in repressing the feminine, the masculine becomes dependent on her.[103] By repressing this feminine moment, the judge tries to channel the feminine without unleashing her full destructive power. But at a heavy cost. Our current era is based on the ideal of freedom actualized by the rule of law, but the masculine objective regime of law must repress its founding feminine moment of subjective freedom. The phallic claim that justice has been achieved frequently serves as a veil to obscure actual injustice. This has been played out literally in the historical repression of women and alienation of men.

EPILOGUE: THE BIRTH OF VENUS

Myth tells us that the Furies were *literally* created by castration. According to Hesiod, the primal parents of all living things were Gaea (Mother Earth) and Uranus (Father Sky). When Uranus proved to be cruel and oppressive, Gaea turned to her most powerful son, Cronus, king of the Titans, for aid. Gaea gave birth to a new element, adamant, and instructed Cronus to make a scythe with it. Cronus obeyed and used the scythe to castrate Uranus.[104] The

103. Jane Gallop explains the illusional nature of masculine freedom and feminine repression in terms of Lacan's notions of metaphor and metonymy.

> Metonymy is servitude; the subject bows under the oppressive weight of the bar. Metaphor is a liberation from that weight. Yet, as Nancy and Lacoue-Labarthe remind us, metaphor 'must borrow the tricks and detours' of metonymy 'in order to produce itself." Feminine metonymy has tricks and detours that, according to Lacan, allow it to 'get around the obstacles of social censorship.' Masculine metaphor may be frank . . . , may be free of the obstacles shackling femininity, but it is dependent on feminine metonymy to '[re]produce itself.' As Lacan puts it a year earlier in his seminar, 'Metonymy is there from the beginning, and it is what makes metaphor possible.' The linearity of language may not be 'sufficient,' but it is 'necessary.' The phallic phase model of thinking (binary opposition between phallus and lack, vertical and horizontal) can applaud metaphor's freedom and demean metonymy's servitude. But the adult sexual model sees the masculine dependency on the feminine, sees the horizontal bar in metaphor's cross.

GALLOP, *supra* note 79, at 129 (citations omitted).

104. HESIOD, *supra* note 63, at 7–8; GRAVES, *supra* note 62, at 39–40. Cronus then became king of the universe. Cronus would eventually be similarly overthrown by his son Zeus. This murderous legacy might explain why Zeus was so terrified by the prophecy concerning Metis's child.

drops of blood that fell from the paternal phallus onto Mother Earth sprang up and became the Furies.[105]

The Furies were therefore the sisters of Aphrodite, the goddess of erotic love. Bowdlerizers prettily state that Aphrodite (literally, "foam born")[106] arose from the sea foam, as in Botticelli's famous painting. This is only half true. According to Hesiod,[107] Cronus threw the castrated paternal phallus into the ocean. The resulting admixture of blood, semen, and spume coagulated to form Aphrodite. Of course, this is consistent with the Lacanian understanding of desire. Desire is the longing to be whole, intact, and inviolate—not to be castrated. Desire is therefore created by castration, in the sense that if we were already whole, there would be nothing to desire.

To say that the Furies, like Aphrodite, are the daughters of castration suggests that the Furies are likewise goddesses of desire.[108] Indeed, the mythical births of the Furies and Aphrodite mirror the Lacanian understanding of the masculine and feminine forms of desire. The myths tell us that when the blood of castration mixed with the traditionally feminine element of Earth, it gave birth to the Furies—goddesses of Thanatos. When it mixed with the traditionally masculine element of Ocean, it gave birth to Aphrodite—goddess of Eros.

At first blush, Lacan seems to present a bleak landscape peopled by deluded, constrained, and castrated men isolated from depressed, destructive, and violated women. Men are paralyzed with fear; women are speechless with grief. Men are bound; women are gagged. Our current Lacanian society is one of contradiction. The freedom that is the essence of personhood can only be actualized in the mutual erotic recognition made possible by law, but law must necessarily repress the freedom that is its founding moment. On the one hand, the fundamental impossibility of this system means that it can never be completely closed, and therefore it necessarily leaves space for growth and movement. On the other hand, the failure of the law is, of course, injustice and lack of freedom, as amply demonstrated in the historical oppression of women and despair of men.

A Hegelian analysis suggests a more hopeful scenario. Internal contra-

105. Hesiod *supra* note 63, at 8; Graves, *supra* note 62, at 39.

106. *Id.* at 49.

107. Hesiod, *supra* note 63, at 8–9; Graves, *supra* note 62, at 49. Hesiod maintains that Aphrodite is called "genial" (smile loving) "because she appeared out of genitals." Hesiod, *supra* note 63, at 9. The translator explains that Hesiod was linking the Greek words for smile (*meid*) and genitals (*meden*). M. L. West, *Explanatory Notes, in* Hesiod, *supra* note 63, 63, 65 n.200.

108. Fagles and Sanford intuit a similar point. The fact that the Furies sprang from Uranus's genitals implies that they have a productive as well as destructive role, that they are goddesses of life as well as death. "They are the paradox of woman. . . . Aeschylus sees them as the force of love-in-hate. . . . The fire of the Furies is Promethean." Fagles & Sanford, *supra* note 23, at 23.

dictions cannot be maintained forever but must eventually be sublated. In Hegel's famous metaphor in the introduction to *The Philosophy of Right,* the owl of Minerva spreads her wings only at the falling of dusk.[109] The dialectic is retroactive in nature. We cannot predict future sublation. We only understand the logic of a completed, or perhaps ongoing, sublation. This is necessarily the fact because the Hegelian dialectic is the story of the unfolding of human freedom. If the precise path of its unfolding were predictable (and therefore predestined or necessary), by definition there would be no freedom.

In the dusk of the early nineteenth century, Minerva's owl revealed to Hegel that the emerging institutions of constitutional liberal states and capitalistic markets were the sublation of the contradictions of the preceding feudal and classical periods. Hegel could see this because he was writing at the end of one era of history, and thus the beginning of another.

At the beginning of a new millennium, the sun is low in the sky of the age that was dawning in Hegel's time. The owl—"that fatal bellman that gives the sternest goodnight"[110]—has not yet set flight, but she is ruffling her feathers. When the blinding glare of the sun of our age begins to dim, we might be able to see more clearly the contradictions that will cause it to set, but perhaps not yet anticipate what the next day will bring. This is because as free subjects *we* must accept the responsibility of deciding what to do tomorrow, albeit within constraints.

Perhaps for the first time in history, the very nature of gender hierarchy is seen by an increasing majority of Americans as fundamentally unjust and unacceptable. The modern mercantile economy, so young in Hegel's time, is rapidly being superseded by a postmodern information economy. The economic structure that supported the modern liberal state and the "traditional" family structure is crumbling. In the industrial revolution, the masculine economic role moved out of the household, which then became the private domain of the feminine. In our time, the feminine economic role is quickly following out of the house, which we are abandoning to our estranged, feral children. These contradictions cannot stand, but how can they be sublated?

As we have seen, Lacanian psychoanalysis posits that the masculine position is created through its abjection of the feminine, and the feminine is created through its abasement by the masculine. The implications of this are that misogynistic institutions are not merely accidental in modern Western society. Rather, a fundamental misogyny of legal institutions and language is essential. Consequently, Lacanian feminists such as myself are frequently

109. HEGEL, THE PHILOSOPHY OF RIGHT, *supra* note 89, at 23.
110. William Shakespeare, *MacBeth,* act 2, scene 2.

confronted with the objection that Lacanian theory suggests that women must subordinate themselves to traditional feminine roles in order to support masculine subjectivity. I believe that the implications of Lacanianism are precisely the opposite.

Lacan, probably unintentionally, subverts rather than supports the sexual status quo. Lacan's fundamental thesis is that sexuality as we know it is neither natural nor inevitable. This does not mean, however, that sexuality is arbitrary. As subjects located in a specific symbolic, we cannot freely change our sexual identity. Sexuality is a masquerade, but not one that we can randomly shed, precisely because there is nothing underneath the masks we wear.

Nevertheless, one implication is that *if* the symbolic order were to change in some fundamental sense, *then* our sexuality would necessarily also change—and vice versa. If men could, in fact, define their subjectivity otherwise then as superiority over an abjected femininity, if women could define their femininity rather than implicitly accepting their definition by men, and if the two sexes could recognize each other as truly equal albeit different, then the very definition of sexual identity would change. This has not yet happened, but, at least for an increasingly large segment of society, it is considered appropriate.

Being a Hegelian, I can only hypothesize that we are at a historical moment when the contradictions of the sexual impasse seem ripe for sublation, but I do not pretend to be able to describe what such a sublation should look like. Hegelianism claims to be the logic of freedom. If the future was perfectly determinate and predictable, we would not be free—we would be totally masculine, with no room for the feminine. If I could predict the future, I would not be a jurist, but a sibyl—like Pythia, who opens *The Eumenides* with her invocation. Rather than engaging in mere scholarship, I would found a religion.

In dialectic reasoning, one begins with a concept, which is then shown to necessarily contain its own negation. The ensuing sublation does not merely resolve the contradiction; it revives and preserves, albeit in a radically altered way, the two original concepts, which threatened to obliterate each other. In our society, the masculine represses and negates the feminine, and the feminine is the radical negativity that lies at the heart of the split masculine subject. The radical freedom of the feminine can today only be understood as the destructive frenzy of *jouissance,* personified by the Furies, which wipes out the old, rather than the fertile possibility of Venus, who brings forth the new. The sublation of sexuality must revive and preserve the feminine, currently negated by the masculine, but must not give into imaginary lures to depict closed, sterile, affirmative femininity. We must find a way to actualize in the symbolic the freedom that is only potential in the real.

We must give rebirth to Venus, but how?

This is the impossible responsibility facing contemporary feminism. It is my thesis that we are historically positioned to recognize the contradiction of a society based on the one hand on a notion of sexuality characterized by hierarchy and the abjection of the feminine, and on the other hand a political and economic system based on the ideal of equality and freedom. From a Lacanian-Hegelian perspective, law is the moment in which sexuality and politics meet. We are therefore positioned to *begin* to consider how to sublate these contradictions and imagine what a new feminine, and therefore a new masculine, might be.

INDEX

Compositor: Binghamton Valley Composition, LLC
Text and display: Baskerville
Printer and binder: Maple-Vail Manufacturing Group